Issues in the Economics
of Immigration

**A National Bureau
of Economic Research
Conference Report**

Issues in the Economics of Immigration

Edited by **George J. Borjas**

The University of Chicago Press

Chicago and London

GEORGE J. BORJAS is the Pforzheimer Professor of Public Policy in the
John F. Kennedy School of Government at Harvard University and a
research associate of the National Bureau of Economic Research.

The University of Chicago Press, Chicago 60637
The University of Chicago Press, Ltd., London
© 2000 by the National Bureau of Economic Research
All rights reserved. Published 2000
Printed in the United States of America
09 08 07 06 05 04 03 02 01 00   1 2 3 4 5
ISBN: 0-226-06631-2 (cloth)

Library of Congress Cataloging-in-Publication Data

Issues in the economics of immigration / edited by George J. Borjas.
     p.   cm.—(A National Bureau of Economic Research
conference report)
  Includes bibliographical references and index.
  ISBN 0-226-06631-2 (cl. : alk. paper)
  1. Emigration and immigration—Economic aspects
Congresses. I. Borjas, George J. II. Series: Conference report
(National Bureau of Economic Research)
JV6217.I77   2000
330.9—dc21   99-39690
                                                 CIP

Contents

Acknowledgments

This volume consists of papers presented at a conference held in Cambridge, Massachusetts, in January 1998. Funding for the project was provided by the Olin Foundation and by the Sarah Scaife Foundation. Funding for individual papers is noted in specific paper acknowledgments.

Any opinions expressed in this volume are those of the respective authors and do not necessarily reflect the views of the National Bureau of Economic Research or the sponsoring organizations.

Introduction

George J. Borjas

There has been a resurgence of immigration in the United States and in many other countries. About 140 million persons—or roughly 2 percent of the world's population—reside in a country where they were not born (Martin 1998). Nearly 9 percent of the population in the United States, 6 percent of the population in Austria, 17 percent in Canada, 11 percent in France, and 17 percent in Switzerland is foreign-born (United Nations 1989, 61). Even Japan, which is thought of as being very homogeneous and geographically immune to immigrants, now reports major problems with illegal immigration. These sizable labor flows have altered economic opportunities for native workers in the host countries, and they have generated a great deal of debate over the economic impact of immigration and over the types of immigration policies that host countries should pursue. This debate over the economic impact of immigration policy is typically centered on three substantive questions. First, How do immigrants perform in the host country's economy? Second, What impact do immigrants have on the employment opportunities of natives? Finally, Which immigration policy most benefits the host country?

The past decade witnessed an explosion in research on many aspects of the economics of immigration. To a large extent, this literature has been motivated by the various policy concerns.[1] The academic studies typically investigate the determinants of the immigration decision by workers in

George J. Borjas is the Pforzheimer Professor of Public Policy in the John F. Kennedy School of Government at Harvard University and a research associate of the National Bureau of Economic Research.

1. There already exist a number of surveys that stress the implications of the empirical findings in the immigration literature, particularly in the U.S. context. These surveys include Borjas (1994a), Friedberg and Hunt (1995), and LaLonde and Topel (1996).

source countries and the impact of that decision on the labor market in the host country. A key insight provided by the existing literature is that the labor market impact of immigration on the host country hinges crucially on how the skills of immigrants compare to those of natives in the host country. And in fact, much of the research effort in the immigration literature has been devoted to: (1) understanding the factors that determine the relative skills of the immigrant flow; (2) measuring the relative skills of immigrants in the host country; and (3) evaluating how relative skill differentials affect economic outcomes.

Reflecting the increasing interest in the economic analysis of immigration, the National Bureau of Economic Research has held three separate research conferences on immigration issues in the past decade. The studies presented in the first two conferences (held in 1987 and 1990) emphasized the labor market impacts of immigration on the United States as well as on a number of other host and source countries. The research presented at these conferences contain studies that analyze various aspects of the economics of immigration, including the decision to migrate, the determinants of assimilation, and the labor market impact of immigration on the United States (see Abowd and Freeman 1991; Borjas and Freeman 1992).

During the time that immigration issues have become one of the core topics of modern labor economics, much has happened to the trends in immigration in the United States. First, the number of legal immigrants entering the United States has increased substantially. The United States is now admitting nearly 1 million legal immigrants annually, as compared to only about 449,000 in the 1970s. Second, the enactment of the Immigration Reform and Control Act (in 1986) failed to curtail the flow of illegal aliens. Finally, the growing concern over the economic and social consequences of legal and illegal immigration has led to drastic policy responses, including the enactment of Proposition 187 by California voters (denying most types of public assistance, including education, to illegal aliens) and the 1996 welfare reform legislation, which banned most noncitizens from receiving many types of public assistance.

This volume presents the research findings of the third NBER conference on immigration. The essays in this volume illustrate how far we have come in analyzing immigration issues in the past decade, but they also show how far away we are from obtaining answers to many policy-relevant questions. Many of the essays address a number of new issues and present new findings. A common theme running through the essays is that the economic impact of immigration on the United States stretches far beyond the labor market. Immigration can affect the education system, the financial well-being of the Social Security system, the costs of controlling crime, and the costs of running the welfare state—and many of these effects are quite subtle, working in ways that have not yet been incorporated in the traditional cost-benefit calculations that attempt to measure whether immigration is a boon or a bane for the United States.

The essays in this volume also represent a significant maturation of the research agenda, suggesting that a new phase in the analysis of the economics of immigration has been entered. The shift has begun away from the question of purely describing the labor market impact of immigration on the United States, toward a more mature analysis that addresses other types of impacts—such as on education, Social Security, and crime. Moreover, even those studies that return to such "old" questions as the assimilation of immigrants do so in a new light, stressing other aspects of the assimilation process (such as employment) or linking the concept of assimilation to the concept of convergence (conditional or otherwise) that plays a large role in studies of the "new growth" literature. Finally, the essays also ask a host of new questions, questions that are sure to motivate much further research in the future, such as stressing the differences between welfare eligibility and welfare recipiency, and a concern over the impact of immigration in the long run, as the children and grandchildren of the immigrants mature and enter the U.S. labor market.

Immigration in the United States

Prior to addressing the specific contributions of the essays in this volume, it is useful to begin with a summary of what earlier research has concluded about the economic impact of immigration on the United States. The size of the immigrant flow has fluctuated dramatically during the past century. The Great Migration occurred between 1881 and 1924, when 25.8 million persons entered the country. Reacting to the increase in immigration and to the widespread perception that the "new" immigrants differed from the old, Congress closed the floodgates in the 1920s by enacting the national-origins quota system. This system restricted the annual flow from Eastern Hemisphere countries to 150,000 immigrants, and allocated the visas according to the ethnic composition of the U.S. population in 1920. As a result, 60 percent of all available visas were awarded to applicants from two countries, Germany and the United Kingdom.[2]

During the 1930s, only 0.5 million immigrants entered the United States. Since then, the number of legal immigrants has increased at the rate of about 1 million per decade and is now nearing the historic levels reached in the early 1900s. By 1998, nearly 1 million persons were being admitted annually. There has also been a steady increase in the number of illegal aliens. The Immigration and Naturalization Service estimates that about 5 million persons were illegally present in the United States in 1996, and that the *net* flow of illegal aliens is on the order of 300,000 persons per year (U.S. Immigration and Naturalization Service 1997, 197).

The size of the immigrant flow has increased not only in absolute terms but also as a percentage of population growth. In fact, the contribution

---

2. Borjas (1994a) presents a more detailed discussion of these trends.

of the new immigration to population growth is fast approaching the level reached during the Great Migration, when immigration accounted for 40 to 50 percent of the change in population. As a result of these trends, the fraction of the population that is foreign-born rose from 4.7 to almost 10 percent between 1970 and 1998.

The huge increase in immigration in recent decades can be attributable partly to changes in U.S. immigration policy. Prior to 1965, immigration was guided by the national-origins quota system. The 1965 amendments to the Immigration and Nationality Act (and subsequent revisions) repealed the national origin restrictions, increased the number of available visas, and made family ties to U.S. residents the key factor that determines whether an applicant is admitted into the country. As a consequence of both the 1965 amendments and major changes in economic and political conditions in the source countries relative to the United States, the national-origin mix of the immigrant flow changed substantially in the past few decades. Over two-thirds of the legal immigrants admitted during the 1950s originated in Europe or Canada, 25 percent originated in Western Hemisphere countries other than Canada, and only 6 percent originated in Asia. By the 1980s, only 13 percent of the immigrants originated in Europe or Canada, 47 percent originated in Western Hemisphere countries other than Canada, and an additional 37 percent originated in Asia.

Responding to the issues raised by these historic changes in the size and composition of the immigrant flow reaching the United States, the academic literature investigating the economic impact of immigration has grown rapidly in the past two decades. This literature has provided important insights into such diverse issues as the process of assimilation, the impact of immigration on the labor market opportunities of native workers, and the fiscal impact of immigration.

The Economic Performance of Immigrants

In 1970, the average immigrant living in the United States actually earned about 1 percent more than the average native. By 1990, the average immigrant in the country earned about 15 percent less. The worsening economic performance of immigrants is partly due to a decline in their relative skills across *successive* waves. The newest immigrants arriving in the country in 1970 earned 17 percent less than natives; by 1990, the newest immigrants earned 32 percent less (Borjas 1994a, 1674).

In short, there has been a precipitous decline in the average skills of the immigrant flow reaching the United States, relative to natives. This historic change in the skill composition of the immigrant population rekindled the debate over immigration policy, and lies at the heart of many of the symptoms of immigration that are the focus of this debate.

Although the direction of the average trend in relative skills is clear, it would be a mistake to interpret the trend as saying that *every* immigrant who entered the country is relatively less skilled. The immigrant population is highly bifurcated; there are many immigrants with few skills and many immigrants who are highly skilled. In other words, immigrants tend to be lumped at both ends of the skill distribution. But the "bump" at the bottom end has become much more pronounced over time.

The poor economic performance of immigrants at the time of entry would have different long-run implications if the immigrant disadvantage diminished over time, as immigrants assimilated into the U.S. labor market. The available evidence, which I discuss in detail in chapter 1 in this volume, suggests that the economic gap between immigrants and natives does not narrow substantially during the immigrants' working lives. It turns out that practically all immigrants, regardless of when they arrived in the country, experience the same sluggish relative wage growth.

The Labor Market Impact of Immigration

Immigrants tend to cluster geographically in a small number of cities and states, and this concentration has increased over time. By 1990, nearly 70 percent of the immigrant population lived in only six states (California, New York, Texas, Florida, New Jersey, and Illinois).

Beginning in the early 1980s, a number of empirical studies began to estimate the impact of immigration on native earnings by comparing the earnings of natives who reside in immigrant cities (such as Los Angeles and San Diego) with the earnings of natives who reside in cities where few immigrants live (such as Atlanta and Pittsburgh) (Grossman 1982; Borjas 1983). The prototypical studies in this literature include the papers by Altonji and Card (1991) and LaLonde and Topel (1991), both published in the first NBER immigration volume (Abowd and Freeman 1991). For the most part, these "spatial correlations" suggested that the average native wage is only slightly lower in labor markets where immigrants tend to cluster. If one city has 10 percent more immigrants than another, the native wage in the city with more immigrants is only about 0.2 percent lower.

This spatial correlation, however, does not necessarily indicate that immigrants have a numerically inconsequential impact on native workers. Suppose, for example, that immigration into California lowers the earnings of natives in California substantially. Native workers are not likely to stand idly by and watch their economic opportunities evaporate. Many will move out of California into other regions, and persons who were considering moving to California will now move somewhere else instead. As native workers respond to immigration by voting with their feet (and hence creating what has already been dubbed "the new white flight"), the adverse impact of immigration on California's labor market is transmitted to the entire economy. In the end, *all* native workers are worse off from immigration, not simply those residing in the areas where immigrants cluster. Filer's (1992) analysis provided what is perhaps the first study to link the native migration decision and the presence of immigrants in local labor markets. Since then, studies by Frey (1995) and Borjas, Freeman, and Katz (1997) indicate that there indeed seems to be a native response to immigration, essentially invalidating the conclusions of the spatial correlations approach.

Because labor (or capital) flows can diffuse the impact of immigration from the affected local labor markets to the national economy, Borjas, Freeman, and Katz (1992) proposed an alternative methodology to estimate the impact. The "factor proportions approach" compares a nation's actual supplies of workers in particular skill groups to those it would have had in the absence of immigration, and then uses outside information on how the wages of particular skill groups respond to increases in supply to compute the relative wage consequences of immigration. This approach predicts that almost half of the 10.9 percentage point decline in the relative wage of high school dropouts observed between 1980 and 1995 can be attributed to immigration. This perspective thus implies that the adverse impact of immigration on the well-being of workers at the bottom end of the skill distribution has been substantial.

Immigration and Welfare

In 1970, immigrants were slightly less likely to receive cash benefits (such as Aid to Families with Dependent Children [AFDC] and Supplemental Security Income [SSI]) than natives. By 1990, however, the fraction of immigrant households receiving public assistance was 9.1 percent, or 1.7 percentage points higher than the fraction of native households (Borjas 1994a, 1701). In fact, if one adds noncash programs (such as Medicaid, food stamps, and housing assistance) to the definition of welfare, it turns out that 21 percent of immigrant households receive some type of aid, as compared to 14 percent of native households, and 10 percent of white, non-Hispanic native households (Borjas and Hilton 1996).

Two distinct factors account for the disproportionate increase in welfare use among immigrant households. Because more recent immigrant waves are less skilled than earlier waves, it is not surprising that more recent immigrant waves are also more likely to use welfare than earlier waves. In addition, the welfare participation rate of a specific immigrant wave *increases* over time. It seems that the assimilation process involves not only learning about labor market opportunities but also learning about the income opportunities provided by the welfare state.

There is little doubt, therefore, that immigrants are making increasing use of public assistance programs. This trend, as well as the expense of providing immigrants with a host of public services, particularly education, has added a new and potentially explosive question to the immigration debate: Do immigrants "pay their way" in the welfare state? A comprehensive study of this issue by the National Academy of Sciences recently concluded that in California, the main destination for immigrants in the post-1965 period, immigration has raised the annual taxes of the typical native household by about $1,200 a year.[3] The fiscal impact of immigration on the affected states, therefore, can be quite severe. Moreover, the welfare reform legislation enacted in 1996 gives states much more leeway in setting benefit levels. States will now "compete" when setting welfare benefits. Immigrant-receiving states, such as California, have a huge incentive to race to the bottom as they attempt to reduce the fiscal burden imposed by the immigration of less-skilled workers.

The NBER Project: A Maturation of the Research Agenda

The papers presented in this volume reflect a maturation of the research agenda on the economics of immigration, illustrating two distinct trends. First, some of the studies that revisit "old" questions, such as assimilation and immigrant welfare use, recast the problems in a way that links the analysis to related questions in other areas of economics. This reformulation, it turns out, teaches us much about the underlying issues. Second, some of the studies address a number of topics that have not received sufficient attention in the immigration literature.

In chapter 1, I provide a new analysis of an old question: What factors determine the trend in the economic performance of immigrants over time, as they assimilate in the United States? My theoretical framework argues that the relationship between the entry wage of immigrants and the subsequent rate of wage growth depends on the technology of the human capital production function, particularly the extent of substitution or complementarity between "pre-existing" human capital and postmigration investments. Complementarity would suggest that higher initial wage levels would be associated with faster wage growth after entry into the United States. This would imply, for instance, that the wages of different immigrant groups would tend to diverge over time.

I stress that the empirical analysis of wage convergence in the immigrant population has much in common with the literature that estimates cross-country regressions to determine if there is convergence in per capita income across countries.[4] These studies typically find that the unadjusted

3. Smith and Edmonston (1997). The National Academy report also estimated the long-run fiscal impact by "tracking" the fiscal consequences over a 300-year period after an immigrant is admitted into the United States (as the descendants of immigrants enter the labor market). This dynamic exercise revealed that admitting one immigrant today yields an $80,000 fiscal surplus at the *national* level. The long-run net benefit from immigration, however, arises solely because the exercise assumes that the federal government will put its fiscal house in order in the year 2016, and pass a huge tax increase to ensure that the debt-GDP ratio remains constant after that point.
4. See, for example, Barro (1991) and Mankiw, Romer, and Weil (1992).

correlation between the growth rate in per capita GDP and the initial level of per capita GDP is positive, but weak. There is, however, "conditional convergence," a strong negative correlation between growth rates and initial levels of per capita income, when the regression controls for measures of the country's human capital endowment. The differentiation between convergence and conditional convergence is also useful for understanding the economic progress of immigrants. As in the economic growth literature, the data reveal a positive unadjusted correlation between the log entry wage of immigrants and the subsequent rate of wage growth. This positive correlation, however, turns negative when one compares immigrant groups who start out with similar human capital endowments. The empirical evidence, therefore, indicates that even though immigrant groups with the same level of human capital will have similar earnings over the long haul, the sizable wage differentials observed among the various immigrant groups at the time of entry may well diverge over time.

Julian R. Betts and Magnus Lofstrom use data drawn from the decennial censuses to study trends in educational attainment and subsequent earnings of immigrants relative to those of natives. An important lesson of the empirical evidence—one that has not been sufficiently appreciated in earlier work—is the importance of differences in educational attainment between immigrants and natives, as well as among immigrant groups, in determining wage differences among the various populations.

Betts and Lofstrom document the familiar result that the gap in educational attainment between immigrants and natives widened between 1970 and 1990, with immigrants experiencing an ever larger disadvantage. More important, they show that much of this widening in the gap is driven by changes in the bottom half of the education distribution, with a larger number of immigrants arriving in the United States with relatively little schooling. The analysis concludes that differences in educational attainment can explain more than half of the observed wage gap between immigrants and natives, and that the rate of return to schooling of natives exceeds the rate of return of immigrants, regardless of whether the schooling was acquired in the United States or abroad.

Betts and Lofstrom also address a question that is sure to attract more attention in the future: Do the increasing number of immigrants and the changes in their relative skills "crowd out" natives from educational opportunities? The authors argue that there is some evidence that immigrants crowd out some natives, particularly at the secondary education level, in the sense that changes in the size of the immigrant population in a particular state are correlated with changes in the educational attainment of natives in that state.

Edward P. Lazear's essay introduces a number of new—and provocative—questions into the immigration literature. In particular, he advances the hypothesis that an important economic benefit from immigration arises because immigrants enhance the "diversity" of the population. La-zear then examines a number of questions that arise from this conjecture: What does diversity mean? To the extent that there are gains from diver-sity, do these gains come through the interaction of individuals from one culture or background with individuals from another culture or back-ground?

Lazear defines a "good" partner in the interaction as one who has different skills, who has skills that are relevant to one's activity (i.e., they are complements), and with whom there can be communication (in terms of culture or language). He then tests some of the theoretical implications using data drawn from the 1990 census. The empirical evidence is quite interesting, and it leads Lazear to conclude that one cannot justify current immigration policy in terms of its impact on diversity. In Lazear's view, the policy fails because it does not promote *enough* diversity. Put differ-ently, the current immigrant flow is dominated by too few cultural or national-origin groups. The empirical work, in fact, suggests that the dif-ferences in the socioeconomic characteristics of immigrants reflect the ef-fects of selection as much as they reflect the underlying characteristics of the populations from which the immigrants are drawn. Balanced immigra-tion, Lazear argues, perhaps implemented through the sale of immigration slots, would do much more to enrich the diversity of the U.S. popula-tion.

To a large extent, the existing literature addresses issues of immigrant assimilation and economic performance by analyzing the trends in the wage differentials between immigrants and natives (or among immigrant groups). Obviously, assimilation influences many other socioeconomic out-comes, and many of these impacts remain unexplored. Edward Funkhous-er's essay uses data drawn from the decennial censuses to analyze the trends in employment of immigrants and natives, in terms of employment rates and hours worked.

Funkhouser's analysis reveals an interesting empirical fact. Even though more recent immigrant waves have relatively lower employment propensities, there is a large increase in employment rates during the initial years following immigration. In short, there is a great deal of convergence in employment rates between immigrants and natives, much more than what is found in age-earnings profiles. Moreover, the convergence in em-ployment rates is larger for immigrants who are more skilled. Because changes in observed measures of skill or the returns to skill do not explain this finding, Funkhouser conjectures that the lack of transferability of hu-man capital may play an important role in the assimilation process during the initial years in the United States. Funkhouser's study raises an impor-tant question for future research: Why does assimilation occur rapidly along some dimensions of socioeconomic outcomes but not others?

Guillermina Jasso, Mark R. Rosenzweig, and James P. Smith use data collected by the Immigration and Naturalization Service (INS) to describe the changes in the quality of the immigrant cohorts admitted between 1972 and 1995. Their unique data set contains information on all new legal immigrants admitted during that period, including the immigrant's occupation and type of visa used to enter the country. These data permit the authors to investigate how the skill composition of the *legal* immigrant population has changed over time, and to relate these trends to underlying changes in immigration policy.

The INS data, like the census data that has been the "work horse" of the literature, do indeed suggest that the average skills of successive immigrant cohorts declined throughout much of the past three decades (with a slight upturn toward the end of the period). Jasso, Rosenzweig, and Smith also show that policy changes in one particular visa category (such as tightening down on fraudulent immigration marriages) tend to spill over into other categories and affect the skill composition of immigrants admitted in those categories.

Although the existing literature has taught us much about the impact of immigration, it is fair to conclude that much of what we have learned focuses on the impact of immigration on the labor market in the current generation. Obviously, immigration has an impact that goes far beyond the labor market and that extends across generations. As a result, there is a growing awareness in the economics literature that a fuller picture of the impact of immigration requires that we analyze the process of social mobility across generations.[5]

David Card, John DiNardo, and Eugena Estes present a comparative perspective on the economic performance of immigrants and their children. Using data from the 1940 and 1970 censuses and from recent Current Population Surveys, they find important links between the economic status of immigrant parents and the status of their U.S.-native-born sons and daughters. Much of this linkage works through education, with the children of more highly educated immigrants having higher levels of education and earning higher wages.

Despite the dramatic shift since 1940 in the country-of-origin composition of the U.S. immigrant population, the authors find that the rate of intergenerational assimilation has not changed much. In particular, the intergenerational correlation linking the average skills of immigrant groups in 1940 and the skills of the second-generation groups in 1970 is roughly of the same magnitude as the correlation linking the skills of immigrants in 1970 and the skills of second-generation workers in the 1990s. This intergenerational correlation is on the order of .4 to .6, depending on whether skills are defined in terms of educational attainment or wages.

There already exists a large literature analyzing the impact of immigra-

---

5. Some exceptions include Borjas (1994b) and Chiswick (1977).

tion on the costs of maintaining the welfare state. For the most part, these studies tend to be "descriptive"—describing the extent of immigrant participation in particular programs and the costs associated with such participation.

Janet Currie's essay raises a number of interesting behavioral questions that future research will need to address. Currie starts by noting that welfare use is particularly high among immigrant children and among the immigrant elderly. Using data from the U.S. National Health Interview Survey, she compares the health insurance coverage and utilization of medical care of children of immigrants and children of the native born, and highlights the importance of differentiating between the eligibility of immigrants to receive particular types of assistance and the "take-up" of such assistance by the immigrant population. Currie's empirical analysis suggests that immigrants have higher eligibility rates but lower take-up rates. In the end, increased Medicaid eligibility is associated with increases in the probability of having obtained at least one doctor's visit in the past year among both immigrant and native children, but there were no effects on the subsequent number of doctor visits. Currie then concludes that the main effect of expanding Medicaid eligibility among children of immigrants was the reduction in the number of children going without any doctor visits.

Although much of the immigration debate stresses the impact of immigration on the welfare system, the increasing number and the changes in the skill composition of the immigrant flow affects many other economic and social institutions, and these effects will be felt by many sectors of U.S. society for many decades to come. As a result, it is important to document the impact of immigration on a variety of American institutions, including Social Security and the criminal justice system. Remarkably, little is known about the short- or long-run effects for either of these systems. The last two essays in this volume set out the framework that can guide the analysis of these important issues and present interesting and provocative empirical evidence.

Alan L. Gustman and Thomas L. Steinmeier report that the income support feature of Social Security disproportionately transfers benefits to immigrants relative to persons born in the United States. Immigrants who have worked in the United States for only a decade or two and who have high incomes gain the most from current benefit calculation procedures, which count all years they lived outside the United States as years of zero earnings. If earnings used to determine Social Security benefits are calculated only over the years immigrants reside in the United States, and benefits are prorated based on the share of a 35- or 40-year base period spent living in the United States, then the progressivity of the Social Security benefit formula would be preserved but would reduce the transfer toward immigrants.

At the same time, Gustman and Steinmeier point out that many immigrants also leave the United States after putting money into the Social Security system, and fail to collect when they retire. This transfer to U.S. taxpayers is substantial.

Finally, using data on new admissions to the California state prisons in the 1980s and 1990s, Kristin F. Butcher and Anne Morrison Piehl find that the foreign born have a very different offense mix than native-born inmates, with foreigners much more likely to be serving time for drug offenses. Butcher and Piehl point out that there have been many changes in the enforcement environment in the past decade, including changes in the level of resources appropriated for enforcement activities targeting deportable aliens. These developments have resulted in much greater involvement of the Immigration and Naturalization Service in the incarceration of the foreign born. By 1996, the definition of deportable person was effectively expanded to cover *all* noncitizens in the California prison system. Throughout the period, those foreign-born inmates designated by the California Department of Corrections to be released to INS custody served substantially longer terms (conditional upon sentence length) than natives or other similar foreigners. These longer terms of incarceration—as the immigrants wait in their jail cells for deportation proceedings—impose substantial costs on the state.

Conclusion

The literature investigating the economic impact of immigration on the United States and on other host countries grew rapidly in the past decade. This explosion of research has substantially increased our understanding of the economics of immigration. The large number of immigrants admitted in the United States in recent decades has already had a major impact on the skill composition of the labor force, might even be responsible for some of the major changes in the wage structure observed in the 1980s, and has had a sizable impact on the cost of maintaining a welfare state.

It is important to stress, however, that the economic impact of today's immigration is not limited to the current generation. Because of the intergenerational link between the skills of parents and children, current immigration policy might already be determining the skill endowment of the labor force for the next two or three generations. An important lesson of the research, therefore, is that immigration has a far-reaching and long-lasting impact. In a sense, we are only beginning to observe the economic consequences of the historic changes in the size, national-origin mix, and skill composition of immigrants admitted to the United States during the past three decades.

References

Abowd, John M., and Richard B. Freeman, eds. 1991. *Immigration, trade, and the labor market.* Chicago: University of Chicago Press.

Altonji, Joseph G., and David Card. 1991. The effects of immigration on the labor market outcomes of less-skilled natives. In *Immigration, trade, and the labor market,* ed. John M. Abowd and Richard B. Freeman, 201–234. Chicago: University of Chicago Press.

Barro, Robert J. 1991. Economic growth in a cross-section of countries. *Quarterly Journal of Economics* 106 (2): 407–33.

Borjas, George J. 1983. The substitutability of black, Hispanic, and white labor. *Economic Inquiry* 21 (1): 93–106.

———. 1994a. The economics of immigration. *Journal of Economic Literature* 32 (4): 1667–717.

———. 1994b. Long-run convergence of ethnic skill differentials: The children and grandchildren of the Great Migration. *Industrial and Labor Relations Review* 47:553–73.

Borjas, George J., and Richard B. Freeman, eds. 1992. *Immigration and the work force: Economic consequences for the United States and source areas.* Chicago: University of Chicago Press.

Borjas, George J., Richard B. Freeman, and Lawrence F. Katz. 1992. On the labor market impacts of immigration and trade. In *Immigration and the work force: Economic consequences for the United States and source areas,* ed. George J. Borjas and Richard B. Freeman, 213–44. Chicago: University of Chicago Press.

———. 1997. How much do immigration and trade affect labor market outcomes? *Brookings Papers on Economic Activity* 1:1–67.

Borjas, George J., and Lynette Hilton. 1996. Immigration and the welfare state: Immigrant participation in means-tested entitlement programs. *Quarterly Journal of Economics* 111 (2): 575–604.

Card, David. 1990. The impact of the Mariel boatlift on the Miami labor market. *Industrial and Labor Relations Review* 43 (2): 245–57.

Chiswick, Barry R. 1977. Sons of immigrants: Are they at an earnings disadvantage? *American Economic Review* 67 (1): 376–80.

Filer, Randall K. 1992. The impact of immigrant arrivals on migratory patterns of native workers. In *Immigration and the work force: Economic consequences for the United States and source areas,* ed. George J. Borjas and Richard B. Freeman, 245–69. Chicago: University of Chicago Press.

Frey, William. 1995. Immigration and internal migration flight from U.S. metropolitan areas: Toward a new demographic balkanization. *Urban Studies* 32: 733–57.

Friedberg, Rachel, and Jennifer Hunt. 1995. The impact of immigration on host country wages, employment and growth. *Journal of Economic Perspectives* 9 (2): 23–44.

Grossman, Jean Baldwin. 1982. The substitutability of natives and immigrants in production. *Review of Economics and Statistics* 54 (4): 596–603.

LaLonde, Robert J., and Robert H. Topel. 1991. Labor market adjustments to increased immigration. In *Immigration, trade, and the labor market,* ed. John M. Abowd and Richard B. Freeman, 167–99. Chicago: University of Chicago Press.

———. 1996. Economic impact of international migration and the economic performance of immigrants. In *Handbook of population and family economics,* ed. Mark R. Rosenzweig and Oded Stark. Amsterdam: North-Holland.

Mankiw, N. Gregory, David Romer, and David N. Weil. 1992. A contribution to the empirics of economic growth. *Quarterly Journal of Economics* 107:407–38.

Martin, Phillip. 1998 *Migration News*. Davis: University of California.

Smith, James P., and Barry Edmonston, eds. 1997. *The new Americans: Economic, demographic, and fiscal effects of immigration*. Washington, D.C.: National Academy Press.

United Nations. 1989. *World population at the turn of the century*. New York: United Nations.

U.S. Immigration and Naturalization Service. 1997. *Statistical yearbook of the Immigration and Naturalization Service*. Washington, D.C.: U.S. Government Printing Office.

1

The Economic Progress of Immigrants

George J. Borjas

1.1 Introduction

The economic impact of immigration depends both on how immigrants perform in the United States when they first enter the country, as well as on their long-run economic prospects. Beginning with Chiswick's (1978) pioneering work, this dual concern has guided much of the empirical research in the economics of immigration.[1] The literature has typically found that immigrants earn less than natives at the time of entry (with the entry wage disadvantage being larger for more recent cohorts), and that the wage gap between immigrants and natives narrows over time as immigrants assimilate into U.S. society. Many studies conclude that the rate of wage convergence between immigrants and natives is not very large, so that the most recent immigrant waves will probably suffer from a substantial wage disadvantage for much of their working lives.

The literature also stresses that there are sizable differences in economic performance among national origin groups (Borjas 1987; LaLonde and Topel 1992; and Funkhouser and Trejo 1995). For the most part, these studies have examined the impact of national origin on the wage *level* of immigrants in the United States, and the data suggest that immigrants who originate in developed countries earn more than immigrants who originate in poorer countries. The sizable wage differentials among na-

George J. Borjas is the Pforzheimer Professor of Public Policy in the John F. Kennedy School of Government at Harvard University and a research associate of the National Bureau of Economic Research.

The author is grateful to Francine Blau and Stephen Trejo for helpful comments and to the Olin Foundation, the Department of Labor, and the National Science Foundation for financial support.

1. Borjas (1994) presents a detailed survey of the literature.

tional origin groups combined with the changing national origin mix of the immigrant population in the United States has been *the* crucial factor in generating the trends in cohort "quality" that have been the subject of intense interest, both in academic studies and in the policy debate.

It turns out that there are also sizable differences in the rate of wage growth experienced by the different national origin groups in the United States (Borjas 1995; Duleep and Regets 1997a, 1997b; Schoeni, McCarthy, and Vernez 1996; and Yuengert 1994). Therefore, it is important to determine if the rate of wage convergence exhibits cohort effects: Do the most recent immigrant cohorts experience either faster or slower wage growth than earlier cohorts? The existing evidence, however, does not settle this issue conclusively. Duleep and Regets (1997b) argue that more recent waves, who have lower entry wages, will experience faster wage growth in the future, while Borjas (1995) and Schoeni, McCarthy, and Vernez (1996) do not find any evidence of cohort effects in the rate of wage growth.

This paper presents a theoretical and empirical study of the rate of economic progress experienced by immigrants. The study uses a human capital framework to motivate and guide the analysis. There seems to be some confusion about whether human capital theory implies wage convergence among the various immigrant groups, in the sense that immigrants who have high wages at the time of entry should experience slower subsequent wage growth. I show that a reasonable set of assumptions can easily generate investment behavior in the immigrant population that leads to wage divergence among groups, with the most skilled groups earning more at the time of entry and experiencing faster wage growth.

The empirical analysis uses the 1970, 1980, and 1990 Public Use Microdata Samples (PUMS) of the decennial census. The empirical analysis of wage convergence in the immigrant population has much in common with the literature that estimates cross-country regressions to determine if there is convergence in per capita income across countries (Barro 1991, 1997; Mankiw, Romer, and Weil 1992; Quah 1993). These studies typically find that the "raw" correlation between the growth rate in per capita GDP and the initial level of per capita GDP is positive, but weak. There is, however, a strong negative correlation between growth rates and initial levels of per capita income when the regression controls for measures of the country's human capital endowment. The data, therefore, reveal *conditional convergence* in per capita income, in the sense that countries that start out with the same human capital endowments will tend to have the same per capita income levels in the long run.

The differentiation between convergence and conditional convergence is extremely useful for understanding the economic progress of immigrants. As in the cross-country studies in the economic growth literature, the raw data reveal a positive correlation between the log entry wage of immigrants and the subsequent rate of wage growth. Furthermore, the same source country characteristics that lead to high entry wages tend to lead to faster wage growth. This positive correlation between entry wages and wage growth, however, turns negative when one compares immigrant groups who start out with similar human capital endowments. The empirical evidence, therefore, indicates that even though immigrant groups with the same level of human capital will have similar earnings over the long haul, the sizable wage differentials observed among the various immigrant groups at the time of entry may well diverge over time.

1.2 Conceptual Framework

What is the relationship between entry wage levels and the rate of economic progress experienced by immigrants? This question is of more than passing interest because the entry wages of immigrant cohorts (relative to natives) have fallen dramatically in recent decades. Borjas (1995) reports that the immigrants who entered the United States between 1965 and 1969 earned about 18 percent less than natives in 1970, while the immigrants who entered between 1985 and 1989 earned 38 percent less than natives in 1990.[2]

If the lower entry wages of more recent cohorts were compensated by a sufficiently higher rate of future wage growth, the present value of the (relative) earnings profiles of immigrants might not be as different as the differences in entry wage levels would suggest. In fact, the direction of the "quality" differential between immigrants and natives could be the opposite of that implied by the trend in entry wages. However, if more recent cohorts have a lower rate of wage growth than earlier cohorts, the long-run implications of the decline in entry wages are amplified. It is important, therefore, to isolate the factors that determine the rate of wage growth of immigrant cohorts, and to determine the trends in the rate of economic progress across successive cohorts.

Beginning with Chiswick (1978), practically all studies of the economic progress of immigrants use the human capital model as a point of departure.[3] The typical discussion argues that immigrants have a relative wage disadvantage at the time of entry because immigrants lack the U.S.-specific skills that are rewarded in the labor market. Moreover, the costs of acquiring human capital in the post migration period (such as becoming proficient in English) are mainly incurred as forgone earnings, so that these initial human capital investments further depress entry wages for immigrants. Over time, as the immigrants reduce their human capital acquisitions and collect the returns on earlier investments, they experience faster wage growth than natives.

This generic restatement of the human capital model seems to suggest

2. These statistics actually refer to log point differentials. The convention of approximating log point differentials by percentage differences will be used throughout most of the paper.
3. Ben-Porath (1967) gives the classic presentation of the life-cycle human capital accumulation model.

that one should expect a negative correlation between entry wages and subsequent wage growth: Faster wage growth results only if immigrants are willing to give up some earnings at the time of entry. This inference, however, is incorrect because it does not account for the dispersion in the human capital stock that exists in the immigrant population at the time of entry.[4] This heterogeneity could easily lead to a *positive* correlation between entry wages and wage growth. A simple two-period model of the human capital accumulation process captures the basic idea.

Let K measure the number of efficiency units that an immigrant has acquired in the source country. Because human capital is not perfectly transferable across countries, a fraction δ of these efficiency units evaporate when the immigrant enters the United States. The number of effective efficiency units that the immigrant can rent out in the U.S. labor market is then given by $E = (1 - \delta)K$. Without loss of generality, suppose that the market-determined rental rate for an efficiency unit is one dollar.

An immigrant lives for two periods after arriving in the United States—the investment period and the payoff period. During the investment period, the immigrant devotes a fraction s of his efficiency units (or of his productive time) to the production of additional human capital. This allocation of effort might be worthwhile because it increases the number of efficiency units available in the payoff period by $g \times 100$ percent. The present value of the immigrant's income stream in the United States equals

$$(1) \qquad V = (1 - \delta)K(1 - s) + \rho[(1 - \delta)K(1 + g)],$$

where ρ is the discounting factor. It is instructive to think of ρ not only as a function of the immigrant's discount rate but also as measuring the probability that the immigrant will stay in the United States (and hence collect the returns on the part of the investments that are U.S.-specific). The parameter ρ, therefore, is smaller when the immigrant has either a high discount rate or a high probability of out-migration.

The human capital production function is:

$$(2) \qquad\qquad gE = (sE)^{\alpha}E^{\beta},$$

where $\alpha < 1$ because of diminishing marginal productivity to human capital investments. Beginning with Ben-Porath (1967), the value of the parameter β has been a matter of debate in the human capital literature. Highly skilled immigrants may be more adept at acquiring additional human capital. This complementarity between pre-existing human capital and the skills acquired in the postmigration period would suggest that β is positive. Because the costs of human capital investments are mostly forgone earnings, however, it may be that highly skilled workers find it

---

4. Many studies in the human capital literature attempt to estimate the correlation between initial earnings and wage growth. See, e.g., Hause (1980), Kearl (1988), and Neumark and Taubman (1995).

very expensive to augment their human capital stock. This "substitutability" would then suggest that β is negative.

The Ben-Porath specification of the human capital production function assumes "neutrality," so that the two effects cancel each other and β is zero.[5] Holding ρ constant, the neutrality assumption states that all workers invest the same *dollar* amount in human capital, regardless of their initial endowment. All workers then get the same *dollar* increase in earnings in the payoff period. As a result, the *dollar* age-earnings profiles of different workers are parallel to each other. The neutrality assumption also implies that the *log* age-earnings profiles of different workers must converge because the payoff from human capital investment is relatively smaller for more-skilled workers.[6]

Most of the empirical work in the human capital literature focuses on the life-cycle trends in log earnings, and analyzes the determinants of the rate of growth of earnings (rather than of the absolute change in earnings). It is, therefore, analytically convenient to define a different type of neutrality in the production function. In particular, rewrite equation (2) as:

$$(3) \qquad\qquad g \;=\; s^{\alpha}\, E^{\,\alpha+\beta-1}.$$

Equation (3) relates the percentage increase in the human capital stock to the fraction of efficiency units that are used for investment purposes during the investment period. Define *relative neutrality* to occur when the relative increase in the human capital stock (g) depends only on the fraction of time devoted to investment (s), and not on the initial level of effective capital. Relative neutrality then occurs when $\alpha + \beta = 1$. If $\alpha + \beta > 1$, the relative returns from the investment (for a given time input) depend positively on the initial level of effective capital, and there is *relative complementarity*. Conversely, if $\alpha + \beta < 1$, the relative returns from the investment are negatively related to the level of initial capital, and there is *relative substitutability*. Not surprisingly, the sign of ($\alpha + \beta - 1$) plays a crucial role in determining the relationship between the log entry wage of immigrants and the subsequent rate of wage growth.

Before proceeding to an analysis of the model, it is worth noting that relative neutrality implies human capital complementarity in the Ben-Porath sense. After all, if the log age-earnings profiles are parallel across different workers, more-skilled workers must be investing more in human capital. An empirical finding of relative neutrality or relative complementarity, therefore, would necessarily imply "Ben-Porath complementarity" in the production of human capital.

Workers choose the rate of human capital investment (s) that maximizes

5. In later work, Ben-Porath (1970) rejected some of the implications of the neutrality assumption. Rosen (1976) presents a model of human capital accumulation that does not rely on the neutrality assumption.

6. Mincer (1974, ch. 4) provides a detailed discussion of the implications of human capital theory for the convergence of dollar and log age-earnings profiles.

the present value of earnings. The first-order condition to the maximization problem implies that:

$$(4) \qquad s = (\alpha\rho)^{1/(1-\alpha)} E^{(\alpha+\beta-1)/(1-\alpha)}.$$

Equation (4) shows that the rate of human capital investment is positively related to the discounting factor, and that the relationship between the rate of human capital investment and initial human capital depends on the sign of $\alpha + \beta - 1$. Suppose that all workers have the same discounting factor ρ. Relative neutrality then implies that all persons allocate the same fraction of time to the production of human capital. Highly skilled workers invest more if there is relative complementarity ($\alpha + \beta > 1$) and invest less if there is relative substitutability ($\alpha + \beta < 1$).

Of course, we seldom have data on the fraction of time that workers allocate to human capital investments. However, we do observe the earnings histories of workers. Let Δ be the *relative* wage growth experienced by an immigrant over his postmigration life cycle:

$$(5) \qquad \Delta = \frac{(1 - \delta)K(1 + g) - (1 - \delta)K(1 - s)}{E} = g + s.$$

It is easy to show that

$$(6) \qquad \left.\frac{d\Delta}{d\rho}\right|_E = \frac{ds}{d\rho}\left(1 + \frac{1}{\rho}\right) > 0.$$

Holding constant the immigrant's initial endowment of human capital, the theory implies that immigrants with a higher ρ (and hence lower discount rates or probabilities of out-migration) experience faster wage growth. The relationship between the rate of wage growth and the initial level of effective human capital, however, is more complicated:

$$(7) \qquad \left.\frac{d\Delta}{dE}\right|_\rho = (\alpha + \beta - 1)\frac{(1 + \alpha\rho)s}{\alpha\rho(1 - \alpha)E}.$$

The correlation between the rate of wage growth and initial human capital depends on the sign of $\alpha + \beta - 1$. If there is relative complementarity in the human capital production function, relative wage growth will be higher for immigrants who have higher levels of effective human capital. In contrast, if there is relative substitutability—and higher levels of effective human capital make it costly to acquire additional human capital—the most-skilled immigrants experience less relative wage growth.

The model can be used to determine the correlation between log entry wages and the rate of wage growth. The log entry wage of the immigrant is

$$(8) \qquad \log w_0 = \log E + \log(1 - s).$$

It is instructive to begin the discussion of the relationship between log w_0 and Δ by considering the simpler case where the only exogenous variation in the immigrant population is in the discounting factor ρ. One can show that

(9)
$$\left.\frac{d\log w_0}{d\rho}\right|_E = \frac{-1}{1-s} \cdot \frac{ds}{d\rho} < 0.$$

A higher discounting factor, therefore, reduces the log entry wage while raising the relative rate of wage growth. Equations (6) and (9) replicate the conceptual experiment where initial earnings vary among workers who have the same initial human capital. This experiment is the basis for many of the discussions of the human capital model. Human capital investment steepens the age-earnings profile by reducing entry wages, raising future wages, and effectively generating a negative correlation between the log entry wage and the rate of wage growth.

However, this negative correlation can potentially break down when the entry wage is lower because the effective level of human capital is itself lower. In particular,

(10)
$$\left.\frac{d\log w_0}{dE}\right|_\rho = \frac{1}{E}\left[1 - \frac{s}{1-s} \cdot \frac{\alpha + \beta - 1}{1 - \alpha}\right].$$

The positive sign of the first term inside the brackets of equation (10) indicates that the larger level of effective human capital raises entry wages simply because the additional skills are valued by American employers. At the same time, the larger human capital endowment alters the rate of human capital investment. Define κ^* as

(11)
$$\kappa^* = \frac{(1 - s)(1 - \alpha)}{s} > 0.$$

By definition, the log entry wage is independent of the initial endowment of human capital when $\alpha + \beta - 1 = \kappa^*$. Figure 1.1 illustrates the four cases that summarize the potential relationship between log entry wages and the rate of wage growth of immigrants:

1. *Relative substitution between pre- and postmigration human capital* ($\alpha + \beta < 1$). Immigrants endowed with a substantial level of effective human capital find it expensive to augment their stock in the United States. There is then a negative correlation between log entry wages and the rate of wage growth. Skilled immigrants invest less, earn more at the time of entry, and have a smaller rate of wage growth.

2. *Relative neutrality in the human capital production function* ($\alpha + \beta = 1$). All workers have the same rate of investment (s). The correlation between the log entry wage and the rate of wage growth is zero.

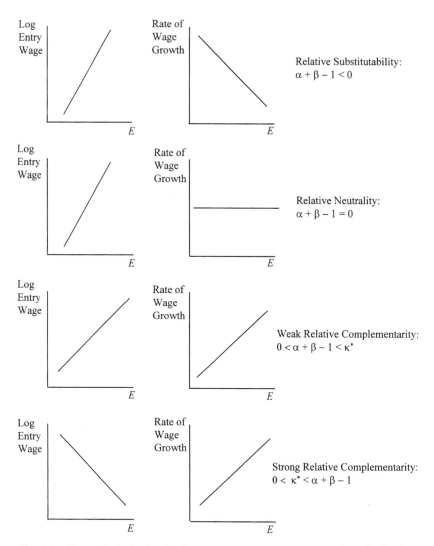

Fig. 1.1   Theoretical relationship between entry wages, wage growth, and effective human capital

3. *Weak relative complementarity in human capital* $(0 < \alpha + \beta - 1 < \kappa^*)$. Skilled immigrants then invest more in human capital, have higher entry wages, and also have a higher rate of wage growth. There is, therefore, a positive correlation between the log entry wage and the rate of wage growth.

4. *Strong relative complementarity in human capital* $(0 < \kappa^* < \alpha + \beta - 1)$. Skilled immigrants invest so much in human capital that they actually earn less at the time of entry, but experience faster wage growth. There

is again a negative correlation between the log entry wage and the rate of wage growth.[7]

The potential relationships between the log entry wage and the rate of wage growth are illustrated in figure 1.1. These cases can be used to construct simple empirical tests that might distinguish among the various possibilities and provide valuable information about the human capital production function faced by immigrants. For example, suppose that there is weak relative complementarity in the production function. The variables that increase the immigrant's effective human capital at the time of entry would then have the same qualitative effect on the log entry wage and on the rate of wage growth. In contrast, if there were relative substitution, then variables that increase effective human capital would have a positive impact on the log entry wage but a negative impact on the rate of wage growth. The empirical analysis presented below suggests that the data is best summarized by a "weak" positive correlation between log entry wages and the rate of wage growth. Put differently, immigrants with high levels of effective human capital experience both higher entry wages and faster economic progress in the United States. This finding suggests that the immigrant human capital production function exhibits weak relative complementarity.[8]

1.3   Data and Basic Trends

The study uses data drawn from the 1970, 1980, and 1990 PUMS. A person is classified as an immigrant if he or she was born in a foreign country; all other workers are classified as natives.[9] I drew a 1 percent random sample from the native population in each of the census years. The immigrant extract comprises a 2 percent random sample in 1970 and a 5 percent random sample in both 1980 and 1990.[10] In each census year,

7. Note that cases 1 and 4 both imply a negative correlation between the log entry wage and the rate of wage growth, but for different reasons. In the case of relative substitutability, the skilled workers earn more at the time of entry and have slower wage growth, while in the case of strong relative complementarity, the skilled workers earn less at the time of entry and have faster wage growth. It is also possible that $\alpha + \beta - 1 = \kappa^*$. In this case, skilled immigrants invest more, but the log entry wage is independent of the level of effective human capital.

8. Although the theoretical framework provides a useful way for thinking about how heterogeneity in the immigrant population generates differences in the short-run and long-run economic performance of immigrant cohorts, the model ignored the link between the migration decision and postmigration human capital investments. A more general analysis would explore how the characteristics of the human capital production function might alter the process that selects the immigrant flow.

9. This definition implies that persons born abroad of American parents and persons born in a U.S. possession are classified as natives.

10. Unlike the earlier census data sets, the 1990 PUMS does not comprise a random sample. All calculations in the 1990 data use the sampling weights.

the study is restricted to men aged 25–64 who work in the civilian sector, are not self-employed, and do not reside in group quarters.

Consider the cohort of immigrants who migrated from country i, in calendar year j, when they were k years old. To calculate the wage for each of the cohorts in the analysis, consider the following individual-level regression model:

$$(12) \qquad \log w_{ijk}(t) = X_{ijk}(t)\beta(t) + v_{ijk}(t) + \varepsilon_{ijk}(t),$$

where $w_{ijk}(t)$ is the hourly wage of cohort (i, j, k) in calendar year t; X is a vector of socioeconomic characteristics (discussed below); $v_{ijk}(t)$ is a fixed effect giving the "adjusted" wage of a person who belongs to the cohort; and $\varepsilon_{ijk}(t)$ is the stochastic error, assumed to be independent from all other variables in the model. The regression model in equation (12) is estimated separately in each census year. To simplify the notation, I denote the adjusted wage of the comparable group of native workers by $v_{n0k}(t)$.[11] Consider initially the model where the standardizing vector X does not contain any variables. The vector of fixed effects in the immigrant population then gives the average log wage in each country-of-origin/year-of-migration/ age-at-arrival cell, while the fixed effect in the native population gives the average log wage of natives in a particular age group. For example, $v_{ijk}(t)$ may give the average 1970 log wage for Mexican immigrants who arrived between 1965 and 1969 and who were 25–34 years old as of 1970. The respective fixed effect $v_{n0k}(t)$ in the native population then gives the average 1970 log wage for natives who were 25–34 years old as of 1970.

Suppose we estimate the cross-section regression model in two different calendar years, say t and t'. We can use the estimated fixed effects to calculate the rate of wage growth of immigrants over the calendar-time interval (t, t') as

$$(13) \qquad \Delta v_{ijk}(t, t') = [v_{ijk}(t') - v_{ijk}(t)].$$

We can also estimate the rate of wage growth of immigrants relative to that of comparable natives as

$$(14) \qquad \Delta \tilde{v}_{ijk}(t, t') = [v_{ijk}(t') - v_{ijk}(t)] - [v_{n0k}(t') - v_{n0k}(t)].$$

If the vector X does not contain any standardizing variables, equation (13) defines the mean rate of wage growth for cohort (i, j, k), and equation (14) defines the cohort's rate of wage growth relative to that observed in a comparably aged group of natives.

I restrict the study to the immigrant cohorts who arrived between 1960

---

11. I obtained the adjusted native wage by simply adding the sample of native workers to the regression in equation (12) and including a vector of dummy variables indicating if the person in a particular age group (k) is native born.

and 1979. The census data define four year-of-migration cohorts within this period: immigrants who arrived in 1960–64, 1965–69, 1970–74, and 1975–79. The immigrant cohorts will also be defined in terms of four age groups, where the age of the immigrant is observed at the time the census is taken: immigrants who are 25–34, 35–44, 45–54, and 55–64 years old.

It is useful to begin by summarizing the broad trends in the rate of wage growth in the immigrant population over the 1970–90 period. The first three columns of table 1.1 report the wage of immigrants—*relative to that of comparably aged natives*—for each of the year-of-migration/age-at-arrival cohorts (aggregated over all national origin groups). Consider the immigrants who arrived in the United States between 1965 and 1969 and were 25–34 years old at the time of the 1970 census enumeration. These immigrants earned 13 percent less than natives who were 25–34 years old in 1970. By 1980, the wage gap between the two groups (who were 10 years older) had narrowed to 6 percent, and by 1990 (when the two groups were 20 years older) to 3 percent. The last two columns of the table report the rate of wage convergence implied by these wage data ($\Delta \tilde{v}_{ijk}(t,\ t')$). This particular cohort experienced a rate of wage convergence of 7 percentage points in the first 10 years after arrival, and of another 4 percentage points in the second 10 years.[12]

The remaining rows of the table reveal roughly the same rate of relative economic progress for many of the cohorts: about 10 percentage points over a 20-year period, with most of the wage convergence taking place in the first 10 years after arrival. Consider, for example, the experience of the group of young men who migrated in the late 1970s. Their relative wage increased by 7 percentage points between 1980 and 1990—the same rate of relative wage growth experienced by the young men who entered between 1965 and 1969 during *their* first 10 years in the country. The data in table 1.1, therefore, do not provide strong evidence for the hypothesis that, on aggregate, there are cohort effects in the rate of wage convergence.[13]

---

12. A potential problem with interpreting the relative wage growth of immigrants as a measure of economic progress is that there were historic changes in the U.S. wage structure during the 1980s, and these changes did not affect all skill groups equally (Murphy and Welch 1992; Katz and Murphy 1992). To control for the changes in the wage structure, La-Londe and Topel (1992) and Borjas (1995) propose "deflating" immigrant wages by measures of the wage change experienced within particular skill groups in the native population. I replicated the analysis presented in this paper using "real" wages that had been deflated by the wage growth experienced by particular age-education groups in the native population. None of the results are affected by this adjustment of the data.

13. The intercensal "tracking" reported in table 1.1 may lead to a biased picture of immigrant economic progress if there is substantial nonrandom out-migration in the immigrant population (Borjas and Bratsberg 1996). Because the sample composition of "stayers" (i.e., persons who remain in the United States) is likely to change over time, the rates of wage convergence reported in the table might reflect both the economic progress of immigrants and the selection bias created by out-migration. Unfortunately, the United States does not collect systematic data on the number or skill composition of the immigrants (and natives) who leave the country.

Table 1.1   **Relative Wages and Wage Growth for Immigrant Cohorts**

Year of Migration/ Age at Arrival	Relative Wage			Rate of Wage Convergence	
	1970	1980	1990	1970–80	1980–90
1960–64 Arrivals					
15–24 in 1970	—	.0105	.0409	—	.0304
		(.0089)	(.0099)		(.0133)
25–34 in 1970	.0310	−.0026	−.0019	−.0336	.0007
	(.0117)	(.0081)	(.0090)	(.0142)	(.0121)
35–44 in 1970	−.0620	−.0693	.0114	−.0073	.0807
	(.0143)	(.0101)	(.0126)	(.0175)	(.0161)
45–54 in 1970	−.1179	−.1140	—	.0039	—
	(.0201)	(.0152)		(.0252)	
1965–69 Arrivals					
15–24 in 1970	—	−.0475	−.0713	—	−.0238
		(.0069)	(.0078)		(.0104)
25–34 in 1970	−.1276	−.0613	−.0255	.0663	.0358
	(.0100)	(.0072)	(.0082)	(.0123)	(.0109)
35–44 in 1970	−.1737	−.1660	−.0919	.0077	.0741
	(.0137)	(.0098)	(.0125)	(.0168)	(.0159)
45–54 in 1970	−.2544	−.2365	—	.0179	—
	(.0200)	(.0153)		(.0252)	
1970–74 Arrivals					
25–34 in 1980	—	−.1212	−.1250	—	−.0038
		(.0054)	(.0060)		(.0081)
35–44 in 1980	—	−.1950	−.1786	—	.0164
		(.0074)	(.0084)		(.0112)
45–54 in 1980	—	−.3008	−.2315	—	.0693
		(.0112)	(.0143)		(.0182)
1975–79 Arrivals					
25–34 in 1980	—	−.2400	−.1688	—	.0712
		(.0051)	(.0058)		(.0077)
35–44 in 1980	—	−.2859	−.2763	—	.0096
		(.0080)	(.0092)		(.0122)
45–54 in 1980	—	−.3545	−.3052	—	.0493
		(.0118)	(.0115)		(.0165)

Note: Standard errors are reported in parentheses.

As noted earlier, one can think of the data reported in table 1.1 as being calculated from the model in equations (12)–(14) where there are no standardizing variables in the vector X. It is of interest to determine the sensitivity of the rate of wage growth in the immigrant population (relative to that of natives) to differences in human capital across the groups, particularly educational attainment. I estimated the regression model in equation (12) including a vector of dummy variables indicating the worker's educational attainment. The dummy variables indicate if the worker has less than 9 years of schooling; 9–11 years; 12 years; 13–15 years; or 16 years or more.

The fixed effects v_{ijk} were then computed at the mean level of educational attainment for the entire immigrant sample.

Table 1.2 reports the education-adjusted log wage levels and rate of wage growth (relative to natives). Not surprisingly, the wage gap between immigrants and natives falls when we control for differences in educational attainment between the two groups. For example, the entry wage of the immigrants who migrated in 1970–74 and were 35–44 years old in 1980 is 20 percent lower than that of natives in the same age group, but it is

Table 1.2   **Relative Wages and Wage Growth for Immigrant Cohorts, Adjusted for Education**

Year of Migration/ Age at Arrival	Relative Wage			Rate of Wage Convergence	
	1970	1980	1990	1970–80	1980–90
1960–64 Arrivals					
15–24 in 1970	—	.0373	.0830	—	.0457
		(.0087)	(.0093)		(.0127)
25–34 in 1970	.0627	.0373	.0507	−.0254	.0134
	(.0113)	(.0078)	(.0084)	(.0137)	(.0115)
35–44 in 1970	−.0298	−.0386	.0535	−.0088	.0921
	(.0133)	(.0096)	(.0118)	(.0164)	(.0152)
45–54 in 1970	−.1201	−.1068	—	.0133	—
	(.0186)	(.0145)		(.0236)	
1965–69 Arrivals					
15–24 in 1970	—	.0323	.0570	—	.0247
		(.0071)	(.0076)		(.0104)
25–34 in 1970	−.1241	−.0329	.0200	.0912	.0529
	(.0098)	(.0070)	(.0077)	(.0120)	(.0104)
35–44 in 1970	−.1663	−.1152	−.0148	.0511	.1004
	(.0128)	(.0094)	(.0117)	(.0159)	(.0150)
45–54 in 1970	−.1997	−.1752	—	.0245	—
	(.0185)	(.0147)		(.0236)	
1970–74 Arrivals					
25–34 in 1980	—	−.0394	.0258	—	.0652
		(.0056)	(.0061)		(.0083)
35–44 in 1980	—	−.1512	−.0890	—	.0622
		(.0073)	(.0080)		(.0108)
45–54 in 1980	—	−.2234	−.1201	—	.1033
		(.0108)	(.0136)		(.0174)
1975–79 Arrivals					
25–34 in 1980	—	−.1868	−.0654	—	.1214
		(.0052)	(.0057)		(.0077)
35–44 in 1980	—	−.2637	−.1863	—	.0774
		(.0078)	(.0087)		(.0117)
45–54 in 1980	—	−.3231	−.2449	—	.0782
		(.0112)	(.0145)		(.0183)

Note: Standard errors are reported in parentheses.

Table 1.3   Rate of Wage Convergence, by Country of Origin

| | Arrived in 1965–69; Was 25–34 Years Old at Arrival: | | Arrived in 1975–79; Was 25–34 Years Old at Arrival: |
Country of Origin	1970–80	1980–90	1980–90
Canada	.029	.238	.174
China	.146	.047	.151
Colombia	−.052	.084	.152
Cuba	.035	−.007	.101
Dominican Republic	.020	.028	.075
Egypt	.438	.301	.402
Germany	.168	.032	−.051
Greece	.022	.079	.110
Hungary	.008	.044	.226
India	.298	.134	.419
Ireland	.022	−.009	.368
Italy	−.053	.138	.157
Jamaica	.048	.036	.130
Korea	.403	.203	.221
Mexico	.147	−.122	−.062
Philippines	.319	.035	.229
Portugal	.073	.153	.099
United Kingdom	.150	.068	.238

only 15 percent lower than that of natives who have the same age and educational attainment. The data also suggests that there is faster wage convergence between immigrants and natives if we adjust for differences in educational attainment. The relative rate of wage growth for the immigrants who arrived in the late 1960s and were 25–34 years old in 1970 was 7 percentage points in the first 10 years, and an additional 4 percentage points in the second 10 years. The education-adjusted rate of wage growth was 9 percentage points in the first 10 years, and another 5 percentage points in the second 10 years.

Not surprisingly, there exist significant differences in economic progress across the various national origin groups. Table 1.3 illustrates this variation by reporting the unadjusted and education-adjusted rates of wage growth for selected national origin groups (relative to natives). Some of the groups exhibit very high rates of wage growth, while other groups do not exhibit *any* economic improvement. Consider, for example, the British immigrants who entered the United States in the late 1960s and were 25–34 years old in 1970. Their relative wage rose by 15 percentage points in the first 10 years after arrival, and by an additional 7 percentage points in the second 10 years. In contrast, the relative wage of the comparable group of immigrants from the Dominican Republic rose by only 2 percentage points in the first 10 years, and by another 3 percentage points in the second 10 years.

1.4 Wage Convergence

The raw data reveal substantial dispersion in the rate of wage convergence experienced by immigrants originating in different countries, arriving at different times and at different ages. The remainder of the empirical analysis attempts to understand the source of these differences.

The dependent variable in this section is $v_{ijk}(t, t')$, the rate of wage growth experienced by a particular immigrant cohort (from country i, arriving in year j, and at age k) over the intercensal 10-year period. The "cross-country" analysis is initially restricted to a sample that contains 85 countries (listed in the appendix), four age groups, and four year-of-migration cohorts. The analysis "stacks" the data. The 85 countries used in the study are chosen because immigrants born in these countries can be matched across two successive censuses, and these countries have sufficiently large numbers of observations in the 1970, 1980, and 1990 censuses to allow reliable estimation of the first-stage regressions in equation (12). The issue of cell size will be discussed in more detail below. About 92 percent of the immigrants who entered the United States between 1960 and 1979 originate in one of these 85 countries.[14]

I now use these data to examine some of the questions raised by the theory.[15] First, what is the correlation between the rate of wage growth and the log entry wage? Consider the convergence regression model:

$$(15) \qquad \Delta v_{ijk}(t, t') = \theta v_{ijk}(t) + \delta_{jk} + \eta_{ijk},$$

where δ_{jk} is a fixed effect indicating if the immigrant cohort arrived in calendar year j at age k; and η is a stochastic error.

A number of technical details about the regression model in equation (15) are worth noting. First, the dependent variable may contain a great deal of sampling error. To account for the heteroscedasticity induced by this sampling error, I weigh all regressions by the factor $(n_t^{-1} + n_{t'}^{-1})^{-1}$, where n_t is the sample size of the cell in census year t. Note that the same

---

14. About 60 percent of the immigrants omitted from the sample did not report a country of origin.

15. The grouped data can also be used to test whether there are cohort effects in the rate of wage growth. Consider a regression model that relates the rate of wage growth of immigrants relative to that of comparably aged natives, $\Delta \tilde{v}_{ijk}(t, t')$, to a vector of variables indicating the time of migration, holding constant the age at migration. This regression reveals that during the first 10 years after migration, the immigrants who migrated in the early 1960s experience the same relative wage growth as those who migrated in the early 1970s; and that the immigrants who migrated in the late 1960s experience the same relative wage growth as those who migrated in the late 1970s. The p-values for these tests are between .4 and .5.

country appears a number of times in the sample and the stochastic error η might contain a country-specific component. The tables, therefore, report White-corrected standard errors that adjust for this sampling frame.

Second, the fixed effect δ_{jk} control for common factors that affect the rate of wage growth of immigrants who arrived at the same time and at the same age. The inclusion of these fixed effects effectively implies that the regression coefficient θ would be numerically identical if the dependent variable had been defined in terms of the rate of wage growth of immigrants relative to that of comparably aged natives, or $\Delta \tilde{v}_{ijk}(t, t')$. The reason is that the native rate of wage growth is constant within a particular age group. The regression results reported below, therefore, can be interpreted as analyzing the determinants of the rate of wage convergence between immigrants and natives.

Finally, to ensure that the convergence regressions use the log entry wage as the independent variable, the analysis is restricted to the rate of wage growth observed during an immigrant cohort's first 10 years in the United States. As a result, the cohorts that arrived in the 1960s contribute only one observation to the sample, giving the wage growth between 1970 and 1980; and the cohorts that arrived in the 1970s also contribute one observation to the sample, giving the wage growth observed between 1980 and 1990. Of course, the wage at time t (the beginning of the decade) is a much better approximation of the entry wage for the immigrants who arrived in the last half of the preceding decade. Consider, for example, the cohort that arrived between 1965 and 1970. Equation (15) then relates the rate of wage growth over the period 1970–80 to the 1970 log wage. The 1970 wage, however, is not as good an approximation of the entry wage for the immigrants who arrived in the first half of the 1960s. I will show below that this rough approximation does not impart a serious bias on the analysis.

Row 1 of table 1.4 reports the relevant coefficients from the convergence regressions. The simplest specification (reported in the first column) reveals a *positive,* though insignificant, correlation between the unadjusted rate of wage growth and the log entry wage of immigrant cohorts. This weak correlation is consistent with the raw data summarized in table 1.1: More recent cohorts, who have much lower entry wages, experience roughly the same rate of wage growth as earlier cohorts. Therefore, there is little reason to expect that the earnings of immigrants who belong to different national origin groups and arrive at different times will converge as they assimilate in the United States. If we take the positive point estimate of θ at face value, the data, in fact, suggest that there might be some divergence over time: The immigrants with the highest entry wages are also the ones who experience the most rapid wage growth. In the context of the model, there seems to be some weak relative complementarity between the skills that immigrants bring into the United States and the skills

Table 1.4   **Estimates of Wage Convergence**

	Regression			
	(1)	(2)	(3)	(4)
1. Unadjusted rate of wage growth ($N = 819$)				
Log entry wage	.1199	−.3893	−.6569	−.8336
	(.1213)	(.0697)	(.0619)	(.0520)
Initial educational attainment	—	.0473	—	.0510
		(.0062)		(.0059)
R^2	.350	.651	.781	.816
2. Education-adjusted rate of wage growth ($N = 819$)				
Log entry wage	−.2623	−.3733	−.8062	−.8341
	(.0911)	(.0537)	(.0550)	(.0411)
Initial educational attainment	—	.0261	—	.0309
		(.0033)		(.0046)
R^2	.421	.653	.805	.824
3. Unadjusted rate of wage growth: Cohorts with large numbers of observations ($N = 409$)				
Log entry wage	.1981	−.3191	−.5774	−.8297
	(.1164)	(.0752)	(.0786)	(.0760)
Initial educational attainment	—	.0446	—	.0597
		(.0064)		(.0079)
R^2	.443	.730	.844	.883
4. Unadjusted rate of wage growth: Cohorts in United States for 5 years or less ($N = 414$)				
Log entry wage	.0493	−.4280	−.7107	−.8239
	(.1207)	(.0736)	(.0673)	(.0647)
Initial educational attainment	—	.0502	—	.0450
		(.0064)		(.0074)
R^2	.301	.648	.820	.840
Includes year-of-migration/ age-at-migration fixed effects	Yes	Yes	Yes	Yes
Includes country-of-origin fixed effects	No	No	Yes	Yes

Note: Dependent variable is rate of wage growth observed in first 10 years in United States. Standard errors are reported in parentheses. The regressions are weighted by $(n_0^{-1} + n_1^{-1})^{-1}$, where n_0 is the number of observations used in calculating the wage at the beginning of the decade, and n_1 is the number of observations used in calculating the wage at the end of the decade.

that they acquire in the postmigration period. This result resembles Mincer's (1974) finding of complementarity between investments in school and investments in on-the-job training.

As the remaining coefficients reported in row 1 of table 1.4 show, however, a simple change in the specification of the regression turns the weak positive coefficient into a significant negative one. Consider the regression model that estimates the rate of *conditional* convergence:

$$(16) \qquad \Delta v_{ijk}(t, t') = \theta^* v_{ijk}(t) + \phi H_{ijk}(t) + \xi_{jk} + \eta_{ijk},$$

where $H_{ijk}(t)$ gives the effective human capital of cohort (i, j, k) at time t. The parameter θ^* estimates the rate of conditional convergence, the rate at which the earnings of different immigrant cohorts converge *if* we hold the initial human capital endowment of the cohorts constant.

Although the census data do not offer precise measures of the cohort's effective human capital at the time of entry, we have information on the average educational attainment of the cohort at time t. Table 1.4 reveals that the coefficient θ^* is strongly negative when the regression adds the cohort's educational attainment, and becomes even more negative if the regression includes country-of-origin fixed effects (which can also be interpreted as determining effective human capital). Holding initial human capital constant, therefore, there is convergence among the various immigrant groups. Moreover, the rate of convergence is economically significant. The regression coefficient of $-.39$ suggests that wage differences among the various immigrant groups (holding initial skills constant) narrow by 32.2 percent within the first decade. If this rate of convergence remained constant over the immigrant's working life, over two-thirds of the initial wage differential would vanish within 30 years. This finding, of course, mirrors the well-known conditional convergence result in the economic growth literature (Barro 1997).

The conditional convergence result is also related to the recent work of Duleep and Regets (1997a, 1997b), who use an alternative way of controlling for education in the analysis. Duleep and Regets define the immigrant cohort not only in terms of country of origin, year of arrival, and age at migration (i.e., a cell in i, j, k) but also in terms of educational attainment (s). In particular, let $v_{ijks}(t)$ be the log wage of an immigrant cohort originating in country i, arriving in calendar year j, migrating at age k, and with s years of schooling. Similarly, let $\Delta v_{ijks}(t, t')$ be the rate of wage growth experienced by this cohort over the time interval (t, t'). To simplify the exposition, suppose that all immigrant cohorts arrive in the same calendar year j and that the wage growth is observed over the same time interval (t, t'). Consider the regression model:

$$(17) \qquad \Delta v_{iks} = \lambda v_{iks} + \xi_k + \omega_{iks},$$

where ω_{iks} is an independent identically distributed (i.i.d.) error term. Duleep and Regets (1997b) show that λ is strongly negative, and they interpret this finding as implying that the decline in skills across successive immigrant cohorts is not as strong as suggested by the trend in entry wages. A negative λ seems to suggest that more recent cohorts will experience faster wage growth in the future and that the present value of the age-earnings profile might not differ much across cohorts.

The key question, however, is whether the coefficient λ estimates the unconditional rate of convergence (θ) or the conditional rate of convergence (θ^*). To see the relationship among the various parameters, rewrite the log entry wage and the rate of wage growth for the (i, k, s) cohort as

$$(18) \qquad v_{iks} = v_{ik} + \varphi_s + e_{iks},$$

$$(19) \qquad \Delta v_{iks} = \Delta v_{ik} = \chi_s + \varepsilon_{iks},$$

where φ_s and χ_s are fixed effects giving the returns to schooling for the log entry wage and the rate of wage growth, respectively; and e_{iks} and ε_{iks} are i.i.d. random variables that are uncorrelated with the other right-hand-side variables in equations (18) and (19). The convergence regression in equation (17) can be rewritten as

$$(20) \qquad \Delta v_{ik} = \lambda v_{ik} + (\lambda \varphi_s - \chi_s) + \xi_k + \omega',$$

where $\omega = \omega_{iks} + \lambda e_{iks} - \varepsilon_{iks}$, and an observation is an (i, k, s) cell. Let $p_{ik}(s)$ be the fraction of the population that has s years of schooling in the immigrant cohort that migrated from country i at age k, and aggregate across schooling groups within this cohort.[16] This aggregation yields

$$(21) \qquad \Delta v_{ik} = \lambda v_{ik} + \sum_s (\lambda \varphi_s - \chi_s) p_{ik}(s) + \xi_k + \overline{\omega}.$$

Equation (21) shows that the convergence regression that uses schooling groups to define the cohort is equivalent to a regression that aggregates across schooling groups but includes variables that indicate the educational attainment of the cohort. As a result, the coefficient λ estimates the extent of conditional convergence across immigrant cohorts, θ^*. It is not surprising, therefore, that Duleep and Regets (1997b) find a great deal of wage convergence across immigrant cohorts since they are implicitly holding constant the human capital endowment at the time of entry.

Row 2 of table 1.4 shows a related way of controlling for educational attainment. The regressions in this panel use earnings data that are adjusted for education in the first stage. In particular, the individual-level regressions in equation (12) include educational attainment as an independent variable. As a result, the log entry wage (v_{ijk}) and the rate of wage growth (Δv_{ijk}) are measured for the worker with the "average" level of schooling. This approach to controlling for differences in education attainment across the groups, therefore, is roughly similar to the Duleep-Regets approach. Not surprisingly, the regression coefficients reported in row 2 of table 1.4 show that the correlation between the rate of wage growth and the log entry

16. The aggregation uses $p_{jk}(s)$ as weights.

wage is strongly negative, regardless of the variables that are included in the regression.

Although interesting, it is important not to over interpret the practical significance of the finding of conditional convergence. Conditional convergence does *not* suggest that immigrant cohorts with lower entry wages experience faster wage growth in the United States. There is, in fact, *no* convergence among the various national origin groups that make up the immigrant population. The *observed* wage gap among the various immigrant cohorts will not narrow over time, but might even increase.

The lesson is clear: The choice of a base group is crucial in any discussion of immigrant economic progress or assimilation. Immigrants who start out with similar endowments of human capital tend to end up with roughly similar wages. But immigrants originating in different countries, in fact, have very different human capital endowments and will tend to end up in very different places in the income distribution.

There are a number of technical problems with the convergence regressions reported in table 1.4 that deserve some discussion. First, many of the cells in the analysis contain relatively few observations. The dependent variable in each cell is constructed from wages reported in two different censuses. Because the 1980 and 1990 immigrant extracts form a 5 percent random sample of the population (and because the immigrant population has grown rapidly over time), the sample size used in the construction of wage levels for the various cells is reasonable for most national origin groups. In particular, 19 observations were used to calculate the 1980 wage for the average cohort, and 24 observations were used to calculate the 1990 wage. The smaller size of the 1970 immigrant extract, however, implies that only 11 observations were used to calculate the 1970 wage for the average cohort.[17]

As noted earlier, all the regressions are weighted by the factor $(n_t^{-1} + n_{t'}^{-1})^{-1}$. I reestimated the regression models using only the cells that are likely to have the least sampling error. In particular, I restricted the analysis to the 50 percent of the cells that have the largest value of the weights. As shown in table 1.4, there is even stronger evidence of a positive correla-

---

17. These averages hide a lot of dispersion in sample size among cells. In calculating the 1980 wage for the 1980–1990 wage growth measure, 25 percent of the cells have 9 or fewer observations, 50 percent have more than 24 observations, and 25 percent have more than 72 observations. In calculating the 1990 wage for the 1980–1990 wage growth measure, 25 percent of the cells have 7 or fewer observations, 50 percent have more than 19 observations, and 25 percent have more than 55 observations. In calculating the 1970 wage for the 1970–1980 wage growth measure, 25 percent of the cells have 5 or fewer observations, 50 percent have more than 11 observations, and 25 percent have more than 30 observations. In calculating the 1980 wage for the 1970–1980 wage growth measure, 25 percent of the cells have 9 or fewer observations, 50 percent have more than 24 observations and 25 percent have more than 71 observations.

tion between entry wage levels and the unadjusted wage growth in this restricted sample. And as before, the positive convergence coefficient turns negative when the regressions control for either educational attainment or country of origin.[18]

A second potential problem is that the log entry wage measures different things for different cohorts. As noted above, the wage observed at the beginning of the decade (time t) is roughly the entry wage for those immigrants who arrived during the 1965–69 or 1975–79 periods. This wage, however, is not the entry wage for immigrants who arrived in either the first half of the 1960s or the first half of the 1970s. Row 4 of table 1.4 shows that the results do not change when the regressions are restricted to the immigrant cohorts that migrated in the last half of a particular decade. The correlation between the log entry wage and the rate of wage growth is positive when no controls are included in the regression, and turns negative when human capital controls are added.

Finally, there is probably measurement error in the log entry wage. Any measurement error in this wage will impart a negative bias on its coefficient (toward -1). The spurious negative correlation arises because the log entry wage appears on both sides of the equation, but with different signs. One can assess the sensitivity of the results to measurement error by using instrumental variables to eliminate the spurious correlation.

The construction of the census data suggests two alternative instruments for the log entry wage. The regressions reported in row 1 of table 1.4 use the rate of wage growth observed for the immigrant cohorts that arrived in 1960–64, 1965–69, 1970–74, or 1975–79. To eliminate the measurement error, we can use the log entry wage of the *preceding* immigrant cohort as an instrument for the entry wage of a particular cohort. Consider, for example, the Mexican immigrants who were 25–34 years old in 1980 and who entered the United States between 1975 and 1979. The proposed instrument would be the wage of Mexican immigrants who were 25–34 in 1980 but who entered the country between 1970 and 1974.[19] The

---

18. To assess the sensitivity of the results to sample size and outlying observations, I estimated a set of unweighted convergence regressions in the sample of immigrant cohorts where I used at least 30 observations to calculate the mean wage of the cohort. The basic convergence coefficient is $-.065$ with a standard error of .05, so that there is essentially no relationship between the rate of wage growth and the log entry wage. The basic conditional convergence coefficient is $-.313$, with a standard error of .06. These regressions have 270 observations. The unweighted results, therefore, are roughly similar to those reported in the text. I also estimated the regressions after omitting the immigrant cohorts that originated in Mexico. The unconditional convergence coefficient in the subsample of cohorts where I used more than 30 observations to calculate the mean wage of the cohort in each census year and where the Mexican cohorts are omitted is $-.097$, with a standard error of .05. The respective conditional convergence coefficient is $-.305$, with a standard error of .06. These regressions have 258 observations.

19. The R^2 for the first-stage regression is .68.

Table 1.5   Estimates of Wage Convergence, Using Instrumental Variables

	OLS		IV	
	(1)	(2)	(3)	(4)
1. Cohorts who migrated between 1965 and 1980[a]				
Log entry wage	.1686	−.3535	.3371	.0146
	(.1091)	(.0786)	(.0918)	(.0862)
Initial educational attainment	—	.0442	—	.0261
		(.0066)		(.0055)
2. Cohorts who migrated between 1960 and 1969[b]				
Log wage in 1980	.1523	−.1284	.2525	.2018
	(.0959)	(.0970)	(.0884)	(.1296)
Educational attainment in 1980	—	.0248	—	.0045
		(.0100)		(.0094)

Note: Standard errors are reported in parentheses. All regressions include a vector of fixed effects indicating the cohort's year of migration/age at arrival. The regressions are weighted by $(n_0^{-1} + n_1^{-1})^{-1}$, where n_0 is the number of observations used in calculating the wage at the beginning of the decade, and n_1 is the number of observations used in calculating the wage at the end of the decade.

[a]Dependent variable is rate of wage growth during first 10 years; instrument is log entry wage for preceding cohort. $N = 402$.

[b]Dependent variable is rate of wage growth between 1980 and 1990; instrument is log entry wage of cohort in 1970. $N = 235$.

construction of this instrument, of course, implies that the immigrants who arrived between 1960 and 1964 do not contribute any observations to the regression (since no preceding cohort is observed for this group).

Row 1 of table 1.5 reports both the ordinary least squares (OLS) and instrumental variables (IV) convergence coefficients in this subsample of the data. The OLS coefficients resemble those reported earlier: There is a positive correlation between the log entry wage and the rate of wage growth in the raw data, and this correlation turns negative once the regression controls for educational attainment. The IV procedure leads to a much stronger positive correlation between the log entry wage and the subsequent rate of wage growth when the regression does not control for initial educational attainment, and it greatly weakens the negative correlation (in fact, it is essentially zero) when the education control is added. The IV estimation, therefore, raises questions about the robustness of the finding of conditional convergence.

These doubts are reinforced when we use an alternative instrument. We have three measures of the wage for the immigrants who arrived between 1960 and 1970. For these immigrants, we can observe their wage in 1970, 1980, and 1990. We can use this subsample of immigrants to estimate a convergence coefficient by regressing the 1980–90 rate of wage growth on the 1980 log wage. The data, however, also allow us to instrument the 1980 wage by the group's 1970 wage.[20] The resulting OLS and IV estimates are reported in row 2 of table 1.5. The IV results show that the correlation between wage levels and wage growth remains positive even after we control for educational attainment.

In sum, there is a positive (although weak) correlation between the log entry wage and the subsequent rate of wage growth across immigrant cohorts. If anything, immigrants who earn high wages at the time of entry experience faster wage growth in the future. This correlation, however, turns negative when the analysis adjusts for differences in initial endowments of human capital, either by including measures of educational attainment or country-of-origin fixed effects. The results, therefore, seem to suggest that there exists conditional convergence in the immigrant population, in the sense that the wages of immigrant groups that have the same initial level of human capital converge over time. However, this finding is not robust to simple attempts to control for the bias introduced by measurement error.

1.5   Immigrant Economic Progress and Source Country Characteristics

As we have seen, there are huge differences in log entry wages across national origin groups. Many studies have found that the initial economic performance of immigrants in the United States is strongly correlated with source country characteristics. For example, Borjas (1987) reports that immigrant wages depend positively on the per capita GDP of the source country and negatively on measures of income inequality. Similarly, Jasso and Rosenzweig (1986) report a positive correlation between immigrant wages and a variable indicating if the country of origin receives a Voice of America broadcast (presumably because these broadcasts provide information about the United States).

Suppose we interpret some of the source country characteristics as rough measures of the effective human capital of immigrant cohorts. The human capital model presented earlier then predicts that the qualitative effects of the source country characteristics on the log entry wage and on the rate of wage growth depend on the extent of relative complementarity or substitutability in the production function. The convergence regressions suggest that the production function exhibits weak relative complementarity between pre-existing human capital and postmigration investments. We would then expect that the source country variables have the *same* qualitative impact on the log entry wage and on the rate of wage growth. To

---

20. The R^2 for the first-stage regression is .73.

examine this theoretical implication, I constructed a data set summarizing various economic characteristics for 75 source countries.[21] The source country characteristics are as follows:

1. *Per capita GDP in the source country.* I used the Penn World Tables (version 5.6) to obtain a measure of per capita GDP in 1960, 1965, 1970, and 1975.[22] These dates were chosen to correspond with the time at which each of the four year-of-migration cohorts left the source country. Immigrants from richer countries tend to earn more in the United States—even after controlling for educational attainment and other observable measures of a worker's skills. Presumably, this correlation arises because the skills acquired in industrialized economies are more easily transferable to the United States. If increases in per capita GDP raise the effective human capital that immigrants bring to the United States *and* if there is weak relative complementarity in the human capital production function, the theory predicts that immigrants originating in richer countries should also have higher rates of wage growth.

2. *The Gini coefficient of the source country's income distribution.* Borjas (1987) has argued that immigrants originating in countries that offer a high rate of return to skills are more likely to be negatively selected, will have a smaller effective human capital stock at the time of migration, and will earn less in the United States. A higher rate of return to skills implies a more disperse distribution of income. The Gini coefficient of the source country's income distribution should then have a negative impact on the rate of wage growth. Deininger and Squire (1996) have constructed various measures of income inequality, including the Gini coefficient, for most countries since 1960. I used these data to obtain measures of the Gini coefficients in four years: 1960, 1965, 1970, and 1975.[23]

3. *A measure of "openness" of the source country's economy.* The openness index is defined as the ratio of exports plus imports to GDP (in percentage terms). I used the Penn World Tables to get this index for the calendar years 1960, 1965, 1970, and 1975. Immigrants originating in countries with open economies are more likely to have some contact with for-

---

21. The 75 countries included in the data below contain about 89 percent of all immigrants enumerated in the census who arrived between 1960 and 1979. A list of the 75 countries in the data is presented in the appendix.

22. The variable used is the real GDP per capita (Laspeyres index) in 1985 international prices.

23. The Gini coefficients are not available for all countries in all the years required. For some countries, for example, there are only two data points over the 1960–1980 period, once in the 1960s and once in the 1970s. In such cases, I used the data point for the 1960s and applied it to both 1960 and 1965, and the data point for the 1970s and applied it to both 1970 and 1975. I did not use any type of linear interpolation in the study, but simply approximated the dates available in the data to the dates required for my analysis. I also reestimated the regressions in the subsample of countries where such approximations were not required and obtained very similar results.

eign industries and economic institutions *prior* to migration, are more likely to have the types of skills that other countries value, and would be expected to have a higher level of effective capital when they enter the United States. Weak relative complementarity in the production function implies that the openness index should be positively correlated with both the log entry wage and the rate of wage growth of immigrant cohorts.

4. *A Herfindahl index measuring how immigrant cohorts cluster geographically once they enter the United States.* It has long been suspected (without much evidence) that residential clustering affects economic opportunities. Define the Herfindahl index for the group of immigrants who arrived from country *i* in year *j* as

$$(22) \qquad\qquad H_{ij} = \sum_r E_{ijr}^2,$$

where E_{ijr} gives the fraction of immigrants from the (i, j) cell who live in state *r*. The Herfindahl index takes on a maximum value of one if all immigrants live in a single state, and it becomes smaller the more randomly the immigrants are distributed over the United States. I use data on states, rather than on metropolitan areas, to calculate the clustering index. The Herfindahl index is sensitive to the number of geographic units, and the number of metropolitan areas identified by the census has grown significantly over time (particularly between 1970 and 1980). The state-based calculation, therefore, makes the Herfindahl index comparable over time. The measures of the Herfindahl index for the immigrant cohorts that arrived in either 1960–64 or 1965–69 are obtained from the 1970 census, while the measures of the index for the cohorts that arrived in 1970–74 or 1975–79 are obtained from the 1980 census.

5. *The distance from the country of origin to the United States (in thousands of miles).*[24] Borjas and Bratsberg (1996) have shown that the return migration rate of immigrants in the United States is negatively correlated with distance from the source country. This empirical finding suggests that immigrants who originate in far-away countries are more likely to view their migration to the United States as permanent, and have greater incentives to invest in U.S.-specific capital. In terms of the theoretical framework, longer distances decrease the probability of out-migration and increase the discounting factor ρ. Distance from the source country, therefore, should have a positive effect on the rate of wage growth.[25]

6. *Political conditions in the country of origin.* Barro and Lee (1994) used the Banks (1986) Cross-National Time-Series Data File to calculate the number of revolutions (per year) that occurred in the various countries in

24. These data are obtained from Fitzpatrick and Madlin (1986).
25. Borjas (1987) shows that distance from the source country (which presumably affects migration costs) can also have a direct effect on effective human capital because it influences the selection of the immigrant flow.

Table 1.6   Log Wage Level and Source Country Characteristics

	Regression			
Variable	(1)	(2)	(3)	(4)
Log per capita GDP	.0862	.1361	.1285	.0531
	(.0299)	(.0222)	(.0928)	(.0707)
Openness index	.0013	−.0001	−.0010	−.0004
	(.0006)	(.0006)	(.0008)	(.0006)
Gini coefficient	−.0047	−.0012	−.0070	−.0019
	(.0015)	(.0015)	(.0057)	(.0040)
Herfindahl index	−.8331	−.3133	−.0639	.1580
	(.1552)	(.1514)	(.1497)	(.1465)
Distance (in 1,000s of miles)	.0163	.0018	—	—
	(.0103)	(.0081)		
Revolutions per year	.0108	−.0105	.0201	−.0062
	(.0493)	(.0391)	(.0555)	(.0318)
Initial educational attainment	—	.0495	—	.0675
		(.0092)		(.0091)
R^2	.770	.845	.879	.906
Includes country-of-origin fixed effects	No	No	Yes	Yes

Note: Sample comprises immigrant cohorts who have been in United States 10 or fewer years. Standard errors are reported in parentheses. All regressions include a vector of dummy variables indicating the cohort's age at arrival and year of migration. The regressions have 966 observations. The regressions are weighted by the number of observations used in calculating the mean log wage.

the periods 1960–64, 1965–69, 1970–74, and 1975–79. Political instability in the country of origin would likely have an impact on the return migration rate, and should again affect the discounting factor. A higher degree of political instability, therefore, would presumably lead to higher rates of wage growth in the United States.

It is useful to begin by documenting that the source country characteristics have effects on the log entry wage that are consistent with those reported in the existing literature. The log entry wage is defined by the fixed effect $v_{ijk}(t)$ calculated in equation (12); it is obtained from the 1970 census for the cohorts that arrived in the 1960s, and from the 1980 census for the cohorts that arrived in the 1970s. The main specification of the log wage regressions is reported in the first column of table 1.6.[26] In general, the results are consistent with the evidence reported in existing studies. Immigrants who originate in richer countries earn more, and immigrants who originate in countries with high levels of income inequality earn less. The regression also reveals that immigrants originating in open economies earn more, and that the immigrant groups who exhibit substantial geo-

26. The regressions are weighted by the cell size.

graphic clustering earn less. The remaining columns of table 1.6 show that the inclusion of educational attainment or of country-of-origin fixed effects weaken many of the coefficients.

The first column of table 1.7 reports the main regression showing the relationship between the rate of wage growth and the source country characteristics. With one important exception, variables that presumably increase the cohort's effective human capital tend to have a positive impact on the rate of wage growth, suggesting weak relative complementarity in the human capital production function. Consider, for example, the index of openness in the source country. Immigrants originating in open economies both earn more and experience faster wage growth. Moreover, the effect is numerically important: A change in the index from 31 to 80, which are the 1975 openness indices for Spain and Jamaica respectively, implies a 7 percentage point increase in the rate of wage growth.

The regressions also indicate that immigrants originating in countries with higher Gini coefficients experience slower wage growth. And again, the effect is numerically important. In 1975, the Gini coefficient for Czechoslovakia was 21, while for Mexico it was 58. This difference in the Gini coefficient implies a 14 percentage point differential in the rate of wage growth.

Table 1.7 also shows that the distance between the source country and the United States, a measure of the difficulty of return migration, has a significant positive effect on the rate of wage growth. Immigrants who originate in a country that is 5,500 miles away will, on average, experience about 6 percentage points greater wage growth than immigrants who come from a country that is 500 miles away. The regression, however, shows that the political instability variable does not play a significant role in determining the rate of wage growth.

The regression also suggests that immigrant clustering reduces the rate of wage growth. The estimated coefficient of the Herfindahl index suggests that a reduction in this index from .25 to .04 (or roughly from the average Herfindahl index in the immigrant population to that found among natives) would increase the rate of wage growth by about 3 percentage points. Of course, the regressions do not tell us *why* this correlation arises. The clustering of immigrants, for instance, may have a direct impact on their economic opportunities simply because the increase in labor supply reduces wages (particularly if immigrants are immobile). Residential segregation, however, may also change the immigrant's effective human capital by reducing the incentives to invest in English language proficiency, or by "tying" the immigrants to specific regions of the country. It would be of great interest to determine the channels through which immigrant clustering slows down the rate of economic progress.

The one anomaly in the regression is the impact of per capita GDP in the source country. This variable has a strong positive effect on the log

Table 1.7   Rate of Wage Growth and Source Country Characteristics

Variable	Regression					
	(1)	(2)	(3)	(4)	(5)	(6)
Log per capita GDP	-.0571	-.0238	-.0428	-.0220	-.0507	-.0445
	(.0147)	(.0886)	(.0155)	(.0878)	(.0235)	(.0234)
Openness index	.0015	.0014	.0011	.0014	.0011	.0010
	(.0003)	(.0014)	(.0003)	(.0014)	(.0005)	(.0005)
Gini coefficient	-.0039	-.0148	-.0031	-.0149	-.0058	-.0043
	(.0009)	(.0077)	(.0007)	(.0078)	(.0017)	(.0014)
Herfindahl index	-.1603	-.4217	-.0343	-.4260	.1166	.2006
	(.0740)	(.1424)	(.0859)	(.1511)	(.1577)	(.1569)
Distance (in 1,000s of miles)	.0110	—	.0077	—	.0186	.0126
	(.0044)		(.0038)		(.0081)	(.0072)
Revolutions per year	.0031	-.0032	-.0066	-.0023	-.0432	-.0482
	(.0229)	(.0362)	(.0211)	(.0360)	(.0375)	(.0369)
Initial educational attainment	—	—	.0119	-.0016	—	.0221
			(.0034)	(.0070)		(.0107)
English proficiency at entry	—	—	—	—	.0915	-.0503
					(.0596)	(.0926)
R^2	.601	.682	.613	.682	.586	.604
Includes year-of-migration/ age-at-arrival fixed effects	Yes	Yes	Yes	Yes	Yes	Yes
Includes country-of-origin fixed effects	No	Yes	No	Yes	No	No

Note: Dependent variable is rate of wage growth observed in first 10 years in United States. Standard errors are reported in parentheses. The regressions in columns (1)–(4) have 749 observations. The regressions in columns (5) and (6) use only the cohort that arrived between 1975 and 1979, and have 219 observations. The regressions are weighted by $(n_0^{-1} + n_1^{-1})^{-1}$, where n_0 is the number of observations used in calculating the wage at the beginning of the decade, and n_1 is the number of observations used in calculating the wage at the end of the decade.

entry wage, but a strong negative effect on the rate of wage growth. The negative correlation reported in the first column of table 1.7, however, turns out to be very sensitive to model specification. Consider, for example, the regressions reported in columns (3) and (4), which add a vector of country-of-origin fixed effects to the specification. Most of the source country variables have the same impact as in the simpler regression, so that a decrease in income inequality *within* the country raises the rate of wage growth of immigrants in the United States. The coefficient of per capita GDP, however, becomes insignificant.

Finally, it is worth noting that the source country characteristics— which, at best, are rough measures of the effective human capital stock of a particular cohort of immigrants—explain about 60 percent of the dispersion in wage growth among the various cohorts. In other words, source country characteristics matter a great deal in determining the rate of wage growth of immigrants in the United States.

The regression specifications reported in columns (3) and (4) of table 1.7 include the average educational attainment of the immigrants at the time of entry. Column (3) implies that a one-year increase in educational attainment increases the rate of wage growth by 1.2 percentage points. Note, however, that the independent impact of educational attainment disappears when the regression includes a vector of country-of-origin fixed effects.

It would be of interest to include measures of English language proficiency in the wage growth regressions. Presumably, persons who know the language would have an easier time adapting in the United States (although this effect could be attenuated by residential segregation). The 1970 U.S. census, however, does not contain any information on English language proficiency, so we cannot observe the initial language skills of the immigrants who arrived in the 1960s. I used the 1980 census to calculate the probability that immigrants who arrived between 1975 and 1979 spoke English well or very well. This statistic was calculated for each cohort by country of origin and age at arrival. The last two columns of table 1.7 report the regression results obtained when one includes this variable in the model (and when the regression is estimated in the subsample of immigrants who migrated in 1975–79). English language proficiency at the time of entry has an independent positive impact on the rate of wage growth, but it does not change the impact of most of the other variables in the model. The last column in the table shows that the impact of English language proficiency becomes insignificant if we control for the educational attainment of the cohort.

In sum, the empirical evidence shows that source country characteristics matter in determining both the entry wage and the subsequent rate of wage growth. Moreover, the same underlying factors that tend to generate higher wages also tend to generate faster wage growth. In effect, the empirical results confirm that there is a positive correlation between the economic performance of immigrants at the time of entry and the rate of economic progress in the United States, so that the human capital production function for immigrants exhibits weak relative complementarity.

1.6 Investments in Education

The previous section documented that the rate of wage growth experienced by immigrants cohorts responded to source country characteristics that proxy for either the effective rate of human capital or the discounting factor. This section shows more directly that source country characteristics do indeed alter the rate of human capital accumulation by examining the determinants of investments in educational attainment in the postmigration period.

I computed the change in educational attainment experienced by each of the immigrant cohorts (by country of origin, year of arrival, and age at migration) during their first 10 years in the United States. I then estimated regressions, identical to those presented in earlier sections, that describe both the extent of convergence in educational attainment across immigrant cohorts and the link between investments in schooling and source country characteristics. The estimated regressions are reported in table 1.8.[27]

The first two columns of the table report the simple convergence regressions by relating the change in educational attainment during the first 10 years to the educational attainment at the time of entry. As with the analysis of wage convergence, the raw correlation is positive, but weak. If the regression also includes a vector of country-of-origin fixed effects, however, these correlations become negative and significant. Not surprisingly, immigrants who originate in the same country of origin (but arrive at different times and at different ages) tend to converge to the same educational attainment. Nevertheless, the main implication of the evidence is that immigrants who have the highest level of effective human capital at the time of entry are also the ones who make the largest postmigration investments, and hence experience the fastest rate of economic progress. Once again, the empirical evidence suggests some complementarity between pre-existing human capital and the rate of human capital accumulation in the United States.

The remaining columns of the table report regressions of the change in educational attainment on the source country characteristics. For the most

27. Not surprisingly, there is a strong positive link between $v_{ijk}(t, t')$, the wage change experienced by a particular cohort during the time interval (t, t'), and the cohort's change in educational attainment. The coefficient from a regression of the wage change on the change in educational attainment in the sample of cohorts used in table 1.8 is .070 (with a standard error of .018), and the R^2 is .402.

Table 1.8   Determinants of Postmigration Investments in Education

	Regression					
Variable	(1)	(2)	(3)	(4)	(5)	(6)
Initial educational attainment	.0209	−.3701	—	−.3773	—	−.0647
	(.0281)	(.0527)		(.0529)		(.0283)
Log per capita GDP	—	—	.7687	1.1772	−.0205	−.0984
			(.3302)	(.5498)	(.0650)	(.0770)
Openness index	—	—	−.0012	−.0045	.0056	.0076
			(.0055)	(.0056)	(.0020)	(.0026)
Gini coefficient	—	—	−.0233	−.0449	−.0154	−.0197
			(.0233)	(.0216)	(.0037)	(.0051)
Herfindahl index	—	—	−.1184	−1.1063	.1464	−.5384
			(.9397)	(.9948)	(.3916)	(.4616)
Distance (in 1,000s of miles)	—	—	—	—	.0022	.0199
					(.0243)	(.0253)
Revolutions per year	—	—	−.1113	.1065	−.0134	.0394
			(.1567)	(.1506)	(.1199)	(.1465)
R^2	.200	.504	.395	.520	.285	.306
Includes year-of-migration/ age-at-arrival fixed effects	Yes	Yes	Yes	Yes	Yes	Yes
Includes country-of-origin fixed effects	No	Yes	Yes	Yes	No	No

Note: Dependent variable is change in educational attainment of immigrant cohort in first 10 years after arrival. Standard errors are reported in parentheses. All regressions include a vector of dummy variables indicating the cohort's age at arrival and year of migration. The regressions in the first two columns have 819 observations, and the regressions in the remaining columns have 749 observations. The regressions are weighted by $(n_0^{-1} + n_1^{-1})^{-1}$, where n_0 is the number of observations used in calculating the education level at the beginning of the decade, and n_1 is the number of observations used in calculating the education level at the end of the decade.

part, the regressions confirm the results reported in the previous section. The source country characteristics tend to affect investments in education in the same way that they affect the rate of wage growth. Immigrants who originate in countries where the income distribution has a large Gini coefficient (and presumably there is a large rate of return to skills) acquire less schooling in the postmigration period; immigrants who originate in open economies acquire more schooling; and immigrants who originate in richer countries acquire less schooling (but this anomalous correlation is not significant).

1.7   Summary

This paper presented a theoretical and empirical study of the determinants of economic progress in the immigrant population. The theoretical framework used the human capital model to derive the relationship between the human capital endowment of immigrants at the time they enter the United States, the entry wage of the immigrant cohort, and the subsequent rate of wage growth. The theory showed that the correlation between initial (log) wages and the rate of wage growth could be positive if there existed some complementarity in the production function for human capital, so that highly skilled immigrants would find it easier to acquire additional human capital in the United States. The potential existence of relative complementarity has practical significance: The sizable skill differentials that are observed among immigrant groups at the time of entry could well widen over time.

The empirical analysis used the 1970, 1980, and 1990 Public Use Microdata Samples of the U.S. census. These data permit the tracking of specific cohorts of immigrants over a 20-year time frame. The immigrant cohorts were defined in terms of national origin, year of migration, and age at arrival. The study generated a number of findings:

1. There is a weak positive correlation between the log entry wage and the rate of wage growth, suggesting some complementarity between the human capital acquired abroad and the human capital that immigrants acquire in the United States. This positive correlation, however, probably turns negative if we compare immigrants who have similar human capital endowments when they enter the United States.

2. There is no evidence that more recent immigrant cohorts, who have lower entry wages, experience faster wage growth.

3. Because of the relative weak complementarity in the human capital production function, the same source country characteristics that improve the economic status of immigrants at the time of entry also lead to larger human capital acquisition in the postmigration period and faster wage growth.

The long-run economic performance of immigrants in the United States plays an important role in any assessment of the economic impact of immigration. The empirical evidence presented in this paper suggests that immigrants who enter the United States with a sizable human capital endowment are also the immigrants who find it easier to adapt and acquire additional skills in their new surroundings. As a result, the process of economic assimilation does not "even out" the playing field in the immigrant population. Instead, the assimilation process may actually increase income inequality among national origin groups in the immigrant population.

Appendix
Countries Used in the Analysis

Note: The countries marked with an asterisk are not included in the analysis that relates the rate of wage growth to source country characteristics.

Africa	El Salvador	Israel
Cape Verde*	Guatemala	Japan
Egypt	Guyana	Jordan
Ethiopia*	Haiti	Korea
Ghana	Honduras	Laos*
Kenya	Jamaica	Lebanon*
Liberia	Mexico	Malaysia
Morocco	Nicaragua	Myanmar
Nigeria	Panama	Pakistan
Sierra Leone	Peru	Philippines
South Africa	Trinidad	Saudi Arabia*
	Uruguay*	Sri Lanka
Americas	Venezuela	Syria*
Argentina		Taiwan
Barbados	*Asia*	Thailand
Bolivia	Afghanistan*	Turkey
Brazil	Bangladesh	Vietnam*
Canada	Cambodia*	
Chile	China	*Europe*
Colombia	Hong Kong	Austria
Costa Rica	India	Belgium
Cuba	Indonesia	Czech
Dominican Republic	Iran	Denmark
Ecuador	Iraq	Finland

France	Poland	USSR
Germany	Portugal	Yugoslavia
Greece	Romania	
Hungary	Spain	*Other*
Ireland	Sweden	Australia
Italy	Switzerland	Fiji
Netherlands	United Kingdom	New Zealand
Norway		

References

Banks, Arthur S. 1986. Cross-national time series data file. Center for Comparative Political Research, State University of New York, Binghamton, N.Y.

Barro, Robert J. 1991. Economic growth in a cross-section of countries. *Quarterly Journal of Economics* 106 (May): 407–33.

———. 1997. *Determinants of economic growth: A cross-country empirical study.* Cambridge, Mass.: MIT Press.

Barro, Robert J., and Jong-Wha Lee. 1994. Sources of economic growth. *Carnegie-Rochester Conference Series on Public Policy* 40:1–46.

Ben-Porath, Yoram. 1967. The production of human capital and the life cycle of earnings. *Journal of Political Economy* 75 (August): 352–65.

———. 1970. The production of human capital over time. In *Education, income, and human capital,* ed. W. Lee Hansen. New York: Columbia University Press.

Borjas, George J. 1985. Assimilation, changes in cohort quality, and the earnings of immigrants. *Journal of Labor Economics* 3 (October): 463–89.

———. 1987. Self-selection and the earnings of immigrants. *American Economic Review* 77 (September): 531–53.

———. 1992. National origin and the skills of immigrants in the postwar period. In *Immigration and the workforce: Economic consequences for the United States and source areas,* ed. George J. Borjas and Richard B. Freeman. Chicago: University of Chicago Press.

———. 1994. The economics of immigration. *Journal of Economic Literature* 32 (December): 1667–717.

———. 1995. Assimilation and changes in cohort quality revisited: What happened to immigrant earnings in the 1980s? *Journal of Labor Economics* 13 (April): 201–45.

Borjas, George J., and Bernt Bratsberg. 1996. Who leaves? The outmigration of the foreign-born. *Review of Economics and Statistics* 78 (February): 165–76.

Borjas, George J., and Richard B. Freeman, eds. 1992. *Immigration and the work force: Economic consequences for the United States and source areas.* Chicago: University of Chicago Press.

Chiswick, Barry R. 1978. The effect of Americanization on the earnings of foreign-born men. *Journal of Political Economy* 86 (October): 897–921.

Deininger, Klaus, and Lyn Squire. 1996. A new data set measuring income inequality. *World Bank Economic Review* 10 (September): 565–92.

Duleep, Harriet Orcutt, and Mark C. Regets. 1997a. Are lower immigrant earnings at entry associated with faster growth? A review. Program for Research on Immigration Policy, Discussion Paper PRIP-UI-44. Washington, D.C.: The Urban Institute.

————. 1997b. Immigrant entry earnings and human capital growth: Evidence from the 1960–1980 censuses. *Research in Labor Economics* 16:297–317.

Fitzpatrick, Gary L., and Marylin J. Madlin. 1986. *Direct line distances.* U.S. ed. London: The Scarecrow Press, Inc.

Funkhouser, Edward, and Stephen J. Trejo. 1995. The labor market skills of recent male immigrants: Evidence from the current population surveys. *Industrial and Labor Relations Review* 48 (July): 792–811.

Hansen, W. Lee, ed. 1970. *Education, income, and human capital.* New York: Columbia University Press.

Hause, John. 1980. The fine structure of earnings and the on-the-job training hypothesis. *Econometrica* 48 (May): 1013–29.

Jasso, Guillermina, and Mark R. Rosenzweig. 1986. What's in a name? Country-of-origin influences on the earnings of immigrants in the United States. *Research in Human Capital and Development* 4:75–106.

Katz, Lawrence F., and Kevin M. Murphy. 1992. Changes in the wage structure, 1963–87: Supply and demand factors. *Quarterly Journal of Economics* 107 (February): 35–78.

Kearl, James R. 1988. The covariance structure of earnings and income, compensatory behavior, and on-the-job investments. *Review of Economics and Statistics* 70 (May): 214–23.

LaLonde, Robert J., and Robert H. Topel. 1992. The assimilation of immigrants in the U.S. labor market. *Immigration and the work force: Economic consequences for the United States and source areas,* ed. George J. Borjas and Richard B. Freeman. Chicago: University of Chicago Press.

Mankiw, N. Gregory, David Romer, and David N. Weil. 1992. A contribution to the empirics of economic growth. *Quarterly Journal of Economics* 107 (May): 407–38.

Mincer, Jacob. 1974. *Schooling, experience, and earnings.* New York: Columbia University Press.

Murphy, Kevin M., and Finis Welch. 1992. The structure of wages. *Quarterly Journal of Economics* 107 (February): 215–326.

Neumark, David, and Paul Taubman. 1995. Why do wage profiles slope upward? Tests of the general human capital model. *Journal of Labor Economics* 13 (October): 736–61.

Quah, Danny. 1993. Galton's fallacy and tests of the convergence hypothesis. *Scandinavian Journal of Economics* 95 (December): 427–43.

Rosen, Sherwin. 1976. A theory of life earnings. *Journal of Political Economy* 84 (2): S45–S67.

Schoeni, Robert F., Kevin F. McCarthy, and Georges Vernez. 1996. *The mixed economic progress of immigrants.* Santa Monica, Calif.: The RAND Corporation.

Summers, Robert, and Alan Heston. 1991. The Penn World table (mark 5): An expanded set of international comparisons, 1950–1988. *Quarterly Journal of Economics* 106:327–68.

Yuengert, Andrew. 1994. Immigrant earnings, relative to what? The importance of earnings function specification and comparison points. *Journal of Applied Econometrics* 9 (January–March): 71–90.

The Educational Attainment
of Immigrants
Trends and Implications

Julian R. Betts and Magnus Lofstrom

2.1 Introduction

Immigration can heavily influence the way in which a country's labor force evolves over time. Recent American experience bears this out. The proportion of immigrants in the adult population, aged 24–64, rose from 4.7 percent in 1970 to 6.2 percent in 1980 and to 7.9 percent in 1990. At the same time, there is a general perception that the educational composition of the immigrant population has changed over the last two decades, with immigrants becoming less skilled relative to native-born Americans. In a string of articles, Borjas has shown that such "cohort" effects are crucial in explaining the rising wage gap between immigrants and natives. (See, e.g., Borjas 1985, 1990.)

This paper has two broad goals. The first is to present a detailed portrait of the educational attainment of immigrants relative to native-born Americans. We will examine the extent to which immigrants' level of education has changed, both in an absolute sense and relative to that of natives, between 1970 and 1990. We also study the dynamics of educational attainment, by comparing and modeling the enrollment behavior of immigrants relative to natives over time. The second broad goal of the paper is to examine the implications of these trends both for immigrants themselves and for natives.

For immigrants, the central question we address is how trends in immi-

Julian R. Betts is associate professor of economics at the University of California, San Diego, and senior fellow at the Public Policy Institute of California. Magnus Lofstrom is a research associate at the Institute for the Study of Labor, Bonn, Germany.

The authors thank George Borjas, Caroline Hoxby, and preconference participants for helpful comments.

grants' educational attainment have affected their earnings relative to earnings of native-born Americans. We focus on modeling the returns to education, allowing for nonlinearities that have not always been addressed in the earlier literature on immigration. For instance, we study the relative size of "sheepskin," or graduation, effects for immigrants and natives, and test the idea that the returns to education depend in part on whether the education was obtained abroad or in the United States. We find these nonlinearities to be of some importance. We also extend the work of Bratsberg and Terrell (1997) by studying the role that traits of the country of origin play in determining the returns to education among immigrants.

Finally, we also study the impact of recent immigration on the educational attainment of natives. While several studies have examined whether inflows of immigrants have altered the wage structure facing natives, there are good reasons to believe that immigration can also affect the level of education that natives acquire. If the arrival of less-skilled immigrants lowers the wages of high school dropouts, it may provide an incentive for natives to acquire more education. But on the other hand, immigrants may "crowd out" natives from education, in part by making schools less effective when many of the students have limited proficiency in English. At the college level, there is the additional possibility that immigrants compete with native minorities for admissions under affirmative action programs. Betts (1998) and Hoxby (1998) provide evidence that immigrants have "crowded out" native minorities at both the high school and college levels. We present further evidence of the extent to which the ratio of immigrants in the local population induces natives to acquire more or less education, using a greater time span than was used in the two previous studies.

2.2   Data

In this paper we use the 1970, 1980, and 1990 U.S. Censuses of Population and Housing. Given the extremely large data set that results from this pooling across three censuses, we extracted a 20 percent randomly selected subsample of native-born Americans from the 5 percent sample of the 1980 and 1990 censuses. All native-born Americans and immigrants from the 1 percent 1970 census are included. Since the 1990 census is not a random sample of the population, sampling weights were used. These were set to the appropriate constants for the 1970 and 1980 censuses. All weights were then adjusted accordingly since not all observations for natives were used. Furthermore, there is a slight variation in the samples used for the tables and analysis presented here. In the first two tables we present summary statistics of educational attainment for males and females. This is the least restrictive sample in which all individuals aged 16–64 from the sample described above are included. For the remainder of the paper, only observations for males are included. Also, wage regressions restrict the sample to include males aged 24–64 who worked the year prior to the census and earned at least $50 in 1989 dollars. Workers for whom census data on age, sex, immigrant status, or education were allocated were deleted. Section 2.5, which examines the impact of immigration on the educational attainment of natives, uses a similar three-census pooled data set that we will describe more fully in the section.

It is important to realize that census data include not only legally admitted immigrants but also foreigners who are temporarily but legally in the United States on visas, as well as a large number of illegal aliens. Warren and Passel (1987) use 1980 census data and Immigration and Naturalization Service (INS) data to estimate that about one half of the 2 million people in the census who report being born in Mexico are illegal immigrants. Borjas, Freeman, and Lang (1991) extend this work by analyzing vital statistics, and they conclude that the 1980 census includes about two thirds of illegal aliens born in Mexico, due to undercounting. We use the census data in the belief that they give the most detailed picture available of all immigrants, regardless of legal status. Of course, it does not speak directly to immigration policy, since some of the immigrants in the sample were not admitted legally. On the other hand, one could equally well use INS data to infer trends in the educational attainment of legally admitted immigrants. Such an approach gives a much better idea of how admission criteria have affected the occupational mix of legally admitted immigrants. But it will necessarily give a less accurate picture of the overall traits of all immigrants in the country. This second approach is adopted by Jasso, Rosenzweig, and Smith in chapter 5 in this volume.

2.3 Trends in Educational Attainment and Enrollment among Natives and Immigrants

2.3.1 Basic Results

We begin by presenting evidence on the distribution of educational attainment among natives and immigrants derived from the 1970, 1980, and 1990 censuses. Table 2.1 shows the mean, 25th, 50th, and 75th percentiles of years of schooling among both groups, for males aged 16–64.[1]

This table reveals some complex patterns. In terms of the mean level

1. The 1990 census codes educational attainment differently from the 1970 and 1980 censuses. In the 1990 data, we recoded years of schooling in the same fashion as Borjas (1995). No school completed, nursery school, and kindergarten are recoded as 0 years of schooling; first through fourth grade are recoded as 2.5 years; fifth through eighth grade as 6.5 years; ninth grade as 9 years; tenth grade as 10 years; eleventh grade or twelfth grade without a high school diploma as 11 years; high school graduate as 12 years; some college, no degree as 13 years; associate degree as 14 years; bachelor's degree as 16 years; master's degree as 17 years; and professional or doctorate degree as 20 years.

Table 2.1   Years of Education, Males Aged 16–64

	Lower Quartile						Upper Quartile					
	1970		1980		1990		1970		1980		1990	
	Native	Immigrant	Native	Immigrant	Native	Immigrant	Native	Immigrant	Native	Immigrant	Native	Immigrant
All	9	8	11	8	12	9	13	13	14	15	14	14
White	10	8	12	10	12	12	13	14	14	16	14	16
Black	8	8	10	11	11	11	12	13	12	14	13	14
Asian	11	9	12	12	12	12	14	16	15	17	16	16
Hispanic	8	6	9	6	11	6.5	12	12	12	12	13	12

	Mean						Median					
	1970		1980		1990		1970		1980		1990	
	Native	Immigrant	Native	Immigrant	Native	Immigrant	Native	Immigrant	Native	Immigrant	Native	Immigrant
All	11.36	10.59	12.42	11.61	12.69	11.28	12	11	12	12	12	12
White	11.63	10.97	12.65	12.51	12.88	13.07	12	12	12	12	13	13
Black	9.49	11.01	11.13	12.19	11.60	12.18	10	12	12	12	12	12
Asian	12.09	11.86	13.26	14.04	13.38	13.45	12	12	12	14	13	13
Hispanic	9.46	8.83	10.89	9.09	11.44	8.86	10	9	12	9	12	10

of education, it does not appear that immigrants became steadily less well educated over time. The mean level of education of immigrants rose slightly from 1970 to 1980 but fell slightly by 1990. Overall, for the 1970–90 period, immigrants became slightly more educated, with a two-thirds of a year increase in years of schooling. The trends for natives are startlingly different, with increases in mean years of schooling in both decades totaling one and one-third years. Immigrants did become less well educated *relative* to natives in both decades, but in *absolute* terms, immigrants' mean level of education rose slightly.

Trends in the median, upper, and lower quartiles reveal considerable heterogeneity in the immigrant population. The drop in the relative level of immigrants' education has been caused by a considerable decline in the relative educational attainment of the lower quartile of immigrants. Between 1970 and 1990, the gap in years of schooling between the 25th percentile immigrant and the 25th percentile native rose from just one year to three years. The data on the median and upper quartiles tell a quite different story. The median level of education of natives remained at 12 years in all three decades; among immigrants, the median level of education rose from 11 to 12 years. The level of education of the 75th percentile immigrant rose from 13 to 14 years between 1970 and 1990, exactly matching the corresponding levels for natives. Furthermore, in 1980 the upper quartile immigrant had 15 years of education, compared to 14 for natives.

In summary, the upper half of the immigrant population has been and continues to be at least as highly educated as the upper half of the native population. The observed decline in the mean level of immigrants' education relative to natives reflects a decline in the relative educational status of the bottom half of the immigrant population.

The table also breaks down the distribution of education among the larger racial/ethnic groups. These calculations show that at all three quantiles, the years of schooling of white, black, and Asian immigrants have increased significantly between 1970 and 1990. Among Hispanics, the mean level of education was far lower than for the other immigrant groups in 1970, and it remained stagnant through the next two decades. The data for the three quantiles show the same stagnation in education among Hispanic immigrants.

Table 2.2 shows the same data, calculated this time for women. The mean level of education among immigrant women increased by more than it did for men over the 1970–90 period, up from 10.05 to 11.06 years. However, this increase is still lower than the one for native women; over the same period, the mean level of education increased from 11.26 to 12.61 for natives. The key trend shown among men seems to hold for women as well: Educational attainment increased among immigrants in absolute terms but declined in relative terms. As for men, the decline in female immigrants' level of education relative to natives has been caused solely by a widening gap in the education in the bottom half of the educational

Table 2.2   **Years of Education, Females Aged 16–64**

Lower Quartile

	1970		1980		1990	
	Native	Immigrant	Native	Immigrant	Native	Immigrant
All	10	8	11	8	12	9
White	10	8	12	10	12	12
Black	8	8	10	10	11	11
Asian	11	9	12	11	12	11
Hispanic	8	6	9	6	10	6.5

Upper Quartile

	1970		1980		1990	
	Native	Immigrant	Native	Immigrant	Native	Immigrant
All	12	12	13	14	13	13
White	12	12	14	14	14	14
Black	12	12	13	13	13	13
Asian	13	15	15	16	16	16
Hispanic	12	12	12	12	13	12

Mean

	1970		1980		1990	
	Native	Immigrant	Native	Immigrant	Native	Immigrant
All	11.26	10.05	12.17	11.00	12.61	11.06
White	11.49	10.40	12.36	11.69	12.77	12.30
Black	10.01	10.29	11.43	11.57	11.96	11.87
Asian	11.91	11.37	12.97	12.39	13.34	12.41
Hispanic	9.24	8.38	10.51	8.97	11.34	9.05

Median

	1970		1980		1990	
	Native	Immigrant	Native	Immigrant	Native	Immigrant
All	12	11	12	12	12	12
White	12	12	12	12	12	12
Black	11	11	12	12	12	12
Asian	12	12	12	12	13	13
Hispanic	10	8	12	9	12	10

Table 2.3   **Mean Years of Total Schooling**

| | Years of Education | | |
Cohort	1970	1980	1990
Arrived 1985–89			12.266
Arrived 1980–84			11.679
Arrived 1975–79		12.254	11.492
Arrived 1970–74		11.492	11.448
Arrived 1965–69	11.313	11.855	12.244
Arrived 1960–64	10.963	12.338	12.721
Arrived 1950–59	10.680	12.376	12.723
Arrived before 1950	10.208	12.351	13.100

Note: Data are from 1970, 1980, and 1990 public use samples of the U.S. census for immigrant men aged 24–64.

distribution. The gap between immigrants and natives increased among the lower quartiles by one year, while there is essentially no difference in educational attainment between immigrants and natives at the median or in the upper quartile.

Although the rest of sections 2.2 and 2.3 focuses on males only, tables 2.1 and 2.2 do establish that the patterns in the relative education of immigrants over time have been quite similar for men and women.

Table 2.3 breaks down mean years of total schooling over the three censuses by arrival cohorts. Comparing cohorts in 1970, the most recent cohort, which arrived during 1965–69, was the most educated cohort, with 11.3 years of education. By 1980 there had been quite a drastic reversal in this pattern, with earlier arrivals in general having a higher level of education than more recent arrivals. The key observation from this table is that the more recently arrived cohorts in the last two censuses have lower average numbers of years of schooling than the less recent cohorts.

Although our findings indicate a slight downward trend of educational attainment among more recent immigrants compared to earlier immigrants, other studies (see, e.g., Jasso, Rosenzweig, and Smith, chap. 5 in this volume, and Funkhouser and Trejo 1995) find a reversal in this trend by the end of the 1980s. Funkhouser and Trejo use data from the Current Population Survey to analyze skills of recent male immigrants. The estimates of skills, however, are very imprecise due to the relatively small sample size and instability of the sample across survey years. The authors acknowledge this and state that the results "should be regarded as suggestive rather than definitive." Our own results in table 2.3 suggest that in 1990 immigrants who arrived between 1985 and 1989 were slightly more highly educated than arrivals from earlier in the 1980s or the 1970s. But some of this difference is probably accounted for by foreign students who enroll in American universities temporarily.

Jasso, Rosenzweig, and Smith utilize INS data to analyze trends in skills of immigrants. The advantage of this data set is that it only includes legal immigrants and the admission criteria of each individual can be identified. However, the disadvantage is that the data set does not contain any information about education or earnings. The authors instead use information on occupation to infer skill levels of immigrants. The finding of a reversal of the downward trend in immigrant skill clearly depends on the accuracy of this method.

The distribution of education in the population is not static. Over time, new cohorts of immigrants and natives enter the working-age population, while others exit. Within cohorts, the level of education is not static either, as people upgrade their skills by deciding to remain in school or to enroll in college. Figure 2.1 shows the proportion of the immigrant and native populations enrolled in school or college in 1970, 1980, and 1990, by age. An interesting pattern emerges. Below the age of 18, the enrollment rate is lower among immigrants in all three decades, but by age 20, this pattern has reversed. As shown in figure 2.1 and in figure 2.2, which continues the graph for those aged 30–64, in virtually all age groups above 20, enrollment rates are higher among immigrants than natives. The enrollment gap is particularly large in 1990, when roughly 10–15 percent of immigrants in their thirties reported being enrolled, compared to about 5–9 percent of natives. This higher enrollment rate suggests that while immigrants'

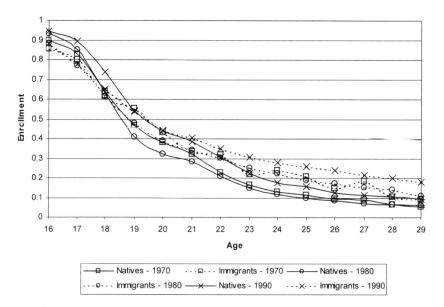

Fig. 2.1   Enrollment rates among native and immigrant men aged 16–29, by year

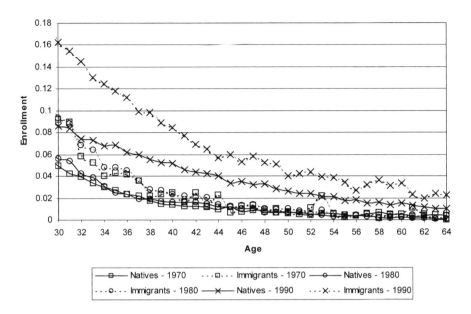

Fig. 2.2   Enrollment rates among native and immigrant men aged 30–64, by year

average level of education is lower, immigrants appear to be more likely to enroll as adults, thereby reducing the gap in education slowly over time within a given age cohort.[2]

Table 2.3 also gives insights into the evolution of education within immigration cohorts over time. Quite different patterns emerge for more recent and less recent cohorts. For the two most recent cohorts in 1980, it appears that the mean schooling level *decreased* over time. However, comparing mean educational attainment between censuses may be somewhat misleading since we had to recode years of schooling for the 1990 census. It is also possible that the decline is due to reverse migration of the relatively more educated immigrants.

In contrast, table 2.3 shows that there has been a mean increase in educational attainment of cohorts arriving before 1970, by between 0.9 and 2.9 years from 1970 to 1990. To check whether these rather large increases in mean levels of schooling are reasonable, and not due to nonrandom return migration, we used the enrollment probabilities from figures 2.1

---

2. One concern is that higher enrollment rates of immigrants simply reflect enrollment in English as a Second Language classes. However, the census form specifically asks respondents whether they are enrolled in regular school, not casual courses. For instance, in the 1980 census respondents were first asked, "What is the highest grade (or year) of regular school the person has ever attended?" Enrollment is inferred by an answer of "Now attending this grade" to the subsequent question, which reads: "Did this person finish the highest grade (or year) attended?"

and 2.2 to calculate the expected increase in education over a 20-year period. This is calculated by the following formula:

$$\sum_{i=20}^{29} \text{Enrollment Probability}_{i,1970} + \sum_{i=30}^{39} \text{Enrollment Probability}_{i,1980},$$

where i is the age and 1970 and 1980 represent the census year. In the above example, the 20-year interval looked at is for an individual who is 20 years old in 1970 and 39 years old in 1989. The expected increase in mean years of schooling for an immigrant in this period is 2.78 years. This is certainly in the range of mean increase in education mentioned above. However, table 2.3 shows that the largest increase in educational attainment over the 20-year period was for the oldest cohort, arrivals before 1950. This group is likely to have a large proportion of individuals who were older than 20 in 1970. If we use the formula above for an immigrant who is 30 in 1970, the predicted increase in schooling is only 0.66 years. It appears that perhaps for the cohort that arrived before 1950, the large apparent gains in mean education over time partly reflect nonrandom return migration whereby less skilled workers returned home over time. But for the cohorts that arrived in the 1950s and 1960s, the observed gains may be genuine.

Immigrants to the United States are likely to have acquired some education in their home country and some after migrating. There is no question in the censuses that asks for this information specifically. However, we can calculate proxies for these as follows, assuming individuals are in school continuously from age six. If an immigrant migrated at an age of six or younger, we assume that all schooling took place in the United States. If the age at migration was between six and the total number of years of schooling plus six, premigration education is set at age at migration minus six and the remainder is assumed to be U.S. education. If age at migration is greater than years of education plus six, it is assumed that all schooling took place abroad.[3]

Mean years of foreign and U.S. schooling for immigrants by arrival cohorts and census year are presented in table 2.4. In 1970, the average immigrant had close to 8 years of foreign schooling and 2.68 years of education obtained in the United States. That is, immigrants had, on average, obtained approximately one-quarter of their schooling in the United States. This composition had changed quite dramatically by 1980. In this year, premigration education had risen to 9.67 years while postmigration education had decreased to 2.4 years. Only one-fifth of total education was obtained in the United States. This was almost exactly the same share of

---

3. This is similar to Chiswick's (1978) approach. He used similar proxies and found no difference between returns to schooling acquired before or after migration, using 1970 census data.

Table 2.4 **Mean Years of Foreign and U.S. Schooling**

Cohort	1970		1980		1990	
	Premigration Education	Postmigration Education	Premigration Education	Postmigration Education	Premigration Education	Postmigration Education
All	7.966	2.684	9.672	2.404	9.515	2.365
Arrived 1985–89					12.253	0.013
Arrived 1980–84					11.501	0.178
Arrived 1975–79			12.240	0.015	10.744	0.748
Arrived 1970–74			11.285	0.207	9.785	1.663
Arrived 1965–69	11.310	0.003	11.165	0.690	8.886	3.357
Arrived 1960–64	10.859	0.103	10.368	1.970	7.844	4.877
Arrived 1950–59	9.833	0.847	7.997	4.379	6.697	6.026
Arrived before 1950	5.185	5.023	7.009	5.342	2.391	10.709

Note: Data are from 1970, 1980, and 1990 public use samples of the U.S. census for immigrant men aged 24–64.

postmigration education to total education that was observed in 1990, when foreign education had decreased slightly to 9.51 years and U.S.-acquired schooling had dropped further to 2.36 years. It is possible that this is simply driven by an increase in immigration in the 1970s and 1980s. Since recently arrived immigrants have obtained most of their schooling in their home country, as is shown in table 2.4, and the proportion of recent immigrants to the total immigrant population has been increasing, the share of postmigration education will consequently decrease.

It is interesting to note that the composition of pre-and postmigration education changes drastically over time for a given arrival cohort. For example, the 1960–64 arrival cohort had only 0.1 years of U.S. education in 1970. In 1980 this had increased to 1.97 years, and by 1990 it was 4.87 years. The large increase in postmigration education within cohorts over time likely reflects a genuine increase in education among immigrants, nonrandom reverse migration, and possibly, recall bias in which immigrants progressively understate the proportion of their education obtained abroad over time. Another plausible reason for the increase is that the older members of a cohort will have lower life expectancy, so that the composition of the cohort shifts over time toward a greater proportion of immigrants who arrived at a younger age. It is these youngest arrivals who are most likely to enroll in American schools and colleges.

Returning to the enrollment rates depicted in figure 2.2, do the higher enrollment rates of older immigrants relative to natives simply arise due to immigrants who have dropped out of school going back to secondary school? Figures 2.3 and 2.4 address this possibility. The figures show that when people are divided into those with and without high school degrees, immigrants in both groups are more likely to be enrolled than are their native counterparts of the same age.[4] Furthermore, approximately two-thirds of the enrollment gap stems from higher college enrollment rates among immigrants.

Enrollment rates are likely to differ among immigrants depending on the number of years they have been in the United States. One obvious reason for this is that immigrants who have been in this country for 15 to 20 years are older than immigrants who arrived more recently. This will be controlled for in linear probability models below. Nonetheless, by look-

---

4. We were concerned that the higher postsecondary enrollment rates among young immigrants might simply reflect international students in the United States temporarily. However, when we redrew figures 2.3 and 2.4 including only immigrants who had been in the United States for more than four years, the same patterns persisted, with the crossover point at roughly an age of 17–18 years. In this subsample, immigrants were found having higher probability of attending both grade school and college for all age groups older than 18 years. This almost exactly replicates the results we got when all immigrants were included. The gap declines roughly by one-fourth for college enrollment for the 21–40 age group and increases slightly for the 16–20 age group. There is very little change in the oldest age group's enrollment probabilities.

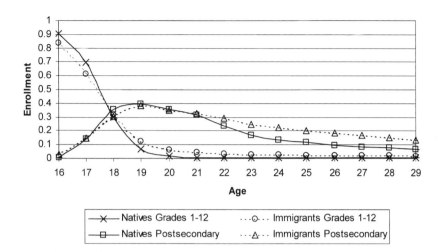

Fig. 2.3   Enrollment rates in grades 1–12 and in postsecondary education among native and immigrant men aged 16–29 (sample averages over 1970, 1980, and 1990 censuses)

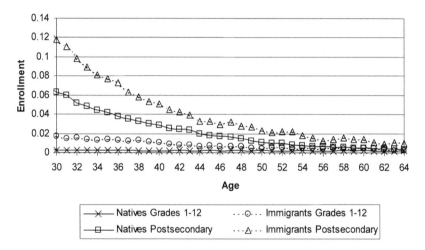

Fig. 2.4   Enrollment rates in grades 1–12 and in postsecondary education among native and immigrant men aged 30–64 (sample averages over 1970, 1980, and 1990 censuses)

ing at the actual enrollment rates, we can observe enrollment behavior of a specific cohort over time. Table 2.5 shows the enrollment rates by arrival cohort. As expected, enrollment rates are highest for the most recently arrived immigrants in all three censuses. It is interesting to note the overall upward trend in enrollment over the two decades. In 1970, 6.4 percent of the most recently arrived cohort, 1965–69 arrivals, were enrolled in school.

Table 2.5   **Enrollment Rates by Arrival Cohort for Males Aged 16–64**

Cohort	Enrollment		
	1970	1980	1990
Arrived 1985–89			0.16508
Arrived 1980–84			0.13436
Arrived 1975–79		0.09309	0.09740
Arrived 1970–74		0.04621	0.07942
Arrived 1965–69	0.06440	0.02887	0.07170
Arrived 1960–64	0.04736	0.03018	0.06530
Arrived 1950–59	0.02896	0.02856	0.05464
Arrived before 1950	0.01299	0.01074	0.05639

Note: Based on 1970, 1980, and 1990 public use samples of the U.S. census.

In contrast, the immigrant cohort who arrived between 1985 and 1989 displayed an enrollment rate of 16.5 percent in 1990. In other words, the newest immigrants were more than 2.5 times more likely to be enrolled in school in 1990 compared to 1970. The table also makes clear that the trend toward higher enrollment rates between 1980 and 1990 has occurred in part *within* cohorts over time.

To find out whether the immigrants who are more or less educated upon arrival enroll in school in the United States, we calculate enrollment rates by premigration education levels. These are shown in table 2.6. It is quite clear that the immigrants who are most likely to enroll in school in the United States are the most highly educated. In 1990, for example, an immigrant who arrived in the United States with at least a high school diploma is 1.5 times more likely to be enrolled in school than a person who arrived with between 9 and less than 12 years of education.

To ensure that these results are not due to a possible inclusion of visa students in the census, we calculated the enrollment rates by both premigration education and arrival cohort (not presented here) for each census. Since visa students are very unlikely to be included in the second most recent cohorts in each census, enrollment rates for these cohorts are likely to reflect enrollment behavior of relatively recently arrived immigrants, as opposed to nonimmigrants such as visa students. In each of the three censuses, immigrants with more than 12 years of education are the most likely to be enrolled in school. This implies that the most highly educated immigrants upon arrival in the United States are indeed the ones most likely to further their education. This supports the findings in the article by Borjas (chap. 1 in this volume), which provide some evidence of complementarity between human capital acquired in the source country and in the United States.

Do higher enrollment rates among immigrants reflect a genuine difference from natives, or do they arise due to systematic variations based on

Table 2.6   **Enrollment Rates by Premigration Education for Males Aged 16–64**

	Enrollment		
Premigration Education	1970	1980	1990
Less than 1 year	0.02290	0.03652	0.09737
1–3 years	0.03488	0.02932	0.04455
3–6 years	0.01369	0.01121	0.10454
6–9 years	0.01361	0.01603	0.07522
9–12 years	0.02610	0.01981	0.09901
12 years	0.01975	0.01136	0.07240
More than 12 and up to 16 years	0.07966	0.08188	0.15700
More than 16 years	0.08641	0.09595	0.13818

Note: Based on 1970, 1980, and 1990 public use samples of the U.S. census.

other observable traits, such as geographic location? A second important question is whether the higher enrollment rates are observed uniformly across all immigrants, regardless of their year of arrival in the United States. Table 2.7 addresses these questions by estimating linear probability models for enrollment.

The probability of overall enrollment is 3 percent higher for immigrants compared to natives when factors such as marital status, geographic location, and age are controlled for. Decomposing enrollment into grades 1 through 12 and college shows that the difference between immigrants and natives is greater for enrollment in higher education. After controlling for observed traits, immigrants are 1 percent more likely to be enrolled in grade school and 2 percent more likely to be enrolled in postsecondary education. Columns 2, 4, and 6 in table 2.7 also control for years since migration, differences across cohorts, and differences between natives and immigrants in the impact of age on enrollment probabilities. The coefficient on the immigrant dummy alone does not indicate the difference in likelihood of enrollment in these models. Instead, the probabilities have to be calculated based on the estimated coefficients. For example, in 1990 a 25-year-old immigrant who has been in the United States for two years, the most recent cohort, is 7 percent more likely to be enrolled in school than a native of the same age. The same individual is 1 percent more likely to be enrolled in grades 1 through 12 and 6 percent more likely to be enrolled in college than a statistically similar native.

Figures 2.5 and 2.6 show the predicted difference in grade school enrollment probabilities between immigrants and natives (i.e., enrollment probability of immigrants minus enrollment probability of natives). Figure 2.5 shows that variations in years since migration can explain little of the difference in enrollment rates in grades 1 through 12, about 2 percent. This, in addition to the relatively flat curve in figure 2.6, indicates that years since migration does not explain much of the difference in enrollment

Table 2.7   OLS Model of the Probability of Enrollment, and Enrollment in Grades 1–12 and in College, for Males Aged 16–64

	Overall Enrollment		Grade 1–12 Enrollment		College Enrollment	
	1	2	3	4	5	6
Constant	3.3089	3.3570	2.8420	2.8784	0.4668	0.4786
	(764.65)	(754.67)	(1,002.7)	(988.08)	(109.89)	(109.54)
1970 census effect	−0.0384	−0.0377	−0.0078	−0.0079	−0.0305	−0.0298
	(−81.87)	(−78.31)	(−25.45)	(−24.96)	(−66.42)	(−63.09)
1980 census effect	−0.0493	−0.0486	−0.0345	−0.0342	−0.0148	−0.0145
	(−112.19)	(−108.92)	(−119.81)	(−116.87)	(−34.34)	(−32.98)
Married	−0.0425	−0.0424	0.0108	0.0108	−0.0533	−0.0532
	(−91.50)	(−91.32)	(35.52)	(35.48)	(−116.91)	(−116.63)
Northeast	0.0125	0.0128	0.0004	0.0004	0.0121	0.0124
	(24.25)	(24.80)	(1.13)	(1.18)	(23.95)	(24.46)
Midwest	0.0144	0.0145	0.0023	0.0023	0.0122	0.0123
	(29.79)	(30.01)	(7.14)	(7.20)	(25.58)	(25.76)
West	0.0164	0.0162	0.0010	0.0010	0.0154	0.0151
	(30.98)	(30.54)	(2.92)	(3.00)	(29.61)	(29.09)
Resides in city	0.0100	0.0102	−0.0035	−0.0034	0.0135	0.0136
	(21.96)	(22.34)	(−11.68)	(−11.54)	(30.16)	(30.44)
Age	−0.2308	−0.2351	−0.2173	−0.2205	−0.0134	−0.0146
	(−614.67)	(−608.00)	(−883.86)	(−870.73)	(−36.42)	(−38.45)
Age^2	0.0053	0.0054	0.0052	0.0053	0.00004	0.0001
	(525.86)	(520.58)	(796.90)	(784.41)	(3.98)	(7.01)
Age^3/10,000	−0.3889	−0.3979	−0.4002	−0.4067	0.0114	0.0088
	(−461.82)	(−457.44)	(−725.67)	(−713.94)	(13.74)	(10.29)
Immigrant	0.0305	−0.7977	0.0092	−0.6640	0.0213	−0.1338
	(40.76)	(−43.30)	(18.73)	(−55.04)	(29.02)	(−7.39)

Age*Immigrant	0.0717	0.0545	0.0172
	(45.73)	(53.05)	(11.18)
Age²*Immigrant	−0.0018	−0.0014	−0.0005
	(−44.08)	(−50.69)	(−11.08)
Age³*Immigrant/10,000	0.1456	0.1100	0.0357
	(41.72)	(48.11)	(10.40)
Years since immigration	−0.0010	0.0039	−0.0049
	(−2.16)	(12.58)	(−10.58)
(Years since immigration)²	0.00002	−0.0002	0.0002
	(1.18)	(−13.71)	(10.34)
(Years since immigration)³/10,000	−.0008	0.0217	−0.0224
	(−0.32)	(13.77)	(−9.51)
Arrived 1980–84	0.0040	0.0159	−0.0119
	(1.20)	(7.32)	(−3.66)
Arrived 1975–79	0.0117	0.0028	0.0089
	(3.88)	(1.44)	(2.99)
Arrived 1970–74	−0.0133	−0.0013	−0.0120
	(−3.65)	(−0.55)	(−3.35)
Arrived 1965–69	−0.0172	−0.0051	−0.0121
	(−5.09)	(−2.29)	(−3.66)
Arrived 1960–64	−0.0173	−0.0051	−0.0122
	(−4.44)	(−2.01)	(−3.17)
Arrived 1950–59	−0.0206	−0.0008	−0.0197
	(−5.09)	(−0.32)	(−4.97)
Arrived before 1950	−0.0162	0.0092	−0.0254
	(−3.06)	(2.66)	(−4.88)
R^2	0.4000 0.4008	0.4112 0.4122	0.1041 0.1044

Note: Based on 1970, 1980, and 1990 public use samples of the U.S. census. *t*-statistics appear in parentheses. $N = 2{,}232{,}284$.

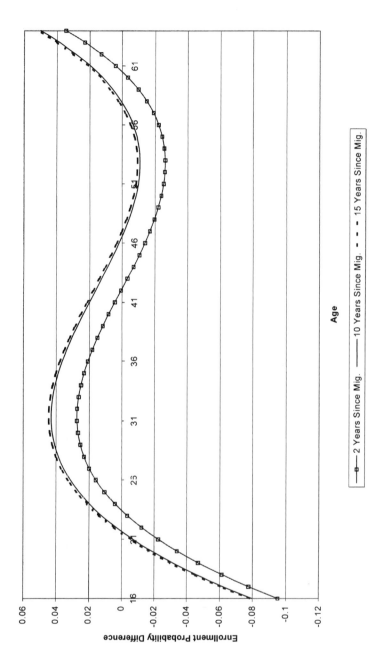

Fig. 2.5 Predicted difference in probability of enrollment in grades 1–12 between immigrants and natives by immigrant's age, 1990 baseline

2 Years Since Mig. ——— 10 Years Since Mig. — - — 15 Years Since Mig.

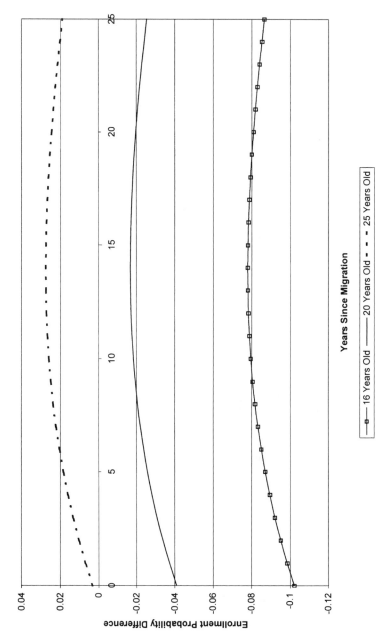

Years Since Migration

- ■ - 16 Years Old ——— 20 Years Old - ■ - 25 Years Old

Fig. 2.6 Predicted difference in probability of enrollment in grades 1–12 between immigrants and natives by years since migration, 1990 baseline

probabilities for grades 1 through 12. Instead, age appears to be the driving force behind the differences. The pattern is complex, but the most striking pattern is lower enrollment rates for immigrants in their teens compared to their native peers.

The relatively low enrollment rates among younger immigrants may indicate that immigrants, in particular from Mexico, do not "drop in" to high school when they arrive in the United States. The average Hispanic immigrant in our sample has fewer than nine years of schooling and has already been out of school for at least one year by the age of 16. Similarly, Vernez and Abrahamse (1996) report that the average Mexican immigrant has only seven years of schooling. It may be hard for these young individuals to perform at the same academic level as their native peers. It is quite possible that they postpone some education until later in life. This would then explain some of the higher enrollment rates in grade school for immigrants in their twenties and thirties.

The predicted difference in enrollment in postsecondary education probabilities between immigrants and natives is quite different from that in grades 1 through 12. Immigrants of all ages are more likely to be enrolled in college than are natives of the same age. These differences are also much more influenced by years since migration than are enrollment probabilities in grade school. This is shown in figures 2.7 and 2.8. Immigrants appear to enroll at a much higher rate relatively early after migrating, regardless of age. The benefits, and possible requirement, of acquiring U.S.-specific human capital in the labor market would give immigrants an incentive to acquire these skills soon after arriving: The earlier these skills are obtained, the longer is the period during which the benefits can be reaped. It should also be noted that the finding that immigrants enroll in postsecondary schooling early after arrival may possibly partially reflect inclusion of visa students in the censuses.

Although immigrants do appear to be more likely to enroll in both secondary and postsecondary education, it is the *level* of education, and not its rate of change, that is a more relevant predictor of an immigrant's economic welfare. Table 2.8 presents two models of years of schooling, along with two models for probability of high school graduation and two models for probability of college graduation.

Immigrants are predicted to have 1.4 fewer years of education compared to natives when age, geographic location, and marital status are taken into account. Although immigrants are 18 percent less likely to graduate from high school, they are not less likely to be college graduates. This again shows that there is great heterogeneity in educational attainment among immigrants; as we showed in tables 2.1 and 2.2, the upper quartile of immigrants is as highly educated as the upper quartile of natives. Column 2 in table 2.8 adds cohort effects, controls for years since migration, and immigrant's age. Immigrants who arrived in the 1950s have 1.5 years more

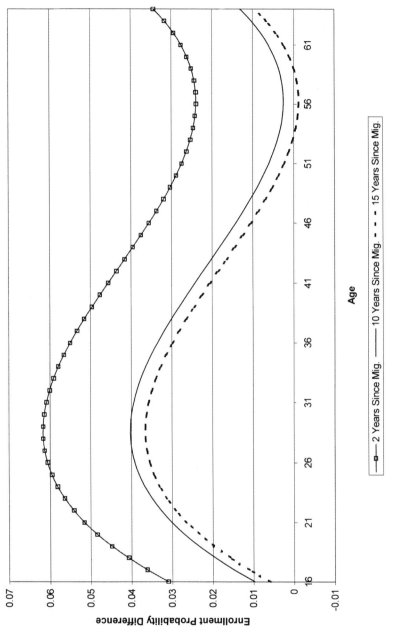

Fig. 2.7 Predicted difference in probability of enrollment in college between immigrants and natives by immigrant's age, 1990 baseline

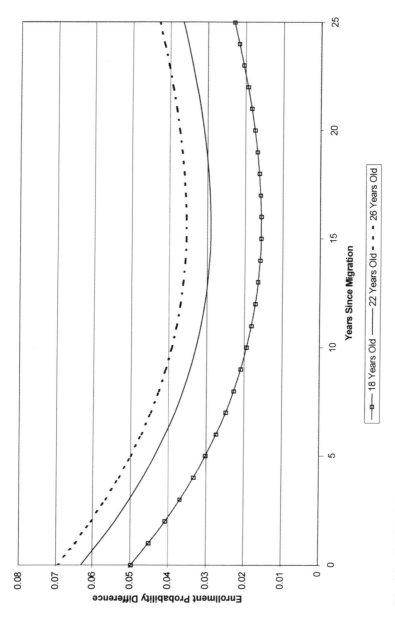

Fig. 2.8 Predicted difference in probability of enrollment in college between immigrants and natives by years since migration, 1990 baseline

Table 2.8   OLS Models of Years of Schooling and Probability of Graduation for Males Aged 16-64

	Education (Years)		High School Graduation (ED ≥ 12)		College Graduation (ED ≥ 16)	
	1	2	3	4	5	6
Constant	1.4345 (29.72)	1.2878 (25.98)	−1.7712 (−264.15)	−1.8191 (−264.16)	−1.0094 (−170.56)	−1.0070 (−165.47)
1970 census effect	−1.1123 (−212.87)	−1.1642 (−217.11)	−0.1621 (−223.30)	−0.1693 (−227.30)	−0.0614 (−95.86)	−0.0630 (−95.69)
1980 census effect	−0.1912 (−39.04)	−0.2324 (−46.68)	−0.0311 (−45.70)	−0.0368 (−53.16)	−0.0114 (−19.03)	−0.0131 (−21.45)
Married	0.3704 (71.48)	0.3736 (72.18)	0.0323 (44.91)	0.0327 (45.45)	0.0148 (23.27)	0.0147 (23.18)
Northeast	0.5854 (101.71)	0.5774 (100.41)	0.0689 (86.21)	0.0677 (84.77)	0.0288 (40.80)	0.0285 (40.40)
Midwest	0.4296 (79.46)	0.4242 (78.55)	0.0664 (88.40)	0.0657 (87.53)	−0.0015 (−2.33)	−0.0016 (−2.43)
West	0.7248 (122.78)	0.7322 (124.17)	0.0955 (116.42)	0.0966 (117.89)	0.0271 (37.40)	0.0274 (37.89)
Resides in city	0.7685 (151.00)	0.7661 (150.71)	0.0690 (97.55)	0.0684 (96.93)	0.0697 (111.61)	0.0695 (111.35)
Age	0.8103 (193.53)	0.8281 (192.18)	0.1977 (339.79)	0.2024 (338.21)	0.0836 (162.87)	0.0839 (158.63)
Age^2	−0.0188 (−167.97)	−0.0193 (−167.28)	−0.0048 (−307.69)	−0.0049 (−306.30)	−0.0018 (−132.88)	−0.0018 (−129.88)
Age^3/10,000	1.2888 (137.24)	1.3313 (137.33)	0.3527 (270.30)	0.3625 (269.18)	0.1227 (106.51)	0.1245 (104.63)
Immigrant	−1.3839 (−165.76)	1.0647 (5.19)	−0.1800 (−155.19)	0.6556 (22.99)	−0.0002 (−0.23)	−0.0941 (−3.73)
Age*Immigrant		−0.2369 (−13.56)		−0.0736 (−30.33)		0.0048 (2.21)

(continued)

Table 2.8   (continued)

	Education (Years)		High School Graduation (ED ≥ 12)		College Graduation (ED ≥ 16)	
	1	2	3	4	5	6
Age²*Immigrant		0.0064 (13.67)		0.0019 (28.70)		0.00004 (0.68)
Age³*Immigrant/10,000		−0.5509 (−14.16)		−0.1449 (−26.82)		−0.0122 (−2.56)
Years since immigration		−0.1136 (−22.66)		−0.0133 (−19.11)		−0.0136 (−22.07)
(Years since immigration)²		0.0055 (24.82)		0.0006 (19.94)		0.0005 (17.66)
(Years since immigration)³/10,000		−0.6451 (−24.61)		−0.0758 (−20.82)		−0.0494 (−15.35)
Arrived 1980–84		0.1162 (3.18)		0.0183 (3.61)		−0.0102 (−2.27)
Arrived 1975–79		0.5190 (15.76)		0.0669 (14.63)		0.0308 (7.62)
Arrived 1970–74		0.5284 (13.27)		0.0689 (12.46)		0.0302 (6.18)
Arrived 1965–69		1.1254 (30.56)		0.1413 (27.62)		0.0500 (11.06)
Arrived 1960–64		1.5204 (35.52)		0.2031 (34.16)		0.0487 (9.26)
Arrived 1950–59		1.5497 (34.97)		0.2197 (35.70)		0.0441 (8.10)
Arrived before 1950		1.4274 (24.64)		0.2136 (26.54)		0.0260 (3.66)
R^2	0.1146	0.1171	0.1437	0.1463	0.0599	0.0605

Note: t-statistics appear in parentheses. Data are from 1970, 1980, and 1990 public use samples of the U.S. census. $N = 2,232,284$.

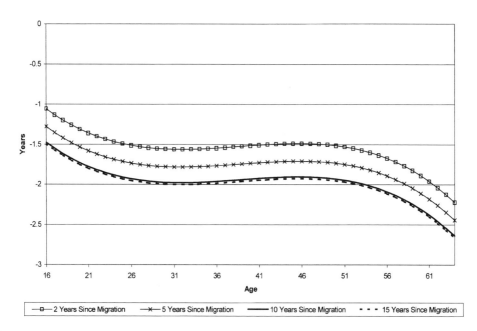

Fig. 2.9   Predicted difference in years of schooling between natives and immigrants, by immigrant's age and years since migration, 1990 baseline and 1975–79 cohort

schooling than the most recent cohort, arrivals between 1985 and 1989. Columns 3–6 show linear probability models for the probability of high school and college graduation. Immigrants who arrived in the 1950s are 22 percent more likely to be high school graduates and 4 percent more likely to have at least a college degree than the most recent cohort. It is interesting to note that although our raw data indicate a slight upward trend in mean years of schooling among immigrants over time, after controlling for immigrants' age, years since immigration, and other traits, this result suggests an absolute decline in the skill level of immigrants across cohorts.

Figure 2.9 displays predicted differences in years of schooling between immigrants and natives by age and years since migration. The number of years spent in the United States seems to have less of an effect on the educational attainment gap than does age. This should not be interpreted as an indication of small cohort effects. The graph in figure 2.9 is for a specific cohort, 1975–79 arrivals with 1990 as baseline. Younger immigrants are predicted to fall further behind natives of the same age until both groups enter their thirties, when immigrants' education catches up slightly with that of natives. Since the coefficients on the cohort variables are increasing with the time since arrival, the graph understates the impact of years since migration. Nonetheless, it appears that, overall, for a given year since migration, the educational gap increases with age. For example, among the most recent immigrants, it seems that the older immigrants are relatively less educated compared to both natives and younger immigrants.

Another way of looking at this question is to think of age at migration, rather than years since migration, as a key determinant of total education acquired.[5] For example, looking at the line for two years since migration in figure 2.9, we see that the younger the person when he immigrates to the United States, the higher will be his level of education in general. See Gonzalez (1997) for an analysis of the effect of age at immigration on the level of education of immigrants. He finds, as implied by our analysis, that immigrants who arrive at an earlier age in the end obtain more years of schooling.

2.3.2   Robustness of the Linear Probability Models

As a test of robustness, the linear probability models of enrollment and graduation presented in tables 2.7 and 2.8 were also estimated by probit. This was done since the enrollment probabilities are quite close to zero for some groups, so that the linearly estimated probabilities may suggest negative probabilities. The probit results for the immigrant variables, including marginal effects, are shown in appendix tables 2A.2 and 2A.3.

The probit results are quite similar with a few relatively minor exceptions discussed below. The simpler enrollment models in table 2A.2—models 1, 3, and 5—show that predicted enrollment probability differences between immigrants and natives do not change very much in the probit models, compared to the least squares models. Immigrants are still more likely to be enrolled in both grade school and postsecondary education. Figures 2.5, 2.6, 2.7, and 2.8 were also re-generated by using the marginal effects from the probit results in the more complex models 4 and 6 (these figures are not presented in this paper). When the marginal effects are evaluated at the means, using the means for immigrants for variables that are specific to immigrants, the figures resemble the original figures quite closely.

The graduation probabilities are also quite similar when the results from the probit models are used. The probit results in models 3 and 5 in table 2A.3 indicate that immigrants are approximately 20.6 percent less likely to be high school graduates and about 0.1 percent less likely to be college graduates, compared to statistically similar natives. The identically defined linear probability models suggest 18 percent and no difference, respectively. Our calculations for predicted graduation probabilities using models 3 and 5 in table 2A.3 show results similar but not identical to the

---

5. Of course, we cannot include age, years since migration, and age at migration in the regression since they are perfectly collinear. Furthermore, the problem of collinearity arises in all our models that include cohort dummies, years since migration, and census years.

derived predictions from the linear models shown in table 2.8. For example, the probit estimates indicate that an immigrant who arrived between 1985 and 1989 is 26.1 percent less likely to be a high school graduate and about 4.4 percent less likely to be a college graduate compared to an immigrant who arrived in the first half of the 1960s. The predicted graduation probabilities derived from the least squares models suggest differences of 20.3 and 4.9 percent, respectively.

Overall, the probit models appear to closely support the estimates from the linear probability models.

2.4   Implications of Recent Trends for the Immigrant-Native Earning Gap

2.4.1   Basic Results

The changes in schooling of immigrants over the last two decades, as described above, are likely to have consequences for the welfare of immigrants. In particular, they may affect how immigrants perform in the labor market. The decline in the relative educational attainment of immigrants is likely to affect the difference between immigrants' and natives' earnings. Table 2.9 shows six models of log weekly earnings. The first two models assume that earnings for immigrants and natives are affected equally by factors such as age and education. Later models do not impose this restriction. The coefficient on the immigrant dummy variable in table 2.9, columns 1 and 2, can be interpreted as the approximate immigrant-native earnings gap. This gap is close to 18 percent when controlling for period effects, geographic location, city residence, and age. However, as shown in model 2, adding variables for education, and education interacted with period effects, narrows the gap to slightly over 7 percent. In other words, the lower levels of schooling of immigrants explain more than half of the wage differential. If we further adjust for differences in returns to education between immigrants and natives, as in model 3, the data suggest that part of the reason why immigrants earn less is that they have significantly lower returns to education.[6]

Model 3 does not capture several important factors that affect earnings. It is not only returns to education that may differ between immigrants and natives. It is quite likely that age affects earnings differently between the two groups. Also, the number of years in the United States and year of arrival, or arrival cohort, is likely to affect wages. Models 4–6 replicate

6. In fact, as an artifact of the specification, the gap is turned into an earnings advantage for immigrants with relatively low schooling levels. For example, in the 1990 sample, immigrants with seven or fewer years of education are predicted to earn more than natives with similar traits. But the vast majority of immigrants have higher levels of education than this; for these immigrants, model 3 indicates that virtually all of the earnings gap with natives can be explained by lower levels of education and lower returns to education among immigrants.

Table 2.9   OLS Models of Log of Weekly Earnings in 1989$ for Males Aged 24–64, Adjusted for Top Coding

Variable	1	2	3	4	5	6
Constant	3.6560	2.9373	2.9002	3.6977	2.9576	2.9175
	(115.28)	(98.35)	(97.09)	(112.72)	(95.69)	(94.39)
1970 census effect	0.0198	0.2932	0.3256	0.0110	0.2802	0.3136
	(15.09)	(60.16)	(65.94)	(8.18)	(56.95)	(60.28)
1980 census effect	0.0384	0.4071	0.4315	0.0317	0.3988	0.4227
	(29.79)	(79.10)	(83.28)	(24.28)	(77.11)	(79.24)
Married	0.2589	0.2433	0.2427	0.2593	0.2434	0.2426
	(192.18)	(192.51)	(192.17)	(192.91)	(192.92)	(192.40)
Northeast	0.1521	0.1176	0.1161	0.1503	0.1167	0.1155
	(103.03)	(84.81)	(83.75)	(102.02)	(84.27)	(83.48)
Midwest	0.1288	0.1063	0.1056	0.1271	0.1051	0.1046
	(92.09)	(80.97)	(80.48)	(91.08)	(80.23)	(79.90)
West	0.1413	0.0968	0.0937	0.1423	0.0974	0.0940
	(92.25)	(67.19)	(65.01)	(93.14)	(67.73)	(65.27)
Resides in city	0.2130	0.1570	0.1548	0.2130	0.1574	0.1553
	(159.40)	(124.59)	(122.80)	(159.73)	(125.13)	(123.47)
Age	0.1183	0.0984	0.0972	0.1159	0.0977	0.0967
	(49.25)	(43.64)	(43.14)	(46.61)	(41.85)	(41.45)
Age^2	−0.0018	−0.0014	−0.0014	−0.0018	−0.0014	−0.0013
	(−31.32)	(−25.31)	(−24.77)	(−29.30)	(−24.03)	(−23.65)
Age^3/10,000	0.0743	0.0488	0.0465	0.0694	0.0463	0.0449
	(16.33)	(11.45)	(10.90)	(14.73)	(10.46)	(10.15)
Immigrant	−0.1663	−0.0739	0.1312	−0.6874	−0.2044	−0.1284
	(−78.91)	(−37.15)	(23.60)	(−5.53)	(−1.75)	(−1.10)
Age*Immigrant				0.0241	−0.0027	0.0076
				(2.57)	(−0.31)	(0.87)

	(1)	(2)	(3)	(4)	(5)
Age²*Immigrant			−0.0007 (−3.16)	−0.0002 (−0.74)	−0.0004 (−1.79)
Age³*Immigrant/10,000			0.0590 (3.34)	0.0233 (1.41)	0.0368 (2.22)
Years since immigration			0.0112 (9.55)	0.0239 (21.83)	0.0213 (18.25)
(Years since immigration)²			−0.00003 (−0.63)	−0.0006 (−11.43)	−0.0004 (−8.05)
(Years since immigration)³/10,000			−0.0138 (−2.18)	0.0454 (7.63)	0.0251 (4.00)
Arrived 1980–84			0.0340 (3.35)	0.0334 (3.51)	0.0336 (3.41)
Arrived 1975–79			0.1038 (10.85)	0.0850 (9.47)	0.0942 (9.07)
Arrived 1970–74			0.1356 (12.59)	0.1057 (10.46)	0.1138 (8.98)
Arrived 1965–69			0.2125 (21.35)	0.1321 (14.13)	0.1411 (10.42)
Arrived 1960–64			0.2721 (24.32)	0.1605 (15.27)	0.1727 (10.79)
Arrived 1950–59			0.2844 (24.72)	0.1667 (15.41)	0.1754 (9.33)
Arrived before 1950			0.2607 (18.33)	0.1383 (10.35)	0.1363 (5.34)
Years of education	0.0780 (283.47)	0.0822 (279.51)		0.0774 (280.28)	0.0815 (267.31)
Education*(1970 census)	−0.0131 (−34.70)	−0.0157 (−40.96)		−0.0124 (−32.82)	−0.0147 (−36.75)

(continued)

Table 2.9 (continued)

Variable	1	2	3	4	5	6
Education*(1980 census)		-0.0266 (-69.51)	-0.0284 (-73.72)		-0.0262 (-68.49)	-0.0278 (-70.11)
Education*(Immigrant)			-0.0183 (-40.35)			-0.0167 (-30.67)
Education*(1970 census)*Immigrant			0.0037 (9.11)			-0.0010 (-1.15)
Education*(1980 census)*Immigrant			0.0011 (3.06)			-0.0025 (-4.72)
R^2	0.1104	0.2183	0.2194	0.1150	0.2215	0.2226
F-test				P-value		
Immigration interacted with education, and immigration interacted with education and period effects = 0			0.0001			0.0001

Note: t-statistics appear in parentheses. Data are from 1970, 1980, and 1990 public use samples of the U.S. census. Observations that are top coded in 1970 and 1980 are multiplied by 1.5. All observations with reported weekly earnings of less than $50 in 1989$ are excluded. $N = 1,244,531$.

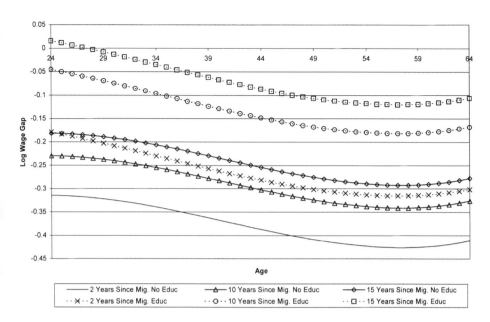

Fig. 2.10   Predicted log wage gap by immigrant's age, without controls for education (*solid lines*) and with controls (*dashed lines*)

the first three models after accounting for such effects. The coefficient on immigrant status alone in columns 4, 5, and 6 cannot be read as the wage gap between the two groups. It is more convenient to analyze the differential by looking at figures 2.10 and 2.11. These show the predicted log wage gap by immigrant's age and years since migration with and without education controls.[7] Note that education can explain much, if not all, of the wage gap for younger immigrants who have been in the United States for at least 10–15 years. Relatively older and recent immigrants exhibit the greatest wage gap. This is an indication that the age at migration matters greatly in determining the immigrant-native earnings gap. The figures suggests that, on average, differences in educational attainment explain about 0.1 log wage points of the observed wage gap, and in some cases substantially more.

There has been a change in returns to education over the past two decades, with an increase in the 1980s after a slight decrease in the 1970s. Returns to education are estimated to be slightly over 8 percent in 1990, as shown in column 2 of table 2.9.[8] In 1980 they were approximately 5.3

7. The lines in figures 2.10 and 2.11 are based on model 4, with no controls for education, and model 6, with controls for education, in table 2.9. The calculations use median years of schooling, 12 years, for lines with controls for education for both immigrants and natives. All lines are calculated based on the 1975–79 arrival cohort.

8. In other words, exp(0.078) = 1.081, indicating a return of 8.1 percent.

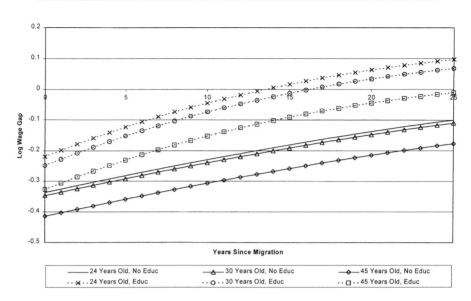

Fig. 2.11   Predicted log wage gap by years since immigration, without controls for education (*solid lines*) and with controls (*dashed lines*)

percent, while in 1970, one year of schooling was associated with a 6.7 percent increase in earnings. Models 3 and 6 show that once the returns to education are allowed to differ between immigrants and natives, the estimated returns for natives are always higher than the returns for immigrants. Models 3 and 6 both show that immigrants, like natives, have experienced cycles in the returns to schooling. However, the two models differ about the extent to which the changes between 1970–90 and 1980–90 have been larger or smaller for natives.

2.4.2   The Importance of Sheepskin Effects

The literature on returns to education has consistently found strong evidence of nonlinearities in the impact of schooling on earnings (Jaeger and Page 1996). Accounting for these effects can alter economic inference considerably. For instance, Heckman, Layne-Farrar, and Todd (1996) show that accounting for sheepskin effects fundamentally changes the conclusion that school spending uniformly affects earnings for all workers. Table 2.10 presents log wage models that incorporate dummies for completing 12 and 16 years of schooling (this corresponds approximately to graduating from high school and college, respectively). These dummy variables are furthermore interacted with period effects and immigration status. Table 2.10, column 2, shows that graduating from 12th grade increases earnings by roughly 7 percent beyond the estimated (log-linear) returns to education. Completing 16 years of schooling adds an additional 15–16 percent to earnings. Both of these coefficients are highly significant.

Table 2.10 OLS Models of Log of Weekly Earnings in 1989$ for Males Aged 24–64 with Sheepskin Effects

Variable	1	2	3	4	5	6
Constant	3.6560	3.1614	3.1146	3.6977	3.1991	3.1422
	(115.28)	(105.01)	(103.15)	(112.72)	(102.74)	(100.54)
1970 census effect	0.0198	0.1752	0.2134	0.0110	0.1443	0.1784
	(15.09)	(23.99)	(28.43)	(8.18)	(19.50)	(22.32)
1980 census effect	0.0384	0.3155	0.3448	0.0317	0.2940	0.3188
	(29.79)	(40.91)	(44.06)	(24.28)	(37.85)	(39.27)
Married	0.2589	0.2436	0.2432	0.2593	0.2438	0.2431
	(192.18)	(193.03)	(192.74)	(192.91)	(193.57)	(193.07)
Northeast	0.1521	0.1190	0.1177	0.1503	0.1180	0.1171
	(103.03)	(85.86)	(84.91)	(102.02)	(85.36)	(84.66)
Midwest	0.1288	0.1086	0.1077	0.1271	0.1076	0.1067
	(92.09)	(82.73)	(82.02)	(91.08)	(82.12)	(81.46)
West	0.1413	0.0984	0.0962	0.1423	0.0993	0.0966
	(92.25)	(68.34)	(66.67)	(93.14)	(69.07)	(67.06)
Resides in city	0.2130	0.1567	0.1552	0.2130	0.1570	0.1557
	(159.40)	(124.50)	(123.27)	(159.73)	(125.01)	(123.97)
Age	0.1183	0.0973	0.0963	0.1159	0.0966	0.0962
	(49.25)	(43.24)	(42.79)	(46.61)	(41.48)	(41.32)
Age^2	−0.0018	−0.0014	−0.0013	−0.0018	−0.0013	−0.0013
	(−31.32)	(−24.88)	(−24.40)	(−29.30)	(−23.61)	(−23.46)
Age^3/10,000	0.0743	0.0468	0.0447	0.0694	0.0441	0.0437
	(16.33)	(10.98)	(10.50)	(14.73)	(9.99)	(9.89)
Immigrant	−0.1663	−0.0870	0.0574	−0.6874	−0.2125	−0.0642
	(−78.91)	(−43.42)	(7.57)	(−5.53)	(−1.82)	(−0.55)
Age*Immigrant				0.0241	−0.0032	−0.0019
				(2.57)	(−0.36)	(−0.22)
Age^2*Immigrant				−0.0007	−0.0002	−0.0002
				(−3.16)	(−0.74)	(−0.90)

(*continued*)

Table 2.10 (continued)

Variable	1	2	3	4	5	6
Age^3*Immigrant/10,000				0.0590	0.0235	0.0246
				(3.34)	(1.42)	(1.49)
Years since immigration				0.0112	0.0227	0.0196
				(9.55)	(20.76)	(16.72)
(Years since immigration)^2				−0.00003	−0.0005	−0.0004
				(−0.63)	(−10.62)	(−8.91)
(Years since immigration)^3/10,000				−0.0138	0.0417	0.0347
				(−2.18)	(7.03)	(5.53)
Arrived 1980–84				0.0340	0.0403	0.0537
				(3.35)	(4.24)	(5.44)
Arrived 1975–79				0.1038	0.0946	0.1252
				(10.85)	(10.54)	(11.99)
Arrived 1970–74				0.1356	0.1205	0.1609
				(12.59)	(11.91)	(12.57)
Arrived 1965–69				0.2125	0.1540	0.2049
				(21.35)	(16.43)	(14.90)
Arrived 1960–64				0.2721	0.1891	0.2549
				(24.32)	(17.94)	(15.67)
Arrived 1950–59				0.2844	0.1981	0.2771
				(24.72)	(18.25)	(14.47)
Arrived before 1950				0.2607	0.1729	0.2721
				(18.33)	(12.90)	(10.46)
Years of education		0.0543	0.0598		0.0522	0.0576
		(93.39)	(93.35)		(89.61)	(87.08)
Education*(Immigrant)			−0.0122			−0.0118
			(−12.64)			(−11.56)
12th grade		0.0697	0.0642		0.0679	0.0645
		(21.36)	(18.89)		(20.84)	(19.01)

	(1)	(2)	(3)		(4)	(5)
16th grade		0.1566 (51.65)	0.1372 (42.34)		0.1688 (55.50)	0.1449 (44.00)
12th grade*(Immigrant)			−0.0347 (−4.86)			−0.0366 (−5.13)
16th grade*(Immigrant)			0.0344 (5.25)			0.0826 (12.52)
Education*(1970 census)		−0.0010 (−1.23)	−0.0045 (−5.45)		0.0011 (1.40)	−0.0015 (−1.74)
Education*(1980 census)		−0.0195 (−23.36)	−0.0221 (−26.14)		−0.0181 (−21.71)	−0.0199 (−23.05)
Education*(1970 census)*Immigrant			0.0043 (10.52)			−0.0045 (−5.20)
Education*(1980 census)*Immigrant			0.0014 (4.00)			−0.0043 (−7.94)
12th grade*(1970 census)		−0.0264 (−5.91)	−0.0236 (−5.22)		−0.250 (−5.60)	−0.257 (−5.70)
16th grade*(1970 census)		−0.0642 (−13.89)	−0.0537 (−11.49)		−0.0759 (−16.38)	−0.0635 (−13.42)
12th grade*(1980 census)		0.0242 (5.15)	0.0263 (5.56)		0.0260 (5.54)	0.0247 (5.22)
16th grade*(1980 census)		−0.0694 (−15.11)	−0.0611 (−13.23)		−0.0775 (−16.84)	−0.0683 (−14.65)
R^2	0.1104	0.2210	0.2216	0.1150	0.2245	0.2251
F-test				*P*-value		
12th and 16th grade effects = 0	0.0001	0.0001	0.0001		0.0001	0.0001
12th and 16th grade effects interacted with immigrant = 0			0.0001			0.0001
All included sheepskin effect coefficients = 0	0.0001	0.0001	0.0001		0.0001	0.0001

Note: t-statistics appear in parentheses. $N = 2,232,284$.

As indicated above, schooling may affect immigrants' earnings differently from natives'. It is therefore necessary to allow for differences in returns to schooling *and* distinct sheepskin effects between the two groups. Column 6 in table 2.10 shows that the sheepskin effect of high school graduation is approximately 6.5 percent for natives but is 3.6 percent lower for immigrants. Remarkably, the lower sheepskin effect for immigrants is reversed for college graduates. The coefficient on the 16th grade sheepskin effect variable interacted with immigrant status is significant and *positive*. This implies that sheepskin effects from graduating college are greater for immigrants than natives. This reversal might reflect the highly selective nature of the flow of college-educated workers into the United States.

The number of years of schooling required to complete high school varies between countries, suggesting that we may have mismeasured the sheepskin effect for graduation from secondary school above. To account for these differences, we reestimated the models in table 2.10 with a dummy variable that is equal to one if the person has completed at least the number of years required to finish secondary schooling in his home country. However, if a person immigrated to the United States before the age of 18 and has completed 12 years or more of education, he is likely to have graduated from a high school in the United States. In these cases we also set the indicator variable equal to one. The data used to determine number of years necessary to finish secondary education are taken from Barro and Lee (1993), whose data we downloaded from the web site of the National Bureau of Economic Research, and from the United Nations Educational, Scientific, and Cultural Organization (UNESCO, 1996). The Barro and Lee data set includes information on duration in years of primary and secondary education in 1965. The UNESCO statistics include data on duration for 1996 and any changes that have taken place between 1980 and 1996.[9]

The regression results for the education variables when using the adjusted sheepskin dummy are presented in appendix table 2A.1. These models were estimated using the same socioeconomic and geographic variables as shown in table 2.10. Since the results for columns 1 and 3 in table 2.10 do not include sheepskin variables and the results are consequently identical, they are not presented in table 2A.1. Using the modified definition of the high school sheepskin effect for immigrants has little effect on the size of the sheepskin effect for college completion or most other coefficients, but it changes the coefficient on the high school dummies dramatically. Columns 3 and 6 in table 2A.1 show that the coefficient on the interaction between the high school dummy and the dummy for immigrants

---

9. Some countries have more than one structure in their educational system that allows for different numbers of years to complete primary and/or secondary education. In these cases, we opted for the ones listed in the main table (i.e., table 3.1).

doubles in size. The coefficient is now slightly larger but opposite in sign to the uninteracted sheepskin effect. In other words, there is no sheepskin effect, or even a slightly negative sheepskin effect, for immigrants who have completed secondary school abroad.

There are a number of ways of interpreting this result. A signaling interpretation might hold that employers pay a premium to those who complete 12 or more years of schooling because they believe that it signals the ability of the worker. At the same time, American employers either do not understand that the number of years required to complete secondary school varies around the world, or they understand these variations but believe that secondary school completion elsewhere does not provide a very good signal of ability. A human capital interpretation of this finding might be that, around the world, there is a strong degree of complementarity between the skills typically imparted during the first 12 years of schooling. Furthermore, American firms find that workers who have completed secondary school abroad, but not exactly 12 years, do not possess exactly the right mix of skills. This second explanation is somewhat strained, in our view. A third interpretation is simply that there is measurement error in the international data we used to redefine the dummy for completion of secondary school. We have no evidence in this regard.

In summary, it appears that the definition of high school completion matters in determining sheepskin effects and that the difference between immigrants and natives is even greater when differences in high school duration are adjusted for. It also supports other findings in this paper that indicate substantial heterogeneity in the immigrant population.

2.4.3 Testing for Variations in the Returns to Premigration and Postmigration Education

Sheepskin effects are not the only possible type of nonlinearity in the returns to education for immigrants. One of the reasons for lower returns to education for immigrants may be that the U.S. labor market discounts schooling acquired abroad. For instance, Friedberg (1996) finds that in the Israeli labor market, returns to education obtained abroad are significantly lower than returns to postmigration education.

We estimate the years of schooling obtained prior to and after immigration to the United States based on the person's age at arrival and years of schooling, under the assumption that a person would have obtained all years of schooling in a continuous period of study. We then estimate wage models with overall years of schooling interacted with a dummy for natives, to show the returns to education for natives, as well as variables measuring the estimated years of pre- and postmigration education for immigrants.

In regressions shown in table 2.11, we find that education acquired after immigration is found to have a larger effect on earnings than is education

Table 2.11   Model to Test for Differences in Returns to Education Obtained in the United States and Abroad for Immigrants

Variable	1	2	3	4	5
Constant	3.6560	2.8876	2.9277	3.6977	2.9177
	(115.28)	(96.71)	(98.11)	(112.72)	(94.39)
1970 census effect	0.0198	0.3231	0.2893	0.0110	0.3130
	(15.09)	(65.46)	(58.06)	(8.18)	(59.98)
1980 census effect	0.0384	0.4307	0.4026	0.0317	0.4224
	(29.79)	(83.12)	(77.36)	(24.28)	(78.89)
Married	0.2589	0.2432	0.2425	0.2593	0.2425
	(192.18)	(192.63)	(192.27)	(192.91)	(192.33)
Northeast	0.1521	0.1161	0.1153	0.1503	0.1155
	(103.03)	(83.77)	(83.27)	(102.02)	(83.44)
Midwest	0.1288	0.1054	0.1047	0.1271	0.1046
	(92.09)	(80.39)	(79.90)	(91.08)	(79.84)
West	0.1413	0.0938	0.0947	0.1423	0.0939
	(92.25)	(65.09)	(65.77)	(93.14)	(65.23)
Resides in city	0.2130	0.1550	0.1551	0.2130	0.1553
	(159.40)	(123.05)	(123.29)	(159.73)	(123.48)
Age	0.1183	0.0980	0.0978	0.1159	0.0967
	(49.25)	(43.50)	(43.47)	(46.61)	(41.46)
Age^2	-0.0018	-0.0014	-0.0014	-0.0018	-0.0013
	(-31.32)	(-25.05)	(-25.20)	(-29.30)	(-23.66)
Age^3/10,000	0.0743	0.0474	0.0481	0.0694	0.0449
	(16.33)	(11.11)	(11.29)	(14.73)	(10.16)
Immigrant	-0.1663	0.1415	-0.1841	-0.6874	-0.0185
	(-78.91)	(25.41)	(-20.21)	(-5.53)	(-0.16)
Age*Immigrant				0.0241	0.00003
				(2.57)	(0.008)

	(1)	(2)	(3)	(4)
Age^2*Immigrant			-0.0007	-0.0002
			(-3.16)	(-1.04)
Age^3*Immigrant/10,000			0.0590	0.0243
			(3.34)	(1.46)
Years since immigration			0.0112	0.0222
			(9.55)	(18.00)
(Years since immigration)^2			-0.00003	-0.0004
			(-0.63)	(-7.37)
(Years since immigration)^3/10,000			-0.0138	0.0234
			(-2.18)	(3.65)
Arrived 1980–84		0.1295	0.0340	0.0300
		(14.95)	(3.35)	(2.98)
Arrived 1975–79		0.2173	0.1038	0.0910
		(25.45)	(10.85)	(8.33)
Arrived 1970–74		0.2939	0.1356	0.1107
		(32.97)	(12.59)	(8.15)
Arrived 1965–69		0.3299	0.2125	0.1404
		(36.50)	(21.35)	(9.47)
Arrived 1960–64		0.4094	0.2721	0.1724
		(42.80)	(24.32)	(9.83)
Arrived 1950–59		0.4565	0.2844	0.1764
		(49.16)	(24.72)	(8.63)
Arrived before 1950		0.4631	0.2607	0.1328
		(44.64)	(18.33)	(4.95)
Education*Native	0.0822	0.0802		0.0815
	(279.31)	(270.52)		(266.47)
Premigration education	0.0596	0.0681		0.0659
	(127.36)	(137.78)		(121.40)

(*continued*)

Table 2.11 (continued)

Variable	1	2	3	4	5
Postmigration education		0.0786	0.0689		0.0606
		(117.71)	(99.47)		(75.44)
Education*Native*(1970 census)		−0.0155	−0.0129		−0.0147
		(−40.49)	(−33.54)		(−36.53)
Education*Native*(1980 census)		−0.0284	−0.0263		−0.0278
		(−73.55)	(−68.02)		(−69.81)
Premigration education*(1970 census)		−0.0104	−0.0253		−0.0155
		(−17.55)	(−38.28)		(−15.92)
Premigration education*(1980 census)		−0.0263	−0.0350		−0.0300
		(−47.97)	(−60.58)		(−45.46)
Postmigration education*(1970 census)		−0.0198	−0.0209		−0.0169
		(−19.40)	(−18.93)		(−14.03)
Postmigration education*(1980 census)		−0.0319	−0.0321		−0.0312
		(−32.67)	(−32.48)		(−30.51)
R^2	0.1104	0.2202	0.2221	0.1150	0.2226
F-test:			*P*-value		
Premigration education = Postmigration education		0.0001	0.2497		0.0001
Pre = Post = Native		0.0001	0.0001		0.0001
Pre = Native		0.0001	0.0001		0.0001
Post = Native		0.0001	0.0001		0.0001

Note: *t*-statistics appear in parentheses. $N = 2{,}232{,}284$.

obtained in the home country. The difference is close to 2 percent, as shown in table 2.10, column 2. It is also very interesting to note that the difference between returns to postmigration education and returns to natives' education is much smaller, one-third of a percent. The null hypothesis of equality in returns between pre- and postmigration education is rejected as indicated by the very low p-values for the f-tests. If we control for cohort effects, as shown in column 3, the difference between the two coefficients becomes insignificant, indicating no difference in returns to pre- and postmigration education. Furthermore, if we allow for differences in the impact of age on earnings between immigrants and natives and control for cohorts and years since migration, as shown in model 5, it appears that education obtained before moving to the United States yields *greater* returns than postmigration education. It is unclear what causes this surprising result. It may partially be explained by differences in rates of return to premigration education due to differences in school quality in the source country. Bratsberg and Terrell (1997) find evidence of such an effect.

The results in table 2.11 are valid only to the extent that our method for allocating total years of schooling in years of postmigration and premigration education is valid. To check this, we analyzed data from the 1976 Survey of Income and Education (SIE). This is the only sufficiently large data set including information on pre- and postmigration education for immigrants in the United States.[10] In this survey, respondents were asked whether they attended school before coming to the United States, and if so, for how many years. Postmigration education is then simply calculated by subtracting premigration education from total years of education. We replicated the sampling procedure from the three censuses with the exception that we included *all* natives and immigrants between the ages of 18 and 64 who earned at least $50 in 1989 dollars. The same models that are presented in table 2.11 were estimated using the SIE data and are shown in table 2.12. For obvious reasons, no period effects or interactions with period effects are included in these models.

The returns to education appear to be about 2–3.5 percent smaller in all models shown in table 2.12 for all three education categories, premigration, postmigration, and native education, when we use the SIE data compared to when we use the census data. However, the SIE data are from the mid-1970s. A closer look at the coefficients for variables interacted with period effects in the regressions using census data indicate that the estimated differences are quite small.

Model 2 in table 2.12 shows that education acquired in the United States by immigrants yields statistically significantly greater returns than does premigration schooling, by about 0.8 percent. When cohort effects are

---

10. We thank George Borjas for suggesting that we use this data set.

Table 2.12   Model to Test for Differences in Returns to Education Obtained in the United States and Abroad for Immigrants, Using 1976 Survey of Income and Education Data

Variable	1	2	3	4	5
Constant	2.2985	2.1925	2.1926	2.2713	2.1768
	(51.81)	(51.21)	(51.22)	(50.08)	(49.74)
Married	0.1837	0.1883	0.1884	0.1840	0.1882
	(43.61)	(46.35)	(46.40)	(43.71)	(46.35)
Northeast	-0.1344	-0.1558	-0.1563	-0.1349	-0.1562
	(-30.10)	(-36.11)	(-36.24)	(-30.23)	(-36.21)
Midwest	0.0201	0.0046	0.0042	0.0194	0.0044
	(4.26)	(1.01)	(0.93)	(4.13)	(0.96)
West	0.0331	-0.0037	-0.0040	0.0324	-0.0039
	(6.96)	(-0.81)	(-0.87)	(6.83)	(-0.84)
Resides in city	0.1399	0.1212	0.1216	0.1411	0.1218
	(40.48)	(36.29)	(36.42)	(40.86)	(36.47)
Age	0.1919	0.1496	0.1499	0.1940	0.1510
	(49.82)	(39.93)	(40.02)	(49.21)	(39.35)
Age^2	-0.0039	-0.0028	-0.0028	-0.0039	-0.0028
	(-37.52)	(-27.89)	(-28.00)	(-37.04)	(-27.50)
Age^3/10,000	0.2450	0.1645	0.1654	0.2481	0.1667
	(28.18)	(19.51)	(19.61)	(27.80)	(19.25)
Immigrant	-0.1004	-0.0096	-0.1147	0.3406	0.3712
	(-13.61)	(-0.44)	(-4.45)	(1.63)	(1.82)
Age*Immigrant				-0.0389	-0.0338
				(-2.23)	(-1.99)
Age^2*Immigrant				0.0008	0.0007
				(1.75)	(1.49)
Age^3*Immigrant/10,000				-0.0571	-0.0442
				(-1.48)	(-1.18)

Years since immigration				−0.0044 (−0.09)	0.0541 (1.07)
(Years since immigration)²				−0.0021 (−0.07)	−0.0291 (−1.07)
(Years since immigration)³/10,000				7.3439 (0.19)	42.037 (1.13)
Arrived 1965–69			0.1028 (4.57)	−0.1081 (−0.18)	−0.5802 (−1.03)
Arrived 1960–64			0.1213 (4.92)	−1.0393 (−0.23)	−4.8568 (−1.14)
Arrived 1950–59			0.1248 (5.96)	−5.1778 (−0.23)	−24.921 (−1.14)
Arrived before 1950			0.1775 (7.59)	−44.924 (−0.21)	−233.48 (−1.14)
Education*Native		0.0484 (84.99)	0.0483 (84.77)		0.0483 (84.69)
Premigration education		0.0421 (24.19)	0.0436 (24.83)		0.0449 (25.07)
Postmigration education		0.0497 (27.09)	0.0463 (24.15)		0.0426 (20.14)
R^2	0.2365	0.2902	0.2906	0.2379	0.2908
F-test:		*P*-value			
Premigration education = Postmigration education		0.0001	0.0897		0.2179
Pre = Post = Native		0.0001	0.0254		0.0289
Pre = Native		0.0005	0.0107		0.0640
Post = Native		0.5037	0.3066		0.0084

Note: *t*-statistics appear in parentheses. Data are from 1976 Survey of Income and Education. Observations that are top coded, in earnings, are multiplied by 1.5. All observations with reported weekly earnings of less than $50 in 1989$ are excluded. $N = 105,468$.

controlled for, as in model 3, the difference in returns between education obtained in the United States and abroad becomes insignificant. This is the same result we reached when performing the same test using the census data, as shown in model 3 in table 2.11. Also, when age is allowed to affect earnings differently for immigrants and natives, and years since migration is controlled for, as in model 5 in table 2.12, we find that the returns to premigration education are greater than the returns to postmigration education. This, too, is what we found when we used the estimated pre- and postmigration education levels from the census data. However, using the SIE data, the difference is insignificant.

The above results from the SIE data show that the relationship between returns to foreign- and U.S.-acquired education is quite similar to what we found when we used the estimated pre- and postmigration education in the three censuses. To check further the validity of the method we used to calculate pre- and postmigration education in the censuses, we ran the same SIE regressions as in table 2.12 but with *estimated* pre- and postmigration education. The estimated foreign- and U.S.-obtained schooling were calculated exactly the same way as for the census data. Table 2.13 presents two specifications, models 3 and 5 from table 2.12, using both the actual and estimated variables. The results are remarkably similar. There is virtually no difference in the estimated coefficients for the education variables. It appears that our method for estimating pre- and postmigration education is valid and leads to robust results.

It is quite possible that returns to education may also vary across different races or ethnicity. Table 2.14 shows the estimated coefficients for returns to education when regression of the same form as table 2.11, column (5), are estimated separately for four different racial/ethnic groups: whites, blacks, Asians, and Hispanics. The groups with the highest and lowest returns are whites and Hispanics, respectively. We ask two questions. First, do the relative returns to pre- and postmigration education among immigrants vary across ethnic groups? Premigration education yields significantly higher returns than postmigration education for two of the groups—whites and Asians. Black and Hispanic immigrants, on the other hand, seem to earn the same return no matter where the education was obtained. Second, how do the returns to education for immigrants differ from those for natives in the same group? Quite remarkably, for Asians we cannot reject the null hypothesis of equal returns at the 5 percent level. Immigrant Asians appear to gain as much from schooling in their home country as U.S.-born Asians gain from their education. For other groups, both pre- and postmigration education for immigrants have lower returns than does education for natives of the same racial/ethnic group. The gap is particularly striking among blacks and Hispanics. Overall, the table makes clear that there is extensive heterogeneity not only in educational attainment among immigrants but also in the gains from education.

Table 2.13   **Model to Test for Differences in Returns to Education Obtained in the United States and Abroad for Immigrants, Using Survey of Income and Education 1976 Data, Actual and Estimated Pre- and Postmigration Education**

Variable	Actual Pre and Post		Estimated Pre and Post	
	3	5	3	5
Constant	2.1926	2.1768	2.1899	2.1768
	(51.22)	(49.74)	(51.12)	(49.74)
Married	0.1884	0.1882	0.1884	0.1882
	(46.40)	(46.35)	(46.40)	(46.35)
Northeast	−0.1563	−0.1562	−0.1563	−0.1562
	(−36.24)	(−36.21)	(−36.23)	(−36.21)
Midwest	0.0042	0.0044	0.0043	0.0044
	(0.93)	(0.96)	(0.94)	(0.96)
West	−0.0040	−0.0039	−0.0040	−0.0039
	(−0.87)	(−0.84)	(−0.87)	(−0.85)
Resides in city	0.1216	0.1218	0.1217	0.1218
	(36.42)	(36.47)	(36.44)	(36.48)
Age	0.1499	0.1510	0.1501	0.1510
	(40.02)	(39.35)	(40.05)	(39.34)
Age^2	−0.0028	−0.0028	−0.0028	−0.0028
	(−28.00)	(−27.50)	(−28.04)	(−27.50)
Age^3/10,000	0.1654	0.1667	0.1658	0.1667
	(19.61)	(19.25)	(19.66)	(19.25)
Immigrant	−0.1147	0.3712	−0.0948	0.4057
	(−4.45)	(1.82)	(−3.68)	(1.95)
Age*Immigrant		−0.0338		−0.0356
		(−1.99)		(−2.06)
Age^2*Immigrant		0.0007		0.0007
		(1.49)		(1.61)
Age^3*Immigrant/10,000		−0.0442		−0.0513
		(−1.18)		(−1.35)
Years since immigration		0.0541		0.0422
		(1.07)		(0.84)
(Years since immigration)^2		−0.0291		−0.0246
		(−1.07)		(−0.91)
(Years since immigration)^3/ 10,000		42.037		37.590
		(1.13)		(1.01)
Arrived 1965–69	0.1028	−0.5802	0.0984	−0.5506
	(4.57)	(−1.03)	(4.37)	(−0.97)
Arrived 1960–64	0.1213	−4.8568	0.1152	−4.4865
	(4.92)	(−1.14)	(4.66)	(−1.05)
Arrived 1950–59	0.1248	−24.921	0.1150	−22.730
	(5.96)	(−1.14)	(5.40)	(−1.04)
Arrived before 1950	0.1775	−233.48	0.1648	−210.80
	(7.59)	(−1.14)	(7.05)	(−1.02)
Education*Native	0.0483	0.0483	0.0483	0.0483
	(84.77)	(84.69)	(84.79)	(84.69)

(*continued*)

Table 2.13   (continued)

Variable	Actual Pre and Post		Estimated Pre and Post	
	3	5	3	5
Premigration education	0.0436	0.0449	0.0430	0.0446
	(24.83)	(25.07)	(24.49)	(24.89)
Postmigration education	0.0463	0.0426	0.0464	0.0413
	(24.15)	(20.14)	(24.07)	(17.36)
R^2	0.2906	0.2908	0.2906	0.2907
F-test:			P-value	
Premigration education = Postmigration education	0.0897	0.2179	0.0358	0.1565
Pre = Post = Native	0.0254	0.0289	0.0076	0.0124
Pre = Native	0.0107	0.0640	0.0039	0.0453
Post = Native	0.3066	0.0084	0.3368	0.0042

Note: t-statistics appear in parentheses. Data are from 1976 Survey of Income and Education. Observations that are top coded, in earnings, are multiplied by 1.5. All observations with reported weekly earnings of less than \$50 in 1989\$ are excluded. $N = 105,468$. The first two columns replicate the results from models 3 and 5 in table 2.12. The final two columns use the same specifications as these models except that we replace actual pre- and postmigration education with estimates based on age at arrival and total years of schooling.

2.4.4 The Impact of Traits of the Source Country on the Returns to Education

The previous tables show mixed evidence about the relative returns to education obtained prior to and after a person immigrates to the United States, and clear evidence that these returns vary by ethnicity. It would be worthwhile to "open up the black box" to find out what characteristics of immigrants' country of origin most affect the returns to education. A plausible hypothesis is that immigrants who come from countries with higher standards of living will have higher returns to education. In such countries, immigrants' parents and peers will be better educated and have higher incomes, which should increase the effectiveness of schooling. Similarly, such countries might be able to afford better schools. It is not clear whether these host-country traits would have a larger effect on the returns to pre- or postmigration education, but it seems more likely to affect education obtained before migrating to the United States.

Here, we are motivated primarily by recent work by Bratsberg and Terrell (1997), who report that the pupil-teacher ratio in immigrants' country of origin is strongly related to the return to years of schooling among immigrants working in the United States. But based on the above hypothesis, we will also condition earnings on GDP per capita and average levels

Table 2.14   **OLS Models of Log of Weekly Earnings by Race/Ethnicity**

	Ethnic Group			
Variable	White	Black	Asian	Hispanic
Education*Native	0.0811	0.0687	0.0704	0.0621
	(229.2)	(57.55)	(35.36)	(67.65)
Premigration education	0.0724	0.0445	0.0724	0.0426
	(64.06)	(15.77)	(80.11)	(61.66)
Postmigration education	0.0619	0.0445	0.0672	0.0445
	(48.91)	(9.82)	(44.26)	(42.41)
Education*Native*	−0.0177	−0.0159	−0.0212	−0.0085
(1970 census)	(−37.82)	(−10.70)	(−8.57)	(−6.59)
Education*Native*	−0.0313	−0.0182	−0.0159	−0.0127
(1980 census)	(−66.39)	(−11.78)	(−7.98)	(−12.28)
Premigration education*	−0.0282	−0.0121	−0.0283	0.0005
(1970 census)	(−18.47)	(−1.99)	(−12.92)	(0.33)
Premigration education*	−0.0386	−0.0243	−0.0194	−0.0088
(1980 census)	(−36.14)	(−7.37)	(−13.18)	(−8.08)
Postmigration education*	−0.0211	−0.0224	−0.0248	−0.0068
(1970 census)	(−14.20)	(−1.88)	(−5.92)	(−2.60)
Postmigration education*	−0.0340	−0.0258	−0.0206	−0.0158
(1980 census)	(−25.31)	(−4.00)	(−8.51)	(−9.59)
R^2	0.2026	0.2118	0.2581	0.2258
N	952,083	85,999	64,175	125,107
F-test		P-value		
Premigration education =				
Postmigration education	0.0001	0.9998	0.0001	0.0785
Pre = Post = Native	0.0001	0.0001	0.0005	0.0001
Post = Native	0.0001	0.0001	0.1556	0.0001
Pre = Native	0.0001	0.0001	0.3245	0.0001

Note: t-statistics appear in parentheses.

of education in the source country as a proxy for the socioeconomic status of the immigrant's family and peer group.

Our data are compiled from three sources. The average years of schooling is collected from Barro and Lee (1993) and covers the period 1960–85. The pupil-teacher ratio in primary schools for the period 1950–80 is collected from Barro and Lee. We also used UNESCO (1994) data to extend the period covered for this variable to 1985. The GDP data is collected from Summers and Heston (1991) and is measured as real GDP per capita in a constant dollars chain index, expressed in international prices with 1985 base for the period 1950–85.

The average years of schooling and GDP per capita are matched to an immigrant's arrival cohort. For example, we use the 1965 data for these variables for an immigrant who arrived between 1965 and 1969. This is done to represent the socioeconomic characteristics of the source country at the time of migration. The pupil-teacher ratio is used to depict school quality and is therefore matched in a slightly different way, using the period the immigrant was most likely in primary school. We calculated the year the person was 10 years old and matched it with the closest year for which data on pupil-teacher ratio exist. For example, if an immigrant was 10 years old in 1963, we used the pupil-teacher ratio for that particular country in 1965. If an individual was 10 years old in 1962, we use data from 1960.

The inclusion of source country traits imposes a limitation on the arrival cohorts that can be included in the regressions. Since data on average years of schooling are limited to no further back than 1960, immigrants who arrived prior to 1960 are dropped. Similarly, since data on the pupil-teacher ratio are limited to 1950 and later, we dropped immigrants who turned 10 before 1947. In order to ensure that the age ranges of immigrants and natives were similar, we applied this same restriction to natives, dropping those born before 1937.

In order to focus on the impact of host-country traits on the earnings of immigrants, these three variables are set to zero for all natives. Our final subsample contains workers from 55 countries, including the United States.

We reestimate models 3 and 5 from table 2.11 on this subsample. Since the earnings of workers from each country are likely to be correlated, and since most of our variation in the source country traits comes from cross-country, as opposed to within-country, variation, we estimate the models by generalized least squares (GLS), adding a random effect for each source country. This treatment will reduce the chance that the t-statistics on the host country traits will be overstated due to within-group correlation.

Table 2.15 presents the results. Models 3a and 5a simply replicate models 3 and 5 from table 2.11. Since the sample is smaller, and since population weights could not be used given that we use a random effect method, the results change slightly. The returns to both pre- and postmigration education are somewhat lower in model 5a in table 2.15 than in the corresponding model 5 in table 2.11.

Regressions labeled 3b and 5b add the pupil-teacher ratio in immigrants' country of origin and the interaction of this variable with years of premigration and postmigration education. In both models, the levels effect and the interaction with education obtained abroad are highly significant, but there is not strong evidence that the pupil-teacher ratio in the source country is strongly related to the returns to education obtained by the immigrant after arrival in the United States. Because the levels and the interaction terms have opposite signs, the derivative of log weekly wages with respect to the pupil-teacher ratio is predicted to be positive for

Table 2.15 Random Effect Models, Including Traits of Immigrants' Country of Origin

Variable	3a	3b	3c	5a	5b	5c
Education*Native	0.0790	0.0794	0.0797	0.0849	0.0849	0.0850
	(222.69)	(223.901)	(224.70)	(218.27)	(218.68)	(219.1)
Premigration education	0.0508	0.1037	0.1016	0.0476	0.0955	0.0847
	(113.68)	(55.777)	(40.706)	(103.793)	(50.961)	(33.58)
Postmigration education	0.0534	0.0648	0.1134	0.0390	0.0442	0.0878
	(82.219)	(28.424)	(30.554)	(50.31)	(18.81)	(23.336)
Education*Native*(1970 census)	−0.0300	−0.0306	−0.0310	−0.0380	−0.0381	−0.0382
	(−41.783)	(−42.566)	(−43.185)	(−50.609)	(−50.76)	(−50.99)
Education*Native*(1980 census)	−0.0262	−0.0271	−0.0278	−0.0382	−0.0384	−0.0385
	(−59.836)	(−61.761)	(−63.101)	(−69.835)	(−70.29)	(−70.66)
Premigration education*(1970 census)	−0.0480	−0.0492	−0.0500	−0.0062	−0.0091	−0.0108
	(−36.447)	(−37.295)	(−37.945)	(−3.574)	(−5.18)	(−6.126)
Premigration education*(1980 census)	−0.0351	−0.0363	−0.0375	−0.0218	−0.0234	−0.0247
	(−65.36)	(−67.396)	(−69.174)	(−34.196)	(−36.39)	(−37.98)
Postmigration education*(1970 census)	0.0222	0.0171	0.0044	0.0045	−0.0024	−0.0146
	(1.271)	(0.978)	(0.253)	(0.258)	(−0.136)	(−0.838)
Postmigration education*(1980 census)	−0.0289	−0.0318	−0.0321	−0.0266	−0.0302	−0.0302
	(−21.468)	(−23.537)	(−23.723)	(−17.335)	(−19.63)	(−19.53)
Pupil-teacher ratio		0.0188	0.0183		0.0166	0.0149
		(27.816)	(25.583)		(24.458)	(20.789)
Premigration education*Pupil-teacher ratio		−0.0014	−0.0012		−0.0013	−0.0010
		(−30.185)	(−24.646)		(−27.29)	(−19.90)

(continued)

Table 2.15 (continued)

Variable	3a	3b	3c	5a	5b	5c
Postmigration education*Pupil-teacher ratio		−0.0001 (−2.114)	−0.0009 (−11.836)		0.0001 (0.865)	−0.0007 (−8.944)
Average years of education			−0.0285 (−4.94)			−0.0344 (−5.922)
Premigration education*Average years of education			0.0026 (7.706)			0.0036 (10.554)
Postmigration education*Average years of education			−0.0008 (−1.655)			0.0004 (0.749)
GDP/Capita			0.0001 (28.532)			0.0001 (27.777)
Premigration education*GDP			−0.000003 (−15.223)			−0.00003 (−14.32)
Postmigration education*GDP			−0.000005 (−12.399)			−0.00005 (−13.47)

Note: t-statistics appear in parentheses. The regressors are identical to those in models 3 and 5 from table 2.11 except for the addition of traits of immigrants' country of origin in models 3b, 3c, 5b, and 5c. Sample size is 692,616. For the immigrants, the means of the new regressors are 37.50 for the pupil-teacher ratio, 4.265 for average years of schooling and 4,446.7 for GDP per capita.

immigrants with less premigration education and negative for those with more premigration education. In model 3b, the derivative is negative for immigrants with 14 or more years of schooling obtained abroad, and in model 5b the crossover point is at 13 years of premigration education. That is, smaller class size benefits the earnings of only those immigrants who have obtained at least some college education before entering the United States. This represents a rather small fraction of immigrants in the sample, for whom mean years of pre- and postmigration education are 9.9 and 1.3 years, respectively. This result is highly similar to recent findings concerning the impact of the pupil-teacher ratio on the earnings of natives. Both Betts (1995) and Heckman, Layne-Farrar, and Todd (1996) find evidence that smaller pupil-teacher ratios are associated with higher earnings only for those with some college education.

In models 3c and 5c we add GDP per capita and average years of education in the immigrant's country of origin, both on their own and interacted with years of schooling obtained abroad and in the United States. The addition of these regressors reduces both the levels of significance and the absolute size of the coefficients on the pupil-teacher ratio and its interaction with premigration education slightly. However, in both models, the pupil-teacher ratio now affects the returns to postmigration education significantly. Given the variation in results between models b and c, it is not clear whether the pupil-teacher ratio in the country of origin really does affect the impact of education obtained by the immigrant in the United States. But both specifications indicate that the pupil-teacher ratio has a larger marginal impact on the returns to premigration education than it does on postmigration education. We find this result quite intuitive.

The average years of educational attainment in the source country is highly significant: The coefficient on the level effect is negative, and the coefficient on its interaction with premigration education is positive. Model 3c suggests that the net effect of higher average educational attainment in the host country on an immigrant's wages becomes positive if the immigrant's own premigration education is 11 or more years. The corresponding crossover point in model 5c is 10 years of education.

GDP per capita in the source country also affects earnings of immigrants significantly. Unlike the other two variables, this trait affects earnings positively for all immigrants, regardless of their level of education. The impact of GDP per capita on earnings in the United States appears to weaken somewhat as the immigrant obtains more education of either type.

Differences in returns to education obtained in the United States and abroad in the above models will partially depend on the three source country traits we control for. This is the case since we interact these characteristics with pre- and postmigration education. We are particularly interested to see at what levels of the pupil-teacher ratio, a measure of school resources in the immigrant's source country, U.S. education yields greater returns than education acquired abroad. In other words, we want to solve for the point at which the partial derivative of the wage equation with respect to premigration education is equal to this partial derivative with respect to postmigration education. We performed the necessary calculations using the returns to education observed in 1990. In model 3b, this happens at approximately the median pupil-teacher ratio of 30.1, among the countries included in the sample. For ratios above this, the returns to postmigration education are greater than for premigration education. The overtaking point in model 5b is slightly higher, at around 37 pupils per teacher. In the more complex models, 3c and 5c, where we also include variables for average years of education and GDP per capita in the source countries, it is also necessary to hold these variables constant to analyze differences in returns to education. In these models we hold average years of education and GDP per capita constant at the median values. The pupil-teacher ratio at which postmigration schooling yields a greater return than premigration education occurs at approximately 30 students per teacher in model 3c. In model 5c, the crossover pointtakes place at a relatively high pupil-teacher ratio of 55. The higher crossover point in model 5c may be due to correlation between pupil-teacher ratio and GDP per capita and/or average years of schooling. The results from all these models indicate, quite intuitively, that returns to education acquired abroad are only greater for immigrants who come from countries with relatively high quality, in the sense of classroom size, of education.

The overall conclusion from this analysis is that the characteristics of the source country affect immigrants' earnings substantially. Reductions in the pupil-teacher ratio and increases in the average level of educational attainment increase earnings of immigrants significantly, but only for the most highly educated workers. (For the pupil-teacher ratio, additional spending on schools increases earnings only for those immigrants with some college education. The effects become zero or opposite in sign for less well educated immigrants.) Both of these variables have a greater impact on the returns to premigration education than to postmigration education. GDP per capita affects earnings positively for all immigrants, although it is the least well educated immigrants for whom the effect is the largest.

2.5   Implications of the Rise in Immigration for the Educational Attainment of Natives: Further Tests of the Crowding Out Hypothesis

The previous section studies the impact of trends in immigrants' educational attainment on immigrants themselves. But it seems likely that the rising gap in educational attainment between immigrants and natives has also affected the lives of natives. Accordingly, we now examine educational outcomes of natives.

Many studies have examined whether immigration has affected the wages of natives. But immigration might also influence natives' own educational attainment. The direction of such effects is theoretically uncertain. Immigrants are likely to increase both the costs and benefits of education to natives. The marginal cost of education for natives may rise due to competition between immigrant and American-born students for school resources. At the same time, the marginal benefit of education for natives may rise if the arrival of relatively unskilled immigrants increases the returns to education.

Two papers have addressed the question of whether immigrants crowd natives out of education. Betts (1998) models the probability of high school graduation among native blacks and Hispanics as a function of the proportion of immigrants in the local population. Using both state-level and metropolitan-level analyses, the paper finds evidence that inflows of immigrants significantly reduce the probability of high school graduation among these two minority groups. Hoxby (1998) tests whether immigrants crowd native-born blacks and Hispanics out of colleges. She, too, finds evidence in favor of the crowding out hypothesis.

In this section, we extend the work in these papers by using pooled 1970, 1980, and 1990 census data. The section extends the work of Betts (1998) and Hoxby (1998) by modeling total years of schooling obtained, rather than just the probability of graduating from high school or the probability of enrolling in college. It further extends earlier work by including 1970 data in addition to data from the 1980 and 1990 censuses. The section extends the earlier work by examining the impact of immigration on the educational attainment of not only blacks and Hispanics but also Asians and whites. (Hoxby's paper, unlike that of Betts, also examines the impact of immigration on natives who are disadvantaged, but it does not explicitly study crowding out for native Asians or whites.) We would expect immigration to have had a more adverse impact on the educational attainment of minorities than of whites, to the extent that immigrant schoolchildren attend the same inner city schools attended by many native minorities. Furthermore, given that white students' test scores tend to be higher than scores of American-born minorities, it is possible that, *within* schools, white students are placed in classes that have relatively few immigrant schoolchildren. For this reason, the presence of children with limited English proficiency (LEP) in schools should have a more adverse effect on the educational attainment of native minorities than on that of whites.

The key hypothesis that we test is that the years of schooling obtained by natives aged 24–30 is unrelated to the proportion of immigrants in the same age group. Betts (1998) examined the probability of high school graduation among those aged 19–25. Since we are interested in the years of schooling obtained eventually by people, we opted for the older 24–30 age group, so as to capture gains in schooling resulting from college attendance.[11] We use the person's current state of residence to attribute the ratio of immigrants to the total population in the age group. This will introduce measurement error if some people live in a different state at the time of the census than the state in which they obtained the bulk of their education. For this reason, we use the subsample of people who report living in the same state five years before the census. We will also report in footnotes the results when the full sample, including movers, was used in the regressions.

For this analysis, we use the full 5 percent samples for each minority group in 1980 and 1990, the full 1 percent sample available in 1970, and a 0.005 percent sample of whites in all years. However, in 1980, information on whether a person was living in the same state five years earlier was available for only one-half of respondents. We adjust our weights accordingly. Unlike the earlier regression analysis in the paper, but following Betts (1998) and Hoxby (1998), we include both men and women in the sample. The inclusion of women, among other things, helps to counteract the loss of observations due to the age restriction on our sample.

In order to control for the traits of the parents of the young people aged 24–30 in our sample, for each ethnic/racial group we examine people in the same ethnic/racial group in the same state who are aged 45–64 and who are not themselves immigrants. For this proxy group for parents, we calculate the average income per capita in 1990 prices and the proportion of people in the groups who are high school dropouts. We also control for the average pupil-teacher ratio in the state in which the person resides. For each age group, we take a simple average of the pupil-teacher ratio for each year in which group members were likely to have been in school. (For instance, for people aged 24–30 in the 1970 census, we take averages of the pupil-teacher ratios between the school years 1946–47 and 1963–64. These data are based on data published by the National Center for Education Statistics [various years] in the *Digest of Education Statistics* and the *Biennial Survey of Education in the United States* [Federal Security Agency, various years].)

We estimate a fixed-effect model that takes account of any unobserved variations in educational attainment of people living in different states:

$$
\text{EDUC}_{ist} = \sum_{j=1}^{49} \text{STATE}_{ist}\,\gamma_j + \alpha_{70}\text{CENSUS70}_{ist} + \alpha_{80}\text{CENSUS80}_{ist}
$$
(1)
$$
+ \beta \text{IMM}_{ist} + X_{ist}\Gamma + \varepsilon_{ist},
$$

---

11. This choice of age group also makes our sample relatively independent of the sample of younger workers chosen by Betts (1998).

where years of schooling for person i living in state s in time t is regressed on state dummies; dummies for census year; the proportion of immigrants in the state's population, both calculated for the age group 24–30; and a vector X_{ist} of personal traits: age and dummy variables for whether the person is female or lives in a city. Based on availability of data on the pupil-teacher ratio, we include all states but Alaska and Hawaii and we also include the District of Columbia. In regressions that do not condition on the pupil-teacher ratio, we include observations from Alaska and Hawaii.

It is important to understand how the impact of immigrants on natives' educational attainment is identified in this model. Regressors include fixed effects for each state and a dummy for two of the three census years. This sweeps out all variation between states and at the same time removes national trends. The variation that remains is the variation within each state across years that is uncorrelated with the national trends. The advantage of this difference on difference model is that it does not simply test for a correlation across states in immigrants' population shares and natives' educational attainment at any one point in time. If immigrants have historically been attracted to certain states that happen to have natives with particularly high or low levels of educational attainment, and if there is an omitted variable that is driving both of these patterns, we would have obtained biased results. Instead, we use *changes* in the immigrant share of the population for each state over time, and the part of this change that varies from national trends, to identify the effects of immigration. There of course remains the possibility that an omitted variable drives state-by-state changes in both immigration and natives' educational attainment, but our approach removes all unobserved state-level effects that are fixed over time, as well as national trends.

Table 2.16 shows the main results. For each ethnic/racial group, two specifications are estimated, with and without the proxies for parental education, parental income, and the pupil-teacher ratio. In all cases the results are consistent: A higher ratio of immigrants in the young population is associated with a significantly lower level of education among natives. The results are little changed when the trio of other variables—proxies for parental income, parental dropout rates, and pupil-teacher ratios—are added, in models 2, 4, and 6.[12]

Numerically, the effects are biggest among Hispanics and Asians, followed by blacks.[13] As expected, the impact on whites is smaller than on American-born minorities. The effects are meaningful. Consider the results based on the more fully specified models. An increase of 0.05 in the

12. The large drop in the number of observations in the more fully specified model for Asians reflects the fact that the pupil-teacher ratio was not available for Hawaii, where a substantial fraction of Asians in the sample lived.

13. Similarly, Betts (1998) finds that immigration has a larger effect on the educational attainment of native Hispanics than of native blacks.

Table 2.16   Models of Years of Schooling Completed by Natives Ages 24-30

	Ethnic/Racial Group							
	Blacks		Hispanics		Asians		Whites	
	1	2	3	4	5	6	7	8
Female	0.2949	0.2950	-0.0843	-0.0838	0.0995	-0.0045	-0.0849	-0.0845
	(26.33)	(26.34)	(-4.41)	(-4.37)	(2.12)	(-0.07)	(-7.29)	(-7.24)
Age	0.0029	0.0026	-0.0394	-0.0392	0.0188	0.0346	0.0261	0.0260
	(1.03)	(0.95)	(-8.24)	(-8.20)	(1.62)	(2.29)	(8.91)	(8.85)
Lives in city	0.6900	0.6760	0.6875	0.6946	0.7743	1.2883	0.5878	0.5849
	(39.74)	(38.63)	(21.48)	(21.57)	(8.97)	(7.49)	(39.07)	(38.72)
1970 census	-1.3520	-0.9759	-2.2765	-2.5498	-1.0879	-0.9799	-0.7309	-0.0127
	(-62.61)	(-7.97)	(-45.92)	(-23.79)	(-7.40)	(-3.04)	(-35.16)	(-0.15)
1980 census	-0.1739	0.0743	-0.6326	-0.8058	0.0914	0.1348	0.0273	0.3950
	(-11.98)	(1.09)	(-19.79)	(-11.57)	(1.16)	(0.74)	(1.80)	(8.49)
Immigrants/ Population (24-30)	-2.1446	-2.0312	-3.3307	-3.3132	-3.6427	-5.7057	-1.2817	-1.1382
	(-8.61)	(-6.34)	(-8.88)	(-7.70)	(-3.95)	(-4.52)	(-5.39)	(-3.48)
Proportion age 45-64 dropout		0.1748		0.2808		0.3091		-2.1723
		(0.54)		(0.98)		(0.39)		(-7.64)
Mean income/1,000 (Age 45-64)		0.0354		0.0056		0.0153		0.0115
		(4.51)		(0.51)		(0.91)		(1.94)
Pupil-teacher ratio		-0.0641		0.0782		-0.1392		-0.0118
		(-5.83)		(3.01)		(-1.47)		(-1.01)
R^2	0.0591	0.0594	0.0809	0.0811	0.0209	0.0195	0.0294	0.0299
N	177,643	177,543	79,891	79,661	11,303	7,444	170,304	169,914

Note: t-statistics are reported in parentheses.

Table 2.17   **Coefficients on Immigration-to-Population Variable in Linear Probability Models of the Probability of Obtaining at Least a High School Diploma, Some College, or a Four-Year College Degree for Natives Aged 24–30**

Group of Natives	High School	Some College	Four Years of College
Blacks	−0.5680	0.007671	0.09973
	(−9.38)	(0.13)	(2.59)
Hispanics	−0.6222	−0.2677	−0.05781
	(−8.52)	(−3.80)	(−1.34)
Asians	−0.4635	−0.9905	−0.3287
	(−3.97)	(−4.81)	(−1.40)
Whites	−0.2645	−0.06122	−0.01518
	(−5.53)	(−0.93)	(−0.28)

Note: Other regressors are as shown in column 2 of table 2.16. *t*-statistics are reported in parentheses.

proportion of immigrants in the young population is predicted to lower average years of education by 0.29 year for Asians, 0.17 year for Hispanics, 0.10 year for blacks, and 0.06 year for whites.[14]

It is also of interest to study more closely the various tiers of education to find out if crowding out occurs solely at the high school level or also at higher levels of schooling. Accordingly, we ran linear probability models for the probability that an individual obtained a high school diploma or higher, some college or higher, or a four-year college degree or higher. (In years before 1990, when the census merely asked people about years of schooling completed, we use 12 or more years of education as a proxy for high school completion, 13 or more years as a proxy for some college, and 16 or more years for a four-year college degree.) The specifications were identical to those in columns 2, 4, and 6 of table 2.16 apart from the dependent variables. The coefficients and *t*-statistics on the immigration-to-population variable for each of the 12 models are shown in table 2.17.

The results in all cases show strong evidence that a rise in the immigrant ratio leads to a rise in the proportion of high school dropouts. But from what tiers of education do these dropouts come? Is the rise in high school dropouts caused by a drop in the number of people with a high school diploma only, or do we observe drops in the numbers of people with some college or four-year college degrees as well? For Hispanics and Asians,

14. The models were also run using both movers and nonmovers. The results were quite similar, although the coefficients on the immigration variable, while remaining highly significant, were typically smaller. The most notable changes were that in model 6 for Asians, the immigration variable became only weakly significant (*t* = −1.82), and in the model for Hispanic students, the perverse sign on the proxy for the parental dropout rate became statistically significant. All of these differences are consistent with the hypothesis that when people who have moved between states in the five years before the census are included, it introduces measurement error in the state-level variables, including the immigration ratio.

a rise in the immigrant ratio is associated with a drop in the proportion of students with some college or four-year college degrees. The association is significant for "some college" only, though. For blacks and whites the share of people with at least some college is insignificantly related to the immigrant ratio. This suggests that the main effect of a rise in immigration for whites and blacks is to discourage those who would have graduated from high school but not attended university from completing high school. These results are borne out by the results for the models of the probability of obtaining a four-year college degree, where there is no significant link to the immigrant ratio for whites. Among blacks, an even stronger result emerges, in which the fraction of young native blacks who obtain a college degree is significantly and *positively* related to the immigrant ratio.

Based on these data, the two groups for which there is evidence that immigration crowds natives out of college are Hispanics and Asians. However, in both cases, the link is significant only when examining students at the sub-baccalaureate level.[15]

Even though the evidence that immigrants crowd natives out of education is stronger at the secondary level than the postsecondary level, census data can shed no light on whether immigration causes natives who do attend postsecondary education to shift between universities. Hoxby (1998) finds evidence that at very selective and extremely selective colleges (with average SAT scores in the observed student population above 1100 and 1200, respectively), immigrants do tend to crowd out American-born minorities. Taken together with the above results based on census data, the implication is that a rise in immigration might not necessarily prevent native minorities from attending four-year colleges, but it may diminish the quality of colleges that they do attend. This finding is extremely relevant for policymakers, given findings by James et al. (1989) and Loury and Garman (1995) that the quality of university attended influences a student's future wages positively.

2.6   Conclusion and Summary

In this paper we present a detailed picture of the educational attainment of immigrants in the United States utilizing data from the three most recent censuses—1970, 1980, and 1990. The paper presents trends in educational attainment and its distribution among natives and immigrants. The

---

15. We also ran these models including people who had moved between states over the last five years. This might be the more appropriate sample for examining crowding out from colleges if many college attendees left home to go to university and still live in the same state at the time of the census. For the most part, the results were quite similar in this larger sample. The only substantive difference was that in the model for college completion among Hispanics, the coefficient and t-statistic changed to -0.091 and 2.53; respectively. Thus, Hispanics are clearly the racial/ethnic group for which the evidence of crowding out across all levels of education is strongest.

main findings are that immigrants' level of education *relative* to natives has declined over the two decades studied, for both males and females. This fall is driven by a widening gap in educational attainment among the bottom half of the educational distribution. But the *absolute* level of education among immigrants rose slightly between 1970 and 1990. Moreover, the top half of the immigrant population is at least as highly educated as the top half of natives. This analysis paints a far more complex picture of the nature of recent immigrants than is commonly given in the press.

We also model enrollment behavior of immigrants relative to natives. Immigrants are found to be more likely to be enrolled in both grades 1–12 and college. This also holds true after we control for socioeconomic characteristics, years since migration, and cohort effects. We infer that immigrants' educational attainment is likely to catch up at least partially to that of similarly aged natives as the immigrants spend more time in the United States.

The paper then analyzes the effects of these trends on immigrants and natives. For immigrants, we examine the wage gap with natives. We find that the lower levels of schooling of immigrants can explain more than half of the immigrant-native wage gap. We also allow for nonlinearities in returns to education. "Sheepskin," or graduation, effects are highly significant. In particular, sheepskin effects for graduating from college are greater for immigrants than natives, but they are smaller for completion of secondary school. When we redefined the sheepskin effect for completion of secondary school based on the actual number of years required in different foreign countries, we found that American employers pay no premium whatsoever to those who have completed secondary school abroad.

This paper also incorporates models allowing for differences in returns to foreign- and U.S.-acquired education. We find that natives' returns to schooling are greater than immigrants' returns to both pre- and postmigration education. In relatively simple models, we find that education acquired after immigrating to the United States brings a greater payoff to immigrants than does education acquired prior to immigrating. But the result is not robust and, in fact, is reversed once we allow age to affect earnings differently between immigrants and natives and control for years since migration and cohort effects. This result also holds when 1976 Survey of Income and Education data are used. This is significant since the latter survey, unlike the census, explicitly asks respondents about the amount of education that they received before and after immigrating to the United States.

Comparisons of returns to pre- and postmigration education reveal differences among ethnic groups. Whites and Asians are found to earn a greater return to education obtained in their source country, while Hispanics display greater returns to U.S.-acquired education than to premigration education, but only weakly so. There appear to be no differences in returns to pre- and postmigration schooling for blacks. We find that traits of the country of origin, such as the pupil-teacher ratio, the average level of education, and GDP per capita, affect earnings of immigrants in mostly intuitive ways. However, a reduction in the pupil-teacher ratio is predicted to increase an immigrant's earnings only if he has obtained some college education.

How have trends in the relative level of education of immigrants and increases in the proportion of immigrants in the population affected the welfare of natives? Keeping to the educational theme of this paper, we extend the work of Betts (1998) and Hoxby (1998) to test whether immigrants "crowd out" natives from secondary and postsecondary schooling. We find evidence in favor of this hypothesis for native blacks, Hispanics, Asians, and whites. Intriguingly, most of the crowding out appears to occur in grade school. However, there is evidence that immigrants crowd native Hispanics and native Asians out of postsecondary as well as secondary education. Although this finding is the third such finding in the literature, all of the analyses to date have used indirect means to infer whether immigrants directly or indirectly dissuade natives from attending educational institutions. More direct studies at the school level would do much to confirm that crowding out occurs.

The paper suggests that education is at the heart of the ongoing debate about immigration policy. The widening gap in relative educational attainment between natives and immigrants appears to have had important consequences for both immigrants and natives. For immigrants, the consequences are directly observed in their wages, with over one-half of the wage gap arising due to the corresponding gap in education. For natives, we find strong evidence that inflows of immigrants have crowded natives, especially minorities, out of schools and, to a lesser extent, colleges.

Appendix

Table 2A.1   **OLS Model of Log of Weekly Earnings in 1989$ for Males Aged 24–64 with Sheepskin Effects, Adjusted for Differences in Years to Complete High School**

Variable	2	3	5	6
Years of education	0.0547	0.0596	0.0527	0.0574
	(94.52)	(93.34)	(90.75)	(87.06)
Education*(Immigrant)		−0.0088		−0.0082
		(−9.57)		(−8.37)
High school graduation	0.0664	0.0651	0.0645	0.0659
	(20.44)	(19.25)	(19.87)	(19.49)
16 Years of schooling	0.1549	0.1380	0.1672	0.1457
	(51.19)	(42.67)	(55.09)	(44.35)
High school graduation*		−0.0696		−0.0753
(Immigrant)		(−10.30)		(−11.11)
16 years of schooling*		0.0267		0.0747
(Immigrant)		(4.14)		(11.51)
Education*(1970 census)	−0.0009	−0.0041	0.0012	−0.0011
	(−1.08)	(−5.03)	(1.46)	(−1.25)
Education*(1980 census)	−0.0196	−0.0219	−0.0183	−0.0197
	(−23.58)	(−26.08)	(−22.02)	(−22.95)
Education*(1970 census)*		0.0041		−0.0046
Immigrant		(10.02)		(−5.29)
Education*(1980 census)*		0.0014		−0.0042
Immigrant		(4.02)		(−7.84)
High school graduation*	−0.0272	−0.0256	−0.0249	−0.0285
(1970 census)	(−6.11)	(−5.71)	(−5.61)	(−6.35)
16 years*(1970 census)	−0.0645	−0.0547	−0.0761	−0.0647
	(−13.98)	(−11.75)	(−16.45)	(−13.72)
High school graduation*	0.0250	0.0256	0.0276	0.0236
(1980 census)	(5.35)	(5.46)	(5.92)	(5.04)
16 years*(1980 census)	−0.0694	−0.0620	−0.0772	−0.0692
	(−15.15)	(−13.46)	(−16.84)	(−14.90)
R^2	0.2209	0.2215	0.2245	0.2251
F-test		*P*-value		
High school graduation and 16 year effects = 0	0.0001	0.0001	0.0001	0.0001
High school graduation and 16 year effects interacted with immigrant = 0		0.0001		0.0001
All included sheepskin effect coefficients = 0	0.0001	0.0001	0.0001	0.0001

Note: *t*-statistics appear in parentheses. $N = 2,232,284$. Column numbers correspond to columns in table 2.10.

Table 2A.2   Probit Model of the Probability of Enrollment, and Enrollment in Grades 1–12 and in College, for Males Aged 16–64

| | Overall Enrollment | | | | Grades 1–12 Enrollment | | | | College Enrollment | | | |
| | 1 | | 2 | | 3 | | 4 | | 5 | | 6 | |
	Coefficient	dp/dx	Coefficient	dp/dx	Coefficient	dp/dx	Coefficient	dp/dx	Coefficient	dp/dx	Coefficient	dp/dx
Immigrant	0.2083 (0.0006)	0.0355	-4.5490 (0.0137)	-0.8096	0.4057 (0.0010)	0.0058	-12.1639 (0.0228)	-0.4227	0.1449 (0.0006)	0.0179	-0.4818 (0.0137)	-0.0614
Age*Immigrant			0.4073 (0.0012)	0.0725			1.1044 (0.0022)	0.0384			0.0441 (0.0012)	0.0056
Age²*Immigrant			-0.0106 (0.0000)	-0.0019			-0.0286 (0.0001)	-0.0010			-0.0006 (0.0000)	-0.0001
Age³*Immigrant/10,000			0.8744 (0.0032)	0.1556			2.8887 (0.0062)	0.0795			0.0147 (0.0031)	0.0019
Years since immigration			-0.0261 (0.0004)	-0.0046			0.0571 (0.0007)	0.0020			-0.0473 (0.0004)	-0.0060
(Years since immigration)²			0.0009 (0.00002)	0.0002			-0.0033 (0.00003)	-0.0001			0.0022 (0.00002)	0.0003
(Years since immigration)³/10,000			-0.0888 (0.0025)	-0.0158			0.4300 (0.0043)	0.0149			-0.2557 (0.0028)	-0.0326
Arrived 1980–84			0.1030 (0.0021)	0.0183			0.1185 (0.0034)	0.0041			0.0362 (0.0022)	0.0046
Arrived 1975–79			0.1805 (0.0019)	0.0321			0.0637 (0.0034)	0.0022			0.1427 (0.0019)	0.0182
Arrived 1970–74			0.0784 (0.0024)	0.0140			-0.0134 (0.0043)	-0.0005			0.0618 (0.0025)	0.0079
Arrived 1965–69			0.0557 (0.0022)	0.0099			-0.0701 (0.0037)	-0.0024			0.0604 (0.0023)	0.0077
Arrived 1960–64			0.0705 (0.0027)	0.0125			-0.0896 (0.0046)	-0.0031			0.0683 (0.0028)	0.0087
Arrived 1950–59			0.0252 (0.0029)	0.0045			-0.1537 (0.0050)	-0.0053			-0.0244 (0.0031)	-0.0031
Arrived before 1950			-0.0963 (0.0047)	-0.0171			-0.1348 (0.0092)	-0.0047			-0.1693 (0.0050)	-0.0216

Note: Based on 1970, 1980, and 1990 public use samples of the U.S. census. All models include the same variables as the models in table 2.7. dp/dx is the marginal effect evaluated at the mean of the population for nonimmigrant variables. For immigrant variables, the mean of the immigrant populations is used. Standard errors appear in parentheses. $N = 2,232,284$.

Table 2A.3   Probit Model of Probability of Graduation for Males Aged 16–64

| | High School Graduation (ED ≥ 12) | | | | College Graduation (ED ≥ 16) | | | |
| | 3 | | 4 | | 5 | | 6 | |
	Coefficient	dp/dx	Coefficient	dp/dx	Coefficient	dp/dx	Coefficient	dp/dx
Immigrant	−0.5687 (0.0004)	−0.2066	2.6910 (0.0096)	1.0727	−0.0059 (0.0004)	−0.0014	0.1725 (0.0152)	0.0399
Age*Immigrant			−0.2842 (0.0008)	−0.1133			−0.0226 (0.0012)	−0.0052
Age²*Immigrant			0.0071 (0.00002)	0.0028			0.0011 (0.00003)	0.0002
Age³*Immigrant/10,000			−0.5482 (0.0018)	−0.2185			−0.1123 (0.0025)	−0.0260
Years since immigration			−0.0402 (0.0002)	−0.0160			−0.0538 (0.0003)	−0.0124
(Years since immigration)²			0.0017 (0.00001)	0.0007			0.0020 (0.00001)	0.0005
(Years since immigration)³/ 10,000			−0.1980 (0.0012)	−0.0789			−0.2145 (0.0015)	−0.0496
Arrived 1980–84			0.0747 (0.0017)	0.0298			−0.0403 (0.0019)	−0.0093
Arrived 1975–79			0.2173 (0.0015)	0.0866			0.1032 (0.0017)	0.0239
Arrived 1970–74			0.2434 (0.0018)	0.0970			0.1070 (0.0021)	0.0247
Arrived 1965–69			0.4630 (0.0017)	0.1846			0.1926 (0.0019)	0.0445
Arrived 1960–64			0.6550 (0.0020)	0.2611			0.1885 (0.0022)	0.0436
Arrived 1950–59			0.7286 (0.0020)	0.2905			0.1809 (0.0023)	0.0418
Arrived before 1950			0.7502 (0.0027)	0.2991			0.1499 (0.0030)	0.0347

Note: Based on 1970, 1980, and 1990 public use samples of the U.S. census. All models include the same variables as the models in table 2.8. dp/dx is the marginal effect evaluated at the mean of the population for nonimmigrant variables. For immigrant variables, the mean of the immigrant populations is used. Standard errors appear in parentheses. $N = 2,232,284$.

References

Barro, Robert J., and Jong-Wha Lee. 1993. International comparisons of educational attainment. *Journal of Monetary Economics* 3:363–94.

Betts, Julian R. 1995. Does school quality matter? Evidence from the National Longitudinal Survey of Youth. *Review of Economics and Statistics* 77:231–50.

———. 1998. Educational crowding out: Do immigrants affect the educational attainment of American minorities? In *Help or hindrance? The economic implications of immigration for African-Americans*, ed. Daniel S. Hamermesh and Frank D. Bean, 253–81. New York: Russell Sage Foundation.

Borjas, George J. 1985. Assimilation changes in cohort quality and the earnings of immigrants. *Journal of Labor Economics* 4:463–89.

———. 1990. *Friends or strangers: The impact of immigrants on the U.S. economy.* New York: Basic Books.

———. 1995. Assimilation changes in cohort quality revisited: What happened to immigrant earnings in the 1980's? *Journal of Labor Economics* 2:201–45.

Borjas, George J., Richard B. Freeman, and Kevin Lang. 1991. Undocumented Mexican-born workers in the United States: How many, how permanent? In *Immigration, trade, and the labor market*, ed. John M. Abowd and Richard B. Freeman, 77–100. Chicago: University of Chicago Press.

Bratsberg, Bernt, and Dek Terrell. 1997. School quality and returns to education of U.S. immigrants. Kansas State University, Manhattan, Kansas.

Chiswick, Barry R. 1978. The effect of Americanization on the earnings of foreign-born men. *Journal of Political Economy* 5:897–921.

Federal Security Agency. Various years. *Biennial survey of education in the United States.* Washington, D.C.: Office of Education.

Friedberg, Rachel M. 1996. You can't take it with you? Immigrant assimilation and the portability of human capital. NBER Working Paper no. 5837. Cambridge, Mass.: National Bureau of Economic Research, November.

Funkhouser, Edward, and Stephen S. Trejo, 1995. The labor market skills of recent male immigrants—evidence from the current population survey. *Industrial and Labor Relations Review* 48 (4): 792–811.

Gonzalez, Arturo. 1997. The education and quality of immigrant children: The impact of age at arrival. Mexican-American Studies and Research Center, University of Arizona, Tucson, Arizona.

Heckman, James, Anne Layne-Farrar, and Petra Todd. 1996. Human capital pricing equations with an application to estimating the effect of schooling quality on earnings. *Review of Economics and Statistics* 4:562–610.

Hoxby, Caroline M. 1998. Do immigrants crowd disadvantaged American natives out of higher education? In *Help or hindrance? The economic implications of immigration for African-Americans*, ed. Daniel S. Hamermesh and Frank D. Bean, 282–321. New York: Russell Sage Foundation.

Jaeger, David A., and Marianne E. Page. 1996. Degrees matter: New evidence on sheepskin effects in the returns to education. *Review of Economics and Statistics* 4:733–40.

James, Estelle, Nabeel Alsalam, Joseph C. Conaty, and Duc-Le To. 1989. College quality and future earnings: Where should you send your child to college? *American Economic Review* 2:247–52.

Loury, Linda Datcher, and David Garman. 1995. College selectivity and earnings. *Journal of Labor Economics* 2:289–308.

National Center for Education Statistics. Various years. *Digest of education statistics.* Washington, D.C.: U.S. Department of Education.

Summers, Robert, and Alan Heston. 1991. The Penn world table (mark 5): An expanded set of international comparisons, 1950–1988. *Quarterly Journal of Economics* 9:327–68.

United Nations Educational, Scientific, and Cultural Organization (UNESCO). Various years. *Statistical yearbook.* Paris: Imprimerie de la Manutention, Mayenne.

Vernez, George, and Allan Abrahamse. 1996. *How immigrants fare in U.S. education.* Santa Monica, Calif.: The RAND Corporation.

Warren, Robert, and Jeffrey S. Passel. 1987. A count of the uncountable: Estimates of undocumented aliens counted in the 1980 census. *Demography* 24:375–93.

3

Diversity and Immigration

Edward P. Lazear

A growing number of studies are attempting to document the effect of immigration on wages of native-born Americans.[1] The emphasis has been on a corollary of standard trade theory. The idea is that the immigrant is paid his marginal product. The inframarginal returns are captured by the complementary factors of production, in this case, natives, who own the capital and complementary labor. The focus on wage effects of immigration is a natural consequence.

Most proponents of immigration, however, argue for the diversity value that immigration confers on the United States. The stew tastes better when the ingredients are varied. The notion that the whole is greater than the sum of the parts derives from interactions between factors that somehow add to creativity or other components of output not captured by the standard production function.

There is something to this argument. It would be surprising to find large gains from immigration associated with bringing in more skilled or unskilled workers. Skill is easily arbitraged by new native-born entrants to the labor market. The limit on the difference between the gains to bringing

Edward P. Lazear is the Jack Steele Parker Professor of Economics and Human Resources Management in the Graduate School of Business at Stanford University. He is also senior fellow at the Hoover Institution and a research associate of the National Bureau of Economic Research.

This research was supported in part by the National Science Foundation. This final version incorporates excellent comments from the discussant, Daniel Hamermesh, and from the author's research assistant, Muhamet Yildiz.

1. Borjas (1994) points out that the gains from immigration accrue to the native population precisely when wages are depressed by the entry of immigrants. Studies of the effects of immigrants on natives' wages include LaLonde and Topel (1991) and Card (1990). The studies generally find small, if any, effects of immigration on the wages of natives.

in a skilled versus an unskilled immigrant is the cost of producing a skilled worker from an unskilled one domestically.

In the traditional model, the gain from immigration results from increases in the population, which enhances the value of capital or other factors owned by natives. There is nothing special about immigration. The argument in favor of immigration is identical to arguing that society benefits when everyone has more children because the child will only capture his marginal product. Inframarginal returns flow to capital and other labor owned by his parents or their contemporaries. Selecting the skill level of immigrants is equivalent to determining whether we want more children who will grow up to be skilled workers or unskilled workers.[2]

Even if constant returns to scale prevails, and even if each immigrant brings with him a proportionate amount of new capital, land is fixed and owned by the native population. Any population increase, native born or immigrant driven, causes the value of land to rise, benefiting the native population.

Fans of immigration might claim that this misses the point. It is possible to argue that gains from immigration derive from having a wider economic "gene pool." With less "inbreeding," our ideas may be better and more creative and we are less likely to exacerbate our mistakes. Although it is politically correct to accept the view that diversity provides benefit, there are few studies to document the magnitude of the gains or even that such gains exist.[3]

Diversity surely carries its costs. Because individuals from different cultures have a more difficult time communicating with one another, diversity reduces trade, at least initially. Lazear (forthcoming) analyzed the effects of diversity on trade reduction but ignored any gains to diversity, per se. If the value of diversity is sufficiently large, then perhaps some of the arguments against a heterogeneous workforce could be mitigated or reversed.

The analysis that follows attempts to take the diversity argument seriously. In some sense, it seems a reductio ad absurdum, both at the theoretical and empirical levels. The conclusion is not that certain countries should be favored because of their contribution to diversity, but rather that the current policy, which has the effect of favoring certain countries, does not enhance diversity. An alternative policy that leads to more balanced immigration would further diversity.

---

2. There is an additional factor. Since parents may care about the well-being of their children more than they do about the well-being of an anonymous immigrant, the wages of the child may enter into the calculation of happiness for the native parent population.

3. See O'Reilly, Williams, and Barsade (1998), who find that the gains from diversity are in fact negative. Because diversity creates conflict, any creativity gains are swamped by those associated with the conflict itself.

Weitzman (1992) models biodiversity. He finds that society does not subsidize the right species in maximizing biodiversity. Other factors, including the "cuteness" of the animal in question, are considerations.

The theoretical analysis builds on the idea that the gains from diversity are greatest when groups have information sets that are disjoint,[4] that are relevant to one another, and that can be learned by the other group at low cost.[5] A more formal model will be presented below, but the intuition can be stated verbally.

First, the diversity gains are greatest when individuals have different information. If information sets are completely disjoint, then members of group A can learn a great deal from group B that they do not already know. If information sets are completely overlapping, then the two groups do not contribute much to each other's knowledge.

Second, the information possessed by the other group must be relevant. For example, the knowledge that an auto mechanic has is quite different from that held by an economist. The information sets are quite distinct and thereby meet the disjointness criterion. But they are not relevant to one another. Knowing how to repair the differential on a 1963 Buick is unlikely to help an economist analyze wage differentials.

Third, even if information sets are disjoint and relevant, they are useless unless they can be understood by the other group. For example, it might be better to express a particular thought in French than in English, but in order for English speakers to get the benefit of this improvement, they must be able to understand French themselves. If it were prohibitively costly to learn the language or obtain the information possessed by the other group, then disjointedness and relevance would have no value.

Diversity is modeled and applied to analyze the choice a country makes about the identity of immigrants. Data from the 1990 census are used to estimate the parameters of the model. The findings are as follows:

1. The current U.S. immigrant flow is inconsistent with diversity. To obtain gains from diversity, it would be necessary to institute a selective immigration policy that eliminates relative-based preferences for immigrants and replaces them with a much more targeted approach. Current American residents may have preferences for their own relatives, per se, but the diversity argument for immigration does not bolster their claims.

2. Ironically, a preference for diversity does not imply a diverse population. When trade with unlike individuals is more valuable than trade with like individuals, the initial population may prefer a homogeneous population of the opposite type. Sale of immigration slots or other transfers may be able to induce the initial population to prefer a heterogeneous population.

3. Groups differ greatly in communication propensity, disjointness, and relevance, the three criteria by which a diverse population can be judged.

4. Hong and Page (1997) focus on the gains from diversity that come about when different agents, each of whom possesses limited ability, work collectively.

5. An informal presentation of these ideas is put forth in Lazear (1998, 310–15).

The current group of immigrants does not do well by any of these criteria. It is possible to select immigrants on the basis of characteristics that would enhance diversity and be consistent with the preferences of the majority of the initial population.

4. Education is an important characteristic, both on the basis of relevance and for communication. As such, an immigration policy that fails to ration slots by price while ignoring the education of immigrants is unlikely to further welfare-enhancing diversity.

5. Immigration policy, more than the underlying characteristics of the countries from which the immigrants are drawn, determines the quality of immigrants observed in the United States. Because the filters are different across groups, immigrants from Japan have lower average levels of education than immigrants from Northern African countries, which is inconsistent with differences in average levels of education in the countries themselves.

6. Balanced immigration, which increases the speed of assimilation, also raises gains from diversity.

3.1   The Model

Let us suppose that there are two groups, A and B. The members of group A have knowledge that spans an interval A_0 to A_1, while the members of group B have knowledge that spans an interval B_0 to B_1. The intervals may be overlapping and the ordering is not important. It is the size of the interval and its overlap that is most important. For simplicity, we reduce knowledge to a scalar variable, x. This is shown in figure 3.1. For example, suppose that the information in question relates to literatures. Then A knows all of the papers on interval A, B knows all of the papers on interval B, and they both know papers on interval AB. As in Lazear (forthcoming), the model is one of random encounter. An individual can encounter one individual per period. This individual is either an A or a B. Initially assume that individuals encounter others based on their proportions in the population—that is; there is no segregation of groups. When an A encounters another A, he can trade with each A receiving surplus equal to

$$(1) \qquad \text{Surplus to each A} \; = \; A_1 - A_0.$$

Trade with another A can yield surplus because two heads or bodies may be better than one, even when they have the same skills or information. For example, it might be impossible for one person to push a stalled car, but two individuals can complete the task.

When a B encounters another B, she can trade with the B, and each B receives surplus equal to

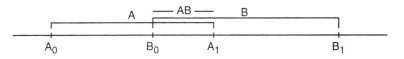

Fig. 3.1   Knowledge

(2) $$\text{Surplus to each B} = B_1 - B_0.$$

Trade between A's and B's may create more or less surplus than trade between homogeneous individuals. The surplus could be greater in a heterogeneous pair than in a homogeneous one because the information sets do not overlap completely.[6] In this situation, A learns B's information, which enhances the value of the trade. If B's information were as valuable to A as another A's information, and vice versa, then trade with a B would yield each trader $B_1 - A_0$ of surplus, which exceeds the value of trade between two homogeneous individuals. The less overlap in information sets, the better. This illustrates that trade is enhanced when the information sets of trading parties are disjoint.

Trade between A's and B's might create less surplus than trade between homogeneous pairs. If the information that B's possess is irrelevant to A's activity, then an encounter with a B would not be valuable to an A. Define θ as a relevance parameter. When $\theta = 1$, everything that B knows is relevant to A. Then a trade between an A and a B yields surplus $B_1 - A_0$ to each trading party. When $\theta = 0$, nothing that B knows is relevant to A. It is possible to define θ as unidirectional. Just because B's information is relevant to A does not mean that A's information is relevant to B. Allowing group-specific relevance parameters would add some realism, but the possibility is ignored to conserve on notation.[7] In general, then, surplus between an A and a B who can communicate with one another is given by

(3)   Surplus to each party from diversified trade $= \theta(B_1 - A_0)$.

Third, even if B's information is different and relevant to A, B and A must be able to communicate in order to share the information.[8] If A and B speak different languages, then either A must learn to speak B or B must learn to speak A (or both) in order to share information. Thus, dis-

---

6. It is assumed that B_0 is never greater than A, to simplify the algebra. This is inessential to any of the results.

7. Logic places a lower bound on θ. If communication were not an issue, then the proportion of B's information that overlaps with A's information must be relevant in order to be consistent with the notion that trade between two A's yields value $A_1 - A_0$ to each party. Since the overlap is $A_1 - B_0$, the lower bound on θ is $(A_1 - B_0) / (B_1 - A_0)$.

8. This is related to the "committee" problem. A large committee possesses more information than any of its individual members, but as the committee gets larger, it becomes impossible to communicate the information. One individual's words drown out another's. This is discussed in Lazear (1998, especially ch. 12).

jointness, relevance, and communication costs determine the value of diversity.

The costliness of communication is modeled by assuming that there is a cost, k_i, for individual i to learn the other language. The distribution function of k is $G_A(k)$ among the A's, and $G_B(k)$ among the B's. It is possible that G_A and G_B are identical, but it is also possible that it is easier for B's to learn A than for A's to learn B, or the converse.

It is now possible to determine how many individuals will learn A and how many will learn B. This depends on the probability of encountering an individual from the opposite group, on the costs of learning, and on the proportion of the opposite group that is bilingual. There is no need for English speakers to learn Spanish if all Spanish speakers also speak English.

Assume only one period. Given that p of the population is A and $1-p$ is B, the expected surplus to a monolingual A is then

(4)   Expected surplus to monolingual A

$$= p(A_1 - A_0) + (1 - p)G_B^* \theta(B_1 - A_0),$$

G_B^* is the equilibrium proportion of B's who can speak A. The first term on the right-hand side is the probability of meeting an A times the surplus associated with meeting an A. The second term on the right-hand side reflects the probability of meeting a B times the surplus associated with meeting a B who can speak A, which depends on disjointness and relevance.

Further, the expected surplus to a bilingual A is

(5)   Expected surplus to bilingual A

$$= p(A_1 - A_0) + (1 - p)\theta(B_1 - A_0) - k_i,$$

because all encounters with B's result in trade. Note that the cost of learning B is subtracted from the gains from trade.

Analogously, the expected surplus to a monolingual B is

(6A)   Expected surplus to monolingual B

$$= (1 - p)(B_1 - B_0) + pG_A^* \theta(B_1 - A_0),$$

and to a bilingual B,

(6B)   Expected surplus to bilingual B

$$= (1 - p)(B_1 - B_0) + p\theta(B_1 - A_0) - k_i.$$

3.2   Gains from Diversity

Since A's are in the majority, and since most A's, as an empirical matter, are monolingual, at least in the current stock of Americans, let us consider whether a monolingual A prefers to meet an A or a B. This gets to the heart of the diversity issue. Normalize $A_1 - A_0$ to be equal to 1. Assume, initially, that $B_1 - B_0$ is equal to $A_1 - A_0$ so that A's and B's receive the same value from trading among themselves.

The difference between meeting a B and an A to a monolingual A is given by

Difference in value of meeting a B instead of an A

$$(7) \qquad\qquad\qquad = \theta G_B^*(B_1 - A_0) - (A_1 - A_0)$$

$$= \theta G_B^*(2 - \Delta) - 1,$$

where Δ is defined as $A_1 - B_0$ and is a measure of overlap, which is the complement of disjointness.[9]

The intuitive statements made earlier come directly from differentiating equation (7). First note that

$$\partial/\partial\Delta = -\theta G_B^* + \theta(2 - \Delta)\partial G_B^*/\partial\Delta.$$

Both terms are negative because $\partial G_B^*/\partial\Delta$ is negative (from eq. [9] below). As overlap decreases, for example, disjointness increases, and so does the gain to diversity. When A's can learn more from B's, they are more anxious to encounter B's.

Second,

$$\partial/\partial\theta = G_B^*(2 - \Delta) + \theta(2 - \Delta)\partial G_B^*/\partial\theta.$$

Both terms are positive because $\partial G_B^*/\partial\theta$ is positive (from eq. [9] below). As relevance rises, so does the advantage of meeting a B over an A.

Third,

$$\partial/\partial G_B^* = \theta(2 - \Delta) \geq 0.$$

When more B's can communicate with A's, the gain to a monolingual A from meeting a B is greater. The cost of learning A is a key determinant of G_B^*, so as more B's find it cheap to learn A, group A's gains from diversity rise.[10]

---

9. If A's and B's were identical and all B's spoke A, then θ would equal 1, Δ would equal 1, and this expression would be equal to zero.

10. Differentiating with respect to G_B^* should be interpreted as a change in the underlying costs of learning a language, which shows up as a change in the equilibrium number of individuals who are bilingual.

Now, the names A and B are arbitrary, except that A's have been defined to be the majority by declaring that $p > \frac{1}{2}$. But nothing in the above derivation has relied on the fact that $p > \frac{1}{2}$. Thus, all statements that relate to A's also relate to B's. Specifically, B's prefer to interact with A's when Δ is low. That is, group A's information is disjoint from group B's information in the sense that A's know much that B's do not know. Further, B's preference for interaction with A rises with θ, the relevance of A's information. Finally, as G_A^*, the proportion of A's who can speak B, rises, B's preference for A's rises. Again, as the cost to A's of learning B declines, the B's gain from diversity rises.

3.3   Parochialism

It is useful to consider the conditions under which B's learn A and vice versa. When are groups cosmopolitan and when are they parochial? First, let us consider when a member of the minority will learn A. Taking the difference of equations (6) and (5), the gain to a B from becoming bilingual is

$$(8) \quad \text{Gain to a B from learning A} = p\,\theta(1 - G_A^*)(B_1 - A_0) - k_i,$$

so that the proportion of B's who learn A are those for whom the right-hand side is positive. Since the distribution function among B's of k_i is $G_B(k_i)$, the proportion of B's who learn A is

$$(9) \quad \text{Proportion of B's who learn A} = G_B[p\,\theta(1 - G_A^*)(B_1 - A_0)].$$

Analogously,

$$(10) \quad \text{Proportion of A's who learn B} = G_A[(1 - p)\,\theta(1 - G_B^*)(B_1 - A_0)].$$

By differentiating equations (9) and (10), the following results obtain under general conditions.[11]

First, an increase in p, the proportion of A's in the population, raises the proportion of B's who learn A. This is the primary result of Lazear (forthcoming). Because there are more A's in the population, being able to speak A allows B to trade with more individuals, which is particularly important when B is a small minority and A is a large majority.

Second, the larger is θ, the greater is the proportion of B's who learn A. When A's knowledge is relevant, it pays for B to learn A.

Third, the smaller is G_A^*, the more likely is B to learn A. A small value of G_A^* means that few A's speak B. Thus, the only way for B to trade with A is for B to learn A.

---

11. The necessary condition is that $p(1 - p)\,\Delta^2\theta^2 G_A G_B < 1$, which is certain to hold as p goes to zero or one.

Finally, the proportion of B's who learn A increases in $B_1 - A_0$, which equals $2 - \Delta$. As the region of information overlap falls—that is, as disjointness rise—so does the value of trading with an A. B types are more likely to learn A when the overlap in information is small.

The population becomes less parochial when disjointness of information is large, when the other group's information is relevant, and when the cost of communication is low.

3.4   Diversity and the Choice of Immigrant Type

It is now possible to consider the primary question. Is there a diversity case for immigration? Let us start by determining which type of individual a country would like to have immigrate.

Initially, there are four types of people in the country. They are monolingual A's, bilingual A's, monolingual B's, and bilingual B's. We assume an egalitarian social welfare function that treats each individual equally and maximizes the sum of surplus across all individuals.

Initially, there are α A's and $(1 - \alpha)$ B's. The equilibrium population will have p A's and $(1 - p)$ B's. The goal is to choose p so as to maximize the welfare of the initial population. Utility of immigrants is ignored.[12]

The utility of an A is given by

(11)
a. Utility of monolingual A $= p(A_1 - A_0) + (1 - p)G_B^* \theta(B_1 - A_0)$,

b. Utility of bilingual A $= p(A_1 - A_0) + (1 - p)\theta(B_1 - A_0) - k_i$,

and that of a B is given by

(12)
a. Utility of monolingual B $= (1 - p)(B_1 - B_0) + pG_A^* \theta(B_1 - A_0)$,

b. Utility of bilingual B $= (1 - p)(B_1 - B_0) + p\theta(B_1 - A_0) - k_i$.

Since there are α A's and $(1 - \alpha)$ B's, the expected utility of the initial population as a function of p, the equilibrium proportions, is

(13)
$$EU(p) = \alpha\{[p(A_1 - A_0) + (1 - p)G_B^* \theta(B_1 - A_0)](1 - G_A^*)$$
$$+ [p(A_1 - A_0) + \theta(1 - p)(B_1 - A_0) - \bar{k}_A]G_A^*\}$$
$$+ (1 - \alpha)\{[(1 - p)(B_1 - B_0) + pG_A^* \theta(B_1 - A_0)](1 - G_B^*)$$
$$+ [(1 - p)(B_1 - B_0) + p\theta(B_1 - A_0) - \bar{k}_B]G_B^*\},$$

12. This is not unreasonable since immigrants who come voluntarily are at least made better off by immigration. Further, since they can choose among many countries, competition will induce them to go to the country that provides the best ratio for them, other things constant.

where G_A^* and G_B^* refer to the equilibrium proportions of A's and B's who learn the other group's language where $\bar{k}_A$ and $\bar{k}_B$ are the conditional expectations of k_i, the average cost of learning the language for A's and B's, respectively, given that they learn the other language. The four terms reflect the utilities of monolingual A's, bilingual A's, monolingual B's, and bilingual B's, weighted by their proportions in population.[13]

To find the optimum p, it is necessary to differentiate equation (13) with respect to p. Intuition is gained, however, by considering some specific cases. First, suppose that it is too costly for either A's or B's to learn the other group's language. Then, $G_A^* = G_B^* = 0$, and equation (13) becomes

$$\alpha p(A_1 - A_0) + (1 - \alpha)(1 - p)(B_1 - B_0).$$

Differentiating with respect to p yields

$$\frac{\partial}{\partial p} = \alpha(A_1 - A_0) - (1 - \alpha)(B_1 - B_0),$$

which is positive as long as $\alpha/(1 - \alpha) > (B_1 - B_0)/(A_1 - A_0)$. For $B_1 - B_0 \leq A_1 - A_0$ this is guaranteed because $\alpha > 1/2$. Then $\partial/\partial p$ is always positive, which means that the optimum level of p is 1. If society were to seek immigrants, it would want those who mimic the majority. Under these circumstances, there is no diversity case for immigration. In fact, the reverse is true. Immigration is valuable, but it is because immigration of majority types would increase homogeneity in society. Homogeneity is the desired outcome when individuals cannot trade with members of the opposite group. Because the A's cannot speak B and the B's cannot speak A, it is best to have only one type of individual. Since A's are initially the majority, welfare maximization implies admitting only A's. Under these circumstances, B's, who cannot communicate with A's, will push for more B's. A consequence is that quite divergent views about immigration policy are likely to result.

The divergence in views is, in part, a result of linearity built into the model. There are no diminishing returns to A's from getting more A's. The gains from trade are independent of the number of individuals who have the relevant skills. If diminishing returns were allowed, corner solutions would be less likely. In particular, it is reasonable that a small group might derive more from an additional member with whom it could trade than a large group. Being alone is quite different from having one friend. The one-hundred-and-first friend makes less difference to one's life than the first. If so, then arguments in favor of the majority type to the exclusion of the minority are weakened. Indeed, in an economy where side payments

---

13. The proportions, G, depend on equilibrium levels, whereas α is the fixed, initial proportion.

are possible (say, by buying immigration rights), all of the nonlinearities would work to affect prices such that an optimal allocation is achieved. This is discussed below.

The strongest case for immigration of minority members can be made when disjointness, relevance, and inexpensive learning prevail. Consider, then, the other extreme, where the cost of learning the other group's language is zero for all individuals. Then, $G_A^* = G_B^* = 1$.[14] Equation (13) is then

$$\alpha[p(A_1 - A_0) + \theta(1 - p)(B_1 - A_0)]$$
$$+ (1 - \alpha)[(1 - p)(B_1 - B_0) + \theta p(B_1 - A_0)].$$

Differentiating with respect to p yields

(14)
$$\frac{\partial}{\partial p} = \alpha[(A_1 - A_0) - \theta(B_1 - A_0)]$$
$$+ (1 - \alpha)[\theta(B_1 - A_0) - (B_1 - B_0)].$$

Suppose, for a moment, that A's and B's have equal information. Then equation (14) becomes

$$\frac{\partial}{\partial p} = (2\alpha - 1)[1 - (B_1 - A_0)\theta]$$

or

$$\frac{\partial}{\partial p} = (2\alpha - 1)[1 - (2 - \Delta)\theta].$$

Since $\alpha > \frac{1}{2}$, the first term is positive. If θ were zero, so that opposite group's information was irrelevant, then $\partial/\partial p$ would always be positive and the optimal p would be 1, as in the case where no one learns the other group's language. Suppose, however, that everything that the other group knows is relevant, so that $\theta = 1$. As long as there is any disjointness at all—that is, as long as overlap is not perfect, so that $\Delta < 1$—the second term is negative, which implies that $\partial/\partial p < 0$ for all values of p. This means that the optimal long-run population would have to be $p = 0$. The initial population would prefer to allow only B's to immigrate because A's get more out of B's than they do out of A's and there are more A's than B's in the initial population.

This produces a surprising implication. Even if there were gains from diversity that outweighed those of trading with one's own type, the implication is that the initial society would want a population of all B's, not a

14. In fact, it is only necessary that one group become bilingual.

diverse population. Homogeneity would be desired, but it would be homogeneity of types in the minority of the initial population. Furthermore, it would be the A's who would prefer this movement to B's; the B's would prefer an opposite movement to A's. The reason is that A's prefer trading with B's, and vice versa. Since there are more A's initially, their preferences win out and the optimum is to admit only B's.

The implication that the society would switch from a majority of A's to unanimity of B's is extreme and is based on the assumption that the initial population can commit to an immigration policy that is maintained in the future. This is unrealistic. If A's were to insist on bringing in only B's, then eventually B's would become the majority. As soon as they outnumbered the A's, they would prefer more A's for the same reason that A's prefer more B's. The majority B's could then institute a policy of admitting only A's, which would hold until A's became the majority, at which point policy would reverse to admit only B's. The equilibrium in a dynamic setting where the majority determines immigration policy is to have a society with half of each type.[15]

The general point is that even when the initial population cares about diversity, it prefers a specific population, not necessarily a diverse population. In some cases, the population preferred by the initial diversity-loving population may be almost completely homogeneous. The immigration rule depends on the size and strength of the various groups, but the message is that the case for diversity as it is generally interpreted is questionable at best on theoretical grounds. Below, it is shown that the case for the current interpretation of diversity fails on empirical grounds as well.[16]

3.5   Immigration and Income

Suppose that we are interested in maximizing GNP or GNP per capita by choosing the number and type of immigrants. Would the solution be the same as that derived above? In general, the answer is no, and the discrepancy between the results in this section and those in the last come about because transfer payments from one group to another have not been allowed.

To maximize GNP per capita, it is sufficient to choose p so as to maximize the net income of the average individual in society, as opposed to the net income of the initial population, which was the criterion expressed in equation (13). To do this, it is necessary to choose p to maximize

---

15. The situation is much more complicated when there are more than two types because the plurality type prefers a smaller minority group but does not have the power to enforce its desires unilaterally.

16. It is, of course, possible to build in a taste for having a mixed society, just for mixture's sake, but there is no underlying reason for this that comes from the usual arguments having to do with the value of diversity. The enriching value of dealing with other types of people is the basis of the model. To assume a taste for diversity on top of this seems a stretch.

$$EU(p) = p\{[p(A_1 - A_0) + (1 - p)G_B^* \theta(B_1 - A_0)](1 - G_A^*)$$

$$+ [p(A_1 - A_0) + \theta(1 - p)(B_1 - A_0) - \overline{k}_A]G_A^*\}$$

(15)

$$+ (1 - p)\{[(1 - p)(B_1 - B_0) + pG_A^* \theta(B_1 - A_0)](1 - G_B^*)$$

$$+ [(1 - p)(B_1 - B_0) + p\theta(B_1 - A_0) - \overline{k}_B]G_B^*\}.$$

The only difference between equations (13) and (15) is that α is replaced by p in (15) to reflect that we wish to maximize the net income of the average individual in society.[17] First consider the case where learning is free, so that $G_A^* = G_B^* = 1$. Also, assume neutrality so that $A_1 - A_0 = B_1 - B_0 = 1$. Then equation (15) becomes

(16) $$EU(p) = p^2 + (1 - p)^2 + 2p\theta(1 - p)(2 - \Delta).$$

Differentiating with respect to p yields

$$\partial/\partial p = (4p - 2)[1 - (2 - \Delta)\theta],$$

and again,

$$\partial^2/\partial^2 p = 4[1 - (2 - \Delta)\theta].$$

The solution to the first order condition is $p = \frac{1}{2}$. This is a maximum when $(2 - \Delta)\theta > 1$, or when trading with unlike individuals has more value than trading with like individuals. When diversity has value and is free, the optimal solution for the economy is to choose immigrants to move in the direction of $p = \frac{1}{2}$. Since $\alpha > \frac{1}{2}$, this necessarily means that minority immigrants are preferred to majority ones.

This result contrasts with that in the previous section, where the utility of the initial population, rather than overall GNP, was allowed. The reason is this: When trading with unlike individuals is better than trading with like individuals, A's want B's and B's want A's. But since there are more A's than B's in the initial population, maximizing the utility of the initial population pushes the outcome to $p = 0$, with all B's (other than the initial group of A's). This does not maximize GNP. Since it does not, it is inefficient and there is opportunity for trade. One way to deal with the discrepancy is to sell immigration slots, discussed below.

It is possible that trading with unlike individuals has less value than trading with like individuals. Then, the second-order condition implies a minimum. Because it was assumed that A's and B's have the same amount of knowledge—that is, $A_1 - A_0 = B_1 - B_0 = 1$—GNP is maximized by choosing either $p = 0$ or $p = 1$. The tie is broken when one group has more information than another. Suppose, for example, that A's are more

---

17. Additionally, k changes because the group of individuals that decides to learn the other language varies with the proportion of each type in the overall population.

educated than B's and that education is positively correlated with information and the value of trade. Then this would tip the balance in favor of A's. The value of $EU(p)$ in equation (16) would be maximized at $p = 1$. Allowing $A_1 - A_0$ to differ from $B_1 - B_0$ turns equation (16) into

$$(17) \quad \begin{aligned} EU(p) &= p[p(A_1 - A_0) + (1 - p)(2 - \Delta)] \\ &+ (1 - p)[(1 - p)(B_1 - B_0) + p(2 - \Delta)], \end{aligned}$$

with first-order condition,

$$(18) \quad \partial/\partial p = 2p(A_1 - A_0) - 2(1 - p)(B_1 - B_0) + (2 - 4p)(2 - \Delta)\theta.$$

Setting equation (18) equal to zero yields

$$p = \frac{(B_1 - B_0) - (2 - \Delta)\theta}{(A_1 - A_0) + (B_1 - B_0) - 2(2 - \Delta)\theta},$$

which solves for $p = \frac{1}{2}$ when B's and A's are symmetric. But if B's have less knowledge than A's, then p moves closer to 1. Some diversity may still be desired. For example, if $A_1 - A_0 = 1.5$, $B_1 - B_0 = .5$, $\Delta = .25$, and $\theta = 1$, then the p that maximizes GNP is 5/6. There is a strong bias toward A's, but complete homogeneity is not desirable.

At the other extreme, when no learning occurs so that $G_A^* = G_B^* = 0$, equation (15) becomes

$$EU(p) = p^2(A_1 - A_0) + (1 - p)^2(B_1 - B_0),$$

which is maximized by setting $p = 1$ if A's know more than B's and $p = 0$ if B's know more than A's. The society should be completely homogeneous because no trade takes place between unlike individuals.[18]

The conclusion of this section is that without transfer payments, the initial population would actually choose immigrants of the opposite type were diversity important. Allowing transfer payments from the new immigrants to the native-born population generally produces an interior solution, but one that favors the group with the most information and skill.

3.6 Selling Immigration Slots

It has been shown that diversity-enhancing immigration may be opposed by the weighted average individual in the initial population[19] even when it would increase overall GNP. Whenever this occurs, there is room for trade. But the ability to buy out the initial population depends on the

---

18. A solution is to have the group that gets the most out of being in the country "buy out" the other group.

19. It is also true that it will be opposed by the median voter since A's are the majority.

number of immigrants that a country can attract and on the population size that is to be tolerated.

If there is a sufficiently large supply of A's who are willing to immigrate under optimal conditions, and of B's who would immigrate even under the solution preferred by the current population, then it is always possible for B's to bribe the initial group of A's into implementing the GNP-maximizing immigration policy. To see this, denote by R_A^* the surplus that goes to each A under the GNP-maximizing strategy, and by R_B^* the surplus that goes to each B under the GNP-maximizing strategy. Denote by R_A' the surplus that goes to each A under the current-population-preferred solution, and analogously by R_B' for B's. Also, let p^* and p' be the equilibrium proportions under the two regimes. The proof that transfers exist, which make all better off, follows.

Since the average person is better off when GNP is maximized, it must be true that

$$R_A^* p^* + R_B^* (1 - p^*) > R_A' p' + R_B' (1 - p'),$$

or that

$$(R_B^* - R_B')(1 - p') > (R_A' - R_A^*) p^*.$$

This implies that

$$(19) \quad (R_B^* - R_B') \frac{B_0 + \dot{B}}{A_0 + B_0 + \dot{A} + \dot{B}} > (R_A' - R_A^*) \frac{A_0}{A_0 + B_0 + \dot{B}},$$

where A_0 and B_0 and are the inital numbers of A's and B's and where $\dot{A}$ and $\dot{B}$ are added to obtain p' in the population. If equation (19) holds, then it must also be true that

$$(R_B^* - R_B')(B_0 + \dot{B}) > (R_A' - R_A^*) A_0.$$

But this condition says that if each B pays $R_B^* - R_B$, this will compensate every initial A for the loss in moving to the GNP-maximizing solution instead of that chosen by the initial population. However, any B who would immigrate when there are p' A's will certainly move when there are p^* A's. Also, if there is a sufficient number of A's who are willing to immigrate under optimal conditions without compensation, the p^* equilibrium can be achieved. This completes the proof.

3.7   The Empirical Case for Diversity

Theory suggests a way by which having a diverse population can enhance the gains from trade. There are costs of diversity, however, in that communication is hindered when everyone does not speak the same language. Do the gains from diversity outweigh the costs?

To determine whether the argument for diversity has any empirical substance, the 1990 census of the United States (1 percent sample) was used. Data are provided on place of birth, ancestry, English fluency, language spoken at home, and standard variables such as age, education, race, and sex.

It is possible to get a sense of how reasonable the diversity argument is by considering the largest non-English-speaking group in the United States, namely Spanish speakers. Forty-eight percent of those in the 1990 census who were born outside the United States are Spanish speakers. Of those, 55 percent report that they speak English well or very well, which will be defined as fluent. Almost all of the native-born population, which is over 90 percent of the United States, speaks English as its first language. Few in this group speak Spanish. Those who do are, for the most part, children of Spanish-speaking immigrants. Thus, for all intents and purposes, communication does not occur between a native-born American and a Spanish-speaking immigrant unless the immigrant is fluent in English. This means that $G_A^* = 0$ and $G_B^* = .55$.

A necessary condition for the diversity case is that trade between an A and a B results in greater expected surplus than that between an A and an A. Defining A's to be all of the English-speaking, native-born population and B's to be the Spanish-speaking immigrants, it is necessary then that

$$\theta(B_1 - A_0)G_B^* > (A_1 - A_0),$$

or that

(20) $$\theta(B_1 - A_0) > 1/G_B^*.$$

Given that $G_A^* = .55$, equation (20) can be written as

(21) $$\theta(B_1 - A_0) > 1.82.$$

Unless the gains from trading across groups exceeds the normalized 1.82, within-group interaction dominates between-group interaction.

Now, equation (21) is a very difficult condition to meet. To see this, consider a quite extreme situation. Suppose, first, that immigrants have neither more nor less information than do native-born Americans, so that $(B_1 - B_0) = (A_1 - A_0) = 1$. Suppose further that information is almost completely disjoint, with only 10 percent overlap, so that $(B_1 - A_0) = 1.9$. This assumption is very favorable to the diversity case. Also suppose that almost all of the information that each side possesses is relevant to the other side. Specifically, A's find all of the information between A_0 and A_1 relevant and 90 percent of the information between A_1 and B_1 relevant. Then the relevance parameter over the interval $B_1 - A_0$ is

$$\theta = 1(1/1.9) + .9(.9/1.9) = .9526.$$

Under these circumstances,

$$\theta(B_1 - A_0) = (.9526)(1.9) = 1.81.$$

Trade between unlike types is not sufficiently valuable to satisfy condition (20). The expected value of diversity is negative.

Intuitively, since only about half of the immigrants can communicate with the native-born population, each actual trade between an immigrant and a native needs to be worth almost twice as much as that between two natives in order to make the value of diversity positive. It is difficult to imagine that the value of the typical trade between native born and immigrant is almost twice that of the typical trade between two natives. Although possible, the conditions under which diversity pays are very strict.

The main reason for this somewhat negative conclusion is that Spanish-speaking immigrants are not very likely to learn English. Were G_B^* close to 1, the requirement in equation (20) would be much easier to satisfy. This suggests that it is useful to look empirically at how G^*, $B_1 - A_0$, and θ vary across groups. The data in the census files allow us to do this.

3.7.1   Communication

Groups differ greatly in their fluency rates. Table 3.1 reports fluency and education levels among immigrants by region of ancestry. Not surprisingly, immigrants from the British Empire have the highest rate of English fluency. Latin Americans, who constitute the largest group of immigrants, have the lowest fluency rate.

More evidence can be presented on variations in G^* by group. Table 3.2 reports the coefficients on country dummies from a logit that has as its dependent variable FLUENT, a dummy equal to 1 if the respondent reported that he or she spoke English very well or well. The logit is run on the sample of individuals living in the United States in 1990 who were born outside the country and are five years of age or older. Excluded are individuals whose native or only language is English. Thus, Canadians, Australians, and the British are out of the sample. (Of course, by the G_B^* criterion, Canadians are ideal immigrants. They may fall short by the disjointness criterion.) This leaves 147,756 observations.

The right-hand variables include age, years in the United States, and place of birth dummies for the countries listed in table 3.2. These countries are the largest suppliers of immigrants, and they are listed in rank order in table 3.2.

First note that 14 of the 18 coefficients are negative. Because the sample size is so large, all coefficients are estimated with great precision. Statistical significance is not an issue. Relative to the base group, which in this case are those who immigrated from a country not listed in table 3.2, these immigrants are less likely to become fluent in English. This is another

Table 3.1　　　　　**Fluency and Education among Immigrants by Region of Ancestry**

Country	Mean
Australia, New Zealand, Canada ($N = 2{,}770$)	
Fluent	.98
Education	11.7
Asia ($N = 35{,}338$)	
Fluent	.76
Education	11.5
Eastern Europe ($N = 11{,}490$)	
Fluent	.86
Education	11.7
Latin America ($N = 66{,}757$)	
Fluent	.56
Education	8.7
Middle East ($N = 5{,}495$)	
Fluent	.85
Education	12.2
North Africa ($N = 574$)	
Fluent	.94
Education	14.1
Not specified ($N = 14{,}653$)	
Fluent	.76
Education	9.8
Other European ($N = 124$)	
Fluent	.96
Education	13.2
Pacific Islander ($N = 416$)	
Fluent	.89
Education	10.9
Sub-Saharan Africa ($N = 1{,}566$)	
Fluent	.94
Education	12.9
South Asia ($N = 4{,}762$)	
Fluent	.91
Education	13.5
Western Europe ($N = 44{,}031$)	
Fluent	.94
Education	11.6
West Indies ($N = 5{,}799$)	
Fluent	.94
Education	11.3
U.S. ancestry (not born in United States) ($N = 647$)	
Fluent	.98
Education	10.5
African American (not born in United States) ($N = 1{,}415$)	
Fluent	.98
Education	10.7
Native American (not born in United States) ($N = 1{,}854$)	
Fluent	.92
Education	12.4

Table 3.2   **Fluency Logit Analysis**

Country	Coefficient in Logit	Change in Probability
Mexico	−2.287329	−0.497723
Non-Mexico Spanish speaking	−1.412393	−0.307337
China	−1.201402	−0.261425
Philippines	1.385355	0.3014532
Vietnam	−0.975913	−0.212359
Italy	−0.940631	−0.204681
Korea	−0.858997	−0.186918
India	0.8852494	0.1926303
Germany	1.124213	0.2446287
Poland	−0.508278	−0.110601
Russia	−0.631468	−0.137408
Taiwan	−0.183816	−0.039998
Japan	−0.787013	−0.171254
Haiti	−0.428511	−0.093244
Iran	0.4914111	0.1069311
Portugal	−1.424866	−0.310051
Greece	−0.815842	−0.177527
Laos	−1.54405	−0.335985
Other coefficients		
Age	−0.064	−0.014
Years in the United States	0.104	0.022

Note: $N = 147{,}756$; log likelihood $= -72{,}679$; overall fluency rate $= .68$.

manifestation of the point made in Lazear (forthcoming). Since these immigrants are from the largest groups, they are the immigrants most likely to encounter individuals with their own backgrounds and therefore are the least likely to learn English.

More important for the purpose here is that there is wide variation across groups. Germans have a predicted fluency probability of .92, whereas Mexicans with the same characteristics have a predicted fluency probability of .37. Older immigrants are less likely to be fluent, consistent with standard human capital predictions. Also, the probability increases by about two percentage points for every additional year that an immigrant is in the United States.

3.7.2   Overlap

The diversity argument relies on the assumption that immigrants have different cultural experiences than native-born Americans and thereby bring new information to the table. But immigrants are not all the same. Some have backgrounds that are very similar to Americans; others are quite different. Although this is difficult to quantify, it is possible to shed some light on the issue by analyzing the ancestry of the American population. These proportions can then be compared to our current flow of immigrants.

Table 3.3 reports the ancestry of a 1/1000 sample of native-born Americans in the 1990 census. The obvious finding from table 3.3 is that about 60 percent of native-born Americans have Western European ancestry. Excluding those who did not specify or who listed U.S. ancestry, the second-largest group consists of African Americans. The third largest group comes from Eastern Europe, followed by Latin American ancestry.

The last column of table 3.3 reports place of birth among the stock of immigrants in 1990. Latin Americans are the largest group, followed by Western Europeans and then by Asians (from East and Southeast Asia). Asian ancestry accounts for less than 1 percent of the native-born population, whereas Latin American ancestry accounts for about 5 percent of native-born Americans. Western Europeans account for 60 percent of the American population. Adding immigrants to the native born drives the Latin American proportion up to around 8 percent and the Asian proportion up to around 3 percent.

Table 3.3   Ancestry among Native-Born Americans in 1990

	N	Frequency in U.S. Population	Frequency of Immigration
By region			
African American	18,382	0.089	0.007
Asia	1,509	0.007	0.178
Australia, New Zealand, Canada	2,262	0.011	0.014
Eastern Europe	12,016	0.058	0.058
Latin America	9,854	0.047	0.338
North Africa	24	0.000	0.003
Native American	6,262	0.030	0.009
Middle East	562	0.003	0.028
Not specified	22,733	0.109	0.074
Other European	381	0.002	0.001
Pacific Islands	285	0.001	0.002
Sub-Saharan Africa	171	0.001	0.008
South Asia	106	0.001	0.024
Stated U.S. ancestry	12,398	0.060	0.003
Western Europe	120,511	0.580	0.223
West Indies	212	0.001	0.029
Total	207,668	1.000	1.000
Selected countries			
China	315	0.002	0.046
Cuba	204	0.001	0.027
Mexico	5,946	0.029	0.197
Philippines	356	0.002	0.041
Vietnam	61	0.000	0.021
Other	200,786	0.967	0.668
Total	207,668	1.000	1.000

The diversity argument suggests that our current immigration policy does not minimize overlap. By the disjointness criterion, the United States admits too many Western Europeans and possibly too many Latin Americans. Asians seem to be the only large group of immigrants that are not already a large part of the American base.

Taken literally, diversity implies that we are accepting the wrong people. For example, underrepresented are North African immigrants. They are the smallest group in the current American population, and there are a significant number of potential immigrants, especially in Egypt, Morocco, and Algeria from which to draw. Indeed, the diversity argument points to a very different immigration policy than the one that is currently in place. Rather than selecting immigrants based on the existence of relatives in the United States, diversity would be served better by doing the opposite. Countries whose residents have the most relatives in the United States are the ones least likely to bring in cultural diversity.

3.7.3 Relevance

The empirical analogue of relevance is somewhat difficult to define. One possibility is that relevance may be related to education. Highly educated immigrants, or at least those with education levels equivalent to those of natives, are more likely to have relevant information than those with much less education. It is unlikely that the details about a particular form of agriculture no longer practiced in the United States are as relevant as information on a new agriculture technique that has been used elsewhere but is not yet practiced in the United States.

It is useful, therefore, to return to table 3.1 and to examine education level by region of origin. It is true, of course, that years of schooling have country-specific meaning. Variations in educational quality and subject matter are likely to be significant across countries. Still, the averages may be instructive.

Somewhat surprisingly, North Africans top the list on average education level. This is almost certainly a result of selective admission. Few and only highly educated North Africans have been successful at obtaining permission to come to the United States. Country-specific evidence is presented in table 3.4, which reports educational attainment (for those no longer in school) by country of origin for large suppliers of immigrants. Immigrants from Mexico have the lowest level of education, and those from India and Taiwan have the highest. Indeed, the highly educated immigrant groups have levels of education that are substantially above the average level among native-born Americans. In 1990, native-born Americans who were not currently enrolled in school and were older than six years old had average levels of education equal to 12.27 years with a standard deviation of 3.08 years.

Again, the differences in education between source countries is as likely

Table 3.4   Mean Levels of Education by Place of Birth

Variable	Observations	Mean	Standard Deviation
Overall	151,888	10.74358	4.76573
Mexico	32,618	7.394307	4.451661
Non-Mexico Spanish speaking	23,599	10.30878	4.50487
China	3,967	10.72044	5.733337
Philippines	7,104	13.17553	3.786291
Vietnam	3,167	10.40101	4.759378
Italy	5,618	9.260413	4.343628
Korea	3,181	12.4967	4.195993
India	3,103	14.83323	4.3834
Germany	6,514	12.33067	3.18601
Poland	3,129	11.10674	4.370777
Russia	2,405	11.58004	4.787556
Taiwan	1,500	14.77033	3.997592
Japan	2,541	13.33806	3.198493
Haiti	1,181	10.46359	4.555955
Iran	1,283	13.86945	4.206208
Portugal	1,549	8.157198	4.717947
Greece	1,575	10.40063	4.338387
Laos	837	6.424134	5.707947

to reflect immigration policy as it is to reflect inherent differences in educational systems or levels. This may be an important point by itself. The characteristics of immigrants in the United States are as likely to reflect the effects of selective immigration policy as they are to reflect the characteristics of the underlying populations from which the individuals are drawn. A policy that is more lenient toward country C than country B will end up with a less qualified pool of immigrants from C than from B, sometimes even when the qualifications of C's are generally higher than those of B's.

The importance of immigration policy in filtering out different groups of immigrants can be seen quite clearly by comparing immigrants from North Africa, whose average education level is 14.1 years, with those from Japan, whose average education level is 13.3 years. The difference observed in the United States between these groups reverses the patterns observed in the native populations and reflects the extreme difficulty of gaining admission to the United States from North Africa.

3.8   Clustering

As mentioned above, the probability of encountering like or unlike individuals is endogenous. In a country that is already as diverse as the United States, it is possible, through geographic mobility, to affect the population with whom trade occurs. Individuals cluster with others of their own type. This is most easily seen by comparing the variable CNTYPCT to the proportion of immigrants in the United States. This variable, discussed in Lazear (forthcoming), measures the proportion of a county's population that is made up of persons who were born in the particular individual's native country.

If immigrants were spread randomly throughout the United States, then the proportion of one's own countrymen encountered would be unrelated to place of residence. Every county would be a microcosm of the United States. For example, 1.7 percent of the people living in the United States in 1990 were born in Mexico. Were they spread randomly throughout the United States, then the average CNTYPCT observed for Mexicans living in the United States would be .017.

Conversely, if Mexican-born immigrants were completely segregated, most counties would have no Mexicans and a few counties would be 100 percent Mexican born. Since CNTYPCT is defined for a specific individual, every Mexican-born immigrant would have a value of CNTYPCT equal to one. That is, every Mexican-born immigrant would reside in a county that consisted entirely of persons born in Mexico.

In fact, the mean value of CNTYPCT among Mexican-born immigrants is .146, much larger than the .017 value that would prevail were Mexican-born immigrants sprinkled randomly throughout the United States. Thus, Mexican immigrants tend to live in more immigrant intensive communities than do natives. The same is true for other large immigrant groups.

The effect of clustering can be examined in another way. A logit identical to that in table 3.2 was run, except that CNTYPCT was included. The coefficient is negative and large. Nonfluent immigrants move to counties with high proportions of individuals from their own countries and they are less likely to learn English. The decision on where to locate is endogenous, and the country coefficients are pushed toward zero when CNTYPCT is included. Taking into account the residential decision reduces the differences between groups because the least-fluent groups are most likely to locate in highly segregated communities. But immigrant groups that segregate pass on fewer of the gains from diversity to the native population.

3.8.1   Diversity Reconsidered

When fluency rates are .55, it is virtually impossible to make a case for diversity. But as the fluency rate rises, the diversity argument makes more sense. Let us consider North African immigrants, whose fluency rate is at .92. Substitution into equation (20) implies that diversity is favored when

$$\theta(B_1 - A_0) > 1.087.$$

Now, suppose that 75 percent of what North Africans know overlaps completely with the native-born American population. Suppose further that the amount of knowledge possessed by natives and by North Africans is the same. Finally, suppose that half of the disjoint information is relevant to native-born Americans. Then, $B_1 = 1.25$, $A_0 = 0$, and

$$\theta = 1(1/1.25) + .5(.25/1.25) = .9,$$

so that

$$\theta(B_1 - A_0) = 1.125,$$

which exceeds the required 1.087. If these assumptions are valid, then diversity, brought about through immigration of North Africans, would be welfare improving to the native population.

The lesson here is that communication between natives and immigrants is the crucial parameter. Unless communication is high, it is virtually impossible to argue in favor of an immigrant group on the basis of gains from diversity. As a practical matter, this means English fluency. Since very few of the native-born American population can be fluent in a large number of other languages, it is necessary that all residents speak a common language.

Of course, it is possible for trade to occur without direct communication. Translators can be used and points of contact between different types of individuals can be minimized. But doing this negates the diversity argument almost by default. An impersonal market, coupled with a few translators, works well to ensure that French wine adorns the tables of American restaurants. But the French vintners need not be U.S. residents for this to occur. The gains from having French vintners teach Californians how to make wine are reaped only when direct communication between the two groups occurs.

Additionally, education and fluency are related. Immigrants, not currently in school, who report that they are fluent in English have average levels of education equal to 11.8 years, whereas those who are not fluent in English have an average education level equal to 7.3 years. Thus, relevance, defined by education level, and communication are likely to be positively related.

Finally, subsequent generations have been ignored. Since virtually all of the children of immigrants are fluent in English, the concerns that were raised in previous sections about English fluency are lessened. On the other hand, children of immigrants who grow up in the United States are less likely to have knowledge and skills that differ from (other) third and subsequent generation Americans. Thus, communication is enhanced when considering children of immigration, but disjointness declines.

3.8.2   Balanced Immigration

The empirical evidence suggest that diversity is enhanced by balanced immigration. Even if one accepts the diversity argument, diversity is useful only when English fluency among immigrants is high. Theory (see Lazear forthcoming) and evidence suggest that individuals who come from countries that make up a small part of the U.S. population are most likely to learn English.

Further, balanced immigration, especially from groups that are not already well represented in the U.S. population, provides the greatest amount of disjointness. If we take the diversity argument seriously, it implies that welfare is enhanced when immigrants come from a large number of underrepresented countries. This suggests that the current policy, which favors relatives of current residents, hinders rather than helps diversity.

Since education is a characteristic that can be screened and selected, there is no obvious reason why countries should be favored or penalized on the basis of the average level of education among their immigrants to the United States. Even though immigrants from Mexico have the lowest average level of educational attainment, nothing prevents the United States from having a policy that favors highly educated Mexican immigrants, if educated immigrants are desired.

Indeed, the lesson learned from this analysis is that current immigration policy is off target if the diversity argument is accepted. Current policy that favors immigrants who have relatives in the United States may have other virtues, but it is likely to grant resident status to those who have significant overlap with the current population, who have low rates of English fluency, and who suffer on the relevance criterion as well.

3.9   Conclusion

A diversity argument can be made for immigration. The desire for diversity is expressed in terms of gains that can be realized by the interaction of individuals who have different backgrounds. Taken literally, the case for diversity is strongest when individuals who differ from the majority confer larger gains from trade on majority members than majority members receive from interacting with their own kind. This argument implies that desirable immigrants come from cultures that are disjoint from current American culture and from cultures that are relevant to Americans. Most important, it is necessary that individuals can communicate with one another. As a practical matter, communication requires a high rate of English fluency among immigrants.

Current immigration policy favors the relatives of U.S. residents. In part, as a result of clustering, this policy has resulted in low fluency rates, which reduces the welfare gains from immigration. Also, because more-educated immigrants are likely to do better on the relevance criterion and because education and English fluency are linked, diversity gains are likely to be positively related to the education levels of the immigrant stock. Related, the results suggest that our immigration policy has resulted in differences in the characteristics of immigrants that reflect the effects of selection as much as they do the underlying characteristics of the populations from which the immigrants are drawn.

The current policy does not lead to an immigrant flow that enhances diversity. Instead, certain countries and cultures are favored at the expense of other countries and cultures. Furthermore, the countries that are the largest suppliers of immigrants are not among the best by the criteria of disjointness, relevance, or communication. A policy that sold immigration slots or one that ranked the specific characteristics of the individual immigrants would be more likely to enhance diversity.

References

Borjas, George J. 1994. The economics of immigration. *Journal of Economic Literature* 32 (4): 1667–717.
Card, David. 1990. The impact of the Mariel boatlift on the Miami labor market. *Industrial and Labor Relations Review* 43 (2): 245–57.
Hong, Lu, and Scott E. Page. 1997. Problem solving by heterogeneous agents. Syracuse University, Syracuse, N.Y.
LaLonde, Robert, and Robert Topel. 1991. Labor market adjustments to increased immigration. In *Immigration, trade and the labor market,* ed. John Abowd and Richard Freeman. Chicago: University of Chicago Press.
Lazear, Edward P. 1998. *Personnel economics for managers.* New York: John Wiley & Sons.
———. Forthcoming. Culture and language. *Journal of Political Economy.*
O'Reilly, Charles, Katherine Williams, and Sigal Barsade. 1998. Group demography and innovation: Does diversity help? In *Research on groups and teams,* vol. 1, ed. E. Mannix and M. Neale. Greenwich, Conn.: JAI Press.
Weitzman, Martin. 1992. On diversity. *Quarterly Journal of Economics* 107 (2): 363–405.

4

Convergence in Employment Rates of Immigrants

Edward Funkhouser

Recent papers (Fry 1996a for males, Schoeni 1998 for females, and Funkhouser and Trejo 1998 for males and females) have used the 1980 and 1990 censuses to document a pattern of employment rates for immigrants in which employment is lower by about 10 percentage points during the first years following entry into the United States. After 6–10 years in the United States, most of the difference in employment rates between immigrant arrival cohorts is eliminated with little subsequent change relative to natives. This concentration of convergence in the initial years following migration contrasts with the pattern for hourly earnings documented by Borjas (1994, 1995) in which convergence is more gradual over a longer period of time. While many of the determinants of employment convergence and wage convergence differ, reservation wages determining employment rates are likely to be based on home country labor market participation or earnings. Many other explanations for low employment rates are also likely to explain subsequent wage convergence as well, but perhaps at different rates—disruption effects, acquisition of human capital, or search in which transferability of skills must be learned may affect employment rates initially until any job is found, but may affect underemployment and wages for a longer period of time. In this paper, I explore several possible explanations for the employment patterns. I use both the 1980 and 1990 census data and, using the empirical techniques utilized extensively for wages of males, follow immigrant arrival cohorts between these two years.

Edward Funkhouser is assistant professor of economics at the University of California, Santa Barbara.

This paper has benefited greatly from previous collaboration with Steve Trejo and the comments of Lawrence Katz and conference participants. Brian Duncan provided excellent research assistance.

I consider four potential explanations for the lower employment rates of immigrants following migration and the rapid convergence to the levels of earlier arrivals during the 1980s.[1] First, employment rates may be related to changes in household demographics—disruption from fertility, child care, or marriage before or after migration. Second, the initial years following migration may be associated with a transition from the culture of labor force participation in the source country toward the culture of labor force participation in the United States. Third, the initial period following migration may be a period of formal or informal investment in skills and substitution away from market activity. These investments could include language acquisition, on-the-job training, and additional years of education, among other things. And finally, skills may not be transferable across countries, and the development of country-specific labor market skills, including the development of labor market networks, contacts, and general knowledge, may be important for immigrants.

For each of the explanations, the approach of this paper is to compare the employment disruptions of groups that are more likely to be affected with the disruption of groups that are less likely to be affected. The organization of the paper is as follows. In the following section, I describe the data and document the pattern of employment disruption in which I am interested. In sections 4.3 through 4.5, I consider the three main explanations that can be examined with these data—household composition, source country characteristics, and skills acquisition. In section 4.6, I summarize the interpretation of my findings. And in section 4.7, I discuss the implications of the findings for estimates of earnings convergence.

4.1   Data

I analyze microlevel data from the 1980 and 1990 U.S. censuses. The sample includes 1 percent of natives and 5 percent of immigrants.[2] To study employment rates following school years and before retirement, the sample is restricted to persons aged 25–59. With these restrictions, there are 664,512 observations for females (190,916 immigrants) and 617,365 observations for males (167,638 immigrants). In 1990, there are 824,549 observations for females (275,378 immigrants) and 788,517 observations for males (265,846 immigrants). In order to follow the same age cohorts, much of the analysis restricts the sample to those between the ages of 25 and 49 in 1980 and those between the ages of 35 and 59 in 1990. With this additional restriction, there are 1,037,347 observations for females and 974,742 observations for males.

---

1. Previous literature has tried to explain differences in levels in employment rates and labor force participation, especially for females. See, for example, MacPherson and Stewart (1989) and Duleep and Sanders (1993).

2. The sample includes 5 percent of persons born in outlying areas of the United States. Persons born abroad of U.S. parents are not included in the sample.

The census questionnaire asks questions related to employment during the previous week and the previous calendar year. For the preceding week, the survey asks about labor force status and, for those who were employed, hours worked. For the preceding calendar year, the survey asks whether the respondent worked and, for those who did, the number of weeks worked and the usual weekly hours. The number of annual hours worked during the preceding calendar year can be approximately calculated as the number of weeks worked multiplied by the usual weekly hours.[3]

In table 4.4 below, I utilize data from the 1 percent Public Use micro sample of the 1960 census and the 1 percent sample (5 percent questionnaire) neighborhood file from the 1970 censuses. In order that the estimates be comparable to those for the 1980–90 period, the sample is restricted in similar ways for the earlier years—persons aged 25–49 in the initial comparison year and 35–59 in the second.[4] In 1960, there is no question on year of arrival, though immigrants that identify their place of residence five years previous to be abroad are members of the 1955–59 arrival cohort to the United States. In the comparison between 1960 and 1970, therefore, employment growth of recent immigrants must be compared to all other immigrants. In the 1970 census, five-year bracket year of arrival is asked of all immigrants.

4.2   Basic Patterns in Employment Outcomes between 1980 and 1990

In this section, I document the convergence in employment rates that occurs for immigrants following their first five years in the United States. In table 4.1, these patterns are shown for several employment outcomes— employment during previous week, employment during previous year, annual hours of work (weeks worked during previous year multiplied by usual hours of work), weeks worked, and usual hours. For each outcome, I calculate the change between the 1980 and 1990 censuses relative to the change for similar natives during the same period. As noted above, the sample is restricted to persons aged 25–49 in 1980 and to persons aged 35–59 in 1990.

The focus of the table is on the change in employment outcomes, and

3. The hourly wage sample includes 697,879 females and 876,761 males. Below, I also utilize two other questions from the census questionnaire. First, in 1980, the census asked the respondent about labor market status in 1975. Second, in both years, the census asked basic earnings information in the preceding year. In the concluding section, I use this information and the information on annual hours to calculate hourly earnings, maintaining consistency in the top codes between the two years.

4. In 1960, the sample includes 296,401 females and 282,878 males between the ages of 25 and 49. In 1970, there are 306,940 females and 288,854 males between the ages of 25 and 49 and 280,593 females and 260,193 males between the ages of 35 and 59 that did not arrive in the United States after 1960 (for comparison with persons aged 25–49 in 1960). In 1980, with the same 1 percent sampling of natives and 5 percent sampling of immigrants, there are 418,382 females and 378,593 males between the ages of 35 and 59 (for comparison with persons aged 25–49 in 1970).

Table 4.1   **Employment Outcomes of Recent Immigrants Relative to Natives, Persons Aged 25–49 in 1980 (35–59 in 1990)**

	Change between 1980 and 1990 Relative to Change for Natives		
	1975–79 Arrival Cohort (1)	1970–74 Arrival Cohort (2)	1965–69 Arrival Cohort (3)
A. Females			
Percent employed previous week	.085	−.010	−.017
	(.004)	(.004)	(.004)
Labor force participation previous week	.091	−.008	−.012
	(.004)	(.004)	(.004)
Percent employed last year	.103	−.002	−.005
	(.004)	(.004)	(.004)
Annual hours	233.880	−15.383	−15.908
	(8.835)	(8.333)	(8.879)
Weeks worked prior year	3.280	−.099	−.333
	(.159)	(.143)	(.147)
Usual weekly hours	−.035	−.038	−.010
	(.126)	(.116)	(.124)
B. Males			
Percent employed previous week	.132	.022	.002
	(.003)	(.003)	(.003)
Labor force participation previous week	.136	.030	.015
	(.003)	(.002)	(.001)
Percent employed last year	.142	.026	.015
	(.003)	(.002)	(.003)
Annual hours	477.117	121.952	32.924
	(7.887)	(7.615)	(8.482)
Weeks worked prior year	4.042	.275	−.183
	(.109)	(.094)	(.102)
Usual weekly hours	1.545	1.404	.315
	(.105)	(.105)	(.115)

convergence relative to natives, of the most recent immigrants. To emphasize these patterns, I present the change in employment outcomes relative to the change for natives for the three most recent five-year arrival groups that can be observed in both the 1980 and 1990 censuses. The patterns for all cohorts—shown in appendix table 4A.1—reveal that nearly all of the significant changes relative to natives can be seen from these comparisons. In column (1) of table 4.1, the relative change for immigrants who arrived between 1975 and 1979—and therefore had 0–5 years of experience in the United States in 1980 and 11–15 years of experience in 1990—is shown. In column (2), the relative change for immigrants who arrived between 1970 and 1974—and therefore had 6–10 years of U.S. experience in

1980—is shown. And finally, the relative change for the immigrant group that arrived between 1965 and 1969 is shown in column (3).

To see how these calculations were made, consider the entry .085 in the first column of the first row for females. From appendix table 4A.1, the employment rate of females in the 1975–79 immigrant arrival cohort aged 25–49 was .484 in 1980. In 1990, the employment rate of females in the 1975–79 immigrant arrival cohort aged 35–59 was .651. This is a change of .167. During the same period, the employment rate of native females aged 25–49 in 1980 and 35–59 in 1990 changed from .613 to .695, or a change of .082. The employment rate of immigrant females in the 1975–79 immigrant arrival cohort grew .085 more than the change for natives.

Appendix table 4A.1 demonstrates the increase for the 1975–79 immigrant arrival cohort in all employment outcomes. Between 1980 and 1990, the proportion of the 1975–79 immigrant cohort employed in the previous week increased .085 more than natives for females and .132 more than natives for males. In contrast, the 1970–74 and 1965–69 arrival cohorts each had changes in employment rates less than those for natives for females and small (.022 and .002) changes greater than those for natives for males.[5] A similar pattern occurs for each employment outcome except usual weekly hours. For each of employment during previous year, weeks worked during the previous year, and annual hours, there is a large increase in employment outcomes for the most recent immigrant group that is not observed for any other immigrant arrival cohort. The different pattern for hours is worth noting. For females, there is no jump in hours for the most recent arrival cohort. For males, there is an increase in hours relative to natives for both the 1975–79 arrival cohort and the 1970–74 arrival cohort.

The contrast of the 1975–79 arrival cohort with earlier arrivals, including those that arrived before 1965, is easily seen in figure 4.1, which demonstrates the pattern for employment rates during the previous week. The change in employment rates relative to natives is shown on the vertical axis for each immigrant arrival cohort along the horizontal axis. The convergence in employment rates between 0–5 years and 11–15 years of U.S. experience is seen for the 1975–79 arrival cohort. For both males and females, there is little change in employment rates relative to natives for all arrival cohorts other than the 1975–79 arrival cohort.

Taken together, these data suggest that an important part of the integration of immigrants into the labor market concerns employment (rather than hours of work) and that, unlike more common views of integration over a long period of time, this integration takes place between the first five years in the United States and the second five years in the United States. Moreover, most of the convergence is the result of the low initial employment rates during the first five years following immigration.

---

5. The results for females presented here are very similar to table 6 of Schoeni (1998).

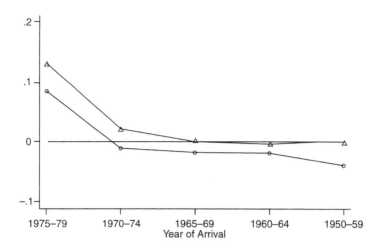

Fig. 4.1   Change in employment rates between 1980 and 1990 relative to natives, males (*triangles*) and females (*circles*)

4.2.1   Detailed Patterns for Employment during Previous Week

In the remainder of the paper, I focus on employment rates during the previous week. This choice is made for two reasons. First, as table 4.1 demonstrates, there are very similar patterns for all of the employment outcomes except hours, and in hours there is no rapid convergence to explain. Second, this is the cleanest measure for comparisons that involve the most recent immigrants. Because the census does not distinguish immigrants that arrived during the census year when asking about employment outcomes during the previous year, there may be confusion regarding to what location these questions refer. For all immigrants, though, employment during the previous week refers to employment outcomes in the United States.

The basic pattern is very robust and is found in a wide variety of subsamples of the data. The pattern is also found in the Current Population Survey for the 1980s, shown in appendix table 4A.4.[6] In table 4.2, I present the results for several subsamples of the census data—based on age, education, and region of origin—using the data for employment during the previous week. The columns are organized as in table 4.1.[7] Without exception, the relative change in employment rates for the 1975–79 arrival

---

6. In November 1979, April 1983, June 1986, and November 1989, the Current Population Survey included a supplement on immigrants. In appendix table 4A.4, employment rates for males aged 25–49 in 1979 are presented for each of these surveys. The one exception to the pattern is that the 1970–74 arrival cohort has low employment rates in both 1979 and 1983.

7. The employment rates from which the entries to table 4.2 are calculated are presented in appendix table 4A.2.

Table 4.2 **Change in Employment Rates Previous Week Relative to Natives, Persons Aged 25–49 in 1980 (35–59 in 1990)**

	Change between 1980 and 1990 Relative to Change for Natives		
	1975–79 Arrival Cohort (1)	1970–74 Arrival Cohort (2)	1965–69 Arrival Cohort (3)
A. Females			
Total	.085	−.010	−.017
	(.004)	(.004)	(.004)
Age 25–39 (35–44)	.065	−.023	−.020
	(.001)	(.005)	(.006)
Age 40–49 (50–59)	.092	−.020	−.003
	(.009)	(.005)	(.007)
High school or less	.055	−.021	−.017
	(.006)	(.004)	(.006)
Some college or more	.165	.035	.004
	(.006)	(.004)	(.007)
Europe	.136	−.004	.008
	(.013)	(.011)	(.008)
Eastern Europe	.122	−.042	.002
	(.019)	(.019)	(.024)
Latin America and Caribbean	.076	−.030	−.020
	(.010)	(.009)	(.009)
Mexico	.023	−.016	−.009
	(.010)	(.008)	(.012)
Asia	.164	.052	.019
	(.009)	(.009)	(.012)
B. Males			
Total	.132	.022	.002
	(.003)	(.003)	(.003)
Age 25–39 (35–49)	.123	.010	−.009
	(.003)	(.003)	(.004)
Age 40–49 (50–59)	.112	.029	.036
	(.007)	(.006)	(.005)
High school or less	.091	.023	.005
	(.004)	(.004)	(.004)
Some college or more	.192	.046	.019
	(.004)	(.004)	(.004)
Europe	.062	.015	.005
	(.009)	(.008)	(.006)
Eastern Europe	.121	.030	−.001
	(.014)	(.017)	(.017)
Latin America and Caribbean	.111	.017	.004
	(.009)	(.007)	(.007)
Mexico	.044	.004	−.010
	(.007)	(.007)	(.007)
Asia	.159	.013	−.020
	(.006)	(.007)	(.008)

cohort is large in magnitude and significantly larger than the change for the 1970–74 arrival cohort. The change relative to natives for the 1970–74 cohorts is small in magnitude for both males and females and positive only for males. Moreover, the change in employment rates for this cohort is significantly different from that for the 1965–69 arrival cohort in only three of the eight subsamples for women (college, Eastern Europe, and Asia) and four of the eight subsamples for males (age 25–39, high school or less, some college or more, and Asia).

Though the pattern is qualitatively similar across subsamples, the magnitude of the employment growth relative to natives does vary, and these differences might point to potential explanations for the patterns. In particular, the change in employment rates for the 1975–79 cohort relative to natives is high for those with more education and those from Asia. The change in employment rates of the 1975–79 cohort relative to natives is low for those with less education and for immigrants from Mexico. For females, immigrants from Europe have a larger magnitude change, while immigrant males from Europe have a lower magnitude change.

4.2.2 Detailed Patterns with Controls

In table 4.3, I present estimates of the convergence in employment rates between 0–5 years of U.S. experience and 6–10 years of U.S. experience derived from pooled regressions of the full sample of persons aged 25–59 in both 1980 and 1990. The regressions include controls for age (five-year brackets), education, race, region of origin of immigrants, year of arrival to the United States (five-year brackets), and a dummy variable for 1990 data in addition to the five-year bracket years of U.S. experience:

$$E_{it} = \alpha + \beta X_{it} + \gamma Y_{it} + \gamma_c C_i + \gamma_o O_i + \pi_t T_{it} + \varepsilon_{it},$$

where the vector X includes age, education, and race variables; Y includes the years of U.S. experience variables; C includes arrival cohort variables; O includes country of origin variables; T includes year of survey variables; and ε_{it} is a random component. The U.S. experience coefficients of interest are identified by the assumption of a common period effect for immigrants and natives, and the assumption that the 1960–64 and 1965–69 cohorts have the same experience effect in 1990. Each entry in the table is the coefficient reported from a separate regression using the indicated sample restrictions.

The results of this estimation confirm the findings of table 4.2 and indicate that the included controls do not much alter the convergence in employment rates of recent immigrants. For females, those with 6–10 years of U.S. experience are predicted to have employment rates 8.9 percentage points higher than those with 0–5 years of U.S. experience. For males, the difference is 11.1 percentage points. The estimates for the subsamples

Table 4.3   **Difference in Employment Rates Previous Week of Immigrants with**
0–5 Years of U.S. Experience and Immigrants with 6–10 Years of
U.S. Experience, with Controls

	Females	Males
Total[a]	.089	.111
	(.014)	(.011)
Age in 1980		
25–39	.091	.103
	(.018)	(.014)
40–49	.096	.094
	(.030)	(.023)
Education		
High school or less	.066	.060
	(.018)	(.016)
Some college or more	.128	.156
	(.021)	(.013)
Europe (vs. white natives)	.117	.065
	(.026)	(.027)
Eastern Europe (vs. white	.156	.060
natives)	(.022)	(.062)
Latin America and Caribbean	.071	.087
(vs. Hispanic natives)	(.022)	(.019)
Mexico (vs. Hispanic natives)	.021	.048
	(.027)	(.019)
Asia (vs. Asian natives)	.145	.130
	(.019)	(.015)

Note: Entries are the coefficient on 6–10 years in the United States relative to 0–5 years in the United States. Other controls include five-year age bracket dummy variables for age, four dummy variables for education (some high school, high school graduate, some college, college graduate; no high school omitted), six race dummy variables (black, Asian, Mexican, Puerto Rican, other Hispanic, and other race), five-year arrival cohort dummy variables for immigrants, a dummy variable for those born in outlying areas, five dummy variables for region of origin (Europe, Eastern Europe and former Soviet Union, Latin America and the Caribbean, Asia, and other countries; Mexico omitted), and a dummy variable for data from the 1990 census.
[a]Total sample size is 1,489,013 for females and 1,405,826 for males.

based on the predicted convergence profile are similar to those in table 4.2 following cohorts over time.

4.2.3   Is the Convergence in Employment Rates
an Artifact of Immigrant Visa Policy?

Because many nonimmigrants to the United States enter the United States under visas in which they are not eligible to work and later adjust their immigration status allowing them to work, it is possible that the observed change in employment rates is an artifact of these changes. During the first five years following entry to the United States, some immigrants do not work, but by the second five years, they report being employed. To examine this possibility, I calculate an approximation of the number of immigrants in the 1975–79 entry cohort that may have entered under a nonwork visa and adjusted status between 1980 and 1984 (6–10 years following immigration). Immigrants in this arrival cohort that adjusted status prior to 1980 would not report lower employment rates at the time of the 1980 census.

The Immigration and Naturalization Service (INS) reports year of arrival for immigrants that adjust their immigration status during any given year. From the data for persons who adjusted their status during the years 1980–84, the number of persons that arrived between 1975 and 1979 can be calculated.[8] During each of these years, the type of entry visa is also reported, though not separately by year of arrival. Approximately 95,000 persons per year adjusted status from the following entry visas: temporary visitors for pleasure (B2), transit aliens (C), students (F1/M1), student spouse or child (F2/M2), exchange visitors (J1) and spouses (J2), and fiancées and children of citizens (K). Applying the calculated distribution of year of entry to these potential adjusters, there are approximately 219,585 immigrants that arrived in the 1975–79 arrival cohort and adjusted status between 1980 and 1984. To make the sample restrictions similar to those utilized for the census, I calculated the proportion of each immigrant arrival cohort between the ages of 25 and 49 for males (20.24 percent) and females (21.39 percent) and assume that this distribution is the same for those who adjusted their status.[9] Thus, approximately 91,412 immigrants—44,453 males and 46,959 females—arrived between 1975 and 1979 between the ages of 25 and 49 and subsequently adjusted status between 1980 and 1984. These are the immigrants that might bias the conclusion from table 4.1.

These 91,412 immigrants represent 6.4 percent of male immigrants in the 1975–79 arrival cohort and 7.3 percent of the female immigrants in this cohort. This is the extreme upper bound to potential bias since all of these persons would have to be not working in 1980 and would have to be working in 1990. Whether this is viewed as a large proportion or a small proportion depends on the proportion of immigrants in this group that change employment status after adjustment. A more reasonable upper bound might be a 50 percentage point increase in the employment rates of these persons between 1980 and 1990. In this scenario, changes in visa status would explain at most 3.2 percent of employment rate changes for males and 3.7 percent for females. Though a sizable group, these adjusters do not explain most of the observed change in employment rates during the first 10 years in the United States.

8. The INS data do not report year of arrival for those who adjust in 1980 and 1981. The distribution of arrival years was calculated based on the years between entry and adjustment observed in the data for 1982–84. The details of the following calculation are available from the author.

9. This age distribution is calculated at year of adjustment, not year of the 1980 census.

4.2.4   Has the Convergence in Employment Rates Changed over Time?

An interesting aspect of the convergence in employment rates is the trend in relative employment rates of immigrants between the 1960s and the 1980s. Previous research by Fry (1996a) reports employment rates by arrival cohort in the 1960, 1970, 1980, and 1990 censuses. Using the sample of all not-in-school males aged 16–59 in the census year, he finds that the most recent immigrant arrival cohorts have employment rates above those of natives with labor market experience similar to the time since immigration of immigrants in both the 1960 and 1970 censuses. He finds that with increased time in the United States, employment rates of the recent arrivals converged downward toward those of natives over the 1960s and 1970s.[10] The pattern above in which recent arrivals have low employment rates relative to natives is similar to that found by Fry for males in the 1980 and 1990 censuses, though he does not find the same convergence over the 1980s. Though Fry focused on changes in entry cohort quality, his findings suggest a change in the pattern of convergence between the 1960s and 1980s as well.

To examine whether Fry's conclusion is present with the same restrictions as those in tables 4.1–4.3, in table 4.4 I provide estimates consistent with those in table 4.2. (The underlying employment rates upon which this table is based are shown in appendix table 4A.3.) In columns (1) and (3), I follow the relative employment rates of the most recent arrival cohort in the 1960 census (1955–59 arrivals) to the 1970 census. As noted above, because the 1960 census does not report year of arrival of immigrants, these recent immigrants are those that resided abroad five years ago in the data for that year. The relative employment rates of all previous immigrants are also reported. In columns (2) and (4), the relative employment rates of the most recent arrival cohort in the 1970 census (1965–69 arrivals) are followed to the 1980 census. The employment rates of the 1960–64 arrival cohort are also reported.

For males (shown in cols. [1] and [2]), the relative increase in employment rates of the most recent immigrant arrival cohort as the level of U.S. experience increases from 0–5 years to 11–15 years is present in the 1960–1970 comparison in column (1) and the 1970–1980 comparison in column (2). Employment rates of recent immigrants increased slightly

10. In a companion paper that focuses on relative inactivity, Fry (1996b) focuses on the cohort effects and finds that more recent cohorts are more likely to be inactive than earlier cohorts. A pattern that may be more similar to that for the 1960 and 1970 censuses in the United States is found by Baker and Benjamin (1997) in their study of female immigrants to Canada. They find little difference between the annual hours of female immigrants and the annual hours of native females. In their study that includes controls and is not directly comparable to either table 4.1 or the paper by Fry, increased time following immigration is associated with an increase in hours of work, all else equal, from the direct effect and a reduction in hours of work as husband income increases. As can be seen from table 4.1, in the U.S. data, there is an important distinction between hours and other employment outcomes.

Table 4.4   **Employment Rates during Previous Week, 1960–80**

	Males		Females	
	1960–70	1970–80	1960–70	1970–80
	(1)	(2)	(3)	(4)
Change Relative to Natives				
Recent immigrants	.034	.075	−.054	.020
	(.009)	(.006)	(.012)	(.013)
Previous immigrants	−.002	.018	−.004	.029
	(.004)	(.006)	(.007)	(.013)
Change of Most Recent Cohort Relative to Previous Immigrants				
Europe	.034	.030	−.109	−.025
	(.014)	(.014)	(.022)	(.020)
Eastern Europe	.028	.029	−.006	.082
	(.026)	(.044)	(.048)	(.061)
Mexico	−.051	.036	−.006	.026
	(.033)	(.030)	(.055)	(.040)
Latin America and Caribbean	.023	.048	−.065	−.024
	(.040)	(.018)	(.054)	(.024)
Asia	.068	.073	.080	−.001
	(.045)	(.028)	(.052)	(.033)

Note: Sample includes persons aged 25–49 in initial year and persons aged 35–59 in final year of comparison.

Recent immigrant is defined as follows: 1960 data, immigrants that resided abroad five years ago; 1970 data (cols. [1] and [3]), 1955–59 arrival cohort; 1970 data (cols. [2] and [4]), 1965–69 arrival cohort; and 1980 data, 1965–69 arrival cohort.

Previous immigrant is defined as follows: columns (1) and (3), all immigrant arrivals before 1955; and columns (2) and (4), 1960–64 arrival cohort.

more than 4 percentage points during each 10-year period, while those of natives remained constant between 1960 and 1970 and declined slightly between 1970 and 1980. The pattern for the 1970–1980 comparison is similar to that observed in table 4.1 for the comparison of 1980 to 1990: Recent immigrants have lower employment rates than natives, while those with 6–10 years of experience have similar or higher employment rates than natives. Over time, the employment rates of recent immigrants catch up to or surpass those of natives.

There is an important difference in the pattern in employment rates prior to the 1980s. Though the relative increase in employment rates for the most recent immigrant arrival cohort is present in the 1960–1970 comparison, the initial employment rate is higher than that of natives. This is because the higher employment rates of recent immigrants from Europe and Mexico offset employment rates that are lower than those of natives for recent immigrants from Latin America and Asia. Over this period, there is overall divergence in the relative employment rates of the recent arrivals; the subsequent increase relative to natives results in employment rates that are even higher than those of natives after 11–15 years of U.S. experience. This aggregate comparison masks wage convergence and resulting employment rates lower than those of natives for recent immigrants from Mexico and Asia during the 1960s and 1970s.

For females (shown in cols. [3] and [4]), the pattern observed in table 4.1 is not present in the earlier periods. In both 1960 and 1970, recent immigrants have higher employment rates than natives or earlier immigrants and the change in the employment rate is less than or equal to that of these other groups. This is especially true for recent immigrants from Eastern Europe and Latin America, while recent immigrants from Mexico and Asia had lower initial employment rates than natives. For recent immigrants from each of the country of origin except Asia, there is a decrease in the magnitude of negative gain relative to natives or a change in sign to positive gain relative to natives between the 1960s and the 1970s.

Over time, there is a consistent pattern in which recent male immigrants have more rapid growth in employment rates than other immigrants or natives. The deficit in employment rates for recent male immigrants has increased since 1960, with the level of employment rates of recent immigrants in each census year falling further below those of natives.[11]

For females, the pattern is not consistent over time. Up until the 1980s, female immigrants had higher employment rates than female natives and lower growth in employment rates. The female pattern, while starting out quite different from males in the decade of the 1960s, looks similar to the pattern for males during the decade of the 1980s.

Though the increase in growth relative to natives and the changing pattern for females do suggest changes over time as a possible source of changes in employment growth, in the remainder of this paper, I focus on explaining the convergence in employment rates between 1980 and 1990.

4.3 The Role of Fertility, Children, and Marital Status in Change in Labor Market Outcomes

In this section, I explore the potential role of fertility, children, and marital status on employment rates. At first glance, these issues would appear to be especially important for females.[12] The evidence in table 4.2,

---

11. Additional evidence supporting this shift is found in the questions on employment status in 1975 in the 1980 census. In this question, for the 1970–74 arrival cohort, there is little change in the employment rate relative to natives between 1975 and 1980. This contrasts with the lower initial employment rates—and subsequent convergence—of the 1975–79 cohort in 1980 and the 1985–89 cohort in 1990. Though selective emigration could explain this pattern, taken together with the evidence from Fry, it is also consistent with a shift in pattern of relative employment rates between the 1970–74 and 1975–79 arrival cohorts. Another possible explanation for the low growth of the 1970–74 cohort between 1975 and 1980 is that employment rates of this cohort took longer to converge to that of natives. This view would be supported by the evidence from the data from the Current Population Survey presented in table 4A.4

12. The paper by Blau (1992) provides evidence on fertility of immigrant females using the 1970 and 1980 U.S. censuses. She shows that that recent immigrants have lower fertility measured by total number of children ever born during the initial years following migration

though, does not support explanations that are particular to females in the childbearing years. First, the patterns are very similar for males and females of all age groups. Second, the pattern for females in the childbearing years (25–39 in 1980) is similar to that for females that are beyond the childbearing years (40–49 in 1980). For each of these comparisons, selection into each sample, based on gender or age, is independent of the fertility or employment outcome. Together, these patterns suggest little potential explanatory role for fertility or child rearing in directly explaining the lower employment rates during the first years following immigration.

But to be certain that household demographics are not explaining the patterns for females and that something else is explaining the pattern for males, I examine two other factors related to household composition for females—presence of children and marital status—using two approaches. First, I use the approach of table 4.1 to follow two samples of the same females over time based on the age of children. The first group consists of those females who had no children in 1980. In 1990, these females either had no children or all of their children were between the ages of zero and nine. The second group consists of those women who only had children aged zero to seven in 1980. These females had children with ages less than 17 in 1990.[13] If disruption from children was a primary determinant of the employment rates of recent immigrants, women without children in 1980 would not experience disruption, while those with children would. Because the same females are followed between 1980 and 1990, there is no selection between the samples.

I also separate the two groups—those with no children in 1980 and those with children aged zero to seven in 1980—into subgroups corresponding to their possible outcomes in 1990. For those with no children in 1980, this includes females with no children in 1990 and those with children in 1990. For those with children aged zero to seven in 1980, this includes those with no additional children in 1990 and those with additional children in 1990. Though these subsamples are self-selected, they may provide additional evidence on the potential role of children in the initial disruption following immigration.

The results of these calculations, shown in table 4.5, strengthen the argument against children playing a large role in the change in relative employment rates of recent immigrants. Female immigrants in the 1975–79 arrival cohort with no children at the time of the 1980 census have employment rates .152 lower than 1970–74 arrivals. By 1990, the two groups have the same employment rates. Similarly, female immigrants in the 1975–79

---

compared to natives. As time in the United States increases, immigrant female fertility approaches that of natives. Funkhouser and Trejo (1998) find similar patterns using the 1980 and 1990 censuses. The results from each of these papers suggest that disruption from the migration process may be more important than assimilation following migration.

13. This age group was chosen so that all children would be living at home in 1990.

Table 4.5   **Employment Rates, 1975–79 Cohort and 1970–74 Cohort, Females**

	Females Aged 25–49 in 1980 (1)	Females Aged 35–59 in 1990 (2)	Change 1980 to 1990 (3)
No Children in 1980 and No Children or All Children aged 0–9 in 1990			
1975–79 cohort	.620	.749	.129
	(.005)	(.008)	(.009)
1970–74 cohort	.772	.740	−.032
	(.006)	(.008)	(.010)
No children			
1975–79 cohort		.754	
		(.008)	
1970–74 cohort		.742	
		(.008)	
All children 0–9			
1975–79 cohort		.656	
		(.008)	
1970–74 cohort		.659	
		(.011)	
All Children Aged 0–7 in 1980 and 10–17 in 1990			
1975–79 cohort	.337	.640	.303
	(.005)	(.005)	(.007)
1970–74 cohort	.468	.647	.179
	(.005)	(.005)	(.007)
All children 10–17			
1975–79 cohort		.710	
		(.009)	
1970–74 cohort		.702	
		(.007)	
Also with children 0–10			
1975–79 cohort		.576	
		(.007)	
1970–74 cohort		.580	
		(.007)	

Note: Entries are employment rates in columns (1) and (2), and change in column (3).

arrival cohort with children only between the ages of zero and seven have employment rates .129 below those of 1970–74 arrivals with children of the same age. By 1990, these two arrival groups also have similar employment rates. Moreover, the employment rates in 1990 are similar between the two arrival cohorts for each of the subgroups reported in column (2).

The second approach is to classify women into four groups—unmarried/no children, married/children, married/no children, and unmarried/children—and look at women of the same age who migrated at different calendar years in each of these groups. Though this comparison is not as clean because it is not possible to follow the same females over time, the result is similar. The main finding from this exercise—not presented in a table—is that the most recent five-year cohort has lower employment rates for each group except the relatively small group of unmarried females with children for all age groups.

Taken together, the evidence in tables 4.2, 4.3, and 4.5 suggest that though household factors may play a role in the level of employment rates, they do not explain the change in relative employment rates as time in the United States increases. This finding contrasts somewhat with the literature, which has focused on these factors to explain the levels of employment and labor force participation rates for females.

4.4   Effect of Source Country Characteristics

I now consider two possibilities related to characteristics in the source country. First, it is possible that the low employment rate following migration and the subsequent jump in employment rates is a phenomenon for immigrants from a small number of countries. Second, it is possible that employment rates upon arrival to the United States are related to labor market activity prior to arrival and, in particular, labor force participation in the country of origin. Figure 4.2 addresses these possibilities.

In the figure, the difference between the growth in employment rates for the 1975–79 arrival cohort and the growth in employment rates for the 1970–74 arrival cohort (without controls) is plotted against the labor force participation in the source country and is shown for both females (fig. 4.2A) and males (fig. 4.2B).[14] Each point represents the data for immigrants from one of the main source countries to the United States denoted by two digit abbreviations. For example, the point for Mexico (ME) shows that the 1975–79 cohort experienced a change in employment rates of .035 for females and .047 for males.[15] The labor force participation, calculated over the entire nonchild population, is .184 for females and .496 for males.

First, examining only the vertical distance of each point, nearly all countries have convergence in employment rates as time in the United States increases. Though immigrants from the main source country, Mexico, experience an increase in employment rates, they are not the only immigrants to do so. In fact, the increase for Mexicans is low relative to that for other countries. Second, there is no clear relationship between the jump in employment rates and the labor force participation in the source country. Though there is a relationship between source country characteristics and the level of labor force participation rates, the lower employment rates of the most recent arrivals relative to earlier arrivals is not related to the source country characteristics. In general, female labor force participation rates are higher in the developed source countries than among immigrants after

---

14. The labor force participation and GNP per capita in the source country around 1990 are taken from World Bank (1990).

15. These numbers differ slightly from those reported in table 4.2 since these calculations do not include the same age restrictions.

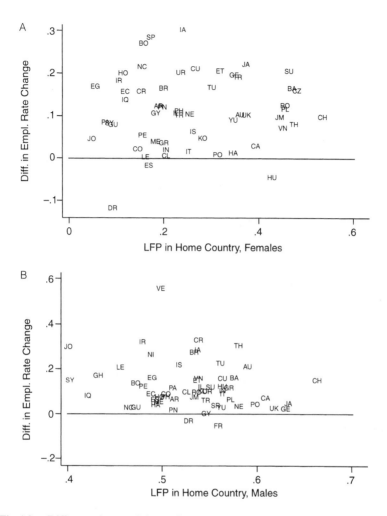

Fig 4.2 **Difference in growth in employment rate between 1970–74 and 1975–79 arrivals and labor force participation in home country, females (*A*) and males (*B*) aged 25–59**

Note: AR = Argentina; AU = Australia; BA = Barbados; BO = Bolivia; BR = Brazil; CA = Canada; CH = China; CL = Chile; CO = Colombia; CR = Costa Rica; CU = Cuba; CZ = Czechoslovakia; DR = Dominican Republic; EC = Ecuador; EG = Egypt; ES = El Salvador; ET = Ethiopia; FR = France; GE = Germany; GH = Ghana; GR = Greece; GU = Guatemala; GY = Guyana; HA = Haiti; HO = Honduras; HU = Hungary; IA = Indonesia; IL = Ireland; IN = India; IQ = Iraq; IR = Iran; IS = Israel; IT = Italy; JA = Japan; JM = Jamaica; JO = Jordan; KO = Korea; LE = Lebanon; ME = Mexico; NC = Nicaragua; NE = Netherlands; NI = Nigeria; PA = Pakistan; PE = Peru; PH = Philippines; PL = Poland; PN = Panama; PO = Portugal; RO = Romania; SP = Spain; SU = USSR; SY = Syria; TH = Thailand; TR = Trinidad; TU = Turkey; UK = United Kingdom; UR = Uruguay; VE = Venezuela; VN = Vietnam; YU = Yugoslavia.

arrival and are lower in the developing source countries. For males, labor force participation rates are higher in all source countries than among immigrants following migration.

I next examine the potential role of source country characteristics more formally in a regression framework. There are two dependent variables reported in these regressions. First, the level of employment rates in 1990 is reported in columns (1) and (2). Second, the difference in the change in employment rates between the 1975–79 arrival cohort and the 1970–74 arrival cohort is shown in columns (3) and (4). These data correspond to those in figure 4.2. Columns (1) and (3) report the results for female employment rates, and columns (2) and (4) report the results for male employment rates. There are 49 countries with complete data for females and 52 countries with data for males.

The two main source country characteristics are labor force participation of nonmigrants of the same gender and the gross national product per capita, each in a year close to 1990.[16] In addition, dummy variables for region of origin are also included. The results are reported in table 4.6. The main finding of the table is that though country characteristics are related to employment levels, they are not correlated with the relative change of employment rates for females. For males, there is a relationship between the level of development and country of origin and the change in employment levels. This pattern in which source country characteristics have no effect on the relative growth in employment rates for females and have an effect for males is the reverse of that that would be expected from an explanation for the change in employment rates based on accumulation of labor market culture.

Though most of the evidence does not suggest a large role for labor market culture in the source country to explain the convergence in employment rates, there are three pieces of evidence that do suggest that the source country is important. First, there is weak correlation (.167, significant at the 80 percent level) between the employment rate jump for females and the employment rate jump for males from the same country of origin. Second, the significance of the region variables in table 4.6 suggests that aspects of the source countries not captured by labor force participation or level of development do have an effect on employment rates subsequent to migration. Third, GNP per capita is a significant determinant of convergence in employment rates for males.

4.5 Role of Skills

There are several pieces of evidence that suggest a potential role for skill in explaining the change in employment rates. First, it was observed in

---

16. Though the immigrants reported in the 1980 and 1990 censuses did not arrive in the United States in 1990, there is consistency across countries in the selection of the data.

Table 4.6   **Relationship between Employment Rates in United States and Source Country Characteristics**

	Employment Rate, Most Recent Five-Year Arrival Cohort		Difference in Growth between 1980 and 1990 for Two Most Recent Arrival Cohorts	
	Females	Males	Females	Males
	1990	1990	1980–90	1980–90
	(1)	(2)	(3)	(4)
Female labor force	.572		.052	
participation	(.149)		(.129)	
Male labor force		.155		−.040
participation		(.279)		(.358)
Log GNP per capita	−.021	.003	−.003	.236
	(.018)	(.013)	(.016)	(.016)
Region (OECD omitted)				
Asia	−.038	−.086	−.015	.179
	(.070)	(.049)	(.061)	(.063)
Latin America	.099	−.018	−.010	.113
	(.054)	(.040)	(.047)	(.051)
Mexico	−.067	.009	−.075	.042
	(.113)	(.084)	(.098)	(.108)
Eastern Europe	−.061	.023	−.091	.082
	(.090)	(.062)	(.078)	(.080)
Other	−.110	−.64	.004	.208
	(.060)	(.047)	(.052)	(.060)
Constant	.502	.720	.120	−.150
	(.165)	(.171)	(.143)	(.220)
Adjusted R^2	.39	.09	−.11	.17
N	49	52	49	52

table 4.2 that the change in employment rates relative to natives is larger for immigrants with more education than for immigrants with less education. Second, the change is greatest for immigrants from Latin America and Asia and is lowest for immigrants from Mexico. Third, there is a correlation in the magnitude of the change relative to natives for male and female immigrants from the same source country. Fourth, GNP per capita is a significant determinant of the change for males, but not for females.[17]

I consider three mechanisms through which skills may be important. First, immigrants may acquire observable skills subsequent to migration, including education and language, during which time employment is lower. Second, labor supply of immigrants may have been responsive to

17. Further evidence is provided by the finding from appendix table 4A.3 that recent immigrants at the time of the 1960 and 1970 censuses—those that arrived before the change in immigration law favoring family reunification—did not experience lower employment immediately following immigration.

the change in the reward to skill in the U.S. labor market during the 1980s. And third, a residual explanation is that skills may not be perfectly transferable between the source country and the United States.

4.5.1   Investment in Skills

The finding that employment rates of more-skilled immigrants are low following migration is consistent with previous literature on human capital formation of immigrants, including the paper by Betts and Lofstrom (chap. 2 in this volume), which has suggested that more-educated workers are more likely to make subsequent investments in human capital. Theories of human capital investment also predict that older workers are less likely to make the investment than younger workers since there is less remaining time to recoup the costs of investment. If the observed change in employment rates for recent immigrants were the result of investment in human capital, the change should be greater for younger workers than for older workers. I examine the consistency of the data with this prediction in table 4.7.

The sample aged 25–49 in 1980 (and 35–59 in 1990) is divided into three age groups (25–34 in 1980, 35–44 in 1980, and 45–49 in 1980) and three education groups (some high school or less, high school graduate, and some college or more). The entries in the table are the change in employment rates of the 1975–79 and 1970–74 immigrant arrival cohorts relative to natives of the same age and education. Though persons can and do change between the education categories, the changes—shown in appendix table 4A.5—are not large enough to offset the patterns in changes in employment rates observed.

The pattern in which the change in employment rates is higher for more-educated workers is observed within each of the three age groups. For the youngest group, the change in employment rates for females in the 1975–79 arrival cohort, aged 25–34 in 1980, and with some college or more is .119 higher than that for similar persons in the 1970–74 arrival cohort. This is significantly greater than the change of .081 for those with exactly a high school diploma. For males in the same age group, the changes are .153 and .064, respectively.

The patterns are very similar for each of the three age groups, noting that the age group 45–49 in 1980 is more imprecisely estimated. They are also very similar across males and females. Though the magnitude of the change in employment rates of those with some college or more for the 25–34-year-olds is slightly higher than the 35–44-year-olds for males and each of the other groups for females, there is not much support for substantial investment in human capital explaining the change in employment rates.

Table 4.7   **Change in Employment Rates Relative to Natives between 1980 and 1990, by Skill and Age Level**

	Females		Males	
	1975–79 Arrival Cohort	1970–74 Arrival Cohort	1975–79 Arrival Cohort	1970–74 Arrival Cohort
Age in 1980	(1)	(2)	(3)	(4)
Age 25–34 (35–44 in 1990)				
Some high school or less	.016	−.032	.088	.021
	(.009)	(.009)	(.009)	(.008)
High school graduate	.061	−.020	.075	.011
	(.010)	(.010)	(.008)	(.008)
Some college or more	.159	.040	.207	.053
	(.007)	(.008)	(.005)	(.005)
Age 35–44 (45–54 in 1990)				
Some high school or less	.051	−.058	.091	.040
	(.013)	(.012)	(.011)	(.009)
High school graduate	.108	.012	.089	.017
	(.015)	(.014)	(.013)	(.010)
Some college or more	.129	.008	.123	.020
	(.012)	(.010)	(.008)	(.006)
Age 45–49 (55–59 in 1990)				
Some high school or less	.064	−.015	.098	−.014
	(.022)	(.020)	(.022)	(.016)
High school graduate	.077	−.007	.158	.100
	(.030)	(.028)	(.027)	(.023)
Some college or more	.233	.010	.144	.045
	(.031)	(.027)	(.017)	(.016)

Note: Entries are change in employment rates between 1980 and 1990 relative to change for natives in same education and age group.

4.5.2   Language Acquisition

I now turn to the role of language acquisition. Since immigrants with less ability to speak English have lower employment rates than those with greater English-speaking ability, if changes in English proficiency are large during the first 5–10 years following migration, this could explain much of the pattern. Moreover, immigrants that arrived in the United States with proficiency in English should not experience low employment during the first years following migration. Initial evidence that the latter may not be the case is the observation that the English-speaking countries in figure 4.2 have high changes in employment rates.

I first examine the relationship between English ability and employment rates without controls in table 4.8. In the census, respondents can be classified as speaking only English or, for those that do not speak only English, speaking English very well, well, not well, or not at all. Because most natives speak only English, I compare the change in employment

Table 4.8   Change in Employment Rates of 1975–79 Arrival Cohort Relative to 1970–74 Arrival Cohort, by English-Speaking Ability

	Females	Males
English only	.083	.067
	(.014)	(.010)
English very well	.086	.116
	(.010)	(.012)
English well	.122	.147
	(.010)	(.012)
English not well	.123	.095
	(.011)	(.012)
English not at all	.024	.086
	(.016)	(.018)

Note: Entries are difference in change in employment rate between 1980 and 1990 for the 1975–79 arrival cohort relative to the 1970–74 arrival cohort calculated for persons with indicated English-speaking ability in each year. Sample is restricted to those aged 25–49 in 1980 and 35–59 in 1990.

rates of the 1975–79 and 1970–74 arrival cohorts directly. The numbers reported in table 4.8 are the difference in the change in employment rates between these two arrival cohorts. For all language levels except females who do not speak English at all, there is a relative increase in employment levels between 1980 and 1990 for the 1975–79 arrival cohort. This includes those who speak only English and those who speak English very well.

In the table, I compare the employment rates of persons of the same English-speaking level in 1980 and 1990. An issue, therefore, is the effect of changes in language ability between the two years, also shown in appendix table 4A.5. Though many immigrants do improve English language skills during the first years following immigration, many do not. Moreover, language acquisition continues well beyond the first 10 years after immigration for many immigrants.[18] Comparison of the magnitudes reveals that the number of immigrants changing language status and the difference in employment rates across language groups are not large enough for the product of the two to explain much of the change in employment rates. The net change over 10 years is a .1 reduction of the 1975–79 arrival cohort in the not well/not at all group and an increase of the same amount in those who speak only English or speak very well. The difference in employment rates between these groups is about .2 for females and .1 for males. Though the within-group changes shown in the table are substantially larger in magnitude, the bias of the composition change is to underestimate the true employment change at the lower levels of English proficiency as immigrants move from lower English proficiency and lower employment rates to higher English ability and higher employment rates.

18. See for example, Funkhouser (1996).

Table 4.9   **Determinants of Employment Rates**

	Coefficient on 6–10 Years U.S. Experience Relative to 0–5 Years	
	Females	Males
1. Restricted across years and nativity without English-speaking ability	.089 (.014)	.111 (.011)
2. Add English-speaking ability	.085 (.014)	.110 (.011)
3. Separate coefficients for age, education, and English across years	.090 (.014)	.111 (.011)
4. Separate coefficients across years and nativity	.083 (.014)	.099 (.011)
N	1,489,013	1,405,826

Note: Entries are coefficient on 6–10 years in the United States relative to 0–5 years in the United States. Other controls in row 1 include five-year age bracket dummy variables for age, four dummy variables for education (some high school, high school graduate, some college, college graduate; no high school omitted), six race dummy variables (black, Asian, Mexican, Puerto Rican, other Hispanic, and other race), five-year arrival cohort dummy variables for immigrants, a dummy variable for those born in outlying areas, five dummy variables for region of origin (Europe, Eastern Europe and former Soviet Union, Latin America and the Caribbean, Asia, and other countries; Mexico omitted), and a dummy variable for data from the 1990 census. In row 2, four dummy variables for English-speaking ability are included. In row 3, the age, education, and English-speaking ability variables are interacted with the year dummy variable. In row 4, these variables are also interacted separately with immigrant status. One additional age group is dropped for immigrants.

4.5.3   Extensions of Table 4.3 and the Changing Returns to Skill

During the 1980s, the return to skill in the United States increased. As a further check on the role of observed human capital formation on employment rates and the possibility that changes in the wage structure affected relative employment rates of immigrants, I extend the regression results of table 4.3. In table 4.9, I add more detailed controls for human capital, beginning with English-speaking ability. The entries in the table are the coefficients on the variable for 6–10 years of U.S. experience from regressions using specifications similar to those in table 4.3. In row 1 of the table, the coefficient from table 4.3 is reported. In row 2, four dummy variables for English-speaking ability are included. I continue the extensions for controls for skills by interacting the human capital variables— age, education, and language ability—with year and nativity. In row 3, separate returns to these variables are included by year of the census. In row (4), separate returns for immigrants and natives are also included.[19]

In the table, there is surprisingly little evidence that skills acquisition or the changing structure of rewards plays a role in the change in employment rates during the first years following arrival in the United States. The pre-

19. Two age group dummy variables are excluded for immigrants.

dicted change in employment rates between 0–5 years of U.S. experience and 6–10 years of U.S. experience ranges between .090 and .083 for females and between .111 and .099 for males.

4.5.4 Discussion

Though investment in skills by immigrants does take place subsequent to immigration, this investment alone does not explain the relative change in employment rates of recent immigrant arrivals. In addition, it is not likely that the changing structure of rewards to skill in the United States during the 1980s can explain the observed patterns. These findings point to a lack of transferability of human and social capital as being important during the initial years following migration. That this lack of transferability is not strongly related to language emphasizes the importance of social capital, including the development of labor market contacts and networks. Though this is a residual explanation, it is consistent with the findings based on the source countries.

4.6 Summary

In this paper, I have utilized the 1980 and 1990 U.S. censuses to examine employment outcomes of recent immigrants. A robust finding is that there is a large increase in employment rates during the initial years following immigration. The findings that the convergence is similar for males and females and for older and younger immigrants make explanations based on gender or age unlikely to explain these patterns. Though labor force culture in the source country—measured by labor force participation rates—is not an important determinant of the change in employment rates after migration, the correlation between the level of development and the change in employment rates and the correlation between the change for males and females from the same country indicate that source country labor markets may be important. The initial disadvantage and subsequent change in employment rates is larger for more-skilled immigrants. Changes in observed measures of skill—experience measured by age, education, or language ability—do not explain the observed patterns. This finding points to lack of transferability of human capital being important during the initial years following migration.

In table 4.4, it was seen that the relative gain in employment rates of recent male immigrants increased between the 1970s and the 1980s. Much of this change is due to the lower initial employment rates of recent male immigrants in the 1980s and 1990s. For females, there was not relative gain during the decades of the 1960s or the 1970s. Though this paper has not provided an explanation for the change in pattern between the 1960s and 1980s, changes in immigration law that favored arrival with skills less transferable than earlier cohorts would be consistent with the main explanation for the pattern over the 1980s presented above.

4.7 Concluding Remark

One of the implications of this paper is that the nonrandom change in the composition of immigrant cohorts between census years may bias estimates of wage convergence for samples that consider only those with positive earnings.[20] Moreover, the recent debate over the possibility that entry earnings are correlated with earnings assimilation (Duleep and Regets 1996) may be the result of the changing composition of immigrant arrival cohorts.

Two pieces of evidence that may provide guidance for future research on this issue are seen from the 1980 question on employment status in 1975 and from reweighting the 1990 data to resemble the composition of 1980. First, though changes in the 1970–74 arrival cohort may not be representative of more recent arrivals because they did not start with a deficit in employment rates, the wage characteristics of those who were not working in 1975 but were working in 1980 can be compared to other earners. For both males and females, these persons have lower earnings than immigrants who worked in both 1975 and 1980.[21] Second, when the 1990 data is reweighted to match the age and education distribution within each arrival cohort in the 1980 data, the growth in earnings is reduced considerably for females but does not change much for males. Together, this initial evidence suggests that changes in the composition of the immigrant population with positive earnings may not bias estimates of earnings convergence for males, though it—along with other labor force participation issues—may be important for females.

20. Friedberg (1993) proposes similar concerns about the composition of immigrant arrival cohorts based on age of arrival.

21. Each of these calculations uses hourly earnings data from the census calculated as annual earnings divided by weeks worked in the previous year and usual hours worked. Those with hourly earnings calculated at less than $1 or greater than $200 in 1980 dollars ($1.66 and $332, respectively, in 1990) were excluded. The 1990 data were recoded so that the top limits match those in 1980. Real dollars were calculated using the consumer price index.

Appendix

Table 4A.1   **Labor Market Outcomes, 1980 and 1990**

| | A. Females | | | |
	Employment Week 1980	Employment Week 1990	Change	Change Relative to Natives
Natives	.613	.695	.082	
	(.001)	(.001)	(.001)	
Outlying areas	.382	.477	.095	.013
	(.004)	(.004)	(.006)	(.006)
1985–89[a]		.494		
		(.003)		
1980–84		.611		
		(.003)		
1975–79	.484	.651	.167	.085
	(.003)	(.003)	(.004)	(.004)
1970–74	.576	.648	.072	−.010
	(.003)	(.003)	(.004)	(.004)
1965–69	.594	.659	.065	−.017
	(.003)	(.003)	(.004)	(.004)
1960–64	.584	.648	.064	−.018
	(.003)	(.003)	(.004)	(.004)
1950–59	.583	.627	.044	−.038
	(.003)	(.003)	(.004)	(.004)
	Participation Week 1980	Participation Week 1990	Change	Change Relative to Natives
Natives	.647	.724	.077	
	(.001)	(.001)	(.001)	
Outlying areas	.429	.530	.101	.024
	(.004)	(.004)	(.006)	(.006)
1985–89		.560		
		(.003)		
1980–84		.669		
		(.003)		
1975–79	.532	.700	.168	.091
	(.003)	(.003)	(.004)	(.004)
1970–74	.624	.693	.069	−.008
	(.003)	(.003)	(.004)	(.004)
1965–69	.637	.702	.065	−.012
	(.003)	(.003)	(.004)	(.004)
1960–64	.622	.684	.062	−.015
	(.003)	(.003)	(.004)	(.004)
1950–59	.617	.657	.040	−.037
	(.003)	(.003)	(.004)	(.004)

	Employment Last Year 1980	Employment Last Year 1990	Change	Change Relative to Natives
Natives	.694	.756	.062	
	(.001)	(.001)	(.001)	
Outlying areas	.429	.529	.100	.038
	(.004)	(.004)	(.006)	(.006)
1985–89		.534		
		(.003)		
1980–84		.672		
		(.003)		
1975–79	.546	.711	.165	.103
	(.003)	(.003)	(.004)	(.004)
1970–74	.648	.708	.060	−.002
	(.003)	(.003)	(.004)	(.004)
1965–69	.660	.717	.057	−.005
	(.003)	(.003)	(.004)	(.004)
1960–64	.651	.706	.055	−.007
	(.003)	(.003)	(.004)	(.004)
1950–59	.648	.687	.0039	−.023
	(.003)	(.003)	(.004)	(.004)

	Usual Hours 1980	Usual Hours 1990	Change	Change Relative to Natives
Natives	35.642	36.989	1.347	
	(.023)	(.023)	(.033)	
Outlying areas	36.339	37.261	.922	−.425
	(.131)	(.121)	(.178)	(.181)
1985–89		38.363		
		(.115)		
1980–84		38.716		
		(.094)		
1975–79	37.427	38.736	1.312	−.035
	(.084)	(.088)	(.122)	(.126)
1970–74	37.410	38.371	1.309	−.038
	(.073)	(.083)	(.111)	(.116)
1965–69	36.604	37.941	1.337	−.010
	(.082)	(.088)	(.120)	(.124)
1960–64	35.904	37.611	1.707	.360
	(.098)	(.101)	(.141)	(.145)
1950–59	35.373	36.514	1.141	−.206
	(.087)	(.094)	(.128)	(.132)

(*continued*)

Table 4A.1   (continued)

	Weeks 1980	Weeks 1990	Change	Change Relative to Natives
Natives	41.752	44.598	2.846	
	(.030)	(.025)	(.039)	
Outlying areas	41.041	43.589	2.548	−.298
	(.190)	(.164)	(.251)	(.254)
1985–89		39.982		
		(.143)		
1980–84		43.503		
		(.104)		
1975–79	38.001	44.127	6.126	3.280
	(.121)	(.095)	(.154)	(.159)
1970–74	41.402	44.149	2.747	−.099
	(.103)	(.092)	(.138)	(.143)
1965–69	42.258	44.771	2.513	−.333
	(.105)	(.095)	(.142)	(.147)
1960–64	41.962	44.987	3.025	.179
	(.125)	(.106)	(.164)	(.169)
1950–59	42.241	44.759	2.518	−.328
	(.108)	(.099)	(.147)	(.152)

	Annual Hours 1980	Annual Hours 1990	Change	Change Relative to Natives
Natives	1,056.969	1,277.504	211.535	
	(1.610)	(1.659)	(2.312)	
Outlying areas	651.142	871.073	219.931	8.396
	(7.316)	(8.471)	(11.929)	(12.151)
1985–89		838.127		
		(6.593)		
1980–84		1,151.900		
		(6.405)		
1975–79	793.628	1,239.043	445.415	233.880
	(5.125)	(6.221)	(8.060)	(8.385)
1970–74	1,024.275	1,220.427	196.152	−15.383
	(5.413)	(5.899)	(8.006)	(8.333)
1965–69	1,045.795	1,241.422	195.627	−15.908
	(5.767)	(6.343)	(8.573)	(8.879)
1960–64	1,005.613	1,217.894	212.281	.746
	(6.589)	(7.127)	(9.706)	(9.978)
1950–59	995.912	1,147.982	152.070	−59.465
	(5.778)	(6.367)	(8.598)	(8.903)

Table 4A.1   (continued)

	B. Males			
	Employment Week 1980	Employment Week 1990	Change	Change Relative to Natives
Natives	.887	.857	−.030	
	(.001)	(.001)	(.001)	
Outlying areas	.774	.722	−.052	−.022
	(.004)	(.004)	(.006)	(.006)
1985–89		.789		
		(.003)		
1980–84		.851		
		(.002)		
1975–79	.783	.885	.102	.132
	(.002)	(.002)	(.003)	(.003)
1970–74	.885	.877	−.008	.022
	(.002)	(.002)	(.003)	(.003)
1965–69	.900	.872	−.028	.002
	(.002)	(.002)	(.003)	(.003)
1960–64	.906	.874	−.032	−.002
	(.002)	(.003)	(.004)	(.004)
1950–59	.902	.872	−.030	−.000
	(.002)	(.002)	(.004)	(.004)
	Participation Week 1980	Participation Week 1990	Change	Change Relative to Natives
Natives	.933	.896	−.037	
	(.001)	(.001)	(.001)	
Outlying areas	.847	.790	−.057	.020
	(.003)	(.004)	(.005)	(.005)
1985–89		.855		
		(.002)		
1980–84		.904		
		(.002)		
1975–79	.835	.934	.099	.136
	(.002)	(.002)	(.003)	(.003)
1970–74	.938	.931	−.007	.030
	(.001)	(.002)	(.002)	(.002)
1965–69	.946	.924	−.022	.015
	(.001)	(.002)	(.002)	(.002)
1960–64	.949	.919	−.030	.007
	(.002)	(.002)	(.003)	(.003)
1950–59	.943	.913	−.030	.007
	(.002)	(.002)	(.003)	(.003)

(*continued*)

Table 4A.1   (continued)

	Employment Last Year 1980	Employment Last Year 1990	Change	Change Relative to Natives
Natives	.942	.910	−.032	
	(.0004)	(.001)	(.001)	
Outlying areas	.824	.781	−.043	−.011
	(.003)	(.004)	(.005)	(.005)
1985–89		.815		
		(.003)		
1980–84		.899		
		(.002)		
1975–79	.823	.933	.110	.142
	(.002)	(.002)	(.003)	(.003)
1970–74	.937	.931	−.006	.026
	(.001)	(.002)	(.002)	(.002)
1965–69	.941	.924	−.017	.015
	(.002)	(.002)	(.003)	(.003)
1960–64	.947	.921	−.026	.006
	(.002)	(.002)	(.003)	(.003)
1950–59	.946	.918	−.028	.004
	(.002)	(.002)	(.003)	(.003)

	Usual Hours 1980	Usual Hours 1990	Change	Change Relative to Natives
Natives	43.546	44.454	.908	
	(.019)	(.020)	(.028)	
Outlying areas	40.400	41.819	1.419	.511
	(.099)	(.105)	(.144)	(.147)
1985–89		42.745		
		(.088)		
1980–84		43.286		
		(.078)		
1975–79	41.442	43.895	2.453	1.545
	(.067)	(.075)	(.101)	(.105)
1970–74	42.048	44.360	2.312	1.404
	(.067)	(.076)	(.101)	(.105)
1965–69	42.742	43.965	1.223	.315
	(.075)	(.083)	(.112)	(.115)
1960–64	43.040	44.256	1.216	.308
	(.088)	(.095)	(.129)	(.132)
1950–59	43.281	44.345	1.064	.156
	(.075)	(.082)	(.111)	(.114)

Table 4A.1 (continued)

	Weeks 1980	Weeks 1990	Change	Change Relative to Natives
Natives	47.886	48.018	.132	
	(.017)	(.018)	(.025)	
Outlying areas	46.170	46.434	.264	.132
	(.112)	(.121)	(.165)	(.167)
1985–89		42.854		
		(.102)		
1980–84		46.390		
		(.071)		
1975–79	42.763	46.937	4.174	4.042
	(.082)	(.067)	(.106)	(.109)
1970–74	46.504	46.911	.407	.275
	(.063)	(.066)	(.091)	(.094)
1965–69	47.300	47.249	−.051	−.183
	(.065)	(.075)	(.099)	(.102)
1960–64	47.688	47.600	−.088	−.220
	(.074)	(.082)	(.110)	(.113)
1950–59	47.876	47.975	.099	−.042
	(.063)	(.070)	(.094)	(.097)

	Annual Hours 1980	Annual Hours 1990	Change	Change Relative to Natives
Natives	1,979.644	1,958.240	−21.404	
	(1.408)	(1.582)	(2.118)	
Outlying areas	1,547.822	1,523.184	−24.638	−3.234
	(8.381)	(9.365)	(12.568)	(12.745)
1985–89		1,511.020		
		(6.848)		
1980–84		1,820.980		
		(5.765)		
1975–79	1,479.570	1,935.283	455.713	477.117
	(5.309)	(5.434)	(7.597)	(7.887)
1970–74	1,848.416	1,948.964	100.548	121.952
	(4.840)	(5.485)	(7.315)	(7.615)
1965–69	1,917.474	1,932.994	15.520	32.924
	(5.378)	(6.207)	(8.213)	(8.482)
1960–64	1,957.394	1,955.410	−2.064	19.340
	(6.232)	(7.132)	(9.470)	(9.704)
1950–59	1,972.413	1,969.215	−3.198	−18.206
	(5.384)	(6.340)	(8.318)	(8.583)

[a]Throughout the table, year ranges refer to immigrant arrival years.

Table 4A.2   Employment Rates Previous Week, Persons Aged 25–49 in 1980 (35–59 in 1990)

	Employment Week 1980	Employment Week 1990	Change	Change Relative to Natives
		A. Females		
Age 25–39 (35–49)				
Natives	.615	.737	.122	
	(.001)	(.001)	(.001)	
Outlying areas	.378	.520	.142	.020
	(.005)	(.005)	(.007)	(.007)
1985–89[a]		.525		
		(.004)		
1980–84		.631		
		(.003)		
1975–79	.481	.668	.187	.065
	(.003)	(.003)	(.004)	(.004)
1970–74	.561	.660	.099	−.023
	(.003)	(.003)	(.004)	(.004)
1965–69	.578	.680	.102	−.020
	(.004)	(.004)	(.006)	(.006)
1960–64	.584	.695	.111	−.011
	(.005)	(.005)	(.007)	(.007)
1950–59	.606	.715	.109	−.013
	(.004)	(.005)	(.006)	(.006)
Age 40–49 (50–59)				
Natives	.609	.599	−.010	
	(.002)	(.001)	(.002)	
Outlying areas	.390	.378	−.012	−.002
	(.007)	(.008)	(.011)	(.011)
1985–89		.389		
		(.007)		
1980–84		.529		
		(.007)		
1975–79	.495	.577	.082	.092
	(.006)	(.007)	(.009)	(.009)
1970–74	.632	.602	−.030	−.020
	(.006)	(.006)	(.008)	(.008)
1965–69	.627	.614	−.013	−.003
	(.005)	(.005)	(.007)	(.007)
1960–64	.585	.594	.009	.019
	(.005)	(.005)	(.007)	(.007)
1950–59	.562	.557	−.005	.005
	(.004)	(.004)	(.006)	(.006)
High school or less				
Natives	.555	.613	.058	
	(.001)	(.001)	(.001)	
Outlying areas	.337	.399	.062	.004
	(.004)	(.005)	(.006)	(.006)
1985–89		.458		
		(.004)		
1980–84		.550		
		(.004)		

Table 4A.2   (continued)

	Employment Week 1980	Employment Week 1990	Change	Change Relative to Natives
1975–79	.461	.574	.113	.055
	(.004)	(.004)	(.006)	(.006)
1970–74	.529	.566	.037	−.021
	(.003)	(.003)	(.004)	(.004)
1965–69	.541	.582	.041	−.017
	(.004)	(.004)	(.006)	(.006)
1960–64	.530	.567	.037	−.021
	(.004)	(.004)	(.006)	(.006)
1950–59	.527	.545	.018	−.040
	(.004)	(.004)	(.006)	(.006)
Some college or more				
Natives	.701	.782	.081	
	(.001)	(.001)	(.001)	
Outlying areas	.606	.734	.128	.047
	(.010)	(.009)	(.013)	(.013)
1985–89		.554		
		(.005)		
1980–84		.718		
		(.005)		
1975–79	.518	.764	.246	.165
	(.004)	(.004)	(.006)	(.006)
1970–74	.663	.779	.116	.035
	(.005)	(.004)	(.006)	(.007)
1965–69	.692	.777	.085	.004
	(.005)	(.005)	(.007)	(.007)
1960–64	.686	.762	.076	−.005
	(.006)	(.005)	(.008)	(.008)
1950–59	.687	.742	.055	−.026
	(.005)	(.005)	(.007)	(.007)
Europe				
White natives	.609	.697	.088	
	(.001)	(.001)	(.001)	
1985–89		.430		
		(.012)		
1980–84		.595		
		(.012)		
1975–79	.445	.659	.214	.136
	(.008)	(.010)	(.013)	(.013)
1970–74	.536	.620	.084	−.004
	(.007)	(.008)	(.011)	(.011)
1965–69	.558	.654	.096	.008
	(.006)	(.006)	(.008)	(.008)
1960–64	.567	.656	.089	.001
	(.006)	(.006)	(.008)	(.008)
1950–59	.581	.634	.053	−.025
	(.004)	(.004)	(.006)	(.006)

(*continued*)

Table 4A.2 (continued)

	Employment Week 1980	Employment Week 1990	Change	Change Relative to Natives
Eastern Europe/Former USSR				
White natives	.609	.697	.088	
	(.001)	(.001)	(.001)	
1985–89		.491		
		(.013)		
1980–84		.722		
		(.014)		
1975–79	.560	.760	.200	.122
	(.013)	(.014)	(.019)	(.019)
1970–74	.645	.691	.046	−.042
	(.018)	(.018)	(.025)	(.019
1965–69	.633	.723	.090	.002
	(.017)	(.017)	(.024)	(.024)
1960–64	.602	.707	.105	.017
	(.018)	(.018)	(.025)	(.025)
1950–59	.589	.626	.037	−.051
	(.012)	(.012)	(.017)	(.017)
Latin America/Caribbean				
Hispanic natives	.522	.579	.057	
	(.003)	(.002)	(.004)	
1985–89		.589		
		(.007)		
1980–84		.651		
		(.006)		
1975–79	.556	.689	.133	.076
	(.007)	(.007)	(.009)	(.010)
1970–74	.636	.680	.054	−.003
	(.006)	(.006)	(.008)	(.009)
1965–69	.651	.688	.037	−.020
	(.005)	(.006)	(.008)	(.009)
1960–64	.650	.701	.049	−.009
	(.007)	(.007)	(.009)	(.010)
1950–59	.643	.680	.047	−.010
	(.011)	(.011)	(.016)	(.016)
Mexico				
Hispanic natives	.522	.579	.057	
	(.003)	(.002)	(.004)	
1985–89		.387		
		(.009)		
1980–84		.454		
		(.008)		
1975–79	.387	.467	.080	.023
	(.007)	(.007)	(.009)	(.010)
1970–74	.437	.478	.041	−.016
	(.006)	(.006)	(.008)	(.008)
1965–69	.445	.494	.049	−.009
	(.008)	(.007)	(.011)	(.012)

Table 4A.2 (continued)

	Employment Week 1980	Employment Week 1990	Change	Change Relative to Natives
1960–64	.441	.485	.044	.013
	(.009)	(.009)	(.013)	(.014)
1950–59	.492	.504	.012	−.045
	(.008)	(.009)	(.012)	(.013)
Asia				
Asian natives	.633	.683	.050	
	(.005)	(.004)	(.006)	
1985–89		.493		
		(.005)		
1980–84		.630		
		(.005)		
1975–79	.501	.715	.214	.164
	(.005)	(.005)	(.007)	(.009)
1970–74	.650	.752	.102	.052
	(.005)	(.005)	(.007)	(.009)
1965–69	.677	.746	.069	.019
	(.007)	(.007)	(.010)	(.012)
1960–64	.678	.670	−.008	−.058
	(.010)	(.010)	(.014)	(.015)
1950–59	.651	.655	.004	−.046
	(.011)	(.010)	(.015)	(.016)
B. Males				
Age 25–39 (40–49)				
Natives	.885	.882	−.003	
	(.001)	(.001)	(.001)	
Outlying areas	.775	.745	−.030	−.027
	(.005)	(.005)	(.007)	(.007)
1985–89		.796		
		(.003)		
1980–84		.861		
		(.002)		
1975–79	.775	.895	.120	.123
	(.002)	(.002)	(.003)	(.003)
1970–74	.880	.887	.007	.010
	(.002)	(.002)	(.003)	(.003)
1965–69	.891	.879	−.012	−.009
	(.002)	(.003)	(.004)	(.004)
1960–64	.895	.893	−.002	.001
	(.003)	(.004)	(.005)	(.005)
1950–59	.889	.902	.003	.006
	(.003)	(.003)	(.004)	(.004)
Age 40–49 (50–59)				
Natives	.893	.800	−.093	
	(.001)	(.001)	(.001)	

(*continued*)

Table 4A.2 (continued)

	Employment Week 1980	Employment Week 1990	Change	Change Relative to Natives
Outlying areas	.770	.666	−.104	−.011
	(.007)	(.008)	(.011)	(.011)
1985–89		.711		
		(.006)		
1980–84		.807		
		(.005)		
1975–79	.815	.834	.019	.112
	(.005)	(.005)	(.007)	(.007)
1970–74	.905	.841	−.064	.029
	(.004)	(.004)	(.006)	(.006)
1965–69	.915	.858	−.057	.036
	(.003)	(.004)	(.005)	(.005)
1960–64	.919	.850	−.069	.024
	(.003)	(.004)	(.005)	(.005)
1950–59	.917	.838	−.079	.014
	(.003)	(.003)	(.004)	(.004)
High school or less				
Natives	.848	.787	−.061	
	(.001)	(.001)	(.001)	
Outlying areas	.754	.854	.100	.161
	(.004)	(.008)	(.009)	(.009)
1985–89		.755		
		(.004)		
1980–84		.807		
		(.003)		
1975–79	.816	.846	.030	.091
	(.003)	(.003)	(.004)	(.004)
1970–74	.877	.839	−.038	.023
	(.002)	(.003)	(.004)	(.004)
1965–69	.881	.825	−.056	.005
	(.003)	(.003)	(.004)	(.004)
1960–64	.883	.826	−.057	.004
	(.003)	(.004)	(.005)	(.005)
1950–59	.879	.813	−.066	−.005
	(.003)	(.003)	(.004)	(.004)
Some college or more				
Natives	.929	.915	−.014	
	(.001)	(.001)	(.001)	
Outlying areas	.860	.854	−.006	.008
	(.009)	(.008)	(.012)	(.012)
1985–89		.808		
		(.004)		
1980–84		.906		
		(.003)		
1975–79	.749	.927	.178	.192
	(.003)	(.003)	(.004)	(.004)
1970–74	.897	.929	.032	.046
	(.003)	(.003)	(.004)	(.004)

Table 4A.2 (continued)

	Employment Week 1980	Employment Week 1990	Change	Change Relative to Natives
1965–69	.925	.930	.005	.019
	(.003)	(.003)	(.004)	(.004)
1960–64	.934	.920	−.014	.000
	(.003)	(.004)	(.005)	(.005)
1950–59	.925	.922	−.003	.011
	(.003)	(.003)	(.004)	(.004)
Europe				
White natives	.904	.877	−.027	
	(.001)	(.001)	(.001)	
1985–89		.878		
		(.010)		
1980–84		.931		
		(.008)		
1975–79	.879	.914	.035	.062
	(.007)	(.006)	(.009)	(.009
1970–74	.903	.891	−.012	.015
	(.005)	(.06)	(.008)	(.008)
1965–69	.917	.895	−.022	.005
	(.004)	(.005)	(.006)	(.006)
1960–64	.922	.888	−.034	−.007
	(.004)	(.005)	(.006)	(.006)
1950–59	.915	.893	−.022	.005
	(.003)	(.004)	(.005)	(.005)
Eastern Europe/Former USSR				
White natives	.904	.877	−.027	
	(.001)	(.001)	(.001)	
1985–89		.669		
		(.010)		
1980–84		.902		
		(.010)		
1975–79	.813	.907	.094	.121
	(.010)	(.010)	(.014)	(.014)
1970–74	.903	.906	.003	.030
	(.011)	(.013)	(.017)	(.017)
1965–69	.928	.900	−.028	−.001
	(.011)	(.013)	(.017)	(.017)
1960–64	.909	.911	.002	.029
	(.011)	(.014)	(.018)	(.018)
1950–59	.919	.867	−.052	−.025
	(.007)	(.008)	(.011)	(.011)
Latin America/Caribbean				
Hispanic natives	.847	.813	−.034	
	(.002)	(.002)	(.003)	
1985–89		.795		
		(.006)		

(*continued*)

Table 4A.2 (continued)

	Employment Week 1980	Employment Week 1990	Change	Change Relative to Natives
1980–84		.837		
		(.004)		
1975–79	.785	.862	.077	.111
	(.006)	(.005)	(.008)	(.009)
1970–74	.881	.864	−.017	.017
	(.004)	(.004)	(.006)	(.007)
1965–69	.886	.856	−.030	.004
	(.004)	(.005)	(.006)	(.007)
1960–64	.911	.813	−.098	−.064
	(.004)	(.006)	(.007)	(.008)
1950–59	.901	.860	−.041	−.007
	(.007)	(.006)	(.009)	(.009)
Mexico				
Hispanic natives	.847	.813	−.034	
	(.002)	(.002)	(.003)	
1985–89		.805		
		(.007)		
1980–84		.846		
		(.006)		
1975–79	.845	.855	.010	.044
	(.005)	(.004)	(.006)	(.007)
1970–74	.877	.847	−.030	.004
	(.004)	(.004)	(.006)	(.007)
1965–69	.873	.829	−.044	−.010
	(.004)	(.005)	(.006)	(.007)
1960–64	.862	.813	−.049	−.015
	(.005)	(.006)	(.008)	(.009)
1950–59	.880	.814	−.066	−.032
	(.005)	(.006)	(.008)	(.009)
Asia				
Asian natives	.880	.877	−.003	
	(.003)	(.003)	(.004)	
1985–89		.769		
		(.005)		
1980–84		.846		
		(.004)		
1975–79	.754	.910	.156	.159
	(.004)	(.003)	(.005)	(.006)
1970–74	.922	.932	.010	.013
	(.004)	(.004)	(.006)	(.007)
1965–69	.947	.924	−.f023	−.020
	(.005)	(.005)	(.007)	(.008)
1960–64	.949	.930	−.019	−.016
	(.007)	(.007)	(.010)	(.011)
1950–59	.912	.908	−.004	−.001
	(.007)	(.008)	(.011)	(.012)

[a]Throughout the table, year ranges refer to immigrant arrival years.

Table 4A.3   **Employment Rates during Previous Week, 1960–80**

	1960 Age 25–49 (1)	1970 Age 35–59 (2)	1970 Age 25–49 (3)	1980 Age 35–59 (4)
A. Females				
Recent immigrants	.401	.456	.484	.603
	(.009)	(.008)	(.008)	(.003)
Previous immigrants	.385	.490	.449	.577
	(.005)	(.005)	(.008)	(.003)
United States				
Possessions	.378	.355	.321	.371
	(.012)	(.013)	(.010)	(.005)
Natives	.384	.493	.469	.568
	(.001)	(.010)	(.010)	(.010)
Europe				
Recent immigrants	.420	.425	.434	.562
	(.014)	(.014)	(.013)	(.007)
Previous immigrants	.382	.496	.411	.564
	(.007)	(.007)	(.012)	(.006)
Eastern Europe				
Recent immigrants	.540	.609	.542	.642
	(.031)	(.031)	(.040)	(.017)
Previous immigrants	.433	.508	.584	.602
	(.012)	(.014)	(.040)	(.016)
Mexico				
Recent immigrants	.308	.362	.306	.417
	(.036)	(.033)	(.028)	(.010)
Previous immigrants	.278	.338	.327	.412
	(.016)	(.019)	(.025)	(.010)
Latin America and Caribbean				
Recent immigrants	.542	.552	.619	.665
	(.030)	(.031)	(.015)	(.006)
Previous immigrants	.492	.567	.573	.643
	(.022)	(.024)	(.017)	(.007)
Asia				
Recent immigrants	.216	.458	.455	.670
	(.024)	(.032)	(.018)	(.008)
Previous immigrants	.348	.510	.426	.642
	(.021)	(.026)	(.024)	(.010)
B. Males				
Recent immigrants	.881	.922	.858	.905
	(.006)	(.006)	(.006)	(.002)
Previous immigrants	.916	.921	.917	.907
	(.003)	(.003)	(.005)	(.002)
United States				
Possessions	.802	.793	.808	.750
	(.010)	(.011)	(.009)	(.005)

(continued)

Table 4A.3 (continued)

	1960 Age 25–49 (1)	1970 Age 35–59 (2)	1970 Age 25–49 (3)	1980 Age 35–59 (4)
Natives	.886	.893	.893	.865
	(.001)	(.001)	(.001)	(.001)
Europe				
Recent immigrants	.912	.947	.899	.908
	(.009)	(.009)	(.008)	(.005)
Previous immigrants	.929	.930	.942	.921
	(.004)	(.005)	(.009)	(.005)
Eastern Europe				
Recent immigrants	.904	.933	.915	.920
	(.016)	(.017)	(.027)	(.012)
Previous immigrants	.918	.919	.907	.883
	(.007)	(.008)	(.029)	(.016)
Mexico				
Recent immigrants	.933	.888	.883	.864
	(.015)	(.023)	(.020)	(.008)
Previous immigrants	.890	.896	.907	.852
	(.010)	(.015)	(.020)	(.007)
Latin America and Caribbean				
Recent immigrants	.850	.926	.862	.899
	(.020)	(.024)	(.011)	(.004)
Previous immigrants	.885	.938	.929	.918
	(.016)	(.019)	(.013)	(.005)
Asia				
Recent immigrants	.689	.798	.774	.959
	(.024)	(.031)	(.016)	(.005)
Previous immigrants	.874	.915	.846	.958
	(.015)	(.017)	(.021)	(.007)

Note: Recent immigrant is defined as follows: column (1), immigrants that resided abroad five years ago; column (2), 1955–59 arrival cohort; column (3), 1965–69 arrival cohort; and column (4), 1965–69 arrival cohort.

Previous immigrant is defined as follows: columns (1) and (2), all immigrant arrivals before 1955; and columns (3) and (4), 1960–64 arrival cohort.

Table 4A.4   **Employment Rates of Males in Current Population Survey**

	1979	1983	1986	1989
Natives	.856	.816	.803	.808
	(.002)	(.003)	(.003)	(.003)
Pre-1960	.851	.837	.829	.789
	(.021)	(.025)	(.028)	(.028)
1960–64	.873	.781	.742	.790
	(.030)	(.031)	(.035)	(.033)
1965–69	.871	.856	.809	.791
	(.024)	(.028)	(.029)	(.030)
1970–74	.808	.784	.807	.827
	(.021)	(.023)	(.024)	(.026)
1975–79	.739	.744	.799	.795
	(.020)	(.026)	(.024)	(.027)
1980–84			.665	.775
			(.025)	(.026)
1985–89				.638
				(.029)
N (immigrants)	1,452	1,504	1,589	1,580
N (natives)	21,472	21,784	20,308	19,543

Note: Sample is males aged 25–49 in 1979, 29–53 in 1983, 32–56 in 1986, and 35–59 in 1989.

Table 4A.5   **Changes in Skill Level between Census Years (Proportion of Arrival Cohort)**

	Females		Males	
	1980	1990	1980	1990
Some college or more				
1975–79	.396	.405	.503	.479
	(.003)	(.003)	(.003)	(.003)
1970–74	.349	.381	.418	.424
	(.003)	(.003)	(.003)	(.003)
High school or more				
1975–79	.617	.651	.660	.677
	(.003)	(.003)	(.003)	(.003)
1970–74	.578	.641	.590	.622
	(.003)	(.003)	(.003)	(.003)
English very well, or only English				
1975–79	.358	.441	.379	.426
	(.003)	(.003)	(.003)	(.003)
1970–74	.421	.492	.433	.486
	(.003)	(.003)	(.003)	(.003)
English well				
1975–79	.242	.258	.271	.279
	(.002)	(.003)	(.002)	(.003)
1970–74	.262	.247	.293	.274
	(.002)	(.003)	(.003)	(.003)
English not well or not at all				
1975–79	.399	.301	.349	.259
	(.003)	(.003)	(.003)	(.003)
1970–74	.317	.261	.274	.240
	(.003)	(.003)	(.003)	(.003)

References

Baker, Michael, and Dwayne Benjamin. 1997. The role of family in immigrants' labor market activity: An evaluation of alternative explanations. *American Economic Review* 87 (4): 705–27.

Blau, Francine. 1992. The fertility of immigrant women: Evidence from high-fertility source countries. In *Immigration and the work force: Economic consequences for the United States and source areas,* ed. George Borjas and Richard Freeman, 93–133. Chicago: University of Chicago Press.

Borjas, George. 1994. The economics of immigration. *Journal of Economic Literature* 32:1667–717.

———. 1995. Assimilation and changes in cohort quality revisited: What happened to immigrant earnings in the 1980s? *Journal of Labor Economics* 13 (2): 201–45.

Duleep, Harriet Orcutt, and Mark Regets. 1996. The elusive concept of immigrant quality: Evidence from 1970–1990. Program for Research on Immigrant Policy, Urban Institute, Washington, D.C.

Duleep, Harriet Orcutt, and Seth Sanders. 1993. The decision to work by married immigrant women. *Industrial and Labor Relations Review* 46 (4): 677–90.

Friedberg, Rachel. 1993. The labor market assimilation of immigrants in the United States: The role of age of arrival. Brown University, Providence, R.I. Mimeograph.

Fry, Richard. 1996a. What explains the decline in relative employment of immigrants? U.S. Department of Labor, Washington, D.C.

———. 1996b. Has the quality of immigrants declined? Evidence from the labor market attachment of immigrants and natives. *Contemporary Economic Policy* 14 (3): 53–70.

Funkhouser, Edward. 1996. How much of immigrant wage assimilation is related to English language acquisition? University of California, Santa Barbara, Calif. Mimeograph.

Funkhouser, Edward, and Stephen Trejo. 1998. The labor market outcomes of female immigrants. In *The immigration debate: Studies on the economic, demographic, and fiscal effects of immigration,* ed. James Smith and Barry Edmonston, 239–88. Washington, D.C.: National Academy Press.

MacPherson, David, and James Stewart. 1989. The labor force participation and earnings profiles of married immigrant females. *Quarterly Review of Economics and Business* 29 (3): 57–72.

Schoeni, Robert. 1998. Labor market assimilation of immigrant women. *Industrial and Labor Relations Review* 51 (3): 483–504.

World Bank. 1990. *Social indicators of development 1990.* Baltimore, Md.: Johns Hopkins University Press.

The Changing Skill of New Immigrants to the United States
Recent Trends and Their Determinants

Guillermina Jasso, Mark R. Rosenzweig, and James P. Smith

5.1 Introduction

An important theme in recent research on immigration is the documentation of trends in the skills of immigrants to the United States compared to those of native-born Americans. While the original interest in that question centered on isolating the "true" life-cycle assimilation process from successive cross-sectional surveys such as the decennial censuses, more recently concern has been expressed that any decline in the relative labor market quality of immigrants is alarming in itself. Less studied has been the issue of the determinants of the changing skills of new U.S. immigrants. As in conventional models of migration, both the number and skill of immigrants to the United States are likely to be influenced by economic and social conditions in origin countries and in the destination country, the United States. However, U.S. immigration flows are also importantly affected by laws governing the number of immigrants who may be admitted and the criteria by which they are selected.

Because the standard sources of data that have been used to study the skill composition of U.S. immigrants, such as census data, do not distinguish among the foreign born by their legal status (legal, illegal, nonimmigrant), we do not know whether any resulting secular trends characterize legal or illegal immigrant flows alone or some unknown amalgam of the

Guillermina Jasso is professor of sociology at New York University. Mark R. Rosenzweig is professor of economics at the University of Pennsylvania. James P. Smith is a senior economist at RAND.

This research was supported in part by the National Institute of Child Health and Human Development, the National Science Foundation, and the Immigration and Naturalization Service under NIH grant no. HD33843. The authors are grateful to John M. Abowd, George J. Borjas, and the anonymous reviewers for useful comments and suggestions.

two. This distinction is important, as levels and trends in the "labor market quality" of legal immigrant flows are quite different from those of illegal immigrants. Proposals to reduce legal immigrant flows in response to concerns about declining immigrant quality could produce the opposite result by reducing high-labor-market-quality legal immigrants and encouraging additional low-labor-market-quality illegal immigrant flows. In addition, conventional surveys do not contain any information on admission criteria (visa type) so that little is known about how changes in U.S. immigration admission criteria have shaped or will shape the composition of legal immigrants. And over the past 25 years, U.S. immigration law has undergone substantial change.

Two fundamental features characterize U.S. immigration law in the period since 1921: First, the United States restricts the number of immigrants (restricting since 1921 the number from the Eastern Hemisphere, and since 1968 the number from the Western Hemisphere). Second, immediate relatives of U.S. citizens are exempt from numerical restriction.[1] Over the years, the United States has altered both the definition of immediate relatives of U.S. citizens (e.g., in 1952 extending to U.S. women citizens the right, already held by men, to sponsor the immigration of an alien spouse outside the numerical limitations) and the system for granting numerically limited visas (e.g., establishing a structure of preference categories in 1965 but not placing the Western Hemisphere under that structure until 1977).

These features of U.S. law combine with the overall attractiveness of the United States to produce a situation that can be described by two facts: (1) More persons would like to immigrate to the United States than current or foreseeable law permits; and (2) whenever the immigration law regime changes, there are winners and losers among the pool of visa applicants. In such a world, we would expect to observe shifts in the number and skill of immigrants, because changes in numerical ceilings within visa categories defining who may enter change the selectivity of the overall immigration regime. For example, the law extending the preference-category system of visa allocation to the Western Hemisphere should produce, mechanically, increases in the number of individuals admitted with preference-category visas, say, as principals in employment-based categories.[2] That same law, however, may induce shifts in the number and skill of

---

1. A few other classes of individuals are also exempt from numerical restriction, some as a permanent feature of U.S. law (e.g., American Indians born in Canada and children born abroad to alien residents), others under temporary provisions (e.g., spouses of IRCA-legalized aliens in the special three-year program in effect in 1992–94). Additionally, special legislation has permitted refugees previously admitted with temporary documents to adjust to permanent resident status outside the numerical limitations.

2. While some visa categories provide visas only for a single individual (e.g., for the spouse of a U.S. citizen or for the parent of a U.S. citizen), other visa categories provide visas for the qualifying immigrant plus his or her spouse and minor children (e.g., for the sibling of a

spouse immigrants, as persons who suddenly find themselves ineligible for a preference-category visa may come to find marriage to a U.S. citizen an attractive alternative.

The objective of this paper is to describe and understand the determinants of changes in the number and quality of new legal immigrants to the United States over the last 25 years. Our main interest is in understanding the behavioral response of potential immigrants to changes in the U.S. immigration law regime (as well as in the origin-country determinants of demand for immigration to the United States) and how these affect and have affected the skill composition of immigrants. By understanding how the composition of legal immigrant flows shifts in response to immigration law changes, particularly in numerically unrestricted immigration categories, a better understanding of the consequences of future immigration reforms may be attained. We assemble a new data set based on annual Immigration and Naturalization Service (INS) records of all new, legal immigrants over the period 1972–95. These data provide information on occupation for many of these immigrants as well as the criteria by which they were admitted. The data thus permit a new examination of the changing skill composition of legal immigrants as well as an investigation of how these changes were influenced by alterations in immigration law regimes and, with additional data, origin-country conditions.

Our principal analytical focus is on the behavior of persons who become immigrants as husbands of U.S. citizens.[3] We choose husband immigrants for three reasons: (1) immigrant spouses of U.S. citizens, being numerically unlimited, provide a clear signal of demand for immigration; (2) men present a more stable unit for studying skill in a period that saw substantial changes in women's labor force participation; and (3) spouse immigrants make up a substantial and growing proportion of all adult immigrants. Over the period we study, the average proportion of all male nonrefugee immigrants aged 21–65 who gained permanent residence by marrying a U.S. citizen was 31 percent, rising from 22 percent in 1972 to

---

U.S. citizen together with the sibling's spouse and minor children). In the latter case, the qualifying individual (i.e., the sibling) is known as the principal. Thus, in the employment-based categories, the principal is the individual who qualifies for the employment-based visa.

3. U.S. citizens who marry (and sponsor the immigration of) foreign-born persons include both native-born U.S. citizens as well as earlier immigrants who have naturalized. The United States has not recorded systematically the nativity of the U.S. citizens who sponsor immigrants; a special study carried out by the U.S. General Accounting Office (GAO) on the sponsors of immediate relatives who immigrated in 1985 indicates that approximately 80 percent of those sponsors of spouses are native-born U.S. citizens. The main source countries of spouses for U.S. citizens are Mexico, the Philippines, the United Kingdom, Canada, and West Germany. Patterns differ by gender, however. For example, although Mexico is the top source of mates for both men and women, the GAO estimates suggest that while Mexico provided almost 30 percent of husbands of U.S. citizens, it provided only about 15 percent of brides of U.S. citizens. Obviously, gender differences in both travel by U.S. citizens (including military service abroad) and U.S. sojourns by foreign-born persons account for the observed differences.

34.4 percent in 1994. The proportion has been as high as 42 percent, in 1986. Understanding the shifts in marital immigration thus provides a great deal of information on overall U.S. immigration. For comparison, and to assess our model, we also examine the number and skill composition of employment-based principal immigrants, a numerically limited category of immigrants that has always been a small proportion of overall immigration but has been increased in size in recent years.

Inspection of our new data indicates, consistent with information from the U.S. censuses and the Current Population Survey (CPS), that since the mid-1980s, the average skill of new, U.S. legal immigrants has been rising relative to that of the U.S. population. An econometric analysis of a panel of country-specific measures of the skill of immigrants based on these data over the period 1972–92 indicates that these changes are due in part to changes in immigration law and to the overall rise in the real purchasing power of countries outside the United States. Our estimates also indicate that changes in restrictions in any visa category have spillover effects on the skill composition of immigrants in other categories due to substitution by prospective immigrants across the immigration routes by which they achieve permanent residence in the United States. Among other results, we find, for example, that the restrictions on fraudulent immigration marriages, which dramatically reduced the number of marital immigrants, lowered the average skill level of immigrants entering via employment categories.

5.2 What Are the Trends in the Labor Market Skills of U.S. Immigrants?

In this section, we revisit the question of what has happened to the skill composition of U.S. immigrants over the past 25 years by providing some new evidence on the skills of legal immigrants for the years 1972–95. Whatever the factual trends in skills of immigrants, there remains an issue of to what extent the trends are determined by changes in the legal structure and rules governing U.S. immigration policy and to what extent trends reflect behavioral choices of immigrants and the U.S. population with whom they interact. We turn to this question in the next section.

The principal evidence on what has been happening to the skills of immigrants has been derived by many researchers from the 1970–90 decennial censuses. Based on this data source, a close to universal consensus has been reached: The labor market skills of new recent immigrants has been declining significantly relative to skills of the native born. For example, the recent National Academy report indicates that the education deficit of recent male immigrants compared to the native born grew from .3 of a year in 1970 to 1.4 years by 1990. Similarly, the new male immigrant wage gap expanded from 17 to 32 percent as measured in the 1970 and 1990 censuses.[4] Similar trends exist for female immigrants.

There are a number of problems with relying solely on decennial census or CPS data to make claims about trends in the characteristics of recent immigrants. First, the samples on which conclusions are drawn may be neither *recent* nor *immigrant*. As is well know, it is not clear whether respondents, in answering the standard question about time since immigration, are referring to their first, last, or most salient time of entry to the United States. Well-intentioned attempts to clarify the meaning of this question may further distort its usefulness for tracking secular trends. It is also well known that some—and perhaps many—sampled respondents in the census or CPS are not new legal immigrants. Demographic studies have shown not only that some fraction of illegal immigrants participate in these surveys but also that those more correctly characterized as nonimmigrants are included in the analytical category "recent immigrants." Since nonimmigrants and illegal immigrants have, on average, relatively short stays in the United States, they are especially numerous among "recent immigrants." This problem is quantitatively important. For example, a recent study estimated that only 52 percent of those who reported that they immigrated since 1990 in the 1995 and 1996 CPSs were legal immigrants (Passel 1999). The rest were either nonimmigrants (10 percent) or illegal immigrants (38 percent). Because there is great additional uncertainty about secular trends in the numbers of such people who appear in our mainstream surveys, our ability to draw unambiguous conclusions is weakened.

There is another, less often mentioned problem with this reliance on census data for this question. The 10-year periodicity between surveys means that the calendar years that end in nine are given enormous weight in our conclusions. If these years are for some reason atypical, we are on treacherous ground indeed. But more importantly, we may well be pointing in the wrong direction about trends in the skills of immigrants by knowing nothing about within-decennial-census trends.

Because of these problems, we take a different approach in this paper to addressing the relative skills of immigrants issue by relying instead on yearly INS data about new "green card" recipients in that year. This data source, described below, has a number of distinct advantages as well as some disadvantages for this question. First, sampling issues do not arise since, with a few exceptions that are noted elsewhere in this paper, these files contain all new green card recipients.[5] Second, unlike the census or

---

4. See Smith and Edmonston (1997).

5. Formally, the INS data for a specified fiscal year cover persons admitted to legal permanent residence during that year; the green card (the "paper" evidence of legal permanent residence) is mailed to the new immigrant a few weeks after admission to permanent residence.

CPS, the population studied is well defined. In these data, new immigrants are defined as that year's new green card recipients. By definition, all such new immigrants are legal immigrants. Third, we also know the visa category under which the new immigrant was admitted. This critical information, unavailable in household surveys, allows us to separate out groups of immigrants by the admission criteria they satisfied. Numerical limits on visa types are one of the most important policy tools in setting immigration policy. Finally, INS data contain new immigrants for all years so that we are not at the mercy of survey-based time intervals.[6]

There is an important disadvantage to the INS data as well. The information available, especially relating to the skills of immigrants, is quite limited. For example, there exist no data on either education or income, the mainstays of economic analyses on this issue. The principal information pertinent to the skill issue is the new immigrant's occupation. Moreover, compared to the detail available in standard household surveys, INS occupation categories are highly aggregated, and a significant proportion of immigrants do not report their occupation. As do the census and CPS, INS occupation categories also undergo periodic revision. Nonetheless, in our view, the advantages of the INS surveys outweigh the disadvantages, especially if the INS data are viewed as a useful complement to standard household surveys.

To construct an index of skill, we first mapped all of the occupational codes in the INS files to a common set of 25 occupational categories, which have been used by the INS starting in 1983.[7] We also mapped the 1970, 1980, and 1990 census occupation codes into these 25 occupational categories. The temporal comparability of this mapping is not exact, an issue to which we return below. Based on the 1980 Public Use Census 1/1000 sample, we obtained the average earnings of all native-born men aged 21–65 working at least 35 hours in a "typical" week and at least 50 weeks in 1979 for each of the 25 occupational categories. These earnings were then assigned to respondents according to which of the 25 occupations they reported. An advantage of our fixed price index for evaluating skills is that any trends indicated by this measure will not be sensitive to the changing prices of skills—a very salient labor market reality during the period from 1970 through the 1990s.

6. The advantages of INS data for studying legal immigrants have not gone wholly unnoticed. Earlier studies of immigrant skills using INS data include Jasso and Rosenzweig (1986, 1988, 1995), Barrett (1996), and Duleep and Regets (1996).

7. The 24-year series of immigrant cohort data available in microfiles from the INS comprises cohorts in which occupation is measured in three distict ways: In fiscal years 1972 and 1973, INS coded occupation using the U.S. 1960 census detailed occupational classification; in fiscal years 1974–82, INS coded occupation using the U.S. 1970 census detailed occupational classification; and since fiscal year 1983, INS has coded occupation using a 25-category classification based on the U.S. 1980 census detailed occupational classification.

Table 5.1   **Average Occupation Income, 1970–90 U.S. Censuses (Recent Immigrants)**

Years of Experience	1970	1980	1990
1–5	19,899	19,002	18,485
1–3	n.a.	n.a.	18,714
4–5	n.a.	n.a.	18,172

5.2.1   Occupational Earnings of the Foreign Born in the 1970–90 Censuses

We first apply the occupational earnings methodology to the decennial census samples of recent male immigrants—those with 1–5 years of immigrant experience. Table 5.1 lists our occupation-imputed average incomes of recent census male immigrants. This series is consistent with our earlier summary of census-based trends. Based on our derived occupation-based income, there was a steady fall in the incomes of new "immigrants." Across the full 20-year span, the income decline was 7.1 percent. This is quite comparable to a decline of 11.9 percent in recent immigrant hourly wages (measured directly in the census files) between 1970 and 1990.[8] This comparability may be especially close since the direct wage measures include the impact of the spreading out in the price of skill.

Additional evidence that our occupation-income series may reasonably characterize time-series trends is contained in table 5.2, which lists average occupation incomes by major region of residence. The first panel in this table documents the changing composition of recent immigrants, at least as revealed in the decennial censuses. The proportion of census-defined recent immigrants of Mexican origin increased significantly (especially between 1970 and 1980) as did immigrants from other North American countries (especially between 1980 and 1990).[9] Europe was the principal region of decline as the fraction of new immigrants who were from European countries fell from 32 percent (1970) to 12 percent (1990). Throughout the entire period, Asians represented a significant fraction of new immigrants.

Not surprisingly, occupation incomes of Mexican-origin immigrants stand out as being particularly low. The rising fraction of immigrants from Mexico over this period indicates that there were nontrivial composition effects in the immigrant pool, an observation that must always be taken into account when describing trends. There were also strong within-region trends in occupation incomes (downward) in the other North American and Asian regions that largely reflect the changing composition of immigration within these regions.

8. See Smith and Edmonston (1997), table 5.2.
9. The principal source of other North American population growth was immigrants from Central America and the Caribbean.

Table 5.2   **Descriptive Statistics, 1970–90 U.S. Censuses (Recent Immigrants)**

Country of Birth	1970	1980	1990
Percent of population			
Mexico	29.6	36.7	37.3
Other North America	5.2	5.0	11.4
South America	7.2	5.2	6.2
Europe	31.8	11.8	11.5
Asia	23.2	36.2	29.7
Africa	1.3	4.0	3.2
Oceania	1.6	0.1	0.7
Average occupation income ($)			
Mexico	17,734	17,187	16,804
Other North America	21,862	19,694	17,843
South America	19,517	19,481	18,361
Europe	19,358	20,282	20,393
Asia	23,290	20,151	20,098
Africa	21,970	21,080	19,959
Oceania	20,264	19,590	20,336
Average education (years)			
Mexico	8.88	8.75	9.26
Other North America	13.06	11.65	10.25
South America	12.05	13.10	12.45
Europe	10.81	12.95	13.93
Asia	14.69	13.80	13.71
Africa	14.52	15.42	14.20
Oceania	9.95	13.64	13.83
All	11.38	11.77	11.62

However, some hint that not all may be so clear and neat is contained in the 1990 column of table 5.1, which separates recent immigrants into the very recent (1–3 years) and the not quite so recent (4–5 years).[10] In that year, more-recent immigrants actually have higher occupation-based incomes than those who reported that they arrived during 1986 and 1985. While this disparity could reflect a rapid and already completed selective out-migration of the more skilled among the original cohort of 1986 and 1985 immigrants, it could also signal some within-period reversal of trend. Although census data cannot resolve this issue, the INS immigrant files are ideally suited for the task.

5.2.2   Occupational Earnings of New Legal Immigrants and the U.S. Population, 1972–95

To assess how the skills of legal immigrants have changed on an annual basis over the period, we use all of the available public use files containing official administrative microdata on persons admitted to legal permanent

---

10. This breakdown is not possible in the 1970 and 1980 censuses.

residence in fiscal years 1972–95 (U.S. Department of Justice 1997).[11] The population covered by the data sets consists of all persons admitted to permanent residence during the fiscal year, including both new arrivals in the United States and persons adjusting their status to permanent residence from some other legal temporary or illegal status, except persons who became permanent residents through the two Immigration Reform and Control Act (IRCA) legalization programs (section 245(a) and special agricultural worker [SAW]).[12] The data sets include information on the immigrant's age, sex, country of birth, visa class, and occupation—the single indicator of skill. For 2 of the 24 years covered by the public use files (fiscal years 1980 and 1981), a subset of the records is missing information on some variables, of which sex and occupation are pertinent to our analysis.[13]

For all years between 1972 and 1995, all new immigrant men aged 21–65 in the INS files were assigned an income based on their reported occupation and 1980 census mean incomes in these occupation cells. To detect trends in relative skills of new immigrants, it is necessary to have a comparison group in each year. The 1972–95 March CPS files were used to obtain this comparison group. From these files, a sample of men aged 21–65 years old were selected and each was assigned an occupation-based income using the same occupation groupings as in the INS.[14]

The occupational earnings for all new immigrants and all CPS men aged 21–65 are presented in figure 5.1A. The CPS income series is straightforward to describe. With the exception of a discrete downward jump in the series between 1982 and 1983, the trend consists of a small but steady rise in CPS male occupation incomes. The timing of the jump is also easy to explain—between 1982 and 1983, CPS switched from the 1970 to the 1980 census occupation coding system. This change represented one of the largest revisions ever undertaken by the census in their occupational coding. While we have attempted to make the coding systems as comparable as possible, strict comparability is simply not attainable.[15] This noncompa-

11. Until 1976, the fiscal year started on 1 July of the preceding year and ended on 30 June; starting in 1977, the fiscal year runs from 1 October of the preceding year to 30 September.

12. INS public use immigrant data files exclude IRCA-legalized persons. IRCA-based adjustments to permanent resident status started in fiscal year 1989, peaked in fiscal year 1991 (over 1 million), and continue at a trickle (e.g., 4,267 in fiscal year 1995). Total IRCA-based adjustments to permanent residence, through fiscal year 1996, number 2,684,892, of whom 59 percent are section 245(a) cases (U.S. Immigration and Naturalization Service 1996).

13. Approximately one-fifth of the records have missing data. For example, among immigrants aged 21–65 admitted with spouse-of-citizen visas, information on sex and occupation is missing for 17.4 percent in fiscal year 1980 and 22.8 percent in fiscal year 1981. In addition, one-third of the records are missing for fiscal year 1988 (see n. 28).

14. Nativity is not available for most of the CPS years. While it is unlikely that the aggregate trends would be affected by the inclusion of immigrants in the CPS files, we also computed a series for non-Hispanic men (a variable that is available in all CPS years). Although the level of the income series for non-Hispanic men is somewhat higher, the time-series trend is identical to that described in the text for all CPS men.

15. For details of the changes, see U.S. Department of Commerce (1989).

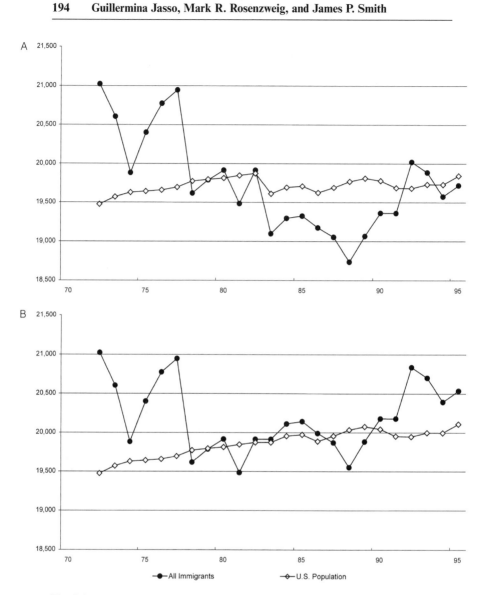

Fig. 5.1   Average occupational income of men 21–65, by year, for U.S. natives and all immigrants: *A*, **actual;** *B*, **revised**

rability produces about a $250 downward shift in the CPS series between 1982 and 1983 and will lead to discrete shifts in the INS income series as well. Putting aside this complication, we see that incomes of the all-male comparison group rise very slowly across these two decades.

This stability in the CPS series stands in sharp contrast to the volatility in the INS income trends for all immigrants. While the INS and CPS income series start out about the same,[16] the INS immigrant series is far less stable and undergoes a pronounced downward shift between 1977 and the mid-1980s.[17] Beginning in the late 1980s, however, the trend reverses and the 1990s witness rising occupation-based incomes of immigrants both absolute and relative to the U.S. male working population. Instead of declining relative quality of immigrants, the decade of the 1990s is more correctly described as one of rising relative immigrant quality. These trends in the earnings of new immigrants do not appear to be sensitive to the choice of census year used to construct the occupational earnings index. Figure 5A.1 in the appendix depicts the occupational earnings of the new immigrants using both the index based on the 1980 census and an alternate index based on the 1990 census. Both series show the downward shift as well as the trend reversal, with the movements slightly more pronounced in the 1990-based series. Either of the two INS occupation income series also demonstrates that the two census years within its time span—1979 and 1989—provide a decidedly unrepresentative portrait of secular trends. The census and INS data do not conflict in their description using these two years—both show a dramatic quality decline. But these years clearly maximize the decline and obviously miss the subsequent recovery.

It has been well documented that even recent immigrants are a very heterogeneous population across many dimensions—income, schooling, and country of origin, to name just a few. A less appreciated—but perhaps more fundamental—manner in which immigrants differ involves the visa categories under which they are admitted. Even if we ignore the impact of trends in illegal immigrants that confound most household surveys, trends in the numbers and characteristics of legal immigrants are an uncertain amalgam of a set of diverse but specific immigration visa categories and the rules and behaviors that are associated with them. The type and number of new immigrants admitted in any year reflect policy decisions about such disparate subjects as refugees, diversity immigrants, family reunification, and needed "skills." Trends in the types of immigrants admitted within these quite disparate categories may reinforce each other during some time periods but counteract each other at other times. Understanding what drives the aggregate trends requires understanding the important subcategories that make up the yearly totals.

The heterogeneity of the categories can be most simply illustrated by subtracting from our aggregate time-series immigrant trend a single category of immigrants—refugees and asylees. Decisions about the number and types of refugees and asylees admitted are mostly not economic, but

---

16. The fact that the series for immigrants and all men are closer than census data would suggest may partly reflect the exclusion of illegal immigrants from the INS data.

17. Note the downward jump in the INS series between 1982 and 1983, a consequence once again of the shift in occupation coding.

a reaction instead to political crises elsewhere and our sense of responsibility to the affected groups. The influx of Vietnamese immigrants after the end of the Vietnam War and Russian immigrants with the collapse of the Soviet Union are but two of the more prominent recent examples. No doubt, other crises will develop in the future in some part of the world and some new mix of refugees will arrive. Consequently, trends in the numbers and "quality" of refugee immigrants are quite episodic in nature and do not reflect long-run trends in nonrefugee U.S. immigration policy, the primary focus of our paper. For this reason, figure 5.2 plots income trends for nonrefugee immigrants.

The occupation income series for nonrefugee immigrants in figure 5.2A differs from that depicted in figure 5.1A in that immigrant incomes are higher and thus immigrant incomes now exceed those obtained in the CPS by even more. This reflects the fact that, on average, refugees are relatively low-skilled and low-income immigrants. They are certainly not typical of the combined family- and employment-based immigrants. In this revised series, there are some sharp year-to-year swings during the mid- to late 1970s, with a particularly sharp drop between 1977 and 1978. Nonetheless, this revised series that excludes refugees also indicates a rise in the "quality" of new immigrants during the 1990s.

Figures 5.1A and 5.2A actually overstate the differences between the labor market quality of native born and immigrant workers. As mentioned above, there is a downward jump in these series beginning in 1982 that is solely due to changes in census occupational coding. One method of eliminating this problem is to force the 1982 incomes to be equal to those in 1983 for both immigrants and native-born workers alike. With these adjusted figures (figs. 5.1B and 5.2B), the quality of legal male immigrants appears to be either equal to or above that of native-born male workers for most of the last 25 years. This is especially so if the very special case of refugees are taken out of the comparison, as in figure 5.2. Legal immigrant labor market quality may have been declining during the 1970s and early 1980s, but this decline started when the labor market quality of legal immigrants was most likely above that of native-born workers. At no point during this period of decline did the labor market quality of male immigrants dip significantly and persistently below that of native-born workers.

5.2.3   Occupational Earnings of Recent Immigrants in the Current Population Survey, 1994–97

Some confirmation of the recent trends documented in the INS surveys about the rising quality of immigrants can be obtained from the March CPS files for the years 1994–97. Starting in 1994, the Current Population Surveys incorporated a number of changes that made these surveys much more useful for immigrant research. In particular, questions were added concerning immigrant status and the number of years since immigration.

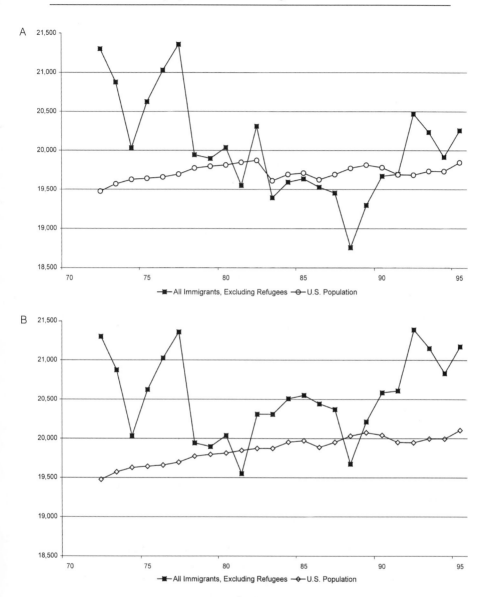

Fig. 5.2   Average occupational income of men 21–65, by year, for U.S. natives and immigrants excluding refugees: *A*, actual; *B*, revised

While containing much smaller sample sizes than the decennial census files, these recent CPS innovations make that data much more useful. Table 5.3 lists occupation-based incomes for recent male immigrants aged 21–65 in these four CPS years. These occupation-based incomes were based on the same categories (and 1980 mean incomes) used to predict incomes in the decennial census and INS files. Consistent with the trends

Table 5.3   Average Occupation Income, 1994–97 CPS (Recent Immigrants)

Years since Immigration	CPS Year			
	1994	1995	1996	1997
All	18,467	18,661	18,751	19,028
1994–current	n.a.	n.a.	19,375	19,156
1992–93	n.a.	n.a.	18,634	18,832
1992–current	18,740	18,853	n.a.	
1990–91	18,608	18,408	18,307	
1988–89	18,168			
N	1,096	845	807	739

in INS data, male immigrant incomes (and hence their quality) rose steadily from 1994 to 1997.

Supporting evidence for the rising quality of recent immigrants is also obtained from the fact that more-recent immigrants in any cross section have higher incomes than those who arrived a few years earlier. It turns out that while for most of the last decade economists have been highlighting the issue of the declining quality of recent immigrants, the quality of new male immigrants has actually been rising.[18]

5.3   U.S. Immigration Law Regimes

To understand the trends and changes in the numbers and skills of new immigrants in the period 1972–95, it is necessary to also understand the features of and changes in U.S. immigration laws. This period lies in the era of worldwide numerical restriction, four years having passed since the Western Hemisphere was brought under the restriction umbrella. For the whole of this period, immigrant visas were allocated under the two-pronged system consisting of numerically unlimited visas for the immediate relatives of U.S. citizens (defined as the spouses, minor children, and parents of adult U.S. citizens) and numerically limited visas for other prospective immigrants. Rules for allocating numerically limited visas, however, changed during the period, as did rules for spouse immigrants; and other legislation produced additional alterations in the law regime. In this section, we briefly describe the major regime changes during the period.

5.3.1   Regime Changes in Allocation of Numerically Restricted Visas

At the start of the period, in 1972, the ceilings on numerically restricted visas were 170,000 for natives of the Eastern Hemisphere (EH) and 120,000 for natives of the Western Hemisphere (WH); and numerically

18. Additional evidence that immigrant skills have turned upward is found in Funkhouser and Trejo (1995) and Barrett (1996).

restricted visas were allocated in two distinct ways, according to hemisphere of origin. For natives of EH countries, the law prescribed a system of preference categories, with country ceilings; the preference categories included four family-based categories, two employment-based categories, a refugee category, and a nonpreference (or residual) category. Each independent country had a 20,000 annual limit. For natives of the Western Hemisphere, there were no country ceilings, and visas were allocated on a first-come, first-served basis, with some employment or asset screening.

Legislation enacted in 1976, effective in 1977, extended the preference-category system and country ceilings to the Western Hemisphere. Initially, each hemisphere retained its own separate ceiling (170,000 for the Eastern Hemisphere and 120,000 for the Western). Legislation enacted in 1978, however, brought both hemispheres under a single worldwide numerical ceiling of 290,000 (exclusive of immediate relatives, refugees, and other special immigrants), effective in fiscal year 1979. Subsequently, the Refugee Act of 1980 removed refugees from the preference-category system and reduced the worldwide ceiling to 270,000, effective in 1981 (with a transition ceiling of 280,000 in fiscal year 1980).

The two employment categories under the 1965–90 preference-category system were the third preference category, designated for "members of the professions of exceptional ability," and the sixth preference category, designated for "workers in skilled or unskilled occupations in which laborers are in short supply in the United States," plus, in both cases, the principals' spouses and minor children. The maximum number of visas allocated to each category was 10 percent of the overall ceiling. Thus, in the years before the worldwide ceiling was established, the ceilings for all occupation-based visas were 34,000 in the Eastern Hemisphere (a continuation of their existing limit) and 24,000 in the Western Hemisphere. In 1979, the worldwide ceiling for these visas was the combined total of 58,000, and in 1981 it was reduced to 54,000 (20 percent of the new worldwide ceiling of 270,000).

The preference-category system itself was radically restructured again by the Immigration Act of 1990, effective in October 1991. Especially relevant to the analysis in this paper was a triple shift in employment-based visas. First, the total number of employment-based visas available to qualified persons plus their accompanying family members was increased from 54,000 under the old law to 120,120—more than a twofold increase.[19] Second, employment-based visas were made available to multinational execu-

19. Under the 1990 act, the number of employment-based visas is 140,000; of this number, however, only 120,120 are for the first three employment preferences, which are the categories corresponding to the old system's employment preference categories. The fourth and fifth employment preference categories in the new law cover a subset of the special immigrant class, which was numerically unlimited in the old law, plus several new classes (U.S. Department of State 1992, appendix F).

tives. Third, the maximum number of employment-based visas available to unskilled principals plus accompanying family members was reduced from 27,000 to 10,00—a 63 percent reduction.[20]

Of the changes within each preference-category system, one is pertinent to an analysis of skill levels, and that is the legislative provision that severely restricted the granting of employment-based visas to foreign physicians. Under the provisions of the Act of 12 October 1976, effective 10 January 1977, physicians are now required to have passed parts I and II of the National Board of Medical Examiners examination as a condition of eligibility for an employment-based visa.[21]

5.3.2 Regime Changes in Allocation of Numerically Unrestricted Visas to Spouses of U.S. Citizens

For the entire period under study, U.S. citizens (of both sexes) were entitled to sponsor the immigration of their foreign spouses outside the numerical limitations. The steep increase in the number of immigrants admitted as spouses of U.S. citizens (hereafter simply "spouse immigrants")—from 25,000 in 1965 to 55,620 in 1975 and 124,093 in 1985—coupled with a suspicion that at least a portion of spouse-immigrant cases were the result of fraudulent marriages, led to enactment of the Immigration Marriage Fraud Amendments in 1986. The 1986 amendments stipulate that spouse immigrants married less than two years receive a conditional visa; to remove the conditional status, such immigrants must apply to the U.S. Immigration and Naturalization Service in the 90-day period preceding the second anniversary of their having been admitted to conditional immigrant status.

5.3.3 Other Changes in the Immigration Law Regime

At the start of the period under study, persons who had lived illegally in the United States since 1948 could petition for adjustment to permanent resident status under the so-called registry provision. During the decade of the 1970s, concern increased that there was a large and growing population of illegal aliens. The Immigration Reform and Control Act (IRCA), enacted in 1986, updated the registry date to 1972 and provided two major legalization programs: (1) a two-phase legalization program for persons who had resided continuously in the United States since before 1982 in an

20. The old law's sixth preference category allowed 27,000 visas to both skilled and unskilled workers in short supply (and accompanying family members). Under the new law, the unskilled portion is allowed 10,000. Thus, under the old law, the maximum number of visas for unskilled workers would be 27,000, in the case where no skilled workers applied.

21. See Jasso and Rosenzweig (1995) for a description of pertinent provisions of the 1976 legislation as well as follow-up legislation, which exempts from the examination requirement physicians who were already practicing in the United States in a nonimmigrant status as of January 1978.

illegal status (the section 245(a) legalizations); and (2) a legalization program for two groups of special agricultural workers (SAWs) who had worked in U.S. agriculture for specified durations in the years 1984–86.[22] The application periods for the two legalization programs were from May 1987 to May 1988 for the pre-1982 applicants and from June 1987 to November 1988 for the SAW applicants (though there were late filings).

During the legalization application period and in its aftermath, two things came to be widely believed: (1) that only a fraction of section 245(a)-eligible aliens came forward, either for fear of the authorities or through inability to pay the processing fees; and (2) that only a fraction of the SAW-legalized aliens had actually worked in agriculture. Evidence in support of the first notion includes the large number of petitions filed by legalized aliens, after adjusting to permanent resident status, to sponsor their spouses and children.[23] As for the second notion, evidence from the National Agricultural Worker Surveys, which have failed to find sufficient SAW-legalized individuals currently working in agriculture, suggests that SAW-legalized persons have left agriculture, if not the United States (Mines, Gabbard, and Steirman 1997).

There were two other changes in the immigration law regime pertinent to analyses of spouse immigrants. First, IRCA-legalized aliens started becoming eligible to naturalize in 1994. Thus, spouses and minor children currently in the numerically limited family second preference visa backlogs would shift to spouses and children of U.S. citizens, introducing to the spouse-of-citizen flow a new segment, starting in fiscal year 1995. Second, the 1990 act instituted more stringent provisions on sponsorship of immigrants, and these became a contractual obligation in 1996, under provisions of the Personal Responsibility and Work Opportunity Reconciliation Act of 1996 and the Illegal Immigration Reform and Immigrant Responsibility Act of 1996.

Finally, there were two major changes in the rules by which foreign-born persons who are eligible for permanent residence and who are already in the United States may adjust their visa status. First, the same law that extended the preference-category system to the Western Hemisphere in 1977 also extended to WH immigrants the right to adjust status in the United States (without returning to their origin country first). Second, legislation enacted in 1995 made it possible for persons eligible for permanent residence but living illegally in the United States to also adjust their status without leaving the country (with payment of a penalty fee).

---

22. For simplicity, the section 245(a) cases will be referred to as "pre-1982" cases.

23. The surge in applications led to enlarged visa backlogs in the family second preference category (which covers the spouses and minor children of permanent resident aliens) and to special legislation desgined to provide relief, such as the three-year legalization dependents transition program and the provision to exempt a portion of them from the country ceiling.

5.4   Immigration Law Regimes and Individual Behavior

In this section we describe the expected effects of the major changes in the immigration law regimes that have occurred in the past 25 years on spouse immigrants and, for contrast, on employment-immigrant principals. To understand the strategic behavior of immigrants, these two immigrant categories stand out. For the vast majority of the world's population who are not candidates for admission to America, because they do not have an existing relative there, these are the only two legal ways to obtain permanent residence. In general, there are both direct and indirect effects of law changes on immigration flows. The direction of direct effects is evident from the provision of law. The direction of indirect effects, however, depends on behavioral responses to the new regime and, in the case of effects on average skill, on differences in the skill configuration between particular pools of prospective immigrants.

Our discussion of how immigration law changes may affect the skill composition of immigrants is based on a few simple assumptions. To illustrate, let there be two categories of legal immigrants (the unrestricted group of spouses of U.S. citizens, N_s, and the numerically restricted employment immigrants, N_e, and one group of illegal immigrants (N_i).[24] The total number of legal immigrants in any year is $N_e + N_s = T_{\text{legal}}$, while the total number of immigrants equals $N_e + N_s + N_i = $ Total. Using S to index the average skill of a given type of immigrant, the average skill of all immigrants can be expressed as a weighted average of the skill of the within-group categories:

$$(1) \qquad S_{\text{legal}} = (N_e/T_{\text{legal}})S_e + (N_s/T_{\text{legal}})S_s$$

for average skill of legal immigrants;

$$(2) \qquad S_{\text{total}} = (N_e/\text{Total})S_e + (N_s/\text{Total})S_s + (N_i/\text{Total})S_i$$

for average skill of all immigrants.

To give some content to these expressions, we assume first that $S_e > S_s > S_i$. This ordering follows because the employment visa categories that screen for skills have a more stringent labor-market-skill threshold than does the spouse category, which in turn has more stringent skill screening than does immigration without any visa (illegal immigration). A prospective immigrant without relatives (siblings, parents, adult children) in the United States faces less-stringent employment skill screening by prospective U.S. mates than via the employment visa route to immigration because, for example, charm, looks, and cooking skills may be less rewarded in the labor market than in the marriage market and can make up for

---

24. This example easily generalizes when there are many visa categories.

deficient earning abilities. Thus, finding a job match that provides a visa is more costly compared with finding a marital match, the lower the prospective immigrant's skill level.

Secondly, we assume that within policy regimes the number of employment visas (N_e) are fixed, while the number of spouse and illegal immigrant flows are free. Prospective immigrants will select the least-cost route to immigration, inducing substitution between these categories as the legal regimes shift or as economic conditions in the United States or in the sending countries vary. The skill distributions of the immigrant categories overlap, and movement between groups on average is from bottom to top (going downward) and from top to bottom (going upward). This ordering is reasonable, since the prospective immigrants most likely to move between groups are those where the skill overlap between the groups is greatest. For example, if there is an increase in the number of illegal immigrants (due to lower enforcement at the border), the spouse immigrants who move into the illegal category will be the least skilled among the spouse immigrants. Similarly, if there is an increase in the number of employment visas available, the spouses who now obtain employment visas on average will be the most skilled (i.e., the most likely to qualify in the employment category) among the spousal immigrants.

This framework implies that there will be two effects of any regime change. The first is a *composition* effect as the relative weights of immigrant categories change. For example, increasing the weight of the employment category will tend to increase the average quality of both legal and total immigrant flows. Similarly, an increase in the relative weight of the illegal immigrants category will reduce the average quality of all immigrants. It may, however, increase the average quality of legal immigrants if some of the low-skill spouse immigrants shift into the illegal category. The second effect of any regime change relates to any within-group alteration in average skill. Our assumptions imply that the skill levels of husband immigrants will be less than those of employment (principal) immigrants on average, as we see in the data, and greater than those of illegal immigrants. Moreover, allowing more illegal immigration (which does not screen for skills) would lead to a shift of higher-skill prospective immigrants out from the marriage route, thus raising the skill level of marital immigrants, while increasing the number of high-skill visas would lower the average skill of the marital immigrants. This latter indirect substitution effect reduces the overall effect of increasing the number of high-skill visas to the extent that those who would have become immigrants via marriage now do so with an employment visa.

We now use these assumptions to discuss how each of the major specific immigration law regime changes that occurred in the period 1972–95 might have affected the numbers and average skill of yearly immigrant flows. We also directly test in section 5.6 how these changes affected the number and skill composition of marital immigrants and the skill composition of employment immigrants. We do not discuss or examine in detail how these law changes affect the numbers of employment principals because the numerical ceilings in this category were usually binding in the years before the 1990 act, so that, aside from direct effects on the ceilings dictated by law, the only possible kind of effect on the number of male employment principals would be due to shifts in sex composition.

5.4.1 Application of the Preference-Category System to the Western Hemisphere (Since Midyear 1977)

By far, the most complicated change involves the integration of the Western Hemisphere into the worldwide preference-category system. The complications stem in part from the possible differential impacts on each hemisphere, subsequent changes in the integration rules, and different treatment of low-skill and high-skill employment visa categories. Before integration, there were no employment visa preference categories in the Western Hemisphere, while the Eastern Hemisphere operated under a total limit of 34,000, divided equally between third and sixth preference visas. In 1977 and 1978, a total ceiling of 24,000 was put in place in the Western Hemisphere (once again, equal division between third and sixth preferences), but there were no changes in the Eastern Hemisphere. Starting in 1979, the two hemispheres were placed under a single limit, initially of 58,000, falling to 56,000 in 1980 and then becoming fixed at 54,000 thereafter. As before, each of those limits were divided equally between the high- and low-skill preference visas. Since the pre-1979 within-hemisphere limits on employment visas may have been more binding on the Eastern Hemisphere, the adoption in 1981 of a common limit could result in an effective increase in the number of Eastern Hemisphere employment visas.

These changes also had an impact on the two main preference categories within the employment visas. As described above, third preference visas are for relatively skilled persons and sixth preference visas are for less-skilled persons. While the post-1981 limits were 27,000 in both third and sixth preferences, there was a much higher demand for third preference visas in the Eastern Hemisphere and a higher demand for the less-skilled sixth preference visas in the Western Hemisphere.

Spouses of U.S. Citizens

Bringing the Western Hemisphere under the preference-category system for allocating numerically limited visas would of course not directly affect the spouse immigrants. However, via behavioral (substitution) mechanisms, WH individuals who previously would have been admitted under the first-come first-served with modified screening regime and who now found themselves without a relative or employer sponsor would become candidates for the spouse route to immigration. Thus, there would immediately be an increase in the number of spouse immigrants from the Western Hemisphere. Given that prior to this law change, the WH immigrants underwent some job screening, we would expect that the numerically limited old-regime WH immigrants had higher skills than spouse immigrants. Accordingly, we would expect that introducing a new flow of previous numerically limited old-regime immigrants into the spouse pool would increase the average skill level of the WH spouse immigrants. In the Eastern Hemisphere, enlargement of the employment visa allotment due to imposition of a worldwide ceiling in 1979 would reduce pressure on the spouse category, inducing a shift from the spouse route to the employment route. Because dual-eligibles would be more skilled than spouses, we would expect a reduction in the average skill level of the EH husband immigrants.

Employment Principals

A direct effect of this law change would be to increase the number of employment principals. Its effect on the skill of employment immigrant principals would depend on whether the "new" WH employment immigrants have higher or lower skills than their EH counterparts. Previous theory and research both indicate the operation of distance as a selection mechanism, and, thus, we would expect that the WH employment principals would be less skilled than the EH employment principals and, therefore, that the effect of the WH law change would be to reduce the skill level of employment principals. Moreover, EH immigrants shifting from the spouse category to the employment category in response to the enlarged visa pool would be of lower average skill than the well-screened EH employment immigrants who had not contemplated the spouse route. Thus, the average skill of employment immigrants should decrease.

5.4.2   Restricting Employment-Based Visas for Physicians (1978)

Relative to the total number of visas, the number of physician employment visas issued before the law change was modest, and hence its decline in numbers would also be modest. For example, the number of physicians admitted with employment visas hovered around 2,000 in 1976 and 1977, declining to about 1,000 in 1978 and to 623 in 1979. Therefore, this law change should have relatively little effect on the total number of employment or spouse visas issued. The major impact stems instead from the changing within-group immigrant quality, which should lower average immigrant quality.

Employment Principals

Since the skill and incomes of physician visa immigrants are much higher than those of other employment visa immigrants, the physician restriction should have a sharp direct negative effect on the average skill level of employment principals. Because there are far fewer employment visas than total legal immigrant visas, the effect on the average quality of employment principals should be larger than any effect in the quality of all legal immigrants.

Spouses of U.S. Citizens

Restricting the access of physicians to employment visas has no direct effect on the number of spouse immigrants, but it might have behavioral substitution effects. Physicians who are now barred from obtaining employment visas may find the spouse route to immigration attractive, thus increasing the number of spouse immigrants and their average skill. However, if the absolute number of individuals involved is small, then these effects may not be noticeable.

5.4.3 IRCA Legalization Programs

Because they deal explicitly with the illegal population, the IRCA legalization programs do not directly affect either employment or spouse immigrants. But IRCA may have had indirect effects on both, by providing an easier route to legal immigration for both potential spouse and employment immigrants. The nature of these indirect effects would depend on the extent to which the IRCA, employment, and husband pools overlap and on the differences between overlapping segments of the pools.

Spouses of U.S. Citizens

To the extent that IRCA-eligibles are relieved of the obligation to meet stringent job screening, the IRCA programs would reduce the number of spouse immigrants. The direct composition effect then is to increase the average quality of non-IRCA legal immigrants.[25] Whether the IRCA programs increased or decreased the average skill of the spouse immigrants would depend on the skill of the IRCA-eligibles relative to the spouse pool. In general, the registry and pre-1982 resident legalized aliens would have had a long enough time to find a mate, and would obviously have been unsuccessful, implying that their skill level was lower than that of other potential mates for U.S. citizen women. The SAW-legalized aliens, on the other hand, might have included interesting, productive, higher-skilled individuals who, with some chutzpah, saw the program as an opportunity to enter the United States, merely by working, or claiming to have worked, a few months in agriculture. If the dual-eligibles were superior to those only eligible for the spouse route, then the IRCA program, which would siphon them off, would reduce the average skill of spouse immigrants. Moreover, if higher-skilled husband-eligibles found the United States less attractive because of the legalization program, then

---

25. Our INS data files do not include IRCA immigrants.

their dropping out of the husband pool would reduce the average skill of husband immigrants.

Employment Principals

The effect of IRCA on the average skill of employment principals is likely to be negligible, as it is unlikely that low-skill IRCA-eligible immigrants were eligible for employment visas and represented in the backlogs in this visa category.

5.4.4   Marriage Fraud Restriction

Marriage fraud provisions reduced the number of immigrants coming under spouse visas. Since spouse visa immigrants are less skilled than employment visa immigrants, the direct composition effect is to increase the average quality of legal immigrant flows. The effect on total immigrant flows is muted as some of the now deterred marriages will probably increase illegal immigrant flows. There are indirect within-group effects as well.

Spouses of U.S. Citizens

The marriage fraud provisions were directed at reducing and should unambiguously reduce, the number of spouse immigrants. Some of the now deterred, more-skilled marriage visa types can try to compete for the still numerically limited employment visas, reducing the average quality of spouse visas. Some of the now deterred, less-skilled marriage visa types can branch into the illegal group, which has no explicit numerical limitation, thus increasing the average quality of spouse visas.

Employment Principals

The marriage fraud provisions, of course, have no direct effect on the number of employment immigrants (which are still numerically fixed), but they may have an indirect effect on skill composition due to substitution. Prior to screening for fraud, a less-skilled immigrant selects the marital route over the employment route. With the marital route costs now higher, some of these lower-skill spouse immigrants would seek employment visas, thus lowering the average skill level of the latter category. The effect of using an employment visa rather than a marriage visa would be to reduce the average skill of employment immigrants.

5.4.5   New Employment Provisions in the 1990 Act

The final regime change concerns the 1990 act, which had two important direct effects—significantly increasing the total number of employment visas issued, while at the same time reducing the number of unskilled employment visas. By assigning higher weight to the relatively high-skilled employment visa categories, the direct compositional effect is to increase the average quality of all legal immigrant and total immigrant flows. In addition, this regime change may have implications due to behavioral substitution effects for flows between categories as well as for within-category immigrant quality.

Employment Principals

The 1990 act dramatically increased the number of visas available to skilled employment immigrants, and equally dramatically reduced the number available to unskilled individuals; it also made visas available to multinational executives. The 1990 act should then unambiguously increase the average skill level of employment principals. If we distinguish between the higher- and lower-skilled subsets of employment principals, then average skill in the higher-skilled subset would increase due to the introduction of multinational executives, while average skill in the lower-skilled subset would increase only if unskilled persons had dominated the category.

Spouses of U.S. Citizens

The more indirect behavioral effects involve the implications for the number and type of spouse visas. Increasing the number of employment visas available should generally reduce the pressure on the spouse route; however, reducing the number of employment visas available for unskilled persons should put pressure on the spouse route. It is an empirical question whether, on net, the change in the employment visa allotment increases or decreases the number of spouse immigrants. The skill level of spouse immigrants should, however, unambiguously decline, as there is a net outflow to the employment visa category of skilled spouses but a net inflow into the spouse visa category of low-skilled employment visas.

To illustrate the effects of the law changes on the numbers of immigrants in the spouse and employment visa categories, we briefly describe their time-series trends. Figure 5.3 plots the numbers of male employment principal immigrants for the years 1972–95, a category, as noted, that has a series of overall binding numerical ceilings. The shape of this plot is thus almost wholly explained by law changes and processing of visas. Although there exist smaller cyclic swings in this series,[26] its principal characteristics are a discrete 50 percent jump in the series between 1981 and 1982 and an even larger (more than two-fold) jump between 1991 and 1992. Both of these changes are the direct consequence of law changes. The 1981–82 shift reflects the impact of the extension of the employment preference

---

26. Although the total numbers of employment visas are fixed within regime, the numbers of male employment visas are not.

E = Employment Principal

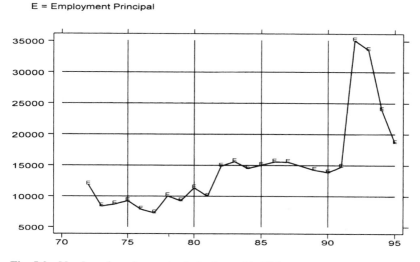

Fig. 5.3   Number of employment principal men 21–65, by year

system to the WH countries. This integration of the Eastern and Western Hemispheres under the same set of rules led to an increase in the total numbers of employment visas allowed. Bringing both hemispheres under a single worldwide ceiling starting in 1980 would result in having more visas available to EH applicants (who had a high demand for them), and indeed, we observe in figure 5.3 an increase in employment principals starting in 1982 (consistent with the usual processing and other delays). Similarly, the 1991–92 shift was the result of the increase in the number of employment visas allowed by legislative change. There was initially a wide pent-up demand for such slots. After some countries met their demand, the numbers of employment visas began to fall.

Figure 5.4 plots the other main series of interest—the numbers of male spouses of U.S. citizens. In contrast to the employment visa category, this series has no explicit numerical limits in any year, a reality that is reflected in the volatility of the numbers. Abstracting from the richness of detail in these swings in the numbers, there are two significant movements that we will highlight. The first is the steady, and eventually large, increase in the numbers of male spousal immigrants from 1981 to 1986, and the second is the somewhat smaller subsequent decline. The major legislative force in the 1981–86 upswing was most likely the placement of the Western Hemisphere under the preference categories. Potential immigrants from some countries were now effectively constrained, and they needed another pathway to become legal immigrant residents in the United States. The major factors in the post-1986 decline were the passage of the marriage fraud

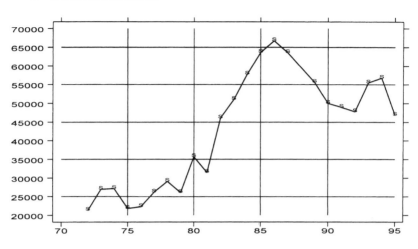

S = Spouse of U.S. Citizen

Fig. 5.4   Number of spouse immigrant men 21–65, by year

amendments, which made such marriages more difficult, and IRCA, which gave some potential immigrants who would have followed the marriage route an alternative path to admission.

Figure 5.5 provides a more detailed description of the changing bite of the numerical ceilings by plotting the number of employment visas issued for each hemisphere along with the sum of the two. The straight horizontal lines in this figure represent the ceilings that were in place in each year. Before 1976, employment visas (and the ceiling of 34,000) were only relevant for the Eastern Hemisphere. By the mid 1970s, EH visas issued were actually below the ceiling, probably due to severe recession in the United States. With integration, employment visas were issued to WH countries. Between 1976 and 1981, there was a growth in employment visas in both hemispheres. In both the Eastern and Western Hemispheres, the growing demand for employment visas did not hit the respective ceilings until 1981. Figure 5.5 shows that when a single ceiling was introduced in 1981, the sharp jump in employment visas was much larger in the Eastern Hemisphere. EH demand for employment visas was far greater than in the Western Hemisphere, so that the introduction of a single ceiling resulted in a de facto relaxation of the EH ceiling. This differential effect between hemispheres suggests that the impact of these changing rules may vary across hemispheres.

Figures 5.6 and 5.7 separate employment visas into their high-skill (third preference) and low-skill (sixth preference) components. These figures demonstrate that the large post-1981 increase in demand in the Eastern Hemisphere were for high-skilled third preference visas while the large

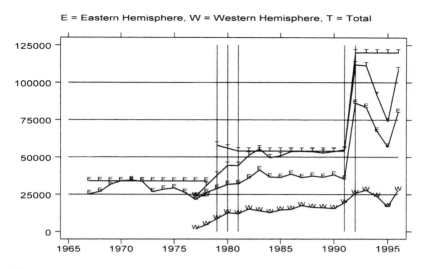

Fig. 5.5   Employment immigrants and ceilings, by hemisphere

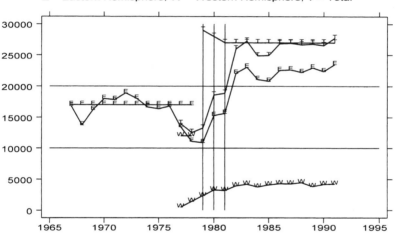

Fig. 5.6   High-skilled employment immigrants and ceilings

shift in the Western Hemisphere was for the low-skill sixth preference visas. To the extent that behavioral substitution is introduced with spouse visas, they are likely to be relatively high-skill EH spouses and low-skill WH spouses.

Figure 5.8 plots time series in the number of spouse visas, separately by hemisphere and, within the Western Hemisphere, separately for Mexico and the rest of the hemisphere. For all three groups, there is a steady climb in the number of such visas following the 1976 integration. However, the

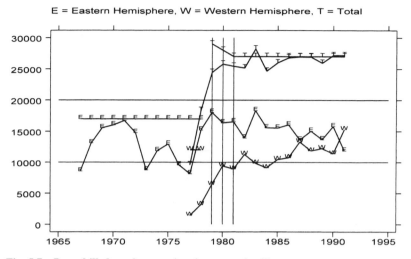

Fig. 5.7   **Low-skilled employment immigrants and ceilings**

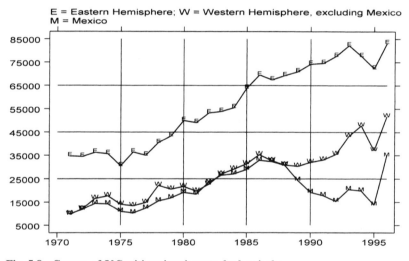

Fig. 5.8   **Spouse-of-U.S.-citizen immigrants, by hemisphere**

sharp decline in marriage visas in the mid- to late 1980s is clearly concentrated in the Western Hemisphere, and within the Western Hemisphere, in Mexico.

5.5   Estimating the Effects of Economic Conditions and Law Changes on Numbers of Immigrants and Their Skill Composition

The annual volume of migration flows, as well as the skill selectivity of migrants who arrive, are not simply consequences of the specific provisions of U.S. immigration laws. Prospective migrants decide to come or not based in part on a comparison of economic conditions in their home countries and in the United States, the costs of migration, and the psychic benefits and costs of living in different places. In a recent paper, we developed a theoretical framework that identifies some of the principal economic forces shaping the economic selectivity of immigrants and the gains they experience from migration.[27] This theoretical framework identifies the interaction between migrant skill heterogeneity and differences in the valuations of skills across countries of the world as important determinants of the numbers of migrants as well as their skill selectivity. For example, holding worker skill levels constant, prospective migrants from countries with low skill prices (relative to the United States) have more to gain from migrating to the United States. Since low skill prices will enable even less-skilled workers to gain from migration, the model also predicts a positive correlation of origin-country-specific skill prices and the average skill of migrants from those countries. Similarly, the high costs of migration will not only reduce the number of migrations but will also increase the average skill of migrants since (at any given skill price) only high-skill migrants will gain enough to justify the move. In summary, this theoretical framework argues that skill price heterogeneity across sending countries, differential direct migration costs, and the selective criteria of U.S. immigration laws influence not only the numbers of migrants from different countries but, selectively, the skill composition of those who migrate.

5.5.1   Data and Measures

To assess how and whether changes in U.S. immigration law regimes and country-specific economic conditions have importantly shaped the changing skill composition of U.S. immigrants, we constructed origin-country-specific data sets for the period 1972–92 that merge information on the new legal immigrants from the INS data sets, information on the major immigration law regimes, and information on the origin-country characteristics of the immigrants.[28] We focus on two subsets of immigrants: spouse-of-citizen immigrants and employment-based principals. The set of spouse immigrants covers all numerically unlimited immediate-relative spouse visas, including fiancé visas and the new visas for widowed persons made available by the 1990 act.[29] The set of employment principals covers the principals in the old system's third and sixth preference categories (for the fiscal years 1972–91) and in the new 1990 act system's

---

27. See Jasso, Rosenzweig, and Smith (1998).

28. We received defective data for fiscal year 1988, such that one-third of the records are missing. Accordingly, we do not use fiscal year 1988 data in this paper, but we will redo all analyses as soon as we receive the correct data set. Moreover, given that data for fiscal years 1980 and 1981 are irremediably incomplete, we control by defining a binary variable for those years (incomplete data).

29. The visa classes included in the spouse set are as follows: IR1, IR6, IF1, MR6, CR1, CR6, CF1, IW1, and IW6.

employment first, second, and third preference categories but, for consistency, excluding visa classes set aside for persons from particular countries.[30]

For each country of origin for each year, we obtained the average occupational earnings, constructed from the reported occupation codes as discussed above for all male immigrants in the relevant visa category aged 21–65. As noted, occupation is the single indicator of skill available in these data. Occupation represents the occupation reported by the immigrant. If the immigrant is obtaining a visa requiring labor certification (for example, if he is an employment-based principal), then the reported occupation is the occupation on which the labor certification is based. Otherwise, occupation refers to the current or last employment in the origin country or in the United States. Because immigrants adjusting their visa status are more likely to report a U.S. occupation and to have some U.S. work experience, we also constructed for each country a variable indicating the proportion of men in the visa category who adjusted their status.[31]

The rate of reporting an occupation has changed over time. It appears to be linked to adjustment of status and to the possibility that the adjusting immigrant is working illegally. Visa applicants who are already in the United States and who are working illegally might be reluctant to provide their occupation on the application forms. To capture trends in reporting bias, we thus constructed a variable indicating the proportion of the immigrants who reported an occupation.

Country-specific skill prices are not directly observable. However, it is possible to infer how skill prices vary across countries with information on the individual earnings and schooling of workers across origin countries and country-specific data on aggregate output, numbers of workers, and average schooling levels.[32] With respect to intercountry skill price variation, among workers with the same schooling and residing in countries with the same output per worker, those workers residing in countries

---

30. As noted in official State Department publications, the old employment categories correspond to the new system's employment first, second, and third categories (U.S. Department of State 1992). Legislation subsequently enacted (in October 1992) provided visas for two country-specific groups: nationals of the People's Republic of China who had been in the United States between 4 June 1989 and 11 April 1990 (mostly students who did not want to return to China after the Tiananmen Square confrontation) and scientists from the independent states of the former Soviet Union and the Baltic States, the visas to be drawn from employment second preference for the Soviet scientists and from the employment third preference for the Chinese students. For comparability with the employment series since 1972, we exclude both of those groups. Accordingly, the visa classes included in the employment principal set are as follows: P31, P36, P61, P66, E11, E12, E13, E16, E17, E18, E21, E26, E31, E32, E36, E37, EW3, and EW8.

31. There is also a variable (not reported in tables 5.6 and 5.7) controlling for missing adjustment status.

32. See Jasso, Rosenzweig, and Smith (1998) for details.

where workers also have average skill levels will have lower skill prices and wages, while among workers with identical schooling levels in countries with the same average worker skill levels, those in countries with higher output per worker will have higher skill prices and observed wages. Given immigrant skill heterogeneity and selectivity due to home-country skill price variation, these results imply that immigrants from countries with high (low) average levels of schooling will have the highest (lowest) skill levels among immigrants with identical schooling levels.

To characterize the origin countries' migration-relevant conditions and to measure skill prices, we use their year-specific gross domestic product (GDP) *per worker* estimates from the Penn World Table, Mark 5.6, and estimates of the average schooling levels of the working-age population in origin countries from Barro and Lee (1996). These country-specific GDP measures were adjusted for purchasing power parity (PPP) and expressed in 1985 U.S. dollars. The series we use omits some countries (notably China, Vietnam, Cuba, and countries of the former Soviet Union). Since the theoretical model is symmetric in terms of attributes of destination and origin countries, our models also include variables measuring time-series variation in GDP per worker and average schooling per worker in the United States.

Table 5.4 provides descriptive statistics for the data sets constructed. Consistent with our assumption about differential screening, the table indicates that, over the period, the average earnings of the husband immigrants, as measured by the occupational income measure, were about 22 percent less than those of all employment principal men, and almost 30 percent less than those of principal immigrant men in the high-skill visa category and less as well, by 7 percent, than those for low-skill employment immigrants. Some of this difference may be due to age, as the average age of the employment immigrants is over five years more (15 percent) than that of the husband immigrants. In addition, a considerably higher proportion of the high-skill employment immigrants adjusted status—66 percent compared with 39 percent for the husband immigrants—so the former group may have more U.S. labor market experience. Not surprising, almost all of the employment immigrants report an occupation, while on average 77 percent of the husband immigrants do so. Finally, over the period, employment immigrants came from larger countries with a higher mean per capita GDP than did the husband immigrants.

5.5.2   Estimation Procedure

Based on the constructed country data set, we estimate the determinants of the country- and year-specific number (per origin country population) and average occupational earnings of immigrant men aged 21–65 who entered by marrying U.S. citizens. We also estimate the determinants of the average occupational earnings of similarly aged men in the

Table 5.4   Characteristics of Legal Male Immigrants Aged 21–65, by Visa Category: 1972–92

Variable	Husbands of U.S. Citizens	Principal Men with Employment Visas		
		All	High Skill	Low Skill
Mean occupational income (1979 US$)	18,943	24,195	27,061	20,466
	(2,039)	(3,902)	(4,492)	(2,801)
Mean age	30.3	35.7	35.1	36.5
	(2.18)	(3.00)	(3.22)	(3.46)
Proportion adjusting status	.389	.529	.659	.360
	(.204)	(.220)	(.236)	(.269)
Proportion reporting an occupation	.770	.971	.965	.976
	(.152)	(.0467)	(.0500)	(.0538)
Mean per capita PPP GDP (1985 US$) of country of birth	5,389	5,663	5,372	6,044
	(3,860)	(4,765)	(5,001)	(4,408)
Mean population size of country of birth (thousands)	68,758	205,567	248,081	149,945
	(48,679)	(331,207)	(357,946)	(283,084)
N	2,369	1,982	1,782	1,811

Note: Standard deviation is in parentheses.

employment visa category, stratified by high- and low-skill immigrants; as discussed above, in these employment regressions, the WH observations start in 1977. The regressors include GDP and average schooling per worker for the origin country and the United States, and the law-regime factors discussed above depicted by sets of dummy variables corresponding to the different regimes. We also include in the specification a cohort term designed to capture a linear time trend and, in the occupational earnings equations, a variable measuring the proportion of immigrants reporting an occupation.[33] The specification also includes country fixed effects, to pick up such time-invariant factors as distance of the country from the United States, language, and unmeasured cultural factors that may affect skill levels of immigrants by country.

In an earlier section, we described in detail the major shifts in U.S. immigration law regimes. Identification of these regime shifts in our statistical model can only flow from calendar year shifts in the underlying relationship. It would be useful to be able to formulate and implement a sharp characterization of the law regimes. However, two factors conspire against such a characterization: First, important law changes sometimes occur together, such as (1) worldwide visa allocation integration and physician restriction, and (2) IRCA legalization and the marriage fraud restrictions. Second, defective data for three years—fiscal years 1980, 1981, 1988, the first two of which are beyond repair—make it necessary to exclude the fiscal year 1988 observations altogether and to define a dummy variable for the 1980 and 1981 years, thus hampering identification of more precise law-regime effects. Fortunately, the coincident regime shifts should have similar effects. Therefore, we characterize the law regimes and estimate their effects with two main binary variables: (1) integration of the two hemispheres into a single worldwide visa allocation system, including the physician restriction provision, equal to one if the year is fiscal year 1977 or later; and (2) IRCA legalization and marriage fraud restriction, equal to one if the year is fiscal year 1987 or later. Each of these variables is defined for one or both hemispheres, as appropriate. For example, in the employment regressions, in which WH observations begin in fiscal year 1977 (when the preference-category system was extended to the Western Hemisphere), the worldwide integration variable is defined only for the Eastern Hemisphere; in the marriage regressions, however, this same variable is defined for both hemispheres.

The data series on the size of the workforce in sending countries is only available up to 1990. Therefore, it is not possible to test for the effect of changes in the 1990 act simultaneously with country-of-origin economic

---

33. Consistent with our discussion above of occupation coding, the skill equation also includes a dummy for the years when the INS coded occupation using the 1960 or 1970 census detailed occupational classifications (fiscal years 1972–82).

Table 5.5   Average Occupational Income among Spouse and Employment
                   Principal Immigrants before and after the 1990 Act: Men Aged 21–65

	Cohort			
Hemisphere of Origin	1990	1991	1992	1993
Spouses of U.S. citizens				
Eastern Hemisphere	20,355	20,613	20,661	20,706
Western Hemisphere	17,868	18,092	18,043	17,572
Employment principals				
Eastern Hemisphere	23,006	23,483	24,043	24,152
Western Hemisphere	20,599	19,179	21,469	21,802

Note: The 1990 act took effect at the start of fiscal year 1992.

conditions. Fortunately, the changes induced by the 1990 act are so large
that its main impact on immigrant quality is not in dispute. This act more
than doubled the number of employment immigrants, so that its principal
composition effect was to raise average immigrant quality. Empirically,
figure 5.5 shows that the large increase in employment visas was concentrated in EH countries. As mentioned above, there were possible within-
group skill effects as well. To examine this question, table 5.5 lists measures of occupation incomes for employment principals and male spouses
in the years immediately before and after the year in which the act became
effective. In addition to the large increase in the numbers of immigrants,
the 1990 act shifted the composition of employment principal immigrants
toward the more skilled. That implication is confirmed in table 5.5 as the
occupation incomes of employment visas in both hemispheres are higher
after the act became effective than before. This increase in occupation
incomes of employment visas was greater in the Western Hemisphere, suggesting that the principal impact on within-group skill may flow from the
restriction on low-skill employment visas—a restriction that was more
relevant in the Western Hemisphere. We also anticipated a larger reduction in the skill of spouse immigrants in the Western Hemisphere since the
reduction in the number of unskilled visas would lead to a greater inflow
of them into the spousal category in the Western Hemisphere.

5.6   Results

Table 5.6 reports the fixed-effects estimates for the husbands of immigrants. The first column lists estimates for the ratio of the number of husband immigrants to the origin-country population, and the second column reports the coefficients for the average occupational earnings of those
immigrants. As explained above, the gains to migration—and consequently the larger the number of migrants per country—are positively re-

Table 5.6   **Estimates: Immigrant Men Admitted as Husbands of U.S. Citizens, 1972–90**

Variable	Immigrants/ Home Country Population	Log of Average Occupational Earnings
Origin country and U.S. economic variables		
Origin-country PPP GDP per worker	−.0162	.0075
(1985 dollars)	(3.33)	(0.39)
Origin-country average ln education	.0065	−.0856
	(1.58)	(3.22)
U.S. GDP per worker (1985$)	−.0099	.0006
	(0.19)	(0.07)
U.S. ln education per worker	−.0899	−.1938
	(2.82)	(0.47)
Time trend	.0016	.0358
	(3.01)	(1.24)
Proportion of immigrants who adjusted	—	−.0075
status		(0.09)
Proportion reporting an occupation	—	−.0130
		(0.27)
1970 occupational categories	—	.0609
		(3.85)
Incomplete data years	−.0153	.0044
	(1.74)	(0.63)
U.S. immigration law regime		
Preference system	−.0024	.0035
	(1.92)	(0.36)
Preference system*WH	.0145	.0345
	(1.39)	(2.21)
Marriage fraud–IRCA legalization	−.0048	.0159
	(2.43)	(2.32)
Marriage fraud–IRCA legalization*WH	.0003	−.0307
	(0.06)	(1.51)

Note: Absolute values of robust t-ratios in parentheses. Number of observations = 2,387. Number of countries = 145. Income observations are weighted by the number of immigrants. WH = Western Hemisphere.

lated to U.S. skill prices and are negatively correlated with skill prices in sending countries. Our empirical estimates for origin-country economic variables support these theoretical expectations. A higher per capita income in the origin country leads to a statistically significant drop in out-migration rates, while (holding constant GDP) an increase in average schooling increases the number of male spouse migrants to the United States. Similarly, an increase in sending-country-specific schooling per worker (holding constant GDP) lowers skill prices and makes immigration more advantageous for lower-skilled workers. This prediction is supported by the statistically significant effect of country schooling in the model for log of average occupational earnings listed in the second column of table 5.6. Not surprisingly, it is more difficult to obtain robust estimates for the U.S. counterpart variables since we must rely on time-series variation in two collinear series (GDP and average schooling per worker) that are common to all sending countries. Yet, even here, we obtain a statistically significant negative effect on U.S. education per worker, implying that lower skill prices in the United States discourage international migration to America. However, we are unable to detect any effects of the U.S. economic variables in the income model, no doubt due to the collinearity in the two variables.

The immigration law regime variables indicate both direct and indirect effects of law-regime changes. As was expected, the regression results in table 5.6 show differential effects by hemisphere. In the Eastern Hemisphere, the integration of preferences leads to an effective increase in employment visas, easing the pressures on marriage visas there. However, applying the preference system to the Western Hemisphere should increase the number of husband immigrants per country (in the Western Hemisphere). Such additional WH immigrants added to the pool at that time were evidently more skilled (there was implicit skill screening of WH applicants before integration), raising the average quality of WH spousal immigrants. However, we find no effect of integration on average quality of spouses in the Eastern Hemisphere.

Similarly, the combined legislation cracking down on marriage fraud and IRCA had a statistically significant depressing effect on the number of spouse immigrants, equally for WH and EH immigrants. If the dominant substitution induced by the lowering of fraudulent marriages is to increase illegals (employment visas), then the average quality of the remaining marriage visas should rise (fall). The impact of fewer prospective immigrants who decide not to marry a U.S. citizen due to IRCA should increase the average quality of the remaining spouse visas. Our empirical estimates indicate that the combined effects of IRCA and movement into illegals dominated for the Eastern Hemisphere (increasing average quality of marriages), while movement into employment may have dominated in the Western Hemisphere, where average quality of marriages declined.

Table 5.7 presents the estimates for the average occupational earnings of the employment immigrants. Decreasing skill prices in sending countries or increasing skill prices in the United States should, through immigrant selectivity, lower the average quality of employment immigrants. The negative estimated coefficient on origin-country ln education and the positive coefficient on U.S. GDP per worker both support this hypothesis. The coefficients estimated in table 5.7 suggest no net effect of expansion in employment immigrants in the Eastern Hemisphere on employment immigrant earnings. This may reflect offsetting effects of the expanding pool lowering within-group quality on the margin and the fact that more-skilled visas were increasingly used in the Eastern Hemisphere. Finally, our re-

Table 5.7   **Fixed Effects Estimates: Log of Average Occupational Earnings for Immigrant Principal Men with Employment Visas, 1972–90**

Variable	All Employment
Origin country and U.S. economic variables	
Origin-country PPP GDP per worker (1985$)	−.0215
	(0.38)
Origin-country average ln education	−.3015
	(3.11)
U.S. GDP per worker (1985$)	.1928
	(1.79)
U.S. ln education per worker	−1.301
	(0.99)
Time trend	−.0146
	(1.35)
Proportion of immigrants who adjusted status	.2676
	(1.20)
Proportion reporting an occupation	.0879
	(0.63)
1970 occupational categories	−.0008
	(0.54)
Incomplete data years	−.0332
	(2.54)
U.S. immigration law regime	
Preference system*EH	.0080
	(0.37)
Marriage fraud–IRCA legalization	−.0293
	(1.20)
Marriage fraud–IRCA legalization*EH	.0669
	(3.77)

Note: Absolute values of robust *t*-ratios in parentheses. Number of observations = 2,387. Number of countries = 145. Income observations are weighted by the number of immigrants. EH = Eastern Hemisphere.

sults in table 5.6 indicated that there may have been an increased flow in the Western Hemisphere into employment visas that lowered the average quality of marriage. The results in table 5.7 indicate, interestingly, that the marriage fraud legislation may have decreased average skill levels in both the husband and employment visa categories for WH immigrants—such immigrants were evidently of above-average skill among spouse immigrants but of below-average skill among employment immigrants. However, the opposite was evidently true for EH immigrants.

5.7   Conclusion

This paper has reexamined one of the central questions in immigration research in the last few decades—secular trends in the "labor market quality" of new immigrants. Based on the conventional surveys used to examine this question, an almost universal consensus had been reached: The labor market quality of new recent immigrants is quite low and has been declining relative to skills of native-born Americans. Despite their widespread use, we argue in this paper that these conventional surveys provide quite flawed data for this question. These data are flawed because it is impossible to determine when the foreign-born population in these conventional surveys actually arrived in the United States and, therefore, how *recent* they actually are. The data are also deficient since a significant fraction of the foreign-born population included in these surveys are not legal immigrants at all, but instead represent an uncertain amalgam of legal, illegal, and nonimmigrant populations. In our view, these data problems are sufficiently serious to call into question most prior research on this question. Another serious problem with most existing research is that, somewhat remarkably, it deals with this issue without any recognition or discussion of the legal rules governing the number of immigrants who may enter and the criteria by which they are selected. In part, this neglect of the legal environment is because conventional labor market surveys do not distinguish the foreign-born population by visa type.

Given these problems with conventional labor market surveys, we turn to an alternative data resource—INS records of legal immigrants over the period 1972–95—that allows us to examine not only the changing skill composition of legal immigrants but also how these changes were influenced by alterations in immigration law regimes and changing economic conditions in sending countries and the United States. These data paint a quite different portrait of the labor market quality of legal immigrants. First, especially if we abstract from the special refugee population, during most of the last 25 years, the labor market quality of male legal immigrants has been as high as or higher than that of male native-born workers. Second, while the relative labor market quality of male legal immigrants was falling during the 1970s and early 1980s, there has been a steady rise in the quality of legal immigrants during the last half of the 1980s and throughout the 1990s.

In this paper, we also examined the reasons for these secular trends in the labor market quality of legal immigrants. In our view, these trends result both from a series of changes in the legal regime governing immigration to the United States and from behavioral choices made by prospective immigrants (and the migrant skill selectivity that results from those choices) in light of changing economic conditions in sending countries and the United States. In addition to a large influx of refugees, there were two regime changes that contributed to the early period of declining labor market quality of immigrants. Legislation enacted in 1976 that extended the preference system to the Western Hemisphere helped produce a large increase in the number of visas for permanent residence obtained by marrying a U.S. citizen. While having little effect on overall numbers, a separate 1976 law severely restricted the granting of employment visas to foreign physicians, thereby lowering the average skill of legal immigrants. Similarly, there were three principal changes in the legal rules that helped produce the post-1986 rise in labor market quality of legal immigrants. First, the Marriage Fraud act led to a decline (especially among residents of Mexico) in the numbers of people who become permanent residents by marrying U.S. citizens. Second, IRCA, by easing one route to legalization, apparently made the alternative path of marriage to U.S. citizens less attractive. Finally, the Immigration Act of 1990 almost tripled the ceilings for the relatively high-skilled employment visas while at the same time reducing the numbers of low-skill employment visas issued.

Legal regime changes alone cannot fully explain secular trends in the numbers and quality of legal immigrants. The annual volume of migration flows and the skill selectivity of migrants who arrive also are based on comparisons of economic conditions in sending countries and the United States. This is especially true in the numerically unrestricted category of those who obtain permanent resident visas by marrying U.S. citizens. The empirical estimates summarized in this paper are consistent with our theoretical framework. First, the volume of migration per capita is positively associated with lower sending-country skill prices. In addition, the average skills of migrants decline as sending-country skill prices (and migration costs) fall relative to those skill prices in the United States. Both our theoretical and empirical models imply that trends in the average labor market quality of immigrants are a negative function of the skill price gap between potential sending countries and the United States. For example, rising skill prices in sending countries (relative to the United States) since the mid-1980s contributed to the rising labor market quality of legal immigrants.

Appendix

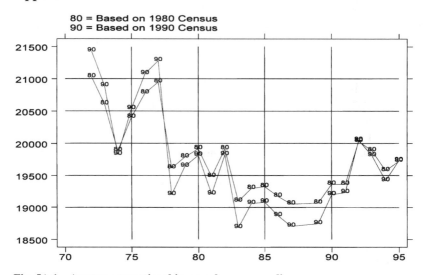

Fig. 5A.1   Average occupational income, by census coding

References

Barrett, Alan. 1996. Did the decline continue? Comparing the labor-market quality of United States immigrants from the late 1970's and late 1980's. *Journal of Population Economics* 9:57–63.

Barro, Robert J., and Jong Wha Lee. 1996. International measures of schooling years and schooling quality. *American Economic Review* 86 (2): 218–23.

Duleep, Harriet Orcutt, and Mark C. Regets. 1996. Admission criteria and immigrant earnings profiles. *International Migration Review* 30:571–90.

Funkhauser, Edward, and Stephen J. Trejo. 1995. The labor market skills of recent male immigrants: Evidence from the Current Population Survey. *Industrial and Labor Relations Review* 48:792–811.

Jasso, Guillermina, Douglas S. Massey, Mark R. Rosenzweig, and James P. Smith. Forthcoming. The New Immigrant Survey Pilot (NIS-P): Overview and new findings about U.S. legal immigrants at admission. *Demography.*

Jasso, Guillermina, and Mark R. Rosenzweig. 1986. What's in a name? Country-of-origin influences on the earnings of immigrants in the United States. *Research in Human Capital and Development* 4:75–106.

———. 1988. How well do U.S. immigrants do? Vintage effects, emigration selectivity, and occupational mobility. *Research in Population Economics* 6:229–53.

———.1995. Do immigrants screened for skills do better than family-reunification immigrants? *International Migration Review* 29:85–111.

Jasso, Guillermina, Mark R. Rosenzweig, and James P. Smith. 1998. Determinants of immigrants' gains from immigration. Paper presented at conference, Immigrants and Their Transition to New Labor Markets. Tel Aviv: Tel Aviv University, March.

Mines, Richard, Susan Gabbard, and Anne Steirman. 1997. A profile of U.S. farm workers: Demographics, household composition, income and use of services. Washington, D.C.: U.S. Department of Labor.

Passel, Jeffrey S. 1999. Undocumented immigration to the United States: Numbers, trends, and characteristics. In *Illegal immigration in America: A reference handbook,* ed. David W. Haines and Karen E. Rosenblum. Westport, Conn.: Greenwood Press.

Smith, James P., and Barry Edmonston, eds. 1997. *The new Americans: Economic, demographic, and fiscal effects of immigration.* Washington, D.C.: National Academy Press.

Summers, Robert, and Alan Heston. 1991. The Penn World Table (Mark 5): An expanded set of international comparisons, 1950–1988. *Quarterly Journal of Economics* 106:327–68.

U.S. Department of Commerce. Bureau of the Census. 1989. The relationship between the 1970 and 1980 industry and occupation classification systems. Technical Paper no. 59. Washington, D.C.: U.S. Government Printing Office.

U.S. Department of Justice. 1997. Immigrants admitted into the United States as legal permanent residents, fiscal year 1972 through fiscal year 1995. Springfield, Va.: National Technical Information Service.

U.S. Department of State. 1992. *1991 report of the Visa Office.* Department of State Publication 9823. Washington, D.C.: Department of State, Bureau of Consular Affairs.

U.S. Immigration and Naturalization Service. 1943–1978. *Annual report of the Immigration and Naturalization Service.* Washington, D.C.: U.S. Government Printing Office.

———. 1979–96. *Statistical yearbook of the Immigration and Naturalization Service.* Washington, D.C.: U.S. Government Printing Office.

The More Things Change
Immigrants and the Children of Immigrants in the 1940s, the 1970s, and the 1990s

David Card, John DiNardo, and Eugena Estes

6.1 Introduction

It is often said that the United States is a country of immigrants. Today, a better description is that the United States is a country of the descendants of immigrants.[1] The upsurge in immigration that began in the mid-1960s is now raising the relative numbers of immigrants and recent descendants of immigrants and shifting the balance back toward the patterns that prevailed earlier in the country's history—especially in the major immigrant-receiving states like California, Texas, and Florida. As was the case with the last big surge of immigration at the turn of the century, recent immigrant inflows have stimulated a wave of research and policy initiatives. Much of the new research focuses on the changing composition of immigrant inflows and on the apparent decline in the relative economic status of immigrants.[2] Perhaps more important from the long-run point of view, however, is the changing economic status of the "second generation"—the offspring of immigrant parents, who now make up 10 percent of all native-born children, and whose own children will constitute a significant fraction of the future population.

David Card is the Class of 1950 Professor of Economics at the University of California, Berkeley, and a research associate of the National Bureau of Economic Research. John DiNardo is associate professor of economics at the University of California, Irvine, and a research associate of the National Bureau of Economic Research. Eugena Estes is a graduate student of economics at Princeton University.

The authors thank seminar participants at the NBER and McMaster University for comments. Card's research was funded in part by a grant from the NICHD.

1. For example, only about 7 percent of adult household heads interviewed in the General Social Survey between 1977 and 1996 are immigrants, but 40 percent report having at least one foreign-born grandparent.

2. See, e.g., Borjas (1985, 1987, 1995).

While there is some research on the "new" second generation, a major stumbling block has been the absence (since the 1970 census) of large-scale data sets that identify the native-born children of immigrants.[3] This gap has been filled very recently by the Current Population Survey (CPS), which added questions on parents' place of birth in 1994. In this paper, we use the recent CPS data together with data from earlier censuses to provide a comparative perspective on the economic performance of immigrants and native-born children of immigrants in 1940, 1970, and today. We also use cohort-level data for different immigrant groups to measure the rate of "intergenerational assimilation" between immigrant fathers and second-generation sons and daughters and to evaluate recent arguments that intergenerational assimilation has slowed down because of changes in the ethnic composition of immigrant inflows and changes in the structure of the U.S. economy.[4]

As our title suggests, our findings reflect a mixture of change and constancy. On the one hand, we find that the well-documented shifts in the origin countries of U.S. immigrants have been associated with a decline in the relative economic status of immigrants as a whole between 1940 and the mid-1990s. We also find some evidence of a decline in the relative status of the second generation, although this is mainly confined to the lower deciles of the wage distribution. At the middle and upper deciles, there is little indication of a shift. On the other hand, we find that the degree of intergenerational assimilation (measured by intergenerational correlations in education or earnings, or by interethnic marriage patterns) has not declined systematically between the cohort of second-generation children raised in the 1940s and 1950s and those raised in the 1960s and 1970s. Moreover, as in the past, second-generation children continue to have higher education and wages than children of comparable U.S.-born parents.

6.2 Background

The changing characteristics of the immigrant and second-generation populations in our sample period (1940–95) reflect the dramatic changes in U.S. immigration policy over the twentieth century, as well as other powerful forces, such as world wars, the Great Depression, political and economic upheavals in Europe, and rapid population growth in the Americas.[5] These various influences are revealed in figure 6.1, which plots annual immigrant inflow rates (the number of documented immigrant arrivals divided by the population) from 1900 to 1990. Most of the immigrants

---

3. See Waldinger and Perlmann (1997) for a review of much of this literature.
4. This argument is advanced in Gans (1992) and Portes and Zhou (1993); also see Waldinger and Perlmann (1997).
5. There are many histories of U.S. immigration; see, for example, Bennett (1963).

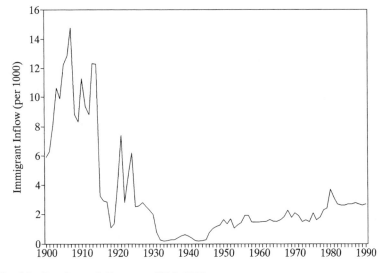

Fig. 6.1   Immigrant inflow rate, 1900–1990

in our 1940 sample had arrived during the massive wave of immigration between 1880 and 1925 and were the "new" immigrants of their time. Many of these were from Russia, Eastern Europe, and Italy and were considered less "desirable" than earlier immigrants from the United Kingdom and Northern Europe.[6] A variety of forces, including populist sentiment against immigration, business opposition stimulated by labor unrest, and the patriotic fervor surrounding the entry of the United States into World War I, led to reductions in immigration during the 1910–20 period. After the war, immigration rates surged, leading to renewed demands for restrictive legislation, which culminated in the Immigrant and Nationality Acts of 1924. These laws capped immigrant inflows and set out the national-origin quotas that were the cornerstone of immigration policy until the 1960s.[7] The effects of the immigrant restrictions are also evident in figure 6.1: Immigrant inflows fell from an average of about 600,000 per year in the early 1920s to about one-half that rate in the late 1920s. With the onset of the Great Depression, immigrant inflows dropped below 50,000 per year by 1932 and remained at similar levels throughout the 1930s.

By contrast, the characteristics of the immigrants in our 1970 census

6. For example, Brigham (1923) developed estimates of the racial composition of immigrants from different source countries. He divided immigrants into four racial categories: "Nordic," "Alpine," "Mediterranean," and "Asian." His analysis suggested that "Alpine" and "Mediterranean" immigrants had lower "intelligence" than "Nordic" immigrants, and on this basis, he argued for limiting immigration from countries with a high fraction of individuals of Mediterranean descent, like Italy, Greece, Portugal, and Spain.

7. There was little confusion about the intent of the policy. A *Los Angeles Times* headline at the time (13 April 1924) read: "Nordic Victory is seen in Drastic Restrictions."

sample reflect the results of the post-1924 restrictions, together with postwar economic and political changes. Indeed, apart from the 1952 McCarran-Walter Acts, which extended special preferences to immigrants with skills deemed urgently needed and put further restrictions on those with "mental, physical, and moral defects," there was comparatively little change in immigration law from 1940 until 1965. Nevertheless, even in this environment the composition of immigrant inflows shifted somewhat, resulting (for example) in a much higher fraction of Mexican immigrants in 1970 than 1940.[8] In addition, refugee arrivals—particularly from Cuba—changed the face of immigration over the period 1925–65.

Finally, the characteristics of our sample of immigrants from the 1990s reflect the influence of the 1965 Immigration Reform Act, which eliminated national-origin quotas and extended special preferences to those with family members already in the United States. This act is widely credited with allowing higher inflow rates and with changing the countries of origin of the "new new" immigrants—away from Europe and toward Asia and South and Central America.

The characteristics of the second-generation populations in our sample period also reflect past immigration policies, albeit with a "generational lag." Thus, the second generation in our 1940 sample—who were born between 1875 and 1920—are a mixture of the children of the "old" (pre-1890) immigrants and the "new" immigrants of the turn of the century. The second generation in our 1970 sample are largely the children of the immigrants who entered the United States during the period 1890–1925; as such, many are the descendants of families who at least began their lives in the United States in relative deprivation (see Waldinger and Perlmann 1997). Finally, the second generation in the mid-1990s are a mixture of children of pre-1965 immigrants; children of Cuban, Hungarian, and Czech refugees; and children of the initial wave of post-1965 immigrants.

6.3   Data Sources and Definitions

6.3.1   Sources

The data for our empirical analysis are taken from the 1940 and 1970 censuses and from pooled 1994, 1995, and 1996 March Current Population Surveys. The 1940 census collected information on immigrant status, education, and earnings for all individuals, but it only collected information on parents' place of birth for one "sample line" person in each household. Thus, most of our analysis for 1940 utilizes the sample-line persons,

---

8. Some of the Mexican inflow can be traced to other aspects of U.S. immigration policy, including the Bracero program, which ended in 1964.

although we also use the full sample of individual records in analyzing the earnings of immigrant fathers.

The 1970 census collected information on both parents' immigrant status and on one parent's place of birth in one of the two versions of the "long form"—the so-called 15 percent sample form. Thus, most of our analysis for 1970 utilizes the 1-in-100 15 percent state samples, although when analyzing the earnings of immigrant fathers, we also use observations in the 1-in-100 5 percent state sample.

Finally, since 1994, the March Current Population Survey has included questions on the place of birth of each individual and his or her parents. Because of the relatively small number of observations in the CPS (compared to the census), we pool information from the 1994, 1995, and 1996 CPSs.[9] We convert the reported earnings information from these three samples into constant 1995 dollars prior to pooling the data.

6.3.2 Definitions

Throughout this paper we distinguish between three mutually exclusive groups: immigrants, individuals born in the U.S. of immigrant parents (the second generation), and others. For simplicity, we refer to the last group as the "third and higher generation," or sometimes as "natives." In the 1970 and 1994–96 samples, we exclude from the immigrant subsample individuals who were born abroad of U.S. parents, and include them instead with the third-and-higher-generation group.[10] We also restrict the definition of the second generation to native-born individuals whose mother *and* father were immigrants. This requirement substantially narrows the second-generation group relative to the alternative of requiring only one immigrant parent. In particular, among adults with at least one immigrant parent, 69 percent had two immigrant parents in the 1940 census, 58 percent had two immigrant parents in the 1970 census, and only 40 percent had two immigrant parents in the 1994–96 CPS.

---

9. We make no adjustments for the overlapping samples in consecutive March surveys. About 40 percent of individuals in each March survey are resurveyed in the following March, and 40 percent were surveyed in the previous year (the other 20 percent are people who either moved into their house in the past 12 months or will move out in the next 12 months). This feature means that our standard errors using the CPS sample are understated by about 17 percent.

10. In the 1994–96 March CPS files, about 8 percent of individuals age 16–66 who were born abroad reported that they had U.S. parents. This is particularly prevalent for individuals born in a few countries, including France (34 percent), Germany (49 percent), England (19 percent), Japan (34 percent), and Canada (22 percent). The fraction of individuals born abroad who had U.S. parents in the 1970 census is comparable to the fraction in the mid-1990s (9.5 percent). In the 1940 census, we experimented with attempting to exclude individuals born abroad of U.S. parents from the foreign-born pool but found that the resulting sample excluded an unusually high fraction of people from some countries.

6.4   Comparisons of Natives, Immigrants, and the Second Generation

6.4.1   Descriptive Overview

We begin our empirical analysis with a descriptive overview of the demographic characteristics and labor market outcomes of the three generational groups in 1940, 1970, and 1994–96. Panel A of table 6.1 presents a variety of data for adult men in the three data sets, while panel B presents comparable data for adult women. Examination of the top row of either panel shows the rather large swings in the relative sizes of the three groups that have occurred in the past 50 years. The fraction of immigrants in the adult population of the United States was about 12 percent in 1940, fell to 5 percent in 1970, and has risen back to about 11 percent in the mid-1990s. Following this pattern, but with a generational lag, the second generation's share of the adult population has fallen steadily from 16 percent in 1940 to 8 percent in 1970 and to 3 percent today.

The changing relative sizes of the three groups were accompanied by notable shifts in their age compositions. In 1940, immigrants were relatively old (reflecting the very low immigrant inflows between 1925 and 1940), while the second and third-and-higher generations had similar age structures. In 1970, both immigrants and the second generation were older than natives, with over a 10-year gap in the average age of the second generation relative to natives. The long-lasting effects of the 1925 Immigration Act are revealed by the very small number of second-generation men or women in the 16–30-year age range in 1970. The resumption of substantial immigrant inflows in the 1970s and 1980s is manifested in the 1990s data by a reversal of the relative ages of immigrants and natives, and by the relatively high fraction of the second generation in the youngest age range.

Although not identical, the relative distributions of education for the native-born, immigrants, and the second generation are roughly similar for men and women. In all three years of our sample, education levels are lowest for immigrants and are roughly similar between natives and the second generation. Interestingly, the mean schooling gap between immigrants and the third-and-higher generation has narrowed slightly over the past 50 years: from 1.9 years in 1940 to 1.4 years in 1994–96 for men; and from 2.5 years in 1940 to 1.4 years in 1994–96 for women. Paradoxically, this convergence in means has occurred at the same time that the immigrant-native gap in the fraction of men or women in the lowest education category has actually risen slightly.

The labor market outcomes in the middle rows of table 6.1 show that native, second generation, and immigrant men have fairly similar employment rates. The one exception to this pattern—the low employment rate of second generation men in 1994–96—is largely an artifact of the

Table 6.1   Characteristics of Natives, Immigrants, and Second-Generation Individuals in 1940, 1970, and 1994–96

	1940			1970			1994–96		
	Natives	Immigrants	2nd Generation	Natives	Immigrants	2nd Generation	Natives	Immigrants	2nd Generation
				A. Men Age 16–66					
Fraction of population	0.71	0.12	0.16	0.87	0.05	0.08	0.86	0.11	0.03
Mean age (years)	35.7	46.7	35.8	36.4	42.8	48.5	38.0	36.9	38.6
Fractions in age range									
16–30 years	0.42	0.10	0.43	0.42	0.26	0.08	0.33	0.36	0.42
31–45 years	0.31	0.32	0.32	0.28	0.28	0.27	0.38	0.39	0.21
46–66 years	0.26	0.57	0.26	0.30	0.46	0.65	0.30	0.25	0.37
Mean years education	8.9	7.0	9.2	11.2	10.5	11.2	13.0	11.6	13.1
Fractions in education range									
<12 years education	0.73	0.85	0.74	0.44	0.50	0.47	0.17	0.35	0.19
12 years education	0.16	0.09	0.16	0.31	0.22	0.29	0.34	0.24	0.27
13–15 years education	0.06	0.03	0.05	0.14	0.12	0.11	0.27	0.17	0.29
16+ years education	0.05	0.04	0.05	0.12	0.16	0.14	0.23	0.23	0.25
Fraction worked last year	0.84	0.85	0.82	0.89	0.89	0.92	0.85	0.84	0.75
Mean annual earnings (1995$)	8,774	11,134	11,910	24,683	27,442	33,582	24,629	20,284	21,779
Mean weekly wage (1995$)	266.0	314.6	303.6	635.1	691.2	800.1	621.4	520.4	638.3
Coefficient of variation of weekly wage	0.74	0.58	0.64	0.63	0.60	0.53	0.73	0.82	0.79
Fraction of workers in overall wage quartiles									
Quartile 1	0.29	0.12	0.17	0.27	0.21	0.11	0.24	0.34	0.28
Quartile 2	0.25	0.25	0.26	0.26	0.27	0.22	0.24	0.30	0.22

(continued)

Table 6.1 (continued)

	1940			1970			1994–96		
	Natives	Immigrants	2nd Generation	Natives	Immigrants	2nd Generation	Natives	Immigrants	2nd Generation
Quartile 3	0.22	0.33	0.29	0.24	0.24	0.30	0.27	0.19	0.23
Quartile 4	0.23	0.30	0.28	0.24	0.28	0.37	0.25	0.17	0.28
Marital status and spouse characteristics									
Fraction married	0.59	0.70	0.53	0.65	0.72	0.81	0.55	0.56	0.47
Nativity of spouse of married individuals									
Native[a]	0.98	0.36	0.91	0.93	0.27	0.54	0.94	0.16	0.67
Immigrant	0.02	0.64	0.09	0.02	0.57	0.08	0.04	0.81	0.17
Second generation	—	—	—	0.05	0.16	0.38	0.02	0.03	0.16
Second generation with matching father's country of birth	—	—	—	—	0.09	0.22	—	0.02	0.11
Sample size	100,674	19,139	23,928	519,644	29,812	46,349	112,125	16,394	4,443
B. Women Age 16–66									
Fraction of population	0.73	0.11	0.16	0.86	0.06	0.08	0.86	0.11	0.03
Mean age (years)	35.5	45.5	35.7	36.9	42.4	48.9	38.3	38.3	39.3
Fractions in age range									
16–30 years	0.43	0.13	0.43	0.41	0.26	0.07	0.32	0.31	0.41
31–45 years	0.31	0.35	0.31	0.28	0.30	0.26	0.37	0.39	0.20
46–66 years	0.25	0.53	0.26	0.31	0.43	0.67	0.31	0.29	0.39
Mean years education	9.3	6.8	9.2	11.2	10.0	10.8	12.9	11.5	12.8
Fractions in education range									
<12 years education	0.67	0.86	0.72	0.41	0.52	0.47	0.15	0.33	0.19

12 years education	0.31	0.27	0.36	0.38	0.29	0.38	0.21	0.10	0.21
13–15 years education	0.30	0.20	0.29	0.09	0.11	0.13	0.05	0.02	0.07
16+ years education	0.20	0.20	0.20	0.06	0.08	0.08	0.03	0.02	0.04
Fraction worked last year	0.64	0.59	0.74	0.53	0.51	0.56	0.34	0.23	0.31
Mean annual earnings (1995$)	12,156	9,912	13,330	9,038	7,754	7,480	4,004	2,529	2,287
Mean weekly wage (1995$)	431.8	383.6	405.1	427.0	402.3	375.6	190.5	186.4	172.5
Coefficient of variation of weekly wage	0.81	0.82	0.77	0.67	0.71	0.73	0.68	0.65	0.79
Fraction of workers in overall wage quartiles									
Quartile 1	0.25	0.26	0.25	0.18	0.20	0.26	0.17	0.16	0.29
Quartile 2	0.23	0.30	0.25	0.23	0.26	0.25	0.27	0.27	0.25
Quartile 3	0.22	0.22	0.25	0.28	0.29	0.26	0.32	0.34	0.23
Quartile 4	0.30	0.21	0.25	0.30	0.25	0.23	0.25	0.23	0.23
Marital status and spouse characteristics									
Fraction married	0.47	0.62	0.55	0.72	0.69	0.64	0.56	0.70	0.61
Nativity of spouse of married individuals									
Native[a]	0.61	0.20	0.95	0.45	0.32	0.92	0.81	0.24	0.97
Immigrant	0.17	0.76	0.03	0.12	0.56	0.02	0.19	0.76	0.03
Second generation	0.22	0.04	0.02	0.43	0.12	0.06	—	—	—
Second generation with matching father's country of birth	0.14	0.02	—	0.24	0.06	—	—	—	—
Sample size	4,769	17,814	121,208	49,234	35,769	551,501	22,826	15,699	102,173

[a] In 1940 sample, native spouses include second generation. In later samples, native spouses exclude second generation.

U-shaped age distribution of this group.[11] Among women the differences are more pronounced: Immigrant women, in particular, have lower employment rates than either second- or third-and-higher-generation women.[12]

A variety of earnings information is presented in table 6.1, including mean annual earnings (for both workers and nonworkers), average weekly earnings (for workers only), and the fractions of each generational group in different aggregate wage quartiles.[13] Looking first at men, the 1940 data show roughly 25 percent higher annual earnings and 15 percent higher weekly wages for immigrants and the second generation than for natives. The second generation-native gap is particularly noteworthy because the two groups have similar age distributions, whereas some of the higher wages of immigrants are presumably attributable to their older age. The 1970 data again show higher earnings for immigrants and the second generation than for natives, although these comparisons must be interpreted carefully given the different age distributions of the three groups. By comparison, immigrants have the lowest annual or weekly earnings of the three generational groups in the 1994–96 data. Indeed, over one-third of immigrant men have weekly wages in the bottom quartile of the overall wage distribution. The same general patterns hold for women, although the percentage wage differentials between the generational groups are typically smaller than those for men. Moreover, immigrant women are far less concentrated at the bottom of the overall wage distribution in the mid-1990s than their male counterparts.

The final rows of table 6.1 present information on an alternative dimension of "success" in the United States: the rate at which members of different generational groups marry outside their own group. Not surprisingly, spouses of third-and-higher-generation men and women are very likely to also be third-and-higher generation. Likewise, the spouses of immigrants are most likely to be immigrants, although the fraction of immigrants married to natives varies over our sample period. In particular, the larger cohorts of immigrants in 1940 and the 1990s are more likely to have immigrant spouses—64 percent and 81 percent, respectively, for men, and 76 percent in both 1940 and 1994–96 for women. The marriage patterns of the second generation are perhaps the most interesting. Second-generation men and women in 1970 and 1994–96 were typically married to natives (i.e., third-and-higher generation), but sizable fractions are married to immigrants and to members of the second generation of the same "ethnic"

---

11. Age-adjusted employment rates for men in the three generational groups are very similar over the sample period.

12. This appears to be inconsistent with evidence from Canada. See Baker and Benjamin (1997).

13. The wage quartiles are calculated using the pooled sample of working natives, immigrants, and second generation (by gender).

group.[14] Interestingly, second-generation men have a slightly higher likelihood of marrying a native than second-generation women.

6.4.2   Relative Wages of Immigrants and Second Generation over Time

As we have noted, comparisons between the relative earnings of natives, immigrants, and the second generation are complicated by changes in the relative age distributions of the three groups. A second confounding factor is the changing geographic distribution of immigrants versus natives. In 1940, immigrants and the second generation were highly concentrated in the northeastern states: 54 percent of immigrants and 45 percent of second-generation adults lived in the Northeast, versus 21 percent of natives. By the mid-1990s immigrants were still slightly more likely to live in the Northeast than natives (23 percent of immigrants versus 19 percent of natives), but the Pacific region had become a more important immigrant focus: 38 percent of immigrants and 28 percent of the second generation lived in the Pacific states compared to only 13 percent of adult natives. Since wages vary systematically across regions, shifts in the geographic distribution of immigrants or second-generation individuals relative to natives would be expected to shift relative wages.

In an effort to parse out the effects of the changing age and geographic distributions among the three generational groups, we performed the simple exercise summarized in table 6.2. We first calculated the joint distributions of age and region for each of the three generational groups in 1940, 1970, and 1994–96 (using five 10-year age intervals and three geographic areas). We then developed a set of weights for the immigrant and second-generation samples in each year that would "reweight" these samples to have the same joint distribution as natives. Finally, we calculated the distributions of log weekly wages for the reweighted samples and constructed the differences relative to natives presented in the right-hand columns of the table.[15]

The effects of the adjustment procedure on the wage distributions of immigrant men are illustrated in figure 6.2. For reference, panel A of the figure presents the densities of log weekly wages of third-and-higher-generation men in 1940, 1970, and 1994–96. The other three panels show the densities of log wages for immigrant men, before and after reweighting the samples to have the same age and regional distributions as native men. As expected, the adjustments are most significant in 1940, when immigrants were older and more heavily concentrated in high-wage regions

14. In the 1970 census we can only determine the place of birth of fathers. We therefore classify all second-generation men and women by the country of origin of their fathers.

15. This procedure can be interpreted as a generalization of the traditional Oaxaca-style regression adjustment method. DiNardo, Fortin, and Lemieux (1996) develop more general reweighting methods that can be applied with continuous covariates.

Table 6.2   Characteristics of Adjusted Log Wage Distributions

	Adjusted Distributions of			Differences Relative to 3rd+ Generation	
	3rd+ Generation	Immigrants	2nd Generation	Immigrants	2nd Generation
A. Men					
1940					
1st quartile	4.87	4.97	5.01	0.10	0.14
Median	5.40	5.46	5.49	0.06	0.09
3rd quartile	5.85	5.85	5.92	0.00	0.07
Std. deviation	0.75	0.69	0.74	−0.06	−0.01
1970					
1st quartile	5.89	5.82	5.98	−0.07	0.09
Median	6.38	6.31	6.44	−0.07	0.06
3rd quartile	6.70	6.70	6.77	0.00	0.07
Std. deviation	0.74	0.73	0.74	−0.01	0.00
1994–96					
1st quartile	5.69	5.46	5.69	−0.23	0.00
Median	6.25	5.92	6.31	−0.33	0.06
3rd quartile	6.74	6.51	6.77	−0.23	0.03
Std. deviation	0.85	0.78	0.83	−0.07	−0.02
B. Women					
1940					
1st quartile	4.48	4.65	4.48	0.17	0.20
Median	5.01	5.04	5.07	0.03	0.06
3rd quartile	5.40	5.33	5.40	−0.07	0.00
Std. deviation	0.75	0.62	0.73	−0.13	−0.07
1970					
1st quartile	5.30	5.36	5.36	0.06	0.06
Median	5.79	5.82	5.82	0.03	0.03
3rd quartile	6.18	6.15	6.21	−0.03	0.03
Std. deviation	0.74	0.70	0.73	−0.04	−0.01
1994–96					
1st quartile	5.20	5.15	5.33	−0.05	0.13
Median	5.82	5.63	5.95	−0.19	0.13
3rd quartile	6.28	6.18	6.44	−0.10	0.16
Std. deviation	0.83	0.81	0.83	−0.02	0.00

Notes: All data pertain to average weekly wages in 1995 dollars. The wage distributions of immigrants and second generation have been reweighted (by age and region cell) using relative weights that give the immigrant and second generation samples the same joint distribution of age and region as the third-and-higher-generation group. See text.

than natives. The effect of reweighting works in a similar direction in 1970 but is of a much smaller magnitude, whereas in the 1994–96 sample, the adjustments are trivial.

The results in table 6.2 point to two main conclusions. First, controlling for age and region, the relative wages of immigrants declined substantially between 1940 and the mid-1990s. For men, the difference in median wages

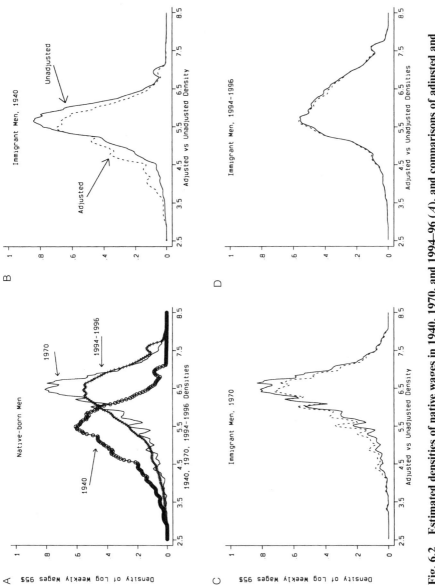

Fig. 6.2 Estimated densities of native wages in 1940, 1970, and 1994–96 (*A*), and comparisons of adjusted and unadjusted densities of immigrant wages (*B–D*)

between immigrants and natives declined by 13 percentage points between 1940 and 1970, and by another 26 percentage points between 1970 and 1994–96. The immigrant-native wage gap at the 25th and 75th percentiles also declined. For women, the difference in median wages between immigrants and natives was stable between 1940 and 1970 but then declined by 24 percentage points between 1970 and 1994–96. Second, in contrast to the pattern for immigrants, any significant decline in the relative wages of the second generation was confined to the lower deciles of the wage distribution. At the median, second-generation men earned 9 percent higher wages than native men in 1940, 6 percent higher wages in 1970, and 6 percent higher wages in 1994–96. At the 25th percentile, however, the second generation's relative wage advantage fell from 14 percent in 1940 to 9 percent in 1970 to 0 in 1994–96. The pattern of wage gaps for women is generally similar, although at the 75th percentile, second-generation women seem to have gained relative to native women (gaps of 0 in 1940, 3 percent in 1970, and 16 percent in 1994–96).

6.4.3 Country-of-Origin Effects

Many previous researchers have noted the decline in the relative earnings of immigrants portrayed in table 6.2 (see, e.g., Borjas 1994). A leading explanation for this change is the shift in the source countries of U.S. immigrants, associated in part with the Immigration Reform Act of 1965. Table 6.3 illustrates the changing composition of the immigrant stocks in 1940, 1970, and 1994–96, along with the corresponding changes in the composition of the second-generation pool. Because of data limitations in the 1970 census, we identify second-generation men and women in this table and throughout the remainder of the paper with the country of origin of their father.

In 1940, most U.S. immigrants were from Europe, the United Kingdom, Ireland, or Canada. The largest group were from Eastern Europe (34 percent), while northern and southern Europe and the U.K.-affiliated countries (the United Kingdom, Ireland, Canada, Australia, and New Zealand) each contributed about one-fifth of the total. By 1970, the fraction of immigrants from Europe (particularly Eastern Europe) had declined substantially, while the fractions from Mexico, South and Central America, and Asia had risen. These trends were amplified over the next 25 years, so that by the mid-1990s nearly 30 percent of immigrants were from Mexico, 25 percent were from Central and South America, and 23 percent were from Asia. Immigrants from the United Kingdom, Ireland, Canada, Australia, and New Zealand—who had made up more than 20 percent of the immigration populations in 1940 and 1970—represent only 6 percent of the 1994–96 sample.

Changes in the composition of the second generation represent a lagged version of the changes for the immigrant population, albeit with addi-

Table 6.3   Country of Origin of Immigrants and Fathers of Second Generation

	1940		1970		1994–96	
	Immigrants	2nd Generation	Immigrants	2nd Generation	Immigrants	2nd Generation
1. Europe, U.K., etc.						
U.K., Ireland, etc.	22.3	15.2	19.9	12.2	5.5	10.6
Northwest Europe	18.8	23.4	14.8	13.4	3.1	18.2
Southwest Europe	17.3	13.3	11.9	22.7	3.2	3.4
Eastern Europe	33.8	27.2	16.3	39.1	4.9	12.2
Subtotal	92.3	79.1	62.9	87.4	16.5	44.5
2. Mexico, Central/South America						
Mexico	3.4	1.4	9.6	5.0	29.1	23.7
Americas	0.5	0.0	4.4	0.2	12.4	4.4
Subtotal	3.8	1.4	13.9	5.2	41.5	28.1
3. Asia						
West Asia	1.4	0.5	2.9	1.3	5.7	2.1
East Asia	1.3	0.3	7.8	2.2	17.6	8.0
Subtotal	2.7	0.9	10.8	3.4	23.4	10.1
4. Caribbean Islands, Africa, other						
Subtotal	1.3	18.6[a]	12.4	4.0	18.7	17.4

Notes: Column entries represent the percentage of immigrants from each country or percentage of second-generation fathers from each country. Based on samples of men and women age 16–66 (see table 6.1 for sample sizes).

[a]In the 1940 census, a large fraction of second-generation individuals have their father's nativity coded as "other."

tional "noise" introduced by differential fertility and intermarriage patterns. For example, Eastern Europeans are the largest second-generation group in 1970, reflecting their importance in the immigrant population a generation earlier. By the mid-1990s, individuals of European or U.K.-related descent are no longer a majority of the second-generation population, and natives with Mexican-born parents represent close to a quarter of the group.

The potential importance of these compositional changes is explored in table 6.4, where we compare the education, wages, and marriage patterns of immigrant and second-generation men and women in four major "country groups." For reference, we also report the outcomes for natives (i.e., the third-and-higher generation). Examination of this table reveals substantial heterogeneity in the outcomes of immigrant and second-generation men and women from different country groups. For example, immigrants from Europe and the U.K.-related countries have consistently higher education and wages than immigrants from Mexico and South and Central America. The sons and daughters of European immigrants likewise have higher education and earnings than the sons and daughters of Mexican and South and Central American immigrants. The changing gaps in education and wages between natives and immigrants are also notable. In 1940, native men and women were better educated than immigrants from any of the four country groups. In 1970, immigrants from Asia were better educated than natives, while in 1994–96, immigrants from the United Kingdom and Europe and from Asia were more highly educated than natives. Thus, the persistent gap in education between immigrants and natives documented in table 6.1 is largely a result of the changing composition of immigrant source countries.

To further illustrate the potential effects of changing immigrant source countries on the wages of immigrants and second-generation individuals relative to natives, table 6.5 presents the mean wages from table 6.4 for each source country expressed as a fraction of the corresponding mean for natives. The most prominent feature of the table is the low level of relative wages for immigrants (and second-generation individuals) from Mexico and South and Central America. This feature suggests that the rise in the fraction of immigrants from Mexico and South and Central America over the past half-century would be expected to generate a decline in the relative economic status of immigrants as a whole. A second interesting aspect of table 6.5 is the time pattern of relative wages for immigrant and second-generation men and women from Mexico and South and Central America. Relative wages of these groups rose from 1940 to 1970 and then fell between 1970 and 1994–96. This inverted-U trend parallels the trend in overall wage inequality for natives (see fig. 6.2 and table 6.1). One explanation for this parallelism is the fact that the relative wages of low-wage groups will tend to rise as overall wage inequality falls (as it

Table 6.4   Comparisons of Education, Earnings, and Marriage Patterns of Natives, Immigrants, and Second-Generation Men and Women

	Men			Women		
	Education	Weekly Wage	Married to Immigrant	Education	Weekly Wage	Married to Immigrant
A. Immigrants versus Natives						
1940						
Europe, U.K., etc.	7.1	324	64.1	6.9	188	74.5
Mexico, Central/South America	5.2	195	61.6	4.9	144	75.0
Asia	7.3	248	74.7	7.3	208	87.5
Caribbean, Africa, other	7.9	254	58.5	6.8	157	78.9
Natives	8.9	266	2.0	9.3	173	3.0
1970						
Europe, U.K., etc.	10.7	762	52.1	10.3	410	51.0
Mexico, Central/South America	8.2	526	60.7	7.9	349	63.5
Asia	12.5	650	69.3	11.4	438	61.7
Caribbean, Africa, other	10.5	581	74.2	9.7	393	74.8
Natives	11.2	635	2.0	11.2	376	2.0
1994–96						
Europe, U.K., etc.	13.4	759	62.3	13.0	455	51.8
Mexico, Central/South America	9.4	366	84.3	9.6	278	85.1
Asia	13.9	646	91.7	13.1	465	81.3
Caribbean, Africa, other	12.8	587	77.1	12.2	399	78.8
Natives	13.0	621	4.0	12.9	405	3.0

(continued)

Table 6.4   (continued)

	Men			Women		
	Education	Weekly Wage	Married to Immigrant	Education	Weekly Wage	Married to Immigrant
	B. Second Generation versus Natives					
1940						
Europe, U.K., etc.	9.4	310	10.6	9.3	194	22.0
Mexico, Central/South America	5.7	138	24.5	5.4	93	42.4
Asia	10.7	258	12.4	10.7	185	48.5
Caribbean, Africa, other	8.7	290	4.4	9.0	178	7.3
Natives	8.9	266	2.0	9.3	173	3.0
1970						
Europe, U.K., etc.	11.3	818	6.9	10.9	430	11.5
Mexico, Central/South America	8.7	571	18.1	8.3	353	22.1
Asia	12.3	782	15.8	11.6	458	17.2
Caribbean, Africa, other	10.9	742	7.9	10.7	427	11.4
Natives	11.2	635	2.0	11.2	376	2.0
1994–96						
Europe, U.K., etc.	13.8	773	9.1	13.3	498	7.6
Mexico, Central/South America	11.7	434	30.7	11.6	316	34.2
Asia	13.5	594	34.2	13.5	473	26.8
Caribbean, Africa, other	13.2	621	19.9	13.2	428	20.0
Natives	13.0	621	4.0	12.9	405	3.0

Notes: Columns show mean education, mean average weekly wage, and percentage of group married to immigrants (among those married). Samples consist of immigrants and second-generation men and women age 16–66.

Table 6.5   **Mean Weekly Wages Relative to Natives by Origin Group**

	Immigrants			Second Generation		
	1940	1970	1994–96	1940	1970	1994–96
	A. Men					
Europe, U.K., etc.	1.22	1.20	1.22	1.17	1.29	1.24
Mexico, Central/South America	0.73	0.83	0.59	0.52	0.90	0.70
Asia	0.93	1.02	1.04	0.97	1.23	0.96
Caribbean and other	0.95	0.91	0.95	1.09	1.17	1.00
	B. Women					
Europe, U.K., etc.	1.09	1.09	1.12	1.12	1.14	1.23
Mexico, Central/South America	0.83	0.93	0.69	0.54	0.94	0.78
Asia	1.20	1.16	1.15	1.07	1.22	1.17
Caribbean and other	0.91	1.05	0.99	1.03	1.14	1.06

Notes: Entries represent ratio of mean weekly wages of origin group to mean weekly wages of natives. Origin groups of second generation are based on father's country of birth.

did between 1940 and 1970) and fall as overall inequality rises (as it did between 1970 and the mid-1990s). Whatever the explanation, examination of table 6.5 suggests that some of the decline in wages of immigrants as a whole between 1970 and 1994–96 may be attributable to a deterioration of the relative earnings of Mexican and South and Central American immigrants.

We can employ the same reweighting techniques used in table 6.2 to more formally evaluate the effects of changing source country composition on the changing relative earnings of immigrants and second-generation individuals. To fix ideas, consider the change in the median log wage of immigrants relative to natives between 1940 and 1970. Let $m(\text{Imm}, 70)$ denote the median wage of immigrants in 1970, and let $m(\text{Native}, 70)$ denote the median wage of natives. Using this notation, the change in the immigrant-native wage gap between 1940 and 1970 is

$$D = m(\text{Imm}, 70) - m(\text{Native}, 70) - [m(\text{Imm}, 40) - m(\text{Native}, 40)].$$

The wage distributions of natives and immigrants may change for a variety of reasons, including changes in the age and geographic distribution of the two populations, and changes in the relative fractions of specific immigrant-origin groups. Let $m(\text{Imm}, 40|70)$ denote the median log wage of immigrants when the sample of 1940 immigrants is reweighted to have the same joint distribution of age, region, and immigrant source countries as in 1970, and let $m(\text{Native}, 40|70)$ denote the median log wage of natives when the sample of 1940 natives is reweighted to have the same joint distribution of age and region as in 1970. The relative change D can be decomposed as

$$D = D_1 + D_2,$$

where

$$D_1 = m(\text{Imm}, 70) - m(\text{Native}, 70)$$
$$- [m(\text{Imm}, 40|70) - m(\text{Native}, 40|70)]$$

and

$$D_2 = m(\text{Imm}, 40|70) - m(\text{Native}, 40|70)$$
$$- [m(\text{Imm}, 40) - m(\text{Native}, 40)].$$

The first of these components represents the change in relative wages that would have occurred if there had been no change in the age or geographic distributions of natives or immigrants and no change in the origin composition of immigrants. The second component represents the difference between the "counterfactual" immigrant-native wage gap in 1940 (constructed to have the 1970 joint distribution of age, region, and immigrant composition) and the actual immigrant-native wage gap in that year.

The elements of D_1 are displayed in table 6.6. In this table, the wage distributions for natives, immigrants, and second-generation individuals have all been calculated using weights that standardize the joint distributions of age (across five age intervals), region (across three regions) and country-of-origin group (across four country groups) back to their 1970 values. (Thus, the 1970 medians, quartiles, and standard deviations are simply the "raw" statistics for the respective generational groups.) The wage gaps relative to natives in the two right-hand columns of the table represent the differences that would have been observed under the assumption of a 1970 distribution for the covariates. Comparing these adjusted wage gaps over time shows the changes in the relative wage gap *holding constant age, region, and origin composition.*

Inspection of the adjusted wage gaps for immigrants in table 6.6 reveals a remarkable degree of stability over time, especially compared to the downward trend in table 6.2. The adjusted median immigrant-native wage gap for men falls from 10 percent in 1940 to 6 percent in 1970 and then rises slightly to 8 percent in 1994–96. The corresponding median gap for women rises from 5 to 7 percent between 1940 and 1994–96. Thus, almost all of the measured decline in the wage gap between immigrants and natives between 1940 and the mid-1990s is attributable to the effects of changing characteristics of immigrants—in particular, the changing fraction of immigrants from different groups of source countries.

The story for the second generation is somewhat different. As is evident from the last column of table 6.6, the second generation–native wage differential (after adjusting for age, region, and origin composition) is always large and quite substantial. At the three points in the distribution reported in the table, the adjusted differentials range from 17 to 57 percent for men and from 9 to 39 percent for women. The existence of a positive

Table 6.6   **Adjusted Log Wage Distributions, Accounting for Changes in Composition of
                   Immigrant and Second-Generation Populations**

	Adjusted Distributions of			Differences Relative to 3rd+ Generation	
	3rd+ Generation	Immigrants	2nd Generation	Immigrants	2nd Generation
A. Men					
1940					
1st quartile	4.88	5.10	5.29	0.22	0.41
Median	5.39	5.49	5.72	0.10	0.33
3rd quartile	5.83	5.82	6.08	−0.01	0.25
Std. deviation	0.75	0.60	0.65	−0.15	−0.10
1970					
1st quartile	5.89	6.00	6.33	0.11	0.44
Median	6.38	6.44	6.58	0.06	0.20
3rd quartile	6.70	6.76	6.87	0.06	0.17
Std. deviation	0.74	0.68	0.58	−0.06	−0.16
1994–96					
1st quartile	5.55	5.69	6.12	0.14	0.57
Median	6.19	6.27	6.65	0.08	0.46
3rd quartile	6.67	6.77	6.96	0.10	0.29
Std. deviation	0.88	0.82	0.75	−0.06	−0.13
B. Women					
1940					
1st quartile	4.47	4.70	4.74	0.23	0.27
Median	4.99	5.04	5.19	0.05	0.20
3rd quartile	5.39	5.37	5.61	−0.02	0.22
Std. deviation	0.75	0.61	0.70	−0.14	−0.05
1970					
1st quartile	5.30	5.47	5.50	0.17	0.20
Median	5.79	5.85	5.94	0.06	0.15
3rd quartile	6.18	6.19	6.27	0.01	0.09
Std. deviation	0.74	0.67	0.66	−0.07	−0.08
1994–96					
1st quartile	5.09	5.24	5.48	0.15	0.39
Median	5.72	5.79	6.10	0.07	0.38
3rd quartile	6.22	6.28	6.57	0.06	0.35
Std. deviation	0.85	0.83	0.82	−0.02	−0.03

Notes: All data pertain to average weekly wages in 1995 dollars. The samples of immigrants and second-generation persons in 1940 and 1994–96 have been reweighted to give these samples the same joint distribution of age, region, and origin composition as in 1970. The samples of natives in 1940 and 1994–96 have been reweighted to give these samples the same joint distribution of age and region as in 1970.

adjusted wage gap between second-generation individuals and natives is consistent with another feature that we will demonstrate below: Conditional on parental background, second-generation men and women have higher education and wages than natives.

Reweighting the second generation in 1940 and 1995 to have the same joint distribution of age, region, and origin as the 1970 second generation has two important impacts on the comparison, both of which substantially raise the second generation–native wage differential relative to the more modest values reported in table 6.2.

First, relative to the native born, the 1970 second generation are considerably older. From table 6.1 it is evident that the mean age differential—which is less than one year in both 1940 and 1994–96—is 12.1 years in 1970. Second, as is evident from table 6.3, the 1970 second-generation sample includes relatively more children of immigrants from Europe and the United Kingdom—who typically fare well in the U.S. labor market—and relatively few children of Mexican or South or Central American immigrants—who typically fare poorly. The net effect of "upweighting" older second-generation people of European descent and "downweighting" younger second-generation people of Mexican and South and Central American descent is particularly striking in 1994–96. At the lowest wage quartile, second-generation men in the reweighted sample earn 57 percent more than native men, while second-generation women earn 39 percent more than natives.

Another notable aspect of the adjusted second generation–native wage gaps in table 6.6 is their evolution over time. Over the period 1940–70, the second generation–native gaps show a general decline. Among women, the declines are relatively modest at all points in the distribution. Among men, the direction and size of the movement is sensitive to the point in the distribution at which the comparison is made, although, on average, the movements are quite modest. (Although we do not report this in table 6.6, the fall in the mean adjusted wage is only 3 percent.)

More interesting is the movement in the adjusted wage gap between 1970 and 1994–96. Unlike the adjusted immigrant-native wage gaps, which were fairly stable over this period, the adjusted second generation–native wage gaps for men and women rose substantially: by 12–26 percent for men, depending on the specific quartile of the wage distribution, and by 19–26 percent for women. Because the weighting adjustments "upweight" older second-generation men and women of European descent—people who would tend to earn above-average wages—some of this rise may be attributable to the rise in overall wage inequality between 1970 and 1994–96 rather than to any shift in the relative position of second-generation workers in the overall wage distribution. As a mechanical matter, a rise in overall inequality will tend to increase the measured wage gaps between the percentiles of the native wage distribution and the percentiles of a sample of relatively high-wage second-generation workers.

An important conclusion that emerges from table 6.6 is that the stability of the wage gaps for second-generation workers that we documented in table 6.2 should be seen as rather surprising, given the changing age and ethnic composition of the second-generation sample between 1970 and the mid-1990s and the trend toward widening wage inequality in the economy as a whole. Despite the rising fractions of second-generation men and women of non-European heritage, and the falling relative age of second-generation workers, they have more or less maintained their relative wage advantage.

6.5   Intergenerational Assimilation

6.5.1   Conceptual Issues

While some immigrants are quite similar to natives, others differ from native-born people in important ways, such as native tongue and level and type of schooling. These differences may be transmitted to the second generation through a variety of mechanisms, including passive channels (such as the home environment) and active channels (such as decisions about schooling).[16] In fact, simple comparisons of second-generation men and women from different backgrounds, such as those in tables 6.4 and 6.5, suggest that the native-born children of immigrants with higher levels of education and earnings tend to have significantly higher levels of education and earnings. This should not be surprising, since even within the native population there is a relatively high "intergenerational correlation" between the education and earnings levels of parents and their children (see Solon [1999] for a recent review).

The strength of the connection between the economic performance of immigrant parents and the outcomes of their native-born children is usefully summarized by a simple descriptive model of the form:

$$(1) \qquad\qquad y_i = a + bx_i + e_i,$$

where y_i is the level of education or wages of child i (adjusted for factors such as age), and x_i is the level of education or wages of his or her father (similarly adjusted). In principle, the outcomes of both the mother and father could be included in this equation. For simplicity, however, and in recognition of the constraints imposed by our data, we focus on the connection between child and father.

In this setup, the "intergenerational assimilation rate" is given by $1 - b$. To see this, note that if $b = 1$, then there is no intergenerational assimilation, since any difference in outcomes between a father and the underlying population is reproduced by his offspring. On the other hand, if $b = 0$, then there is complete intergenerational assimilation, since regardless of the outcomes of the father, his offspring will have the mean characteristics of the overall population. More generally, if $0 < b < 1$, then a fraction

---

16. Mechanisms of intergenerational transmission are studied by Becker and Tomes (1986).

$1 - b$ of the difference between the father's outcome and the population mean for the father's generation is closed in the next generation.

We lack data on the education or earnings of the parents of second-generation children. Instead, following Borjas (1993), we rely on a grouping estimation strategy to estimate equation (1). This method proceeds as follows. First, we estimate mean education or earnings levels (adjusted for age, etc.) for immigrant men in 1940 or 1970 by country of origin. Second, we estimate mean education or earnings levels (adjusted for age, etc.) for second-generation men or women in 1970 or 1994–96 by their father's country of origin. Third, we regress the mean outcomes for the second generation in a specific origin group on the outcomes of the immigrant men in the same group from the preceding census sample. There is clearly some slippage in this method because (for example) not all immigrant men in 1940 had children who appear in our sample in 1970, nor do all children have fathers who were potentially sampled in 1940. The method can be refined to reduce this slippage by restricting the immigrant men to those married to immigrants and having children between the ages of 0 and 15, and restricting the second generation samples to individuals of the "right" age to match with these children. Ignoring slippage in the definitions of the father's and children's cohorts, however, this grouping method will yield consistent estimates of the coefficient b.

It is interesting to ask how the degree of intergenerational correlation between immigrant fathers and their native-born children might differ from the degree of correlation between native fathers and their children. A natural assumption is that the intergenerational correlation is the same; that is, the rate of intergenerational assimilation between immigrants and the second generation is merely a particular manifestation of a more general process of intergenerational transmission. Solon (1992) and Zimmerman (1992), using the Panel Study of Income Dynamics and the National Longitudinal Study of Youth, respectively, for example, estimate several different variants of equation (1) using samples of mainly native-born men. Both papers report estimates of the parameter b between 0.4 and 0.5, suggesting an intergenerational assimilation rate of between 0.5 and 0.6.

There are at least two reasons why one might expect estimates of b based on the children of immigrants to be different from this. First, there may be a stronger or weaker connection between the observed characteristics of an immigrant father and the true underlying characteristics of the family. For example, suppose that the true model generating children's outcomes includes both the father's and mother's education (or wages):

$$y_i = a + bx_i + cz_i + e_i,$$

where z_i is the mother's outcome. In this case, a regression of the child's outcomes on the father's will yield a coefficient with probability limit

$$b + c\frac{\text{Cov}(x_i, z_i)}{\text{Var}(x_i)}.$$

Thus, if immigrant parents are more likely to have similar economic outcomes or levels of education than native-born parents, our estimates of b will be higher than those calculated from a similar regression on the general population.

A second reason is the possibility of "ethnic human capital" that has been raised by Borjas (1992), among others. The ethnic human capital model specifies that the outcome of a child may be affected by the education or economic well-being of other parents from the same country of origin, perhaps because of "neighborhood effects." To formalize this model, we distinguish between individuals (indexed by i) and origin groups (indexed by j). A model with ethnic human capital specifies that

$$(2) \qquad y_{i,j} = a + bx_{i,j} + dx_j + e_{i,j},$$

where $y_{i,j}$ is the outcome for child i in group j; $x_{i,j}$ is the outcome of his or her father; and x_j is the mean outcome of origin group j. A standard microlevel regression of $y_{i,j}$ on $x_{i,j}$ will yield a coefficient with probability limit

$$b + d\frac{\text{Cov}(x_{i,j}, x_j)}{\text{Var}(x_{i,j})} = b + d\frac{\text{Var}(x_j)}{\text{Var}(x_{i,j})},$$

and will be upward biased for b if $d > 0$. If ethnic human capital effects are larger for the children of immigrants than for other children (because immigrants are more likely to live in enclaves, or because immigrant's children are more strongly affected by their parents' peer group), then the upward bias will be *bigger* for second-generation children than for the general population, leading to a higher intergenerational correlation.

Moreover, the use of grouped estimation strategy will exacerbate this bias. To see this, note that equation (2) implies that the probability limit of the coefficient from a regression of y_j on x_j is $b + d$, which is greater than $b + d [\text{Var}(x_j)]/[\text{Var}(x_{i,j})]$, since $\text{Var}(x_j) < \text{Var}(x_{i,j})$. A similar argument suggests that the bias induced by any unobserved error component in the residual $e_{i,j}$ that happens to be correlated with x_j will be accentuated in the grouped regression relative to a microlevel regression.

A final aspect of the grouped estimation strategy is that it "solves" the attenuation problem that arises in the corresponding microlevel regression if parental outcomes are reported with error, or if income is measured in only one year but a father's permanent income is the conceptually appropriate determinant of his children's success.[17] To see this, note that any

17. This point is emphasized by Solon (1992, 1999) and Zimmerman (1992).

individual-specific transitory income fluctuations or measurement errors are "averaged out" of the mean for the origin group. Thus, intergenerational correlations of income obtained from a grouped estimation method are most comparable to the estimates obtained from microlevel regressions that use instrumental variables methods or multiple years of data to isolate the correlation between children's outcomes and their father's permanent income.

6.5.2   Estimation Results

We applied the grouped estimation method described above to estimate intergenerational correlations between immigrant fathers in 1940 and 1970 and second-generation sons and daughters in 1970 and 1994–96. We focus on two outcomes for fathers—mean education and mean log weekly wages—and three outcomes for children—mean education, mean log weekly wages, and a measure of marriage assimilation described below. Given the sample sizes available in our data sets, we aggregated some countries into groups and arrived at a total of 34 countries (or country groups) between 1940 and 1970, and 33 countries (or country groups) between 1970 and 1994–96. The countries are listed in table 6A.1, along with the outcome measures we use.

For the immigrant fathers, we constructed age- and region-adjusted education and earnings outcomes for each country of origin by regressing education or log weekly earnings on origin dummies, region dummies, and origin dummies interacted with age and age-squared.[18] We then used the estimated age profiles to obtain predicted education or earnings levels for each origin group at age 40. As described in the data section, we use all available observations in the 1940 census (not just the sample-line individuals) and two 1 percent samples of the 1970 census to obtain more reliable estimates of the outcomes of immigrant fathers. For the second-generation sons and daughters we constructed age- and region-adjusted education and earnings outcomes by regressing education or log weekly earnings on origin dummies, region dummies, and a quadratic age function.[19] We then predicted education or earnings levels for each origin group at age 40.

Our estimates of the intergenerational correlations in wages and education are presented in table 6.7, while figures 6.3 and 6.4 plot the adjusted wages of second-generation sons and daughters against the adjusted wages of immigrant men. Inspection of the estimation results and figures suggests that there are strong links between the education and earnings of immigrant fathers and the outcomes of their native-born children. Countries with higher immigrant earnings (such as Germany and the United

---

18. We restricted our attention to men age 24–66 in order to help stabilize the estimates.

19. As with the immigrant fathers, we restricted our attention to men and women age 24–66.

Table 6.7	**Relationship between Education and Earnings of Immigrant Fathers and Education and Earnings of Second-Generation Sons and Daughters**							
	Second-Generation Sons				Second-Generation Daughters			
	Education		Log Wage		Education		Log Wage	
	(1)	(2)	(3)	(4)	(5)	(6)	(7)	(8)
			A. 1940–70					
Mean education	0.41	—	0.03	—	0.47	—	0.02	—
of fathers	(0.10)		(.01)		(0.08)		(0.01)	
Mean log wage	—	4.74	—	0.44	—	4.78	—	0.21
of fathers		(0.68)		(0.05)		(0.56)		(0.06)
R^2	0.35	0.60	0.24	0.72	0.51	0.69	0.12	0.25
			B. 1970–95					
Mean education	0.43	—	0.06	—	0.42	—	0.05	—
of fathers	(0.05)		(0.01)		(0.04)		(0.01)	
Mean log wage	—	4.50	—	0.62	—	4.05	—	0.50
of fathers		(0.72)		(0.12)		(0.67)		(0.13)
R^2	0.68	0.56	0.51	0.45	0.76	0.54	0.54	0.33

Notes: Estimated on immigrant group-level means using weighted least squares. Groups are indentified by father's country of origin. Education and wage outcomes are adjusted for age (see text). There are 34 country of origin groups in the 1940–70 analysis and 33 in the 1970–95 analysis. Group weight is the sum of the number of sons and daughters (age 24–66) observed for the group. Standard errors are in parentheses.

Kingdom) have higher second-generation earnings, while countries with lower immigrant earnings (notably Mexico) have lower second-generation earnings. Using education as the outcome measure for fathers and children, the estimates of the intergenerational coefficient b in equation (1) are very stable, with a range from 0.41 to 0.47. Using wages as the outcome measure the estimates of b are more variable, ranging from 0.21 to 0.62. The relatively low coefficient for second-generation daughters in 1970 may reflect the fact that many women in this cohort had limited attachment to the labor market.[20] By comparison, the coefficient for the later sample of daughters is much larger and closer to the estimate for sons.

Table 6.7 also reports regressions of the second generation's education (or earnings) on the father's earnings (or education). The coefficients linking father's wages to children's education are large and relatively stable over time. The coefficients linking father's education to children's earnings are more variable, although for both sons and daughters the coefficient seems to have risen between 1970 and 1994–96. This is consistent with the relatively stable intergenerational correlations of education shown in table

20. In addition, unlike the other estimates we report, the results for the wages of second-generation daughters in 1970 are very sensitive to whether or not weights are used in estimation.

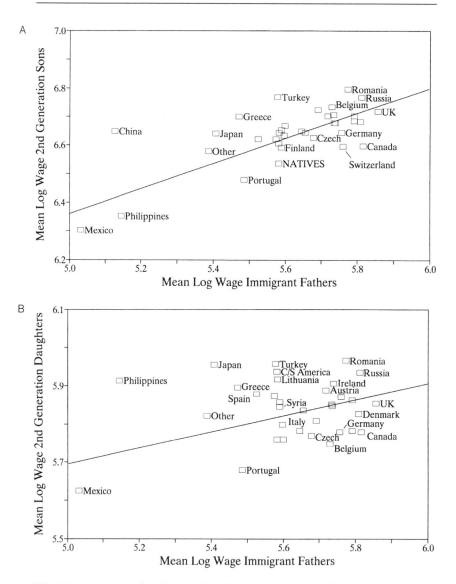

Fig. 6.3   Intergenerational correlations between the wages of immigrant fathers in 1940 and the wages of second-generation sons (*A*) and daughters (*B*) in 1970
Note: *A*, weighted OLS regression line shown, slope = 0.44; *B*, weighted OLS regression line shown, slope = 0.21.

6.7, along with the well-known rise in the economic payoff to education over the past 25 years.

Although they are not used in the estimation, we have added the data for native fathers and their children to figures 6.3 and 6. 4. An interesting feature of all four graphs is that native children earn 15–20 percent less

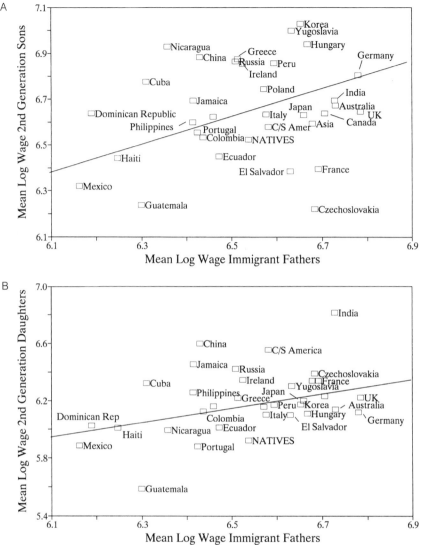

Fig. 6.4 Intergenerational correlations between the wages of immigrant fathers in 1970 and the wages of second-generation sons (*A*) and daughters (*B*) in 1994–96
Note: *A*, weighted OLS regression line shown, slope = 0.62; *B*, weighted OLS regression line shown, slope = 0.50.

than one would expect, given their fathers' earnings and the patterns for second-generation children. A similar feature is evident for education: Native men and women have 0.8 to 1.4 fewer years of education than would be predicted form their fathers' education level and the pattern of second-generation education outcomes. An implication of this gap is that even if

Table 6.8   Further Evidence on the Relation between Immigrant Fathers and Outcomes of Second-Generation Sons and Daughters

	Second-Generation Sons		Second-Generation Daughters	
	Education (1)	Log Wage (2)	Education (3)	Log Wage (4)
A. 1940–70				
Mean education	0.12	−0.00	0.21	0.00
of fathers	(0.10)	(0.01)	(0.07)	(0.01)
Mean log wage	4.08	0.46	3.65	0.20
of fathers	(0.86)	(0.06)	(0.65)	(0.08)
R^2	0.62	0.72	0.75	0.26
B. 1970–95				
Mean education	0.36	0.04	0.43	0.07
of fathers	(0.10)	(0.02)	(0.08)	(0.02)
Mean log wage	0.94	0.20	−0.18	−0.16
of fathers	(1.19)	(0.22)	(0.94)	(0.20)
R^2	0.69	0.53	0.76	0.55

Notes: Estimated on immigrant group-level means using weighted least squares. Groups are indentified by father's country of origin. Education and outcomes are adjusted for age (see text). There are 34 country of origin groups in the 1940–70 analysis and 33 in the 1970–95 analysis. Group weight is the sum of the number of sons and daughters (age 24–66) observed for the group. Standard errors are in parentheses.

immigrants have somewhat lower education or earnings than natives, their children will surpass the children of natives.[21]

A question raised by the estimated models in table 6.7 is whether the education and earnings of second-generation children are more strongly affected by the education or earnings of their fathers. To answer this question, we fit the models in table 6.8, which include both outcome measures for the fathers. For the 1940–70 generation, the data suggest that a father's earnings are more important than his education, although both variables are significant in the model for second-generation daughters' education. In contrast, the data for the 1970–95 generation suggest that a father's education is the key determinant of the second generation's success. Holding constant education, differences in father's earnings exert no significant effect on the second generation's education or earnings outcomes. We are unsure whether this difference between the 1940–70 cohort and the

21. We have checked this implication using micro data from the pooled 1977–96 General Social Survey, which contains information on father's education and nativity for about 15,300 men and women. A regression of education on father's education, age controls, and dummies for immigrants and second-generation individuals yields a coefficient of 0.31 on father's education and 0.79 (standard error 0.12) on the second generation dummy. We suspect that the father's education coefficient is biased down by about 20 percent by measurement error. If we force the coefficient on father's education to equal 0.40, the estimated second generation dummy rises to 0.90 years (standard error 0.12).

1970–95 cohort reflects changes in behavior, changes in the economic importance of education, or changes in the relative reliability of measured education and earnings differences across different immigrant groups in the 1940 and 1970 censuses.

Another question raised by the findings in table 6.7 is whether all of the effect of father's education or earnings is subsumed in the educational attainment of the second generation, or whether father's outcomes exert an independent effect on the wages of the second generation, controlling for the second generation's education. To answer this question, we fit a series of models for the wages of the second generation that included the education of the second generation and outcomes of the fathers. The results are summarized in table 6.9. Columns (1) and (5) of the table show simple models that include only the second generation's education. These estimates tend to be only slightly higher than corresponding microlevel estimates fit to the same samples of second-generation men and women in 1970 and 1994–96.[22] The models in the other columns add father's wages and education, alone and together, to this basic specification. For the 1940–70 cohort, there is some indication that even controlling for the second generation's education, father's wages and education matter. However, the signs of the effects differ between second-generation sons and daughters. For the 1970–95 cohort, on the other hand, the father outcome variables are individually (and jointly) insignificant determinants of wages, controlling for the education of the second generation.

Taken in combination with the findings in table 6.8, the results for the most recent cohort in table 6.9 point to a very simple model of the intergenerational transmission mechanism. According to the estimates in table 6.8, only father's education matters in the education or wage outcomes of the 1970–95 second generation cohort. Moreover, fathers' outcomes only directly affect the education of the second generation in this cohort. For this cohort, at least, the strong intergenerational linkages between immigrant fathers and their native-born children work only through education.

6.5.3 Marriage Assimilation

A different perspective on intergenerational assimilation is provided by the marriage patterns of second-generation sons and daughters. A child of immigrants can either marry a native, another child of immigrants, or an immigrant. A simple index of "marriage assimilation" is the fraction of second-generation men or women who marry natives, minus the fraction who marry immigrants. This index treats marriage to natives as a "positive" outcome and marriage to immigrants as a "negative" outcome.

---

22. The corresponding microlevel returns to education (controlling for a cubic in experience) for the second-generation samples are 0.064 (men, 1970); 0.065 (women, 1970); 0.121 (men, 1994–96); and 0.102 (women, 1994–96).

Table 6.9   Effects of Own Education and Father's Wages and Education on Average Weekly Earnings of Second-Generation Sons and Daughters

	Second-Generation Sons				Second-Generation Daughters			
	(1)	(2)	(3)	(4)	(5)	(6)	(7)	(8)
	A. 1940–70							
Mean education of group	0.080	0.061	0.085	0.065	0.057	0.087	0.080	0.106
	(0.005)	(0.007)	(0.006)	(0.006)	(0.008)	(0.013)	(0.010)	(0.013)
Mean log wage of fathers	—	0.154	—	0.198	—	-0.207	—	-0.192
		(0.043)		(0.039)		(0.074)		(0.065)
Mean education of fathers	—	—	-0.006	-0.012	—	—	-0.021	-0.019
			(0.004)	(0.003)			(0.007)	(0.006)
R^2	0.88	0.92	0.89	0.94	0.62	0.70	0.71	0.78
	B. 1970–95							
Mean education of group	0.132	0.125	0.130	0.128	0.135	0.150	0.146	0.144
	(0.014)	(0.021)	(0.025)	(0.025)	(0.014)	(0.201)	(0.030)	(0.030)
Mean log wage of fathers	—	0.059	—	0.080	—	-0.109	—	-0.133
		(0.128)		(0.168)		(0.118)		(0.155)
Mean education of fathers	—	—	0.002	-0.003	—	—	-0.006	0.005
			(0.031)	(0.017)			(0.014)	(0.019)
R^2	0.74	0.74	0.74	0.74	0.74	0.75	0.74	0.75

Notes: See notes to table 6.7. Dependent variable is mean log weekly earnings of second-generation sons or daughters (age 24–66). Standard errors are in parentheses.

We used information on the nativity of the spouses of married second-generation individuals in each of the origin groups analyzed in tables 6.7–6.9 to construct the marriage assimilation index. We then plotted the index for each origin group against the levels of education and wages of immigrant fathers, and fit the regression models shown in table 6.10.

Despite its ad hoc nature, the marriage index is very highly correlated with other measures of second generation success. As shown in figure 6.5, the sons and daughters of better-educated immigrant fathers have higher marriage assimilation indexes. Closer inspection of the data for individual countries revealed an exception to this general pattern for the children of immigrants from Asian countries. For example, second-generation Japanese children had very low marriage assimilation rates in 1970, despite the relatively high level of their father's education (see fig. 6.5). This impression is confirmed by the regression models in table 6.10, which show a substantial improvement in fit once an indicator for Asian origin groups is added.

As with the education and earnings outcomes of the second generation, there are some differences in the effects of father's education and wages for different cohorts of second-generation children. The effects of father's education on marriage assimilation rates are similar between men and women and are fairly stable over time (see cols. [2] and [6]). By comparison, the effects of father's earnings increase substantially between the 1940–70 cohort and the 1970–95 cohort. Moreover, in the earlier cohort, father's education seems to matter more than father's earnings, while in the later cohort, the reverse is true. Nevertheless, the marriage patterns of second-generation men and women generally confirm the existence of a strong linkage between the economic well-being of immigrant fathers and the degree of assimilation achieved by their children.

6.5.4   Comparison with Previous Estimates

How do our estimates of the degree of intergenerational correlation between immigrant fathers and their native-born children compare with other estimates? Our most easily compared estimates are those based on the log wages of the two generations. Like Borjas (1993), who analyzed the intergenerational correlation between immigrant fathers in 1940 and second-generation sons in 1970, we find fairly high correlations between the earnings of immigrants fathers and their children: in the range of 0.4 to 0.6. These are on the high side of estimates in the intergenerational correlation literature, potentially for the reasons discussed earlier.

The intergenerational correlations of education are lower and more stable (in the range of 0.40 to 0.45). A reasonable benchmark for comparison with these estimates is obtainable from the General Social Survey (GSS), which collects a yearly sample of data on adult household heads, including information on their father's education. Using the 1972–96 samples for

Table 6.10 Relationship between Education and Earnings of Immigrant Fathers and Marriage Assimilation of Second-Generation Sons and Daughters

	Second-Generation Sons				Second-Generation Daughters			
	(1)	(2)	(3)	(4)	(5)	(6)	(7)	(8)
A. 1940–70								
Mean education of fathers	0.055	0.062	—	0.068	0.074	0.081	—	0.100
	(0.011)	(0.009)		(0.012)	(0.012)	(0.011)		(0.014)
Mean log wage of fathers	—	—	0.34	−0.08	—	—	0.37	−0.24
			(0.11)	(0.11)			(0.15)	(0.13)
Indicator for Asian country	—	−0.39	−0.20	−0.42	—	−0.40	−0.16	−0.49
		(0.09)	(0.13)	(0.10)		(0.11)	(0.16)	(0.11)
R^2	0.43	0.64	0.31	0.65	0.52	0.67	0.22	0.70
B. 1970–95								
Mean education of fathers	0.045	0.065	—	−0.024	0.053	0.070	—	−0.019
	(0.018)	(0.015)		(0.026)	(0.017)	(0.015)		(0.026)
Mean log wage of fathers	—	—	0.89	1.13	—	—	0.94	1.13
			(0.14)	(0.29)			(0.14)	(0.28)
Indicator for Asian country	—	−0.59	−0.48	−0.41	—	−0.48	−0.35	−0.31
		(0.14)	(0.11)	(0.12)		(0.12)	(0.11)	(0.12)
R^2	0.16	0.48	0.65	0.66	0.24	0.46	0.65	0.65

Notes: Dependent variable is the fraction of married second-generation sons or daughters whose spouse is third or higher generation, minus the fraction whose spouse is an immigrant. Estimated on immigrant group-level means using weighted least squares. Groups are identified by father's country of origin. There are 34 country of origin groups in the 1940–70 analysis and 33 in the 1970–95 analysis. Group weight is the sum of the number of sons and daughters (age 24–66) observed for the group. Standard errors are in parentheses.

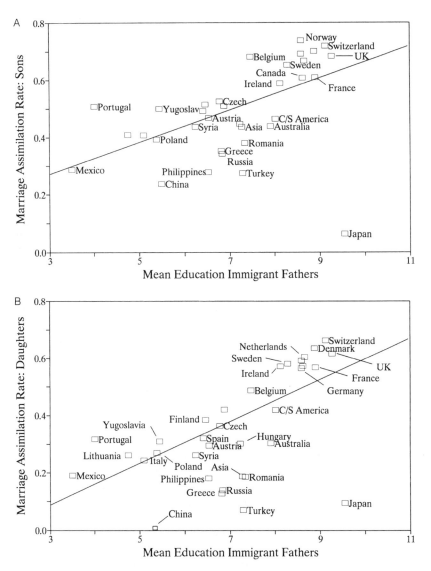

Fig. 6.5   Father's education in 1940 and marriage assimilation rates of second-generation sons (*A*) and daughters (*B*) in 1970

men and women who reported their father's education (a total sample of 19,520 observations), we regressed each person's education on their father's education, dummies for gender and sample year, and a cubic function of age. The estimated coefficient is 0.318 (standard error 0.005); the model explains about 25 percent of the variance in education. While this estimate is lower than the ones in table 6.7, it is important to account for the potential effects of measurement error. Ashenfelter and Rouse (1998) study the correlation in twins' reports of their parents' education, and estimate that the reliability of father's education is about 0.80. Combining this estimate with the GSS estimate, a microlevel regression for the effect of father's education on his son's or daughter's education implies an effect of 0.40 (= 0.318/.80). This estimate is remarkably close to our estimates based on the correlation between the education of second-generation men and women of different ancestries and the education of immigrant men in the same origin groups 25 or 30 years earlier.

6.5.5   Assessment

What do the intergenerational models in tables 6.7–6.10 imply about changes in the rate of intergenerational assimilation over time? On the one hand, our estimates of the intergenerational transmission of educational attainment (cols. [1], [2], [5], and [6] in table 6.7) show remarkable stability between 1940–70 and 1970–95. Based on these patterns, one might conclude that rates of intergenerational assimilation have not changed much. On the other hand, the implied estimates of the intergenerational *assimilation* coefficient for wages are uniformly *lower* in 1970–95 than in 1940–70. Thus, the intergenerational patterns of wages suggest that children of the immigrants born in the early part of this century assimilated faster than the children of the immigrants born in the later part of this century. Indeed, the magnitude of the estimates of the effect of the father's wage in 1970 on the wages of his son or daughter in 1995 is more than twice as large as the effect of the father's wage in 1940 on the wages of his son or daughter in 1970.

Any comparison of rates of intergenerational assimilation based on patterns of wages must be interpreted very carefully, however, in light of the recurring "theme" throughout this paper that the status of specific groups may be affected by overall shifts in wage inequality over time. If the dispersion in overall wages is changing over time, then the measured rate of intergenerational assimilation may change even if there are no changes in the relative ranking of second-generation workers in the overall wage distribution.

This point is illustrated in the following simple model. Let w_{i1} and w_{i2} represent the mean wages of first- and second-generation workers from family or ethnic group i, and assume that

$$(3) \qquad\qquad w_{i1} = \gamma_1 z_{i1},$$

$$(4) \qquad\qquad w_{i2} = \gamma_2 z_{i2},$$

$$(5) \qquad\qquad z_{i2} = \rho z_{i1},$$

where z_{i1} and z_{i2} refer to some latent index of "human capital" of the two groups, and γ_1 and γ_2 refer to the rates of transformation between human capital and observed wages for the first and second generation (or, loosely, the "prices" of human capital faced by members of the first and second generation). A larger value for γ implies that for a given distribution of z, the observed distribution of wages is more unequal.

In this one-factor model, one minus the intergenerational assimilation coefficient (the simple regression coefficient from a regression of child's wage on parent's wage) is equal to

$$\frac{\text{Cov}(w_{i1}, w_{i2})}{\text{Var}(w_{i1})} = \frac{\gamma_{i1}\gamma_{i2}\,\text{Cov}(z_{i1}, z_{i2})}{(\gamma_{i1})^2\,\text{Var}(z_{i1})} = \frac{\gamma_{i2}}{\gamma_{i1}}\rho.$$

It is therefore apparent that the magnitude of the measured intergenerational assimilation rate will vary as the variance of wages conditional on the single factor varies. In particular, if the distribution of wages is more unequal for parents than for children—the case for 1940 parents and their offspring in 1970—the rate of assimilation will be faster than when the distribution of wages is more unequal for the children than the parents— the case for 1970 immigrants and their offspring in 1995.

Moreover, under the assumption that the variance of the latent variable z has been constant across time, we can test the hypothesis that the intergenerational transmission process has remained unchanged over the period 1940–96. Given the simple one-factor model described above, a test for constancy involves a comparison of the simple correlation coefficient r across time, where

$$r \equiv \frac{\text{Cov}(w_{i1}, w_{i2})}{\sqrt{\text{Var}(w_{i1})\text{Var}(w_{i2})}} = \rho,$$

which does not depend on the values taken by γ.

For men, the value of ρ is 0.847 in 1970–40 and 0.853 in 1995–70. The comparable values for women are 0.503 and 0.575, respectively. At any conventional level of significance, the equality of ρ in the two time periods cannot be rejected for either men or women.[23] Given the substantial social, political, and economic changes over the last half-century, the relative stability of the intergenerational correlation in wages is noteworthy. We conclude that the fundamental determinants of the rate of assimilation of immigrant children have not changed much, although the measured par-

---

23. We performed the test by using Fisher's transformation: $z = .5 \log [(1 + \rho)/(1 - \rho)]$, which under suitable conditions is distributed normally with variance approximately equal to $1/(n - 3)$.

tial correlations between the wages of immigrant children and their second-generation children have been affected by changes in overall wage inequality.

6.6   Conclusions

We have used data from the 1940 and 1970 censuses and the 1994–96 Current Population Surveys to construct an economic history of the labor market status of immigrants and their children. Our main findings are easy to summarize: Despite changes in the legal environment for immigration and major changes in the origin countries of immigrants, the relative status of immigrant children has been remarkably constant. Indeed, we find that the rate of intergenerational "assimilation" in educational attainment has remained stable over the last 50 years and that the rate of intergenerational "assimilation" in earnings has also remained constant, apart from an effect of widening overall wage inequality.

A related finding is that the children of immigrants tend to have noticeably higher education and wages than the children of natives, controlling for parental background. This gap accounts for the relatively high labor market status of the second generation today, even though an increasing fraction of today's second generation are the children of immigrants from the lowest-paid immigrant groups. Other things equal, being a child of immigrants is associated with greater socioeconomic success in the United States.

Appendix

Table 6A.1   Earnings, Education, and Marriage Patterns of Immigrant Men in 1940 and Second-Generation Men and Women in 1970

| | Immigrant Men Age 24–66, 1940 | | | | Second-Generation Men Age 24–66, 1970 | | | | | Second Generation Women Age 24–66, 1970 | | | | |
| | | | Fraction Married to | | | | Fraction Married to | | | | | Fraction Married to | | |
	Mean Log Wage	Years School	Same Immigrants	Natives	Mean Log Wage	Years School	Same Immigrants	Same 2nd Generation	Natives	Mean Log Wage	Years School	Same Immigrants	Same 2nd Generation	3rd+ Generation
Asia nec	5.57	7.3	0.36	0.29	6.62	12.6	0.06	0.18	0.55	5.87	11.9	0.10	0.23	0.35
Austria	5.72	6.5	0.53	0.31	6.70	12.3	0.01	0.12	0.53	5.89	11.6	0.02	0.15	0.40
Belgium	5.73	7.5	0.57	0.31	6.73	11.4	0.01	0.07	0.72	5.75	11.2	0.07	0.09	0.58
Canada	5.82	8.6	0.31	0.63	6.60	11.4	0.07	0.10	0.70	5.78	11.4	0.05	0.13	0.65
Central/South America nec	5.58	8.0	0.08	0.60	6.61	10.3	0.13	0.00	0.66	5.94	10.5	0.05	0.00	0.55
China	5.13	5.5	0.78	0.18	6.65	12.8	0.09	0.28	0.44	6.19	12.4	0.33	0.27	0.32
Czechoslovakia	5.68	6.8	0.67	0.28	6.62	11.6	0.02	0.16	0.57	5.77	11.0	0.05	0.19	0.45
Denmark	5.81	8.9	0.41	0.46	6.68	12.5	0.00	0.04	0.75	5.83	12.5	0.01	0.06	0.71
Europe nec	5.69	7.9	0.29	0.45	6.72	12.3	0.00	0.16	0.51	5.81	11.6	0.03	0.18	0.41
Finland	5.59	6.5	0.63	0.31	6.59	11.7	0.03	0.24	0.56	5.86	11.9	0.05	0.25	0.50
France	5.73	8.9	0.31	0.53	6.71	12.1	0.02	0.03	0.69	5.85	12.1	0.01	0.02	0.67
Germany	5.76	8.6	0.48	0.43	6.64	11.8	0.02	0.05	0.75	5.78	11.6	0.04	0.08	0.66
Greece	5.47	6.8	0.58	0.37	6.70	12.9	0.07	0.25	0.48	5.90	12.0	0.18	0.30	0.34
Hungary	5.74	7.2	0.66	0.24	6.68	11.8	0.02	0.14	0.51	5.85	11.3	0.05	0.15	0.42
Ireland	5.74	8.1	0.60	0.31	6.68	12.7	0.03	0.11	0.67	5.91	12.3	0.03	0.12	0.64
Italy	5.60	5.1	0.68	0.29	6.63	11.2	0.04	0.34	0.48	5.80	10.8	0.11	0.39	0.38
Japan	5.41	9.5	0.88	0.10	6.64	12.6	0.14	0.56	0.23	5.96	11.7	0.09	0.63	0.21
Lithuania	5.58	4.7	0.70	0.16	6.64	12.4	0.01	0.17	0.45	5.92	11.6	0.03	0.20	0.36
Mexico	5.03	3.5	0.64	0.34	6.30	8.2	0.16	0.33	0.47	5.63	7.7	0.20	0.35	0.41

(*continued*)

Table 6A.1 (continued)

| | Immigrant Men Age 24–66, 1940 | | | | Second-Generation Men Age 24–66, 1970 | | | | | Second Generation Women Age 24–66, 1970 | | | | |
| | Mean Log Wage | Years School | Fraction Married to | | Mean Log Wage | Years School | Fraction Married to | | | Mean Log Wage | Years School | Fraction Married to | | |
			Same Immigrants	Natives			Same Immigrants	Same 2nd Generation	Natives			Same Immigrants	Same 2nd Generation	3rd+ Generation
Netherlands	5.65	8.7	0.41	0.51	6.65	11.5	0.01	0.13	0.72	5.78	11.3	0.05	0.15	0.68
Norway	5.79	8.6	0.48	0.43	6.68	12.3	0.01	0.05	0.79	5.78	12.4	0.03	0.08	0.67
Caribbean/ Africa/other	5.39	6.9	0.51	0.41	6.58	11.3	0.03	0.13	0.59	5.82	11.0	0.04	0.12	0.53
Philippines	5.15	6.5	0.08	0.89	6.35	10.5	0.14	0.22	0.51	5.91	10.5	0.26	0.18	0.47
Poland	5.65	5.4	0.68	0.23	6.64	11.5	0.02	0.28	0.45	5.84	10.9	0.04	0.30	0.36
Portugal	5.49	4.0	0.56	0.36	6.48	9.6	0.05	0.22	0.59	5.68	9.7	0.12	0.23	0.46
Romania	5.77	7.3	0.52	0.24	6.80	13.3	0.02	0.05	0.46	5.97	12.4	0.02	0.06	0.35
Russia	5.81	6.8	0.59	0.27	6.77	13.5	0.02	0.31	0.42	5.94	12.5	0.06	0.34	0.29
Spain	5.52	6.4	0.49	0.36	6.62	11.4	0.04	0.10	0.61	5.88	11.1	0.08	0.09	0.51
Sweden	5.79	8.3	0.44	0.47	6.70	12.6	0.01	0.07	0.71	5.86	12.7	0.03	0.10	0.67
Switzerland	5.76	9.1	0.33	0.39	6.59	12.0	0.02	0.03	0.75	5.87	12.5	0.03	0.04	0.75
Syria	5.59	6.2	0.69	0.29	6.65	12.4	0.02	0.20	0.54	5.85	11.3	0.07	0.22	0.41
Turkey	5.58	7.3	0.63	0.22	6.77	13.1	0.04	0.23	0.39	5.96	12.5	0.11	0.22	0.27
United Kingdom	5.86	9.3	0.40	0.49	6.72	12.6	0.02	0.04	0.75	5.85	12.3	0.03	0.05	0.70
Yugoslavia	5.60	5.4	0.65	0.27	6.67	11.7	0.02	0.17	0.56	5.76	11.2	0.06	0.19	0.42

Notes: For immigrant men, fraction married to "same immigrants" is the fraction of married men whose spouse is an immigrant from the same country; and fraction married to natives is the fraction of married men whose spouse is native born. For second-generation men and women, fraction married to "same immigrants" is the fraction of married people whose spouse is an immigrant from the same country as their father; fraction married to same 2nd generation is the fraction of married people whose spouse is second generation and whose father-in-law was born in the same country as their father; and fraction married to 3rd+ generation is the fraction of married people whose spouse is native born with native-born parents.

Asia nec are Asian countries other than those listed separately. Central/South America nec are countries in Central or South America not listed separately. Europe nec are European countries not listed separately, plus Australia and New Zealand. Caribbean/Africa/other includes countries in the Caribbean and Africa not listed separately, plus all other countries not included in other categories.

Table 6A.2 Earnings, Education, and Marriage Patterns of Immigrant Men in 1970 and Second-Generation Men and Women in 1994–96

| | Immigrant Men Age 24–66, 1970 | | | | Second Generation Men Age 24–66, 1994–96 | | | | | Second Generation Women Age 24–66, 1994–96 | | | | |
| | Mean Log Wage | Years School | Fraction Married to | | Mean Log Wage | Years School | Fraction Married to | | | Mean Log Wage | Years School | Fraction Married to | | |
			Same Immigrants	Natives			Same Immigrants	Same 2nd Generation	Natives			Same Immigrants	Same 2nd Generation	3rd+ Generation
Asia nec	6.68	13.4	0.42	0.27	6.59	15.2	0.16	0.13	0.56	6.34	14.8	0.12	0.11	0.38
Canada	6.70	11.7	0.33	0.48	6.64	14.2	0.01	0.07	0.75	6.23	13.5	0.00	0.09	0.81
Central/South America nec	6.58	11.7	0.51	0.24	6.58	13.3	0.33	0.00	0.44	6.56	14.0	0.03	0.00	0.85
China	6.43	10.9	0.69	0.13	6.88	15.3	0.02	0.09	0.42	6.60	14.6	0.00	0.17	0.65
Colombia	6.44	12.6	0.68	0.20	6.53	13.8	0.00	0.00	0.87	6.13	13.6	0.29	0.00	0.71
Cuba	6.31	11.0	0.84	0.08	6.78	13.8	0.25	0.37	0.31	6.32	14.3	0.15	0.24	0.45
Czechoslovakia	6.68	12.1	0.25	0.27	6.22	14.6	0.00	0.00	0.85	6.39	14.1	0.00	0.00	0.89
Dominican Republic	6.19	8.8	0.78	0.14	6.64	13.2	0.10	0.12	0.66	6.03	12.7	0.15	0.14	0.42
Ecuador	6.47	11.9	0.52	0.26	6.45	13.3	0.44	0.17	0.39	6.01	13.3	0.00	0.11	0.63
El Salvador	6.63	11.5	0.78	0.19	6.39	13.5	0.32	0.00	0.61	6.10	12.4	0.06	0.00	0.87
Europe nec	6.73	12.2	0.33	0.30	6.67	15.0	0.01	0.01	0.84	6.14	14.5	0.01	0.05	0.69
France	6.69	11.9	0.31	0.38	6.39	14.5	0.00	0.04	0.71	6.34	14.2	0.00	0.06	0.75
Germany	6.78	12.4	0.45	0.29	6.80	14.8	0.02	0.10	0.74	6.12	14.0	0.01	0.14	0.78
Greece	6.51	10.2	0.51	0.21	6.88	15.7	0.04	0.11	0.72	6.22	14.0	0.16	0.35	0.35
Guatemala	6.30	13.3	0.36	0.33	6.24	14.2	0.00	0.00	0.46	5.59	10.7	0.00	0.00	0.00
Haiti	6.25	11.5	0.82	0.10	6.44	11.9	0.00	0.29	0.71	6.01	14.0	0.26	0.30	0.44
Hungary	6.67	11.9	0.37	0.26	6.94	14.9	0.00	0.00	0.88	6.11	13.9	0.00	0.00	0.66
India	6.73	15.2	0.60	0.21	6.69	15.9	0.00	0.23	0.37	6.81	15.2	0.11	0.13	0.43

(continued)

Table 6A.2 (continued)

	Immigrant Men Age 24–66, 1970		Fraction Married to		Second Generation Men Age 24–66, 1994–96		Fraction Married to			Second Generation Women Age 24–66, 1994–96		Fraction Married to		
	Mean Log Wage	Years School	Same Immigrants	Natives	Mean Log Wage	Years School	Same Immigrants	Same 2nd Generation	Natives	Mean Log Wage	Years School	Same Immigrants	Same 2nd Generation	3rd+ Generation
Ireland	6.52	10.9	0.51	0.27	6.86	14.7	0.09	0.05	0.75	6.35	14.5	0.06	0.04	0.69
Italy	6.57	9.0	0.42	0.22	6.63	13.7	0.02	0.13	0.77	6.11	13.3	0.05	0.21	0.63
Jamaica	6.41	10.9	0.57	0.27	6.69	14.3	0.73	0.00	0.27	6.46	13.0	0.29	0.00	0.71
Japan	6.66	13.8	0.56	0.16	6.63	15.0	0.24	0.19	0.57	6.20	14.8	0.09	0.53	0.38
Korea	6.65	17.3	0.76	0.13	7.03	16.1	0.72	0.00	0.28	6.18	16.6	0.00	0.00	0.00
Mexico	6.16	6.0	0.54	0.25	6.32	11.9	0.25	0.21	0.50	5.89	11.6	0.28	0.20	0.48
Nicaragua	6.36	10.3	0.71	0.07	6.93	13.9	0.27	0.00	0.51	5.99	12.9	0.00	0.00	0.48
Caribbean/ Africa/other	6.46	10.5	0.30	0.33	6.62	14.4	0.04	0.10	0.76	6.16	13.9	0.07	0.11	0.74
Peru	6.59	12.4	0.46	0.41	6.86	15.9	0.37	0.00	0.36	6.17	13.0	0.00	0.00	0.83
Philippines	6.41	10.9	0.59	0.25	6.60	14.3	0.27	0.26	0.43	6.26	14.0	0.18	0.23	0.50
Poland	6.57	10.3	0.41	0.14	6.74	15.1	0.00	0.10	0.77	6.16	14.2	0.02	0.16	0.61
Portugal	6.42	7.1	0.63	0.16	6.55	13.4	0.05	0.32	0.55	5.88	12.0	0.05	0.36	0.56
Russia	6.51	10.8	0.31	0.15	6.86	16.1	0.01	0.10	0.72	6.42	15.3	0.00	0.21	0.61
United Kingdom	6.78	12.8	0.34	0.42	6.65	13.5	0.01	0.00	0.84	6.22	14.1	0.02	0.00	0.88
Yugoslavia	6.63	9.9	0.51	0.20	7.00	14.6	0.00	0.00	0.74	6.31	14.3	0.00	0.07	0.66

Notes: For immigrant men, fraction married to "same immigrants" is the fraction of married men whose spouse is an immigrant from the same country; and fraction married to natives is the fraction of married men whose spouse is native born. For second-generation men and women, fraction married to "same immigrants" is the fraction of married people whose spouse is an immigrant from the same country as their father; fraction married to same 2nd generation is the fraction of married people whose spouse is second generation and whose father-in-law was born in the same country as their father; and fraction married to 3rd+ generation is the fraction of married people whose spouse is native born with native-born parents.

Asia nec are Asian countries other than those listed separately. Central/South America nec are countries in Central or South America not listed separately. Europe nec are European countries not listed separately, plus Australia and New Zealand. Caribbean/Africa/other includes countries in the Caribbean and Africa not listed separately, plus all other countries not included in other categories.

References

Ashenfelter, Orley, and Cecilia E. Rouse. 1998. Income, schooling, and ability: Evidence from a new sample of twins. *Quarterly Journal of Economics* 113 (1): 253–84.

Baker, Michael, and Dwayne Benjamin. 1994. The performance of immigrants in the Canadian labor market. *Journal of Labor Economics* 12 (3): 369–405.

———. 1997. The role of the family in immigrants' labor market activity: An evaluation of alternative explanations. *American Economic Review* 87:705–27.

Becker, Gary S., and Nigel Tomes. 1986. Human capital and the rise and fall of families. *Journal of Labor Economics* 4 (3): S1–S39.

Bennett, Marion T. 1963. *American immigration policies: A history.* Washington, D.C.: Public Affairs Press.

Borjas, George J. 1985. Assimilation, changes in cohort quality, and the earnings of immigrants. *Journal of Labor Economics* 3:463–89.

———. 1987. Self-selection and the earnings of immigrants. *American Economic Review* 77 (4): 531–53.

———. 1992. Ethnic capital and intergenerational mobility. *Quarterly Journal of Economics* 107 (1): 123–50.

———. 1993. The intergenerational mobility of immigrants. *Journal of Labor Economics* 11 (1): 113–35.

———. 1994. The economics of immigration. *Journal of Economic Literature* 32 (4): 1667–717.

———. 1995. Assimilation and changes in cohort quality revisited: What happened to immigrant earnings in the 1980s? *Journal of Labor Economics* 13: 201–45.

Brigham, Carl Campbell. 1923. *A study of American intelligence.* Princeton, N.J.: Princeton University Press.

DiNardo, John, Nicole Fortin, and Thomas Lemieux. 1996. Labor market institutions and the distribution of wages, 1973–1993: A semi-parametric approach. *Econometrica* 64 (5): 1001–45.

Gans, Herbert. 1992. Second generation decline—Scenarios for the economic and ethnic futures of the post-1965 American immigrants. *Ethnic and Racial Studies* 15 (2): 173–92.

Portes, Alejandro, and Min Zhou. 1993. The new second generation: Segmented assimilation and its variants among post-1965 immigrant youth. *Annals of the American Academy of Political and Social Science* 530:74–96.

Solon, Gary. 1992. Intergenerational income mobility in the United States. *American Economic Review* 82 (3): 393–408.

———. 1999. Intergenerational mobility in the labor market. In *Handbook of labor economics,* vol. 4, ed. Orley Ashenfelter and David Card. Amsterdam: North Holland.

Waldinger, Robert, and Joel Perlmann. 1997. Second generations: Past, present, and future. Jerome Levy Economics Institute Working Paper no. 200. Annandale-on-Hudson, N.Y.: Jerome Levy Institute of Bard College.

Zimmerman, David. 1992. Regression toward mediocrity in economic stature. *American Economic Review* 82 (3): 409–29.

7

Do Children of Immigrants Make Differential Use of Public Health Insurance?

Janet Currie

The fraction of the U.S. population that is foreign born has risen dramatically over the past two decades from 4.7 percent in 1970 to 7.9 percent in 1990 (Banister 1994). First- and second-generation children of immigrants are the fastest-growing segment of the U.S. population under age 15; by 2010, it is estimated that 20 percent of school-aged children will be children of recent immigrants (Lamberg 1996). By 1997, 1 in every 6 children (12 million) were immigrants or had immigrant parents (Hernandez and Charney 1998).

The increased inflow of immigrants has been accompanied by growing concern about the cost of social services used by immigrants and their families. Many previous studies have shown that because immigrants tend to be poorer than the native born, their children are more likely to be eligible for welfare programs (Blau 1984; Borjas 1990; Borjas and Hilton 1996; Jensen 1988; Tienda and Jensen 1986; Trejo 1992). Concern about

Janet Currie is professor of economics at the University of California, Los Angeles. She is a consultant with the Labor and Population group at RAND; a research associate of the National Bureau of Economic Research and a member of their research program on Children and Families; a faculty associate at the Chicago/Northwestern Poverty Center; and a member of the Canadian Institute of Advanced Research. She recently served on the National Academy of Sciences panel on the Health and Well-Being of Immigrant Children.

Michael Baker, George Borjas, David Card, David Cutler, Martin Dooley, Rachel Friedberg, Jon Gruber, Wei-Yin Hu, Christopher Jencks, Lawrence Katz, James Poterba, Jon Skinner, and seminar participants at Queen's University, the NBER, UNC–Chapel Hill, and the University of Arizona provided many helpful comments. Thanks also to Aaron Yelowitz for supplying the data for table 7C.1. Graciela Teruel and Luis Rubalcava provided excellent research assistance. Financial support from the Alfred P. Sloan Foundation, UCLA's Center for American Politics and Public Policy, and from the NIH under grant no. R01HD31722-01A2 is gratefully acknowledged. The views expressed are the author's and should not be attributed to these institutions.

the fiscal burden imposed by immigrants provided the impetus for certain provisions of the passage of the Personal Responsibility and Work Opportunity Reconciliation Act of 1996 (P.L. 104-193). This bill will sharply curtail the availability of welfare benefits for immigrants. It is estimated that of the projected $56 billion in federal funds the law will save over the next six years, almost half will come from a reduction of payments to immigrants (Fix and Zimmerman 1997).

Medicaid, a system of public health insurance for poor women and children, is one of the more costly social programs available to the families of immigrants. In recent years, the United States spent about $3.4 billion annually on cash welfare payments to children under the Aid to Families with Dependent Children (AFDC) program (Clark 1994), and $5.5 billion on payments to children of immigrants under the Medicaid program.[1] The new law will ban legal immigrants from Medicaid for five years after their arrival in the United States, after which time states will have the authority to decide whether or not they will be eligible. Undocumented immigrants have never been eligible for coverage of routine care under the Medicaid program. All immigrants will continue to be eligible for coverage of emergency medical care and for public health assistance (immunizations and treatment of communicable diseases). Refugees and citizen children of immigrants will also remain eligible for Medicaid coverage.

Although the law is likely to reduce Medicaid coverage, it is difficult to predict the effect it will have on either health care costs or public health because these more important outcomes are determined by utilization of care rather than by insurance coverage per se. Medicaid differs in a fundamental way from other welfare programs, because it is possible for uncovered individuals to receive emergency services that are paid for by the program ex post (while it is not possible for example, for someone ineligible for cash assistance to legally receive cash benefits). The evidence presented in this paper is consistent with the previous evidence that because of their characteristics, immigrants are more likely than nonimmigrants to be eligible for Medicaid. However, it suggests that making children ineligible for Medicaid coverage will reduce the use of relatively low-cost routine preventive care, without having much impact on the utilization of more costly services.

The rest of the paper is laid out as follows: Necessary background information about the Medicaid program and a discussion of its effects on the incentives facing eligible immigrants and nonimmigrants is given in section 7.1. Section 7.2 outlines the instrumental variables strategy. The data

1. By way of comparison, the entire budget for AFDC was approximately $22 billion annually. AFDC has recently been replaced with the Temporary Aid for Needy Families (TANF) program. According to Clark (1994), Medicaid expenditures for immigrants total $16.6 billion. Since two-thirds of Medicaid expenditures are on the elderly, this implies that $5.5 billion is spent on children.

are described in section 7.3. Section 7.4 provides the empirical results, while section 7.5 concludes.

7.1   The Medicaid Expansions and Incentives for Immigrants and Nonimmigrants

Historically, eligibility for Medicaid was closely tied to the receipt of cash welfare payments under the Aid to Families with Dependent Children program. Hence, eligibility was effectively limited to very low income women and children in single parent families. Beginning in 1984, states were first permitted and then required to extend Medicaid coverage to other groups of children. By 1992, states were required to cover children below age 6 in families with incomes up to 133 percent of the federal poverty line, and children between ages 6 and 19 with family incomes up to 100 percent of the poverty line; states also had the option of covering infants up to 185 percent of the poverty line.[2] A list of the relevant statutes is given in appendix B.

The important point to note is that states took up these options at different rates, so that there was a great deal of variation across states in both the income thresholds and the age limits governing Medicaid eligibility. Table 7C.1 in appendix C shows the maximum age covered by Medicaid in each state at three different points in time, as well as the maximum income limit that applied to any child made eligible by the expansions (the oldest child eligible was generally subject to a less-generous income cutoff). Older children remained eligible if their families received AFDC. The table shows that as of January 1988, 26 states had taken advantage of the options described above to extend Medicaid eligibility to previously ineligible children. By December 1989, all 50 states had expanded Medicaid eligibility—however, states like Colorado covered only infants in families with incomes up to 75 percent of the poverty line, while more generous states, like California, covered children up to age 5 in families with incomes up to 100 percent of the poverty line, and covered infants in families with incomes up to 185 percent of the poverty line.

By December 1991, most states had been required by the federal government to increase the age limits and income limits still further. Table 7.1 illustrates the growing uniformity in the way that children were treated in three states that began the period with widely differing eligibility criteria: California, Texas, and New Jersey. This variation in eligibility thresholds by state, year, and age of child will be exploited to identify the effects of Medicaid eligibility.

2. States received federal matching funds for coverage of these groups. However, some states have extended coverage to children above 200 percent of the poverty line, using only state funds.

Table 7.1   **Eligibility for Medicaid by Age and Percentage of Federal Poverty Line:**
California, Texas, and New Jersey

	January 1988		December 1989		December 1991	
	Age	Percentage of Federal Poverty Line	Age	Percentage of Federal Poverty Line	Age	Percentage of Federal Poverty Line
California		75[a]	<1	185	<1	185
			1–5	133	1–5	133
			6+	75	6–8	100
					9+	75
Texas		22[a]	<1	130	<1	185
			1–3	100	1–5	133
			4+	22	6–8	100
					9+	22
New Jersey		50[a]	<2	100	<1	185
			3+	50	1–5	133
					6–8	100
					9+	50

Note: Children born after 30 September 1983 were eligible for Medicaid if their families were income eligible for AFDC. Older children were eligible only if their parents actually qualified for AFDC (i.e., met all other requirements as well as income eligibility). By 1989, states were required to cover children through age six if their families were income eligible for AFDC.

[a]The 75 percent, 22 percent, and 50 percent figures are based on the maximum AFDC benefit levels for these states.

A large literature documents the fact that eligible individuals do not always take up public assistance—for example, only about two-thirds of those eligible for AFDC or unemployment insurance receive benefits (Blank and Card 1991; Blank and Ruggles 1993). The probability of taking up benefits should be systematically related to the relative costs and benefits of being covered. For example, as Blank and Card suggest, those who expect to be unemployed for only a short spell may be less likely to apply for or receive benefits. The available preexpansion evidence suggests that although take-up of Medicaid among children on AFDC is high, only about one-quarter of children eligible through other aspects of the program (e.g., under the Ribicoff provisions) took up coverage (Shore-Sheppard 1996).

It is not unreasonable to suppose that immigrant parents face higher costs of enrolling their children in the Medicaid program than nonimmigrants. First, the General Accounting Office (U.S. GAO 1994) reports that many applications are denied and that half of all denials occur because the applicant failed to supply supporting documentation (such as birth certificates or pay stubs) or failed to keep all of the necessary appointments. It may be more difficult for immigrants to follow these procedures. Second, although citizen children are eligible for all Medicaid services, and even undocumented children are eligible for emergency services under the Medicaid program, immigrant parents may fear harassment by authorities, particularly if they or other family members are themselves undocumented. Third, the residential segregation of many immigrants may make it difficult to get to an enrollment center. Fourth, language barriers may make the enrollment process more difficult.

It is also possible that the benefits of formal enrollment are not as great as they might at first appear, because it is often possible for eligible children to obtain acute services even if they are not formally covered at the time that services are rendered. The GAO gives the following example: "The child of a single, uninsured, working mother incurred a $20,000 hospital bill. . . . The hospital referred this case to an enrollment vendor firm after determining that it was a potential Medicaid case. After contacting the mother, the firm initiated and submitted a Medicaid application. The firm gave the applicant a list of verification items she would have to provide. However, the applicant did not provide the requested items and Medicaid coverage was denied. Upon learning of the denial, the firm contacted the applicant twice weekly for a period of two months to get her to cooperate. . . . Eventually, the applicant responded and submitted the verification items and a signed power of attorney to the firm. . . . The signed power of attorney allowed the firm to appeal the denial successfully" (U.S. GAO, 24). In this example, the child became covered by Medicaid for a time. But eligibility must be periodically reestablished in order to retain coverage, and one suspects that this child's coverage might have been particularly likely to lapse subsequently.

Hence, immigrant parents with an eligible child have two options: They can choose to incur the transactions costs and become covered. The Medicaid program will then cover the costs of both preventive care and acute care for their child. Alternatively, they may choose to forgo the transactions costs and remain uncovered, knowing that acute care will be provided under the Medicaid program as necessary. Viewed in a dynamic context, parents who face higher transactions costs may simply choose to enroll their children less often than other parents. For example, instead of keeping children continuously enrolled, which requires going through an administrative procedure at least every six months, they might choose to enroll their children only when they needed to take them to the doctor for some form of routine care.

The role of transactions costs is depicted in figure 7.1, which shows the trade-off between expenditures on health insurance for children and expenditures on other child goods. An eligible child whose family faces no transactions costs becomes covered by the program and is able to consume at point M1. A family facing high transactions costs can choose to become enrolled and consume at point M4, or it can choose to forgo coverage and consume slightly less health insurance at point M2. Thus, if parents have

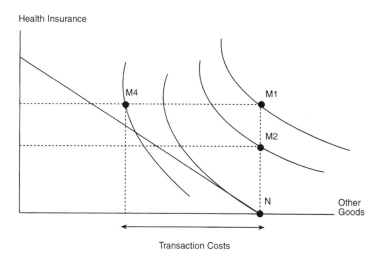

Health Insurance

M4

M1

M2

N

Other
Goods

Transaction Costs

Fig. 7.1   The role of transactions costs

preferences like those depicted in the figure and immigrant parents face higher transactions costs than nonimmigrant parents, then their eligible children will be less likely to become formally covered.

Parents of eligible children may also have another decision to make: whether or not to take up Medicaid coverage for their children and drop the child's private health insurance coverage. Cutler and Gruber (1996) emphasize that public insurance could "crowd out" private insurance in this way. Alternatively, they point out that employers might stop offering private insurance of employees' dependents if substantial numbers of them were to become covered under public programs. Immigrant parents may be more likely than nonimmigrants to work for small, low-wage employers who offer insurance at less favorable rates than large employers, or who do not offer it at all.

This situation is illustrated in figure 7.2, in which immigrant parents are assumed to face a flatter trade-off between health insurance for their children and other child goods than other parents. Given these opportunities, immigrant parents will consume less child health insurance than nonimmigrant parents in the absence of Medicaid eligibility (compare point A to point B). Now consider what happens when the child becomes Medicaid eligible, assuming that the transactions costs associated with becoming covered are similar to those described in figure 7.1. Native-born parents with the preferences shown in figure 7.2 do not change their insurance arrangements; the private insurance they are purchasing is far superior to what is available under Medicaid. Immigrant parents, on the other hand, are made better off by moving to M2 (eligible but not covered). Although the health insurance offered at M2 is inferior to what was being purchased

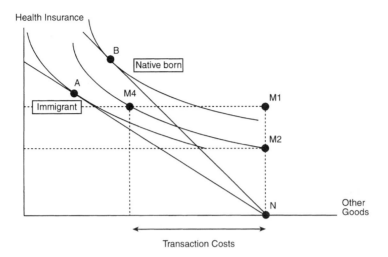

Fig. 7.2   The role of differential opportunities

previously, the cost savings allow a more than offsetting increase in the consumption of other child goods. In the data, a movement from A to M2 will appear as an increase in the fraction of children who are uninsured.

These diagrams implicitly assume that being eligible for Medicaid coverage of acute services is better than not being insured at all (i.e., that point M2 is higher than point N). Since some emergency care is likely to be available to all children in the United States, one may question this assumption. However, there is considerable evidence that suggests that hospitals are able to determine relatively quickly whether someone is likely to be Medicaid eligible. For example, Piper, Ray, and Griffin (1990) found that a 1985 expansion of Medicaid eligibility to married pregnant women in Tennessee increased Medicaid enrollments, but that most of this increase is likely to have occurred at the time of the delivery. And it is well known that insured patients receive more intensive treatment than uninsured patients along a number of margins (cf. Hadley, Steinberg, and Feder 1991; Wenneker, Weissman, and Epstein 1990; and Currie and Gruber 1997). Hence, it seems likely that patients who are eligible for Medicaid will receive better care (and receive it with greater certainty) than those who are not, even if the latter do receive some acute care.

In summary, these diagrams suggest that if immigrant parents face differences in transactions costs and/or opportunities relative to native-born parents, then they will make different choices about health insurance. Among parents who were not purchasing private health insurance for their children previously, increases in Medicaid eligibility will be associated with larger increases in formal coverage among children of the native born than among children of immigrants. And among parents who were purchasing private health insurance to begin with, increases in eligibility for Medicaid will be more likely to cause "crowding out" among immigrants than among nonimmigrants.[3]

It is more difficult to make predictions about the relationship between utilization and eligibility among immigrants and nonimmigrants. If eligible children of immigrants are less likely to be formally covered than children of nonimmigrants, then utilization of nonacute services is less likely to be paid for by Medicaid. On the other hand, if the main difference between immigrants and nonimmigrants is that the former are less likely to be continuously covered, we might see little difference in the utilization of routine care because immigrants may simply bunch care during periods when they are covered. In the case of hospitalizations, eligibility is arguably a more important determinant than coverage given that a hospital that treats an eligible but uncovered child can receive reimbursement from Medicaid ex post.

Although the preceding discussion assumes that immigrant and native-born parents have similar preferences, it is possible that there are systematic cultural differences in attitudes toward the utilization of medical care. For example, eligible immigrant parents might be less likely to enroll in Medicaid because they value the available services less than native-born parents. It is also possible that immigrant parents have less information about these programs; Currie and Gruber (1996b) conclude that lack of information about welfare programs among the working poor may be an important barrier to take-up of coverage. However, as we shall see, such cultural or informational explanations are not particularly consistent with the findings of this study: Children of immigrant parents actually show larger changes in the utilization of basic medical care when they become Medicaid eligible than do children of the native born.

7.2   Methods

The main empirical problem involved in investigating the effects of Medicaid eligibility on coverage and utilization is that those children who are most likely to be eligible are least likely to take up coverage or to use services, given health status. They are also more likely to be ill. Currie and Gruber (1996b) describe the construction of a detailed simulation model that uses information about state rules, the child's age, and family charac-

---

3. Both diagrams illustrate the fact that even if the child is not formally covered, the family may be made better off when the child becomes Medicaid eligible. Since the utilization of medical care given health status is known to be a normal good, one would expect some of this increase in household "income" to translate into an increase in the number of visits. However, it is difficult to judge how large this income effect should be, given measurement error in income and the fact that we do not know the value of Medicaid eligibility to the family.

teristics to impute individual Medicaid eligibility.[4] They estimate that between 1989 and 1992, the fraction of children less than 15 years of age who were eligible for Medicaid increased from 20.4 to 31.2 percent, and that all but 2.1 percentage points of this increase can be attributed to changes in state Medicaid rules as opposed to changes in economic conditions or demographics.

In what follows, the Currie-Gruber imputation program is used to determine individual eligibility. This measure is included in linear probability models of health insurance coverage and the utilization of medical care below. However, these ordinary least squares (OLS) estimates are subject to two sources of bias. The first is omitted variables bias. In addition to eligibility, all of the models include observable variables associated with Medicaid eligibility, such as the absence of a male household head, income, the number of children in the family, and the age of the child (through single year of age dummies). Also controlled for are family income; the child's gender, race, and ethnicity; whether he or she is the oldest child; the number of siblings; the education of the mother and (if present) the father; whether the mother or father was the respondent; the presence of other adult relatives; and whether the family lives in a central city or rural area.

Even after conditioning on this detailed set of controls, however, persons who are eligible for Medicaid may have other characteristics that make them less likely to take up Medicaid coverage or to utilize medical care. For example, they may be more likely to live in areas with limited access to physicians (cf. Fossett et al. 1992; Fossett and Peterson 1989). In this case, OLS estimates of the effects of eligibility on coverage and utilization would be biased toward zero. If these omitted factors are more important for immigrants than for nonimmigrants, then estimates for immigrants may be more severely affected by these biases than estimates for nonimmigrants.

The second problem is that there may be substantial measurement error in the eligibility indicator, given limitations of the National Health Interview Survey (NHIS) income data that are discussed below. Such measurement error would normally be expected to bias the estimated effect of eligibility toward zero. Since Medicaid coverage is also self-reported (with some verification of the holding of Medicaid cards by interviewers), it may also be measured with error. An additional measurement problem is that children of immigrants who are themselves undocumented are ineligible

---

4. They use data from the National Health Interview Survey and the Current Population Survey. In these data sets, it is necessary to impute eligibility at the time of the survey on the basis of annual income. Devine and Heckman (1994) conduct a comparison of eligibility simulations using the CPS to some constructed using the Survey of Income and Program Participation (SIPP), which has monthly income data. They conclude that CPS-based simulations of eligibility for training programs produce estimates remarkably similar to those using the SIPP.

for Medicaid coverage of nonemergency services, and it is not possible to identify these children.[5]

Hence, in addition to the OLS estimates, instrumental variables (IV) estimates are presented below. The aim of the instrumental variables procedure is to abstract from characteristics of the child and/or family that may be correlated with eligibility, survey response error, and the dependent variables, and to achieve identification using only legislative variation in Medicaid policy. One way to do this would be to instrument imputed individual eligibility in the NHIS using the fraction of children in the same state, year, and age who are eligible, calculated using the Current Population Survey (CPS). This instrument would capture differences in Medicaid eligibility across states, years, and age groups, and would purge the regression of individual-level sources of variation in eligibility.

This approach would run into two problems in practice, however. First, the CPS is simply not large enough to permit reliable estimation of the fraction of children eligible in each state, year, and age category. Second, these estimates could be biased by the omission of characteristics of state, year, and age groups that are correlated both with the fraction eligible and with utilization or health. For example, if infants in a given state and year were particularly poor, they might have both higher eligibility levels and fewer doctor's visits, resulting in a downward bias in estimates of the effects of eligibility on utilization.

In order to address these problems, an instrument that varies only with the legislative environment, and not with its economic or demographic conditions, was developed. This instrument was constructed by first selecting a national random sample of 300 children for each single year of age (0 to 14) from the CPS, in each year, and then using the Currie-Gruber program to calculate the fraction of this national sample of children who would have been eligible for Medicaid in each state and year.[6] This measure can be thought of as a convenient summary of the legislation affecting the Medicaid eligibility of children in each state, year, and age group. In what follows, we use linear probability models for ease of computation and for consistency of this instrumental variables procedure (Heckman and MaCurdy 1985).

---

5. It is difficult to estimate the fraction of children of immigrants who are themselves undocumented. Estimates based on the 1990 census suggest that 3 in 20 immigrants are undocumented (Banister 1994). However, many undocumented adult immigrants have citizen children who are entitled to services under the Medicaid program. It is also unclear that the undocumented are accurately counted in a survey such as the NHIS.

6. That is, how many of the 300 one-year-olds would be eligible if they all lived in California, how many would be eligible if they all lived in Massachusetts, and so forth. The sample size of 300 was chosen due to data and computational constraints. In order to assess the severity of potential problems due to sampling variability, the instrument was constructed twice, using two different random samples. The correlation between the two instruments was 0.97.

In principle, this instrumental variables strategy overcomes the econometric difficulties noted above—the model is purged of endogeneity bias and of biases due to individual-level omitted variables that are correlated with both eligibility and outcomes. To the extent that the measurement error in the instrument is uncorrelated with the measurement error in the individual eligibility measure, this procedure also surmounts the measurement error problem.[7] Finally, using a national random sample eliminates the effects of state- and year-specific economic conditions that might be correlated with both eligibility and with utilization; the problem of small age/year/state cell sizes is also eliminated. This instrument is strongly correlated with individual eligibility, among both natives and immigrants— the t-statistic is over 10 in the first-stage equations.

Of course, using legislation as the source of identifying variation raises the question of whether laws can be treated as exogenous variables. It is possible, for example, that states raise eligibility for Medicaid in response to poor outcomes among children. It is important to note that much of the identifying variation used in this paper is a result of federal mandates and is therefore outside the control of state governments. States differed widely in their propensity to take up optional Medicaid expansions prior to 1989. Hence, states started with differing levels of generosity, a fact that can be controlled for by including state fixed effects in the empirical model. Between 1989 and 1992, however, even the most recalcitrant states were forced to extend Medicaid coverage to meet federal standards, with the result that greater uniformity across states was achieved. Thus, although New Hampshire and Minnesota ended up with similar programs in 1992, New Hampshire expanded eligibility much more rapidly over this period as federal mandates began to bite. Note that possible legislative endogeneity would be a potentially far greater problem if, instead of simulating the fraction eligible for Medicaid, various state rules that help to determine eligibility, such as maximum AFDC benefit levels, had been used. The problem is that benefit levels in other programs may be correlated with other characteristics of states that affect the utilization of health care and insurance coverage.

The models estimated in this paper all take the following form:

$$\text{OUTCOME} = \beta_0 + \beta_1 \text{ELIG} + \beta_2 \text{PARIMMIG} + \beta_3 \text{PARELIG}$$

(1)
$$+ \beta_4 X + \beta_5 \text{STATE} + \beta_6 \text{YEAR} + \beta_7 \text{CHILDAGE}$$

$$+ \beta_8 \text{AGEYEAR} + \beta_9 \text{STATEAGE} + \varepsilon,$$

---

7. If the measurement error stems mainly from random individual response error, then measurement error in the CPS instrument will be uncorrelated with that in the NHIS data, especially given the fact that the measure calculated using the CPS is the average eligibility for a large group.

where OUTCOME is an indicator for either insurance status or utilization, ELIG is an indicator equal to one if the child is eligible for Medicaid, PARIMMIG is an indicator equal to one if at least one parent is an immigrant, PARELIG is an interaction term equal to one if the child is eligible and a parent is an immigrant, and X is a vector of additional explanatory variables. In addition, the models all include state fixed effects and a full set of dummy variables for calendar years and for each child's single year of age. These variables control for variables such as secular trends in utilization rates or changes in the recommended schedule of visits for various age groups. Interactions between five broad age groups and the year dummies, and between the five age groups and the state of residence are also included.[8]

In this framework, we can test for whether eligible immigrants behave similarly to eligible natives by looking at whether $\beta_1 + \beta_2 + \beta_3 = \beta_1$. In principal, it would be possible to estimate a fully interacted model in which all of the coefficients were allowed to vary with immigrant status. In practice, it was found that this had little effect on the inferences that could be drawn from OLS estimates of the effects of eligibility. However, the two-stage least squares (TSLS) estimates were much less precisely estimated in the fully interacted model, which may reflect the difficulties involved in trying to draw many inferences about differences between immigrants and natives from a relatively small sample of immigrants.

7.3   Data

The National Health Interview Survey (NHIS) interviews a large, nationally representative cross section of American families each year.[9] The baseline survey collects information about demographic characteristics and family income. There are also a number of questions about the utilization of medical care over the previous year. These data cover approximately 100,000 individuals and 30,000 children less than age 15 in each year. This age cutoff was chosen in order to avoid issues arising from the fact that teens may become eligible for Medicaid due to pregnancy.

Beginning in 1989, the NHIS has asked all non-native-born adults in the household how long they have lived in the United States. Using this information, it is possible to determine whether either the mother or father

---

8. The five groups are: less than 1; greater than or equal to 2 and less than or equal to 4; greater than or equal to 5 and less than or equal to 7; greater than or equal to 8 and less than or equal to 10; and greater than or equal to 11. All of the children in the sample are 14 or under.

9. The models estimated in this paper are unweighted but include controls for key variables used in stratifying the sample such as race, central city residence, and rural residence. The inclusion of these variables results in estimates similar to those that would be obtained by weighting (Dumouchel and Duncan 1983).

of the child is an immigrant.[10] The relatively few respondents who answer that they don't know how long they have been in the United States are also treated as immigrants. Sixteen percent of the sample children have at least one parent who is an immigrant.

The NHIS fields supplements that ask additional questions about health insurance status every three years. Insurance supplements were fielded in 1989 and 1992, years that neatly bracket much of the increase in Medicaid eligibility for low-income children. Using these supplements, it is possible to determine whether the child was covered by private insurance or Medicaid or was uninsured at the time of the interview.[11]

Information from the main NHIS survey can be used to impute Medicaid eligibility to each child, although there are several problems to be overcome. First, family income is missing for a number of households, as shown in table 7C.2. Missing income data are imputed by using CPS data to estimate regressions of income on household characteristics, and then using the regression coefficients to calculate income for NHIS households with similar characteristics. The census Bureau uses a similar procedure to impute missing data in the CPS. These estimates were calculated separately for each year.[12]

Second, when family income is reported, it is reported in brackets. This is less of a problem than it might first appear because it causes problems

10. In principal, one could distinguish between the effects of having an immigrant father and the effects of having an immigrant mother. However, 83 percent of children who had at least one immigrant parent had a mother who was an immigrant, while 70 percent of these children had an immigrant father. Thus, there is a high degree of correlation between the two measures, and it proved impossible to separate these effects.

11. The questions about private health insurance coverage and no insurance coverage are straightforward. The 1989 insurance supplement asks four questions about public health insurance coverage. Parents are asked whether each child received Medicaid in the past 12 months, has a Medicaid card, is covered by some other type of public assistance program that pays for health care, or is covered by any type of public assistance health insurance coverage. In 1989, for example, 7,287 respondents reported receiving Medicaid in the past 12 months; 7,319 said they had a Medicaid card (and this was verified for 4,534 individuals); 8,072 said that they were covered by public assistance health insurance coverage; and 686 said that they were covered by some form of public assistance health insurance coverage other than Medicaid. Hence, the most inclusive definition of Medicaid coverage, which is the one adopted here, is to count as Medicaid covered anyone who received public assistance health insurance that was not of some "other" type. This leaves 7,386 individuals, which is not very different than what would be obtained using the least inclusive measure—the 7,287 individuals who reported "receiving" Medicaid in 1989. Experimentation with other possible measures of Medicaid coverage produced results similar to those reported below. The 1992 supplement simply asks about Medicaid coverage. The existence of "other" public health insurance programs accounts for the fact that the effects of eligibility on Medicaid coverage, private health insurance coverage, and no insurance coverage may not sum to zero.

12. For most of the missing observations, we know whether income was greater than or less than $20,000, so I can impute income within those subsamples. The imputation regressions fit fairly well; the R^2s for the yearly regressions estimated using all individuals average 0.45. For those with incomes below $20,000, the R^2s average 0.32; while for those with incomes above $20,000, the R^2s average 0.25.

only when the Medicaid cutoff falls in the middle of the family's reported income bracket, and the income brackets are in $1,000 increments if income is less than $20,000.[13] Two approaches to this problem were tried. The first involved predicting income within the bracket using regressions estimated using the CPS, as described above. The second method involved choosing a random number within the bracket. Since the estimated fraction eligible was very similar under both approaches, the simpler method was used. The estimated models control for income brackets rather than the noisy imputed income measure, and interactions between the (nominal) income brackets and the year dummies are included in order to account for inflation. The omitted income category in all the models estimated below is "missing."

A third problem is that there is no information about the distribution of income across family members, or about income sources. This lack of information is potentially problematic because, for example, some portion of earnings, but not other types of income, can be disregarded from total family income in determining AFDC eligibility, which in turn affects Medicaid eligibility. In this paper, these disregards are applied to total income, under the assumption that most family income comes from earnings, especially in poor families.[14] These limitations of the NHIS income data do not seem to lead to any systematic measurement problems; the resulting annual eligibility rate in the NHIS is similar to that calculated using the CPS in terms of both levels and the time-series trend.[15]

This paper focuses on three measures of the utilization of medical services over the past year: whether or not the child had a doctor's visit in the past year; the number of doctor's visits if the child had any visits; and whether or not the child was hospitalized in the past year.[16] Since the utilization measures are available in every year, the data set available for examining utilization is approximately twice as large as that available for examining insurance coverage.

Pediatric guidelines recommend at least one doctor's visit per year for all of the children in the sample, so that the absence of a doctor's visit in the previous year is suggestive of an access problem, regardless of underlying morbidity. If the marginal benefit of doctor's visits is decreasing in the number of visits (which seems reasonable if children who get any visits

13. For incomes over $20,000 and less than $50,000 the brackets are in increments of $5,000. The last bracket is for incomes over $50,000.

14. In the 1984 CPS, 75 percent of the average child's family income comes from his or her parents' earnings.

15. In the years 1989 to 1992, the percentages of children eligible for Medicaid in the NHIS data were 19.3, 25.2, 27.5, and 31.5 percent, respectively. These numbers are very close to those calculated from the CPS.

16. Although the NHIS asks many other questions about utilization, most pertain to a two-week window. Even in a sample as large as the NHIS, this sampling scheme yields very small samples of immigrant children who have received specific services.

receive some necessary preventive care), then this first visit is also the most important from the point of view of the child's health. Nevertheless, it is interesting to examine the number of doctor's visits conditional on the child receiving care, since the cost of care will be increasing in the number of visits. Because this distribution is highly skewed to the right, the analysis focuses on the log of the number of doctor's visits.

We examine hospitalizations primarily because they are so much more expensive than doctor's visits and, hence, account for a disproportionate share of Medicaid costs. For example, the U.S. House of Representatives (1993) reports that in 1991, the Medicaid program spent $5.4 billion on inpatient hospital services for AFDC children, and only $1.5 billion on physician services.[17] However, approximately 80 percent of children receive a doctor's visit in any given year, while only 3–5 percent of children are hospitalized. Hence, inferences about differences in hospitalization rates between immigrants and nonimmigrants are based on small sample sizes.

An overview of the data on eligibility, coverage, and utilization is shown in table 7.2. All means are calculated using sample weights.[18] The first row of table 7.2 indicates that 35 percent of immigrant children are Medicaid eligible, compared to 21 percent of the children of the native born. This evidence is consistent with previous work that shows that immigrants are more likely than natives to be eligible for social programs. The second row of table 7.2 suggests that although a slightly higher fraction of immigrant children are currently covered by Medicaid (18 percent compared to 14 percent of children of the native born), average take-up rates conditional on eligibility are actually lower among immigrants: Approximately 50 percent of the Medicaid-eligible immigrant children are covered compared to 66 percent of eligible children of the native born. Immigrant children are also less likely to be covered by private health insurance, with the result that 25 percent of the immigrant children are without health insurance coverage compared to 12 percent of other children.

This large difference in the probability of having health insurance coverage is associated with relatively small differences in the utilization of care, however. The second panel of table 7.2 indicates that 19 percent of immigrant children went without a visit in the 12 months prior to the survey, whether or not they were Medicaid eligible. The comparable figures for

17. Some of these physician services would have been rendered in hospitals.
18. An earlier version of this paper broke out children with at least one parent who immigrated less than 10 years ago. In principle, a comparison of these "new" immigrants with all immigrants is of interest because of evidence that new immigrants are less skilled than previous cohorts (Borjas 1990) and because new arrivals may be less familiar with Medicaid and may face higher transactions costs of enrolling in the program. However, even in a sample as large as the NHIS, there are relatively few children of new immigrants, making it difficult to judge the effects of assimilation. Leclere, Jensen, and Biddlecom (1994) find that among adults, recent immigrants are less likely than either the native born or immigrants of longer duration to receive timely health care.

Table 7.2   **Eligibility, Coverage, and Utilization in the NHIS**

Insurance Status		
	All Natives	All Immigrants
Number of observations	49,979	8,934
Medicaid eligible	.21	.35
Medicaid coverage	.14	.18
Private health insurance	.72	.56
No insurance	.12	.25
Fraction eligible in child's state/age/year	.25	.28

Utilization of Medical Care				
	All Natives		All Immigrants	
	Medicaid Eligible	Not Medicaid Eligible	Medicaid Eligible	Not Medicaid Eligible
Number of observations	25,577	81,374	7,852	12,394
No visit in past year	.15	.16	.19	.19
Number of doctor's visits last year if any visits	5.83 (.083)	5.24 (.047)	4.50 (.127)	4.12 (.067)
Hospitalized in past year	.07	.04	.04	.03

Utilization of Medical Care by Income and Insurance Status					
	All Natives			All Immigrants		
	Income <$20,000	Income $20,000–$40,000	Income $40,000+	Income <$20,000	Income $20,000–$40,000	Income $40,000+
Medicaid covered						
Number of observations	7,081	750	153	1,654	145	46
No visit in past year	.13	.10	.08	.12	.10	.15
Number of doctor's visits last year if any visits	7.04 (.20)	11.52 (.89)	5.74 (.53)	5.51 (.34)	3.50 (.28)	4.92 (.53)
Hospitalized in past year	.08	.11	.10	.06	.05	0
Private insurance						
Number of observations	8,647	12,419	14,203	1,271	1,625	1,911
No visit in past year	.19	.16	.11	.18	.19	.13
Number of doctor's visits last year if any visits	4.75 (.12)	4.80 (.09)	5.47 (.11)	4.00 (.26)	3.97 (.16)	4.41 (.14)
Hospitalized in past year	.04	.04	.04	.04	.03	.03

Note: Standard errors in parentheses. Means calculated using annual weights. Means for insurance status are calculated using data from 1989 to 1992 only, whereas means for utilization are calculated using 1989, 1990, 1991, and 1992 data.

children of the native born are 15 percent for Medicaid eligibles and 16 percent for noneligibles, indicating that the differences between natives and immigrants are much greater than the differences between the insured and uninsured. Conditional on having had at least one visit, Medicaid-eligible children had slightly more visits. But the difference of 0.4 or 0.6 more visits is much smaller than the raw differences between children of the native born and children of immigrants, which are on the order of 1.1 to 1.3 visits. The largest difference between those who are Medicaid eligible and those who are not is in terms of hospitalizations—native children on Medicaid are almost twice as likely to be hospitalized as those who are not covered.

The third panel of table 7.2 shows differences in utilization by insurance status and income. These figures lend support to the view that the private insurance policies held by many low-income households may be less desirable than Medicaid. For example, among natives, 13 percent of Medicaid households with incomes less than $20,000 (the vast majority of Medicaid households) went without a doctor's visit in the past year. The comparable figure for privately insured households is 19 percent. It is only in privately insured households with incomes over $40,000 per year that the incidence of going without doctor's visits falls below the Medicaid rate. A similar pattern is evident in immigrant households. Within income brackets, children on Medicaid tend to receive more doctor visits conditional on any visits than the privately insured. And among the privately insured, number of doctor visits increases with income, which may be (at least in part) a reflection of the generosity of the insurance coverage.

What remains to be seen is how much of these raw differences can be explained by the characteristics of immigrant children and their families. Some additional characteristics of children of immigrants and children of the native born and their families are shown in table 7C.2. As others have noted, immigrant parents are less skilled on average than other parents. Immigrant families also are poorer, have more children, are more likely to have other adults present in addition to the parents, are less likely to be female headed, and are more likely to live in central cities than other families. These differences will be controlled for in the models estimated below. Thus, these models focus on the differences between immigrants and similar natives, rather than on the differences between immigrants and all natives.

7.4 Results

7.4.1 Effects of Eligibility on Insurance Coverage

This section investigates the relationship between Medicaid eligibility and type of insurance coverage among children of immigrants and children of the native born. Ordinary least squares models of the probability of Medicaid coverage are shown in the first three columns of table 7.3. Table 7.1 indicated that immigrants were more likely to be eligible for Medicaid, but had lower take-up rates conditional on eligibility. Controlling for observable characteristics does not change this finding. The first row of table 7.3 indicates that becoming eligible for Medicaid increases the probability of coverage among children of the native born by 21 percentage points. The effect of eligibility is somewhat smaller among immigrants, as indicated by the negative interaction between eligibility and an indicator equal to one if the parent is an immigrant. The coefficient on the "parent immigrant" indicator is also significantly negative, indicating that children of immigrant parents are less likely to be enrolled in Medicaid conditional on observable characteristics. An F-test soundly rejected the null hypothesis that the combined effect of the parent immigrant indicator and the interaction was zero; hence, we conclude that eligible immigrants are significantly less likely than similar eligible natives to take up Medicaid coverage. The point estimates suggest that becoming eligible increases the probability of coverage by 18 percentage points among children of immigrants rather than 21 percentage points.[19]

The OLS estimates for private insurance coverage and the probability of noninsurance suggest that among natives, most of the increase in Medicaid coverage that accompanies eligibility increases comes at the expense of private health insurance coverage, while among immigrants, some families are dropping or losing private health insurance and becoming uninsured.

There is some evidence in table 7.3 that the transactions costs of applying for Medicaid matter, since children in larger families are more likely to be covered than other children (transactions costs imply that there are economies of scale involved in applying for Medicaid). Also, children in central cities where it may be easier to apply are more likely to be covered. Finally, there appears to be a strong seasonal effect: Medicaid coverage falls in winter and spring relative to summer and fall. This pattern suggests that many parents sign children up for Medicaid in summer and fall in order to get routine care such as immunizations that schools mandate. Then, six months later when children must be recertified (in most states), the parents do not renew the child's coverage.

The remaining rows of table 7.3 show that, for the most part, coverage

---

19. I have also estimated models that exclude parent's education, income, and measures of family structure. These models ask whether take-up is similar among immigrants and all natives, rather than focusing on *similar* natives. The pattern found is qualitatively similar to that reported in table 7.3, although the estimated effects of eligibility are larger for both natives and immigrants. For example, eligibility is estimated to increase the probability of Medicaid coverage by 32 percentage points among natives, but by only 22 percentage points among children of immigrants.

Table 7.3   Effects of Eligibility on Insurance Coverage

	OLS			TSLS		
	Medicaid (1)	Private (2)	No Insurance (3)	Medicaid (4)	Private (5)	No Insurance (6)
Medicaid	.206	−.192	−.006	.182	.021	−.206
	(.005)	(.006)	(.022)	(.050)	(.063)	(.060)
Parent immigrant and Medicaid eligible	−.033	−.030	.045	−.018	.050	−.057
	(.007)	(.009)	(.009)	(.023)	(.030)	(.028)
Parent immigrant	−.024	−.022	.040	−.028	−.051	.075
	(.005)	(.006)	(.005)	(.008)	(.010)	(.010)
Child male	−.001	−.001	.003	−.001	.000	.002
	(.002)	(.003)	(.003)	(.002)	(.003)	(.003)
Black	.054	−.047	.007	.055	−.051	.100
	(.004)	(.005)	(.005)	(.004)	(.006)	(.005)
Hispanic	−.000	−.028	.030	−.001	−.040	.043
	(.005)	(.006)	(.006)	(.005)	(.006)	(.006)
Mother high school dropout	.068	−.107	.024	.068	−.118	.035
	(.004)	(.005)	(.004)	(.004)	(.005)	(.005)
Mother some college	−.032	.051	−.017	−.033	.057	−.023
	(.003)	(.004)	(.004)	(.004)	(.004)	(.004)
Male head high school dropout	−.004	−.085	.082	−.004	−.094	.091
	(.004)	(.005)	(.005)	(.005)	(.006)	(.005)
Male head some college	.008	.015	−.022	.008	.016	−.023
	(.004)	(.004)	(.004)	(.004)	(.004)	(.004)

(*continued*)

Table 7.3 (continued)

	OLS			TSLS		
	Medicaid (1)	Private (2)	No Insurance (3)	Medicaid (4)	Private (5)	No Insurance (6)
Child is eldest	.019	−.018	−.003	.019	−.023	.002
	(.003)	(.004)	(.004)	(.003)	(.004)	(.004)
Number of siblings	.022	−.023	−.003	.024	−.037	.011
	(.001)	(.002)	(.002)	(.003)	(.004)	(.004)
No male head	.119	−.004	−.139	.120	−.006	−.138
	(.006)	(.007)	(.007)	(.006)	(.008)	(.007)
Mother is respondent	.117	.367	−.008	.116	.361	−.001
	(.009)	(.011)	(.010)	(.009)	(.011)	(.011)
Male head is respondent	.085	.395	−.010	.084	.393	−.007
	(.009)	(.012)	(.011)	(.009)	(.012)	(.011)
Other adult female relatives in household	−.004	−.066	.062	−.004	−.076	.072
	(.007)	(.008)	(.008)	(.007)	(.009)	(.008)
Other adult male relatives in household	−.041	−.050	.081	−.041	−.054	.085
	(.008)	(.010)	(.009)	(.008)	(.010)	(.010)
Income <$10,000	.203	−.254	.074	.216	−.388	.201
	(.008)	(.010)	(.009)	(.030)	(.038)	(.036)
Income $10,000–$19,999	.012	−.086	.085	.012	−.093	.092
	(.007)	(.008)	(.008)	(.007)	(.009)	(.008)
Income $20,000–$29,999	−.013	.069	−.064	−.017	.106	−.100
	(.007)	(.008)	(.008)	(.010)	(.013)	(.008)
Income $30,000–$39,999	−.011	.141	−.133	−.015	.177	−.168
	(.007)	(.009)	(.008)	(.010)	(.013)	(.013)

Income $40,000–$49,999	−.005	.140	−.138	−.008	.174	−.170
	(.007)	(.010)	(.009)	(.010)	(.013)	(.013)
Income ≥$50,000	−.005	.150	−.138	−.002	.183	−.182
	(.007)	(.009)	(.009)	(.010)	(.013)	(.012)
Central city	.034	−.034	−.002	.034	−.038	.002
	(.003)	(.004)	(.004)	(.003)	(.004)	(.004)
Rural area	−.001	−.016	.020	−.001	−.021	.024
	(.004)	(.004)	(.004)	(.004)	(.005)	(.004)
Winter	−.014	−.003	.014	−.013	−.002	.012
	(.004)	(.004)	(.004)	(.004)	(.005)	(.004)
Spring	−.006	.007	−.002	−.006	.008	−.003
	(.003)	(.004)	(.004)	(.003)	(.004)	(.004)
Summer	.004	.000	−.007	.004	.001	−.007
	(.003)	(.004)	(.004)	(.003)	(.004)	(.004)
Intercept	−.032	.317	.226	−.046	.281	.274
	(.018)	(.023)	(.022)	(.020)	(.027)	(.025)
R^2	.41	.45	.14	.40	.43	.13
Number of observations (thousands)	51.930	51.930	51.930	51.930	51.930	51.930

Note: Standard errors in parentheses. All models also include additional dummy variables for states, years, and ages; interactions between ages, states, and years; and interactions between income brackets and survey year as described in the text. The omitted income category is "missing."

varies with child and family characteristics as one might expect. For example, children of richer parents are less likely to be covered, while children of less-educated parents are more likely to be covered. One noteworthy finding is that the probability of coverage is much higher in families without a male head. This differential may reflect the fact that families on AFDC are already familiar with the welfare system and, in most cases, are already covered by Medicaid. Finally, although they are not shown, the age dummies included in the regression indicate that younger children are more likely to have coverage, other things being equal. This result may reflect a higher perceived benefit of regular medical care for younger children, or more illnesses requiring care.

As discussed above, it is possible that OLS estimates of the effects of becoming eligible under the Medicaid expansions reflect omitted variables that are correlated with both eligibility and coverage. Suppose, for example, that some children are both more likely to be eligible and more likely to have been covered by Medicaid in the absence of the Medicaid expansions, perhaps because they receive AFDC benefits or because their parents are refugees. In this case, the estimated effect of making someone eligible for Medicaid under the expansions would be biased upward. Similarly, it is easy to see that OLS estimates of the effect of eligibility on private health insurance coverage are likely to be biased downward, while those on being uninsured are likely to be biased upward; that is, the same children who are most likely to be made eligible for Medicaid are least likely to have private health insurance coverage and most likely to be uninsured.

The remaining three columns of table 7.3 show TSLS estimates of the effects of eligibility on insurance coverage. The estimated effects of eligibility on Medicaid coverage are remarkably robust. Once again, it appears that eligibility raises the probability of Medicaid coverage more among natives than among immigrants (18 percentage points compared to 14 percentage points), and the point estimates are similar to those obtained via OLS. However, instrumenting has a large effect on the estimated effects of eligibility on private health insurance and the probability of being uninsured. While the OLS estimates suggested substantial crowding out of private insurance, the TSLS estimates indicate that most of the gain in Medicaid coverage is in fact coming from the uninsured population.

Are these TSLS estimates reasonable? Note first that although the standard errors are large, the changes in the point estimates are also large. Thus, it is not the case that the effect of eligibility on private insurance becomes statistically insignificant in the TSLS specification solely because of the increase in the size of the standard errors. Still, it is possible that trends in the private health insurance market (e.g., concerns about increasing numbers of uninsured among the "working poor") drove some of the expansions of Medicaid eligibility, which would call these TSLS estimates of the size of crowding out into question.

One crude specification check involves excluding variables such as parent's education and income from the TSLS models. If these characteristics are uncorrelated with the fraction eligible in the state, then the instrumental variables strategy remains valid, and one should obtain the same TSLS estimates of the effects of Medicaid eligibility whether or not these variables are included. In fact, the results for Medicaid coverage are qualitatively similar (e.g., larger effects on Medicaid coverage among natives than among immigrants), but all of the estimated effects of Medicaid eligibility are larger in absolute value, and the effect of Medicaid eligibility on private health insurance coverage has the wrong sign. Thus, there is some evidence that individual characteristics that affect insurance coverage are correlated with the fraction eligible instrument. If these characteristics are not adequately controlled for in the specifications shown in table 7.3, then the instrument may be invalid.

In any case, the estimated effect of eligibility on Medicaid may seem low compared to take-up rates of approximately two-thirds for programs such as AFDC or food stamps. One reason for low take-up rates may be that many of the newly eligible were already covered by private health insurance. A second consideration is that many of the newly eligible were unfamiliar with welfare programs in general and unaware that it was now possible for them to qualify for Medicaid without being on welfare. Third, given transactions costs, many eligibles may not enroll until they have an urgent need for health care, leading them to cycle on and off the rolls. Short, Cantor, and Monheit (1988) found that only 43 percent of Medicaid patients stayed on the program for a continuous 32-month period and that over half of those leaving the program remained uninsured. Cycling will cause the fraction covered to be smaller than the fraction eligible in a cross section.

It is important to keep in mind that these effects are identified using recent changes in Medicaid eligibility, so they should be interpreted as the effect that similar changes or reductions in Medicaid eligibility would have. Evidently, barring all immigrants from receiving Medicaid would have some effect on coverage rates, since some immigrants are in fact covered, as shown in table 7.2.

7.4.2 Effects on Utilization

The discussion of figures 7.1 and 7.2 highlighted the fact that even if children do not take up Medicaid coverage, becoming eligible for Medicaid is likely to make their families better off, and may therefore have some effect on the consumption of medical care. Alternatively, if we think about the problem from a dynamic point of view, it is clear that eligibility may be more tightly linked to utilization in the past year than Medicaid coverage if children cycle in and out of coverage as needed. This section investigates the effects of eligibility on utilization of care.

The first column of table 7.4 shows linear probability models of the effects of eligibility on the probability that a child went without a doctor's visit in the past 12 months. As discussed above, this is the cleanest measure of utilization of health care available in the NHIS since children who do not see a doctor at all are likely to have a true access problem and to go without necessary preventive care. Becoming eligible for Medicaid is associated with an increase in the utilization of care. The insignificant interaction of immigrant status and eligibility suggests that becoming eligible has the same effect on all children. However, immigrant parents are about 3 percentage points less likely to have taken their child for a visit in the last year, and the increases in eligibility do not seem to have affected this gap.

The second column of table 7.4 suggests that while children of immigrants have fewer doctor's visits than children of the native born, becoming eligible for Medicaid has little effect on the number of doctor's visits among either group, given that they had at least one visit.

Finally, the third column of table 7.4 indicates that while children of immigrants are slightly less likely to be hospitalized than other children, becoming eligible for Medicaid increases hospitalizations only among children of the native born. This result is difficult to interpret because hospitalizations are likely to reflect supply as well as demand factors. It is possible, for example, that immigrants tend to live near hospitals that supply indigent care, whereas children of the native born tend to live near hospitals that primarily treat the insured. In this case, increases in Medicaid eligibility among previously uninsured children would increase access to hospital care among the native born but not among immigrants. It is also possible that some changes in hospitalization patterns associated with changes in insurance coverage reflect increases in unnecessary hospitalizations.

The remaining columns of table 7.4 highlight the fact that many observable characteristics have different effects on utilization than they have on coverage. For example, black children are more likely to have Medicaid coverage, but they are less likely to have received any visits in the past year. Similarly, table 7.3 showed that children in large families were more likely to be covered, while table 7.4 indicates that children in smaller families are more likely to have had a doctor's visit; the latter effect may reflect parental diligence with respect to scheduling the first child's checkups that is relaxed for later children, or the classic Becker (1981) child quality/quantity trade-off.[20] And although coverage rates were highest for children with less-educated and poorer parents, the probability of receiving any doctor's visits was also lowest for these children. These latter results are consistent with previous evidence that doctor's visits are a normal good,

20. Alternatively, larger families have lower per capita incomes and may therefore purchase fewer normal goods such as health care.

Table 7.4 Effects of Eligibility on the Utilization of Care

	OLS			TSLS		
	No Visits (1)	Ln (Number of visits) (2)	Number of Hospitalizations (3)	No Visits (4)	Ln (Number of visits) (5)	Number of Hospitalizations (6)
Medicaid	-.022 (.004)	-.013 (.010)	.009 (.002)	-.077 (.025)	.082 (.062)	.041 (.012)
Parent immigrant and Medicaid eligible	-.012 (.007)	.015 (.016)	-.008 (.003)	-.087 (.021)	.026 (.051)	-.039 (.010)
Parent immigrant	.027 (.004)	-.115 (.010)	-.004 (.002)	.050 (.007)	-.120 (.017)	.005 (.003)
Child male	-.003 (.002)	.030 (.005)	.008 (.001)	-.003 (.002)	.030 (.005)	.008 (.001)
Black	.038 (.004)	-.215 (.008)	-.005 (.002)	.037 (.004)	-.218 (.009)	-.007 (.002)
Hispanic	.005 (.004)	-.023 (.010)	.002 (.002)	.012 (.004)	-.025 (.010)	.004 (.002)
Mother high school dropout	.023 (.003)	-.008 (.008)	.004 (.002)	.028 (.004)	-.014 (.009)	.002 (.002)
Mother some college	-.030 (.003)	.043 (.007)	-.002 (.001)	-.031 (.003)	.046 (.007)	-.001 (.001)
Male head high school dropout	.021 (.004)	.004 (.009)	-.001 (.002)	.026 (.004)	-.001 (.010)	-.002 (.002)

(*continued*)

Table 7.4 (continued)

	OLS			TSLS		
	No Visits (1)	Ln (Number of visits) (2)	Number of Hospitalizations (3)	No Visits (4)	Ln (Number of visits) (5)	Number of Hospitalizations (6)
Male head some college	−.025 (.003)	.052 (.008)	−.002 (.002)	−.025 (.003)	.053 (.008)	−.002 (.002)
Child is eldest	−.023 (.003)	.061 (.006)	.000 (.001)	−.021 (.003)	.059 (.007)	−.000 (.001)
Number of siblings	.015 (.001)	−.037 (.003)	−.002 (.001)	.020 (.002)	−.043 (.005)	−.003 (.001)
No male head	−.042 (.005)	.067 (.012)	.004 (.002)	−.044 (.005)	.066 (.013)	.003 (.002)
Mother is respondent	−.004 (.008)	−.005 (.019)	−.001 (.004)	−.001 (.008)	−.006 (.019)	−.001 (.004)
Male head is respondent	.012 (.009)	−.030 (.020)	−.005 (.004)	.014 (.009)	−.031 (.020)	−.004 (.004)
Other adult female relatives in household	−.006 (.006)	.005 (.014)	−.002 (.003)	−.003 (.006)	.002 (.014)	−.002 (.003)
Other adult male relatives in household	.027 (.007)	−.046 (.016)	−.006 (.003)	.030 (.007)	−.048 (.017)	−.005 (.003)
Income <$10,000	−.005 (.013)	.124 (.023)	.005 (.004)	.023 (.014)	.090 (.035)	−.007 (.007)
Income $10,000–$19,999	−.017 (.012)	.060 (.020)	.002 (.004)	.004 (.006)	.067 (.015)	.000 (.003)
Income $20,000–$29,999	.014 (.012)	.068 (.020)	.003 (.006)	−.032 (.006)	.086 (.015)	.008 (.003)

	(1)	(2)	(3)	(4)	(5)	(6)
Income $30,000–$39,999	−.028	.077	.002	−.059	.111	.011
	(.012)	(.021)	(.006)	(.008)	(.018)	(.004)
Income $40,000–$49,999	.013	.119	−.010	−.077	.123	.009
	(.013)	(.022)	(.006)	(.008)	(.019)	(.004)
Income ≥$50,000	.005	.161	−.005	−.081	.165	.007
	(.012)	(.021)	(.006)	(.007)	(.018)	(.003)
Central city	−.013	.021	−.001	−.011	.019	−.001
	(.003)	(.007)	(.001)	(.003)	(.007)	(.001)
Rural area	.025	.013	.008	.025	.011	.008
	(.003)	(.008)	(.002)	(.003)	(.008)	(.002)
Winter	−.002	.046	.002	−.003	.047	.002
	(.003)	(.008)	(.002)	(.003)	(.008)	(.002)
Spring	.001	.020	.002	.000	.021	.002
	(.003)	(.007)	(.001)	(.003)	(.007)	(.001)
Summer	.003	−.014	.002	.002	−.014	.002
	(.003)	(.007)	(.001)	(.003)	(.007)	(.001)
Intercept	.113	1.321	.094	.141	1.230	.086
	(.015)	(.035)	(.007)	(.016)	(.039)	(.008)
R^2	.09	.12	.02	.09	.12	.02
Number of observations (thousands)	112.456	91.534	112.818	112.456	91.534	112.818

Note: Standard errors in parentheses. All models also include additional dummy variables for states, years, and ages; interactions between ages, states, and years; and interactions between income brackets and survey year as described in the text. The omitted income category is "missing."

and one that more educated parents tend to value more (cf. Currie and Thomas 1995).

As discussed above, these OLS estimates of the effects of eligibility are likely to be biased toward zero if eligible children are those who are most likely to go without medical care for unobservable reasons. TSLS estimates of the effect of eligibility on utilization appear in the last three rows of table 7.4. Column (4) suggests that OLS estimates of the effects of Medicaid eligibility on the probability of "no visits" are indeed biased toward zero. Moreover, the bias appears to be greater for immigrants than for natives, since the probability of going without a visit declines by 8 percentage points among eligible natives but by 11 percentage points among eligible immigrants, and this difference is statistically significant. Recall that eligible immigrants were less likely to take up Medicaid coverage than eligible natives, yet they are more likely to receive at least one doctor's visit. The juxtaposition of these results supports the view that immigrants face greater transactions costs than natives and hence spend more time without formal Medicaid coverage. On the other hand, neither the OLS or TSLS results show any effect of eligibility on the number of doctor visits conditional on the child having had at least one visit.

Finally, OLS estimates of the effects of eligibility on hospitalizations also appear to be biased toward zero, though instrumenting does not change the qualitative finding that eligibility increases hospitalizations among natives but not among children of immigrants. The effect for children of the native born is large (implying a 100 percent increase in hospitalizations) but consistent with what was shown in the means in table 7.2.

A specification check similar to that described above was conducted for the models shown in table 7.4. That is, the TSLS models were reestimated excluding variables such as parent's education, income, and family structure. The resulting estimates were extremely similar to those reported in table 7.4. Thus, there is little evidence that these measurable individual characteristics are correlated with both utilization of care and the fraction eligible instrument in a way that would invalidate the instrument. The conclusion that can be drawn is that the TSLS results regarding utilization are more robust than those regarding insurance coverage. In particular, it is difficult to draw any conclusions regarding the extent to which public insurance has crowded out private insurance using these data.

7.5   Discussion and Conclusions

This paper demonstrates that children of immigrants are more likely than other children to be eligible for Medicaid. Despite higher eligibility levels, the fraction of children covered by Medicaid is only slightly higher among immigrant children, which indicates that immigrants have lower average take-up rates. Moreover, recent eligibility expansions increased coverage more among natives than among immigrants, and this is true whether or not characteristics such as parental education, income, and family structure are controlled for.

The eligibility expansions had quite different effects on the utilization of care, suggesting that a narrow focus on coverage can lead to quite misleading assessments of the costs and benefits of extending eligibility. Becoming eligible for Medicaid reduced the probability that a child went without a doctor's visit in the past year dramatically for both immigrants and nonimmigrants. On the other hand, becoming eligible was not associated with an increase in the number of doctor's visits given at least one visit among either group of children, and it was associated with greater increases in hospitalization rates among children of the native born but not among children of immigrants.

Thus, among immigrants, the main effect of becoming eligible for Medicaid was to reduce the number of children going without any doctor's visits. As discussed above, in 1997 there were 12 million children with at least one immigrant parent. If we follow table 7.2 and assume that 35 percent of these children are eligible for Medicaid, then if Medicaid caused 11 percent of these children to receive an additional doctor visit at a cost of $50 per visit, the total bill would be approximately $2.3 million dollars per year.

Hence, the *marginal cost* of extending Medicaid eligibility to children of immigrants appears to have been small. These results do not imply that the total cost of providing Medicaid to immigrant children is insignificant; as discussed above, the United States has been spending on the order of $5.5 billion per year on Medicaid payments for children of immigrants. The key point is that reducing Medicaid eligibility for these children will not necessarily save money as long as children remain eligible for costly emergency care. In fact, costs could increase if lack of preventive care eventually increases the number of emergency cases.

Appendix A
Simulating Medicaid Eligibility

This appendix describes the procedure for imputing the Medicaid eligibility of individuals in the CPS and NHIS. The sources for information on state Medicaid options are the National Governors' Association (various years) and Congressional Research Service (1988, 1993).

Eligibility for AFDC

In order to qualify for AFDC, the child's family must satisfy three tests: (1) gross income must not exceed 1.85 times the state needs standard, (2) the gross income less certain "disregards" must be below the state needs standard, and (3) the gross income less the disregards, less a portion of their earnings, must be below the state's payment standard.

The disregards can be computed as follows. Beginning in October 1981, the allowance for work and child care expenses was $75 per month for work expenses and a maximum of $160 per child for child care costs. These allowances were not changed until the Family Support Act of 1988, which raised the allowances to $90 for work expenses and $175 per child for child care expenses, effective 1 October 1989. In addition, a portion of earned income was disregarded. In 1984, women were allowed to keep $30 plus one-third of earned income for 4 months. From 1985 onward, individuals who would have become ineligible for AFDC (and hence for Medicaid) after the 4 months were allowed to remain eligible for Medicaid for an additional 9 to 15 months depending on the state. We modeled this by assuming that for Medicaid eligibility purposes, women were allowed to keep the $30 and one-third of earned income for a year. The aim was to consistently model the maximum amount that a person could have received while remaining eligible for Medicaid coverage under AFDC.

One difficulty in implementing these rules in the NHIS is that the disregards apply only to earned income and one cannot distinguish between earned income and other income. It is therefore assumed that all household income is earned. This assumption yielded AFDC eligibility findings in the NHIS that were similar to those from the CPS, where there are data on individual earnings by source.

The second set of rules that must be evaluated to see if a child is eligible for AFDC are rules relating to family structure. Eligibility under the traditional program requires that the child reside in a female-headed household. However, children in two-parent households may still have been eligible under the AFDC-UP program. Eligibility for AFDC-UP is conditional on both current employment status and work history. We obtained data on AFDC-UP regulations from Hilary Hoynes. In addition, some states covered families with Medicaid if they had an unemployed head, even if there was no AFDC coverage; these states are identified in National Governors' Association (various years).

Lacking longitudinal data on work histories, it is assumed in the CPS that families are eligible if the state has a program and the spouse had worked less than 40 weeks in the previous year. In the NHIS it is only possible to determine whether or not the spouse is currently unemployed. Hence, the estimate of the AFDC-UP caseload is biased upward because it is not possible to determine whether those who are unemployed have been attached to the labor force long enough to qualify for AFDC-UP. Still, our estimates of the size of the AFDC-UP caseload appear to be reasonable, as about 1 in 20 AFDC eligibles are estimated to qualify through that program, matching the ratio reported in administrative data.

Eligibility under State Medically Needy Programs

In some states, children in families with incomes too high for AFDC could qualify for Medicaid under state Medically Needy programs. Income thresholds for these programs could be set no higher than 133 percent of the state's needs standard for AFDC. Families could "spend down" to these thresholds by subtracting their medical expenditures from their gross incomes (less disregards); if they did so, then Medicaid would pay the remainder of their medical expenses. In order to qualify, however, families must have high medical expenditures for several consecutive months (the "spend down period"). There is no way to determine which families have had such high medical spending in the CPS, and I do not do so in the NHIS, since eligibility would then be a direct function of utilization and health. As an approximation, eligibility thresholds are set to the Medically Needy levels in states with this program. Data on Medically Needy coverage and thresholds are from National Governors' Association (various years).

Eligibility for Ribicoff Children

Ribicoff children are those who would qualify for AFDC given income criteria alone, but who do not qualify for reasons of family structure. States may or may not choose to cover children under this optional program. In states that do cover them, the family structure requirements are ignored and screening is done only on income. Some states cover selected groups of children (such as only those in two-parent families, or only those in institutions). However, it was not possible to obtain precise information on the groups of children covered. Hence, a state is counted as a "Ribicoff state" only if it covers all categories of children, as reported by the National Governors' Association. Currie and Gruber also tried calling all of the states to obtain information about their Ribicoff children program; the resulting information appeared unreliable, since almost every state said that they had a program, whereas secondary sources report that coverage is much more selective. Using the state self-reported coverage yielded similar results to those reported in the paper.

Eligibility under the Medicaid Expansions

See appendix B for a summary of the relevant legislation. If family income and the child's age were less than the cutoffs, it was assumed that the child was eligible. One important question is whether states apply AFDC disregards when computing a family's eligibility for the expansions. Discussions with several state and federal Medicaid administrators suggested that such disregards were generally applied, so they were used in our eligibility calculations. Calculating eligibility without the disregards yielded a significantly smaller effect of the expansions, but the regression results were quite similar.

Appendix B
The Medicaid Expansions

Deficit Reconciliation Act, 1984. Effective 1 October 1984. Required states to extend Medicaid coverage to children born after 30 September 1983, if those children lived in families that were income eligible for AFDC.

Omnibus Budget Reconciliation Act, 1986. Effective 1 April 1987. Permitted states to extend Medicaid coverage to children in families with incomes below the federal poverty level. Beginning in fiscal year 1988, states could increase the age cutoff by one year each year, until all children under age five were covered.

Omnibus Budget Reconciliation Act, 1987. Effective 1 July 1988. Permitted states to cover children under age 2, 3, 4, or 5 who were born after 30 September 1983. Effective 1 October 1988, states could expand coverage to children under age 8 born after 30 September 1983. Allows states to extend Medicaid eligibility to infants up to one year of age in families with incomes up to 185 percent of the federal poverty level. States were *required* to cover children through age 5 in fiscal year 1989, and through age 6 in fiscal year 1990, if the families met AFDC income standards.

Medicare Catastrophic Coverage Act, 1988. Effective 1 July 1989, states were required to cover infants up to one year of age in families with incomes less than 75 percent of the federal poverty level. Effective 1 July 1990, the income threshold was raised to 100 percent of the poverty level.

Family Support Act, 1988. Effective 1 April 1990. States were required to continue Medicaid coverage for 12 months among families who had received AFDC in 3 of the previous 6 months but who had become ineligible because of earnings.

Omnibus Budget Reconciliation Act, 1989. Effective 1 April 1990. Required states to extend Medicaid eligibility to children up to age 6 with family incomes up to 133 percent of the federal poverty line.

Omnibus Budget Reconciliation Act, 1990. Effective 1 July 1991. States were required to cover all children under age 19 who were born after 30 September 1983, and whose family incomes were below 100 percent of the federal poverty level.

Appendix C

Table 7C.1   State Medical Eligibility Thresholds for Children

State	January 1988		December 1989		December 1991	
	Age Limit	MEDICAID%	Age Limit	MEDICAID%	Age Limit	MEDICAID%
Alabama			1	185	8	133
Alaska			2	100	8	133
Arizona	1	100	2	100	8	140
Arkansas	2	75	7	100	8	185
California			5	185	8	185
Colorado			1	75	8	133
Connecticut	0.5	100	2.5	185	8	185
Delaware	0.5	100	2.5	100	8	160
D.C.	1	100	2	100	8	185
Florida	1.5	100	5	100	8	150
Georgia	0.5	100	3	100	8	133
Hawaii			4	100	8	185
Idaho			1	75	8	133
Illinois			1	100	8	133
Indiana			3	100	8	150
Iowa	0.5	100	5.5	185	8	185
Kansas			5	150	8	150
Kentucky	1.5	100	2	125	8	185
Louisiana			6	100	8	133
Maine			5	185	8	185
Maryland	0.5	100	6	185	8	185
Massachusetts	0.5	100	5	185	8	185
Michigan	1	100	3	185	8	185
Minnesota			6	185	8	185
Mississippi	1.5	100	5	185	8	185

(*continued*)

Table 7C.1   (continued)

State	January 1988		December 1989		December 1991	
	Age Limit	MEDICAID%	Age Limit	MEDICAID%	Age Limit	MEDICAID%
Missouri	0.5	100	3	100	8	133
Montana			1	100	8	133
Nebraska			5	100	8	133
Nevada			1	75	8	133
New Hampshire			1	75	8	133
New Jersey	1	100	2	100	8	185
New Mexico	1	100	3	100	8	185
New York			1	185	8	185
North Carolina	1.5	100	7	100	8	185
North Dakota			1	75	8	133
Ohio			1	100	8	133
Oklahoma	1	100	3	100	8	133
Oregon	1.5	85	3	100	8	133
Pennsylvania	1.5	100	6	100	8	133
Rhode Island	1.5	100	6	185	8	185
South Carolina	1.5	100	6	185	8	185
South Dakota			1	100	8	133
Tennessee	1.5	100	6	100	8	185
Texas			3	130	8	185
Utah			1	100	8	133
Vermont	1.5	100	6	225	8	225
Virginia			1	100	8	133
Washington	1.5	100	8	185	8	185
West Virginia	0.5	100	6	150	8	150
Wisconsin			1	130	8	155
Wyoming			1	100	8	133

Source: Yelowitz (1995).

Note: The age limit represents the oldest that a child could be (at a given point in time) and still be eligible under the expansions. MEDICAID% represents the maximum income limit for an infant (the maximum for an older child is less).

Table 7C.2   **Child and Family Characteristics in the NHIS**

	Natives	Immigrants
Child age	6.86	6.55
	(.90)	(2.04)
Child male	.51	.51
Child black	.17	.09
Child Hispanic	.05	.43
Mother less than 12 years education	.18	.42
Mother some college	.37	.33
Male head less than 12 years education[a]	.15	.37
Male head some college[a]	.47	.39
Male head employed[a]	.92	.88
Female head employed	.58	.54
No male head	.22	.16
Child oldest/only child	.55	.50
No. of siblings in household	1.26	1.56
	(.23)	(.63)
Mother is respondent	.30	.30
Male head is respondent[a]	.69	.72
Other adult female relative in household	.03	.10
Other adult male relative in household	.02	.07
Central city	.23	.46
Rural	.26	.07
Household Income Category		
$10,000 or less	.11	.14
$10,001–$20,000	.15	.21
$20,001–$30,000	.16	.15
$30,001–$40,000	.15	.11
$40,001–$50,000	.12	.08
Greater than $50,000	.19	.16
Missing	.12	.15

Note: Standard errors in parentheses. Means calculated using annual weights.
[a]The mean is calculated conditional on there being a male head.

References

Banister, Judith. 1994. International perspectives on United States immigration. Paper presented to the Population Association of America, Miami, Florida.

Becker, Gary. 1981. *A treatise on the family.* Cambridge, Mass.: Harvard University Press.

Blank, Rebecca, and David Card. 1991. Recent trends in insured and uninsured employment: Is there an explanation? *Quarterly Journal of Economics* 106: 1157–90.

Blank, Rebecca, and Patricia Ruggles. 1993. When do women use AFDC and food stamps? The dynamics of eligibility vs. participation. NBER Working Paper no. 4429. Cambridge, Mass.: National Bureau of Economic Research.

Blau, Francine. 1984. The use of transfer payments by immigrants. *Industrial and Labor Relations Review* 37 (2): 222–39.

Bloom, Daniel, Sharon Parrott, Isaac Shapiro, and David Super. 1995. *The personal responsibility act: An analysis.* Washington D.C.: Center on Budget and Policy Priorities.

Borjas, George J. 1990. *Friends or strangers: The impact of immigrants on the U.S. economy.* New York: Basic Books.

Borjas, George J., and Lynette Hilton. 1996. Immigration and the welfare state: Immigrant participation in means-tested entitlement programs. *Quarterly Journal of Economics* 111 (2): 575–604.

Clark, Rebecca. 1994. *The costs of providing public assistance and education to immigrants.* Washington, D.C.: The Urban Institute.

Congressional Research Service. 1988. *Medicaid source book: Background data and analysis.* Washington, D.C.: U.S. Government Printing Office.

———. 1993. *Medicaid source book: Background data and analysis.* Washington, D.C.: U.S. Government Printing Office.

Currie, Janet, and Jonathan Gruber. 1996a. Saving babies: The efficacy and cost of recent changes in the Medicaid eligibility of pregnant women. *Journal of Political Economy* 104 (6): 1263–96.

———. 1996b. Health insurance eligibility, utilization of medical care, and child health. *Quarterly Journal of Economics* 111 (2): 431–66.

———. 1997. The technology of birth: Health insurance, medical interventions, and infant health. NBER Working Paper no. 5985. Cambridge, Mass.: National Bureau of Economic Research.

Currie, Janet, Jonathan Gruber, and Michael Fischer. 1995. Physician payments and infant health: Effect of increases in Medicaid reimbursements. *American Economic Review* 85 (2): 106–11.

Currie, Janet, and Duncan Thomas. 1995. Medical care for children: Public insurance, private insurance, and racial differences in utilization. *Journal of Human Resources* 30:135–62.

Cutler, David, and Jonathan Gruber. 1996. Does public insurance crowd out private insurance? *Quarterly Journal of Economics* 111 (2): 391–430.

Devine, Theresa J., and James Heckman. 1994. The consequences of eligibility rules for a social program: A study of the Job Training Partnership Act (JTPA). University of Chicago, Department of Economics, June.

Dumouchel, William, and Greg Duncan. 1983. Using sample survey weights in multiple regression analyses of stratified samples. *Journal of the American Statistical Associations* 78 (383): 535–43.

Fix, Michael, and Wendy Zimmerman. 1997. Welfare reform: A new immigrant policy for the U.S. Washington, D.C.: The Urban Institute.

Fossett, James W., Janet D. Perloff, Phillip R. Kletke, and John A. Peterson. 1992. Medicaid and access to child health care in Chicago. *Journal of Health Politics, Policy, and Law* 17:273–98.

Fossett, James W., and John A. Peterson. 1989. Physician supply and Medicaid participation: The causes of market failure. *Medical Care* 27:386–96.

Hadley, Jack, E. P. Steinberg, and J. Feder. 1991. Comparison of uninsured and privately insured hospital patients: Condition on admission, resource use, and outcome. *Journal of the American Medical Association* 265:374–79.

Heckman, James. 1990. Alternative approaches to the evaluation of social programs: Econometric and experimental methods. Paper presented to the World Congress of the Econometric Society, Barcelona, Spain.

Heckman, James, and Thomas MaCurdy. 1985. A simultaneous equations linear probability model. *Canadian Journal of Economics* 18 (1): 28–37.

Hernandez, Donald, and Evan Charney, eds. 1998. *The health and well-being of children of immigrants.* Washington, D.C.: National Academy Press.

Jensen, Leif. 1988. Patterns of immigration and public assistance utilization, 1970–1980. *International Migration Review* 22 (1): 51–83.

Kemper, Kathi. 1988. Medically inappropriate hospital use in a pediatric population. *New England Journal of Medicine* 318 (16): 1033–37.

Lamberg, L. 1996. Nationwide study of health and coping among immigrant children. *Journal of the American Medical Association* 276 (18): 1455–56.

Leclere, Felicia, Lief Jensen, and Ann Biddlecom. 1994. Health care utilization, family context, and adaptation among immigrants to the United States. *Journal of Health and Social Behavior* 35:370–84.

Mitchell, Janet, and Rachel Schurman. 1984. Physician participation in Medicaid revisited. *Medical Care* 29:645–53.

National Governors' Association. Various years. *A catalogue of state Medicaid program changes.* Washington, D.C.: National Governors' Association.

Newhouse, Joseph. 1993. Medical care costs: How much welfare loss? *Journal of Economic Perspectives* 6:23–42.

Piper, Joyce, W. A. Ray, and M. R. Griffin. 1990. Effects of Medicaid eligibility expansion on prenatal care and pregnancy outcomes in Tennessee. *Journal of the American Medical Association* 264:2219–23.

Shore-Sheppard, Lara. 1996. Stemming the tide? The effect of expanding Medicaid eligibility on health insurance coverage. Princeton University Industrial Relations Section Working Paper no. 361. Princeton, N.J.: Princeton University.

Short, Pamela, Joel Cantor, and Alan Monheit. 1988. The dynamics of Medicaid enrollment. *Inquiry* 25:504–16.

Thomas, Duncan, and John Strauss. 1995. Human resources: Empirical modeling of household and family decisions. In *Handbook of development economics,* ed. T. N. Srinivasan and Jere Behrman. Amsterdam: North-Holland.

Tienda, Marta, and Lief Jensen. 1986. Immigration and public assistance participation: Dispelling the myth of dependency. *Social Science Research* 15 (4): 372–400.

Trejo, Stephen. 1992. Immigrant welfare recipiency: Recent trends and future implications. *Contemporary Policy Issues* 10:44–53.

U.S. General Accounting Office. 1994. *Health care reform: Potential difficulties in determining eligibility for low-income people.* Report no. GAO/HEHS-94-176. Washington, D.C.: U.S. Government Printing Office.

U.S. House of Representatives. Committee on Ways and Means. 1993. *Overview of entitlement programs.* Washington, D.C.: U.S. Government Printing Office.

U.S. National Commission on the International Year of the Child. 1980. *Report to the president.* Washington, D.C.: U.S. Government Printing Office.

Wenneker, Mark, J. S. Weissman, and H. M. Epstein. 1990. The association of payer with utilization of cardiac procedures in Massachusetts. *Journal of the American Medical Association* 2461:1255–60.

White, Halbert. 1980. A heteroskedasticity-consistent covariance matrix and a direct test for heteroskedasticity. *Econometrica* 48:817–38.

Yelowitz, Aaron S. 1995. The Medicaid notch, labor supply and welfare participation: Evidence from eligibility expansions. *Quarterly Journal of Economics* 110 (4): 909–40.

Social Security Benefits of
Immigrants and U.S. Born

Alan L. Gustman and Thomas L. Steinmeier

8.1   Introduction

Social Security is often billed as a retirement insurance plan where benefits are earned based on payroll tax contributions. But there also is a transfer component to Social Security. The benefit formula is designed to transfer benefits disproportionately to families with a history of low lifetime earnings. This paper finds that the income support feature of Social Security disproportionately transfers benefits to immigrants relative to U.S. born *with identical earnings* in all years the immigrants have been in the United States. Moreover, immigrants who have been in the United States for a decade or two and who have relatively high earnings benefit disproportionately. A method for prorating the benefits of immigrants based on time in the United States is discussed. Prorating would provide similar rates of return under Social Security to U.S.- and foreign-born individuals with similar earnings in each year of work. Paradoxically, although the foreign born have a higher return to their Social Security taxes than the U.S. born, even in the absence of reform, it is in the interest of the U.S. born for immigrants to have been included in Social Security.

Alan L. Gustman is the Loren M. Berry Professor of Economics at Dartmouth College and a research associate of the National Bureau of Economic Research. Thomas L. Steinmeier is professor of economics at Texas Tech University.

Gustman and Steinmeier received support from the National Institute on Aging. In addition, support for Gustman was provided by a Rockefeller Center Fellowship at Dartmouth College. The authors thank Richard Freeman, Dean Leimer, Lawrence Thompson, and conference participants for their helpful comments, and Emily Loudon for her research assistance. A longer version of this paper, available as NBER Working Paper no. 6478, with the same title, provides additional tables and calculations.

Even though immigrants receive a better deal under Social Security than U.S. born, the immigrants just reaching retirement age will have contributed more to Social Security than they will receive in benefits.

Why do immigrants receive a better return on Social Security taxes paid than U.S. born? For those reaching retirement age today, when lifetime earnings history is calculated for purposes of determining Social Security benefits, a simple average is taken of the highest 35 years of real covered earnings. When average covered earnings is computed for immigrants who have spent fewer than 35 years in the United States, the average includes zeros for years spent outside the United States. Accordingly, immigrants who have been in the United States for only a part of their working lives are treated by the Social Security system as having lower average earnings than the average of the yearly earnings they in fact report. Because the Social Security benefit formula redistributes benefits toward those with a low lifetime earnings history, and years spent outside the country are counted as years of zero earnings, Social Security taxes paid by immigrants generate a higher return than do the taxes paid by U.S. born.

In the sections below, we explore the structure of the current Social Security system, its consequences for benefits and taxes paid by immigrants and U.S. born, and the effects of prorating benefits on the differences in returns realized by each group. The Social Security benefit formula is examined in section 8.2, and its implications for redistribution of benefits among U.S.- and foreign-born individuals are explored. Section 8.3 discusses the effects of adopting an alternative benefit structure for immigrants, where benefits are prorated on the basis of time spent in the United States. Labor force patterns and earnings distributions for immigrants and U.S. born, as reported by respondents to the Health and Retirement Study (HRS), are contrasted in section 8.4. Section 8.5 presents findings based on the matched Social Security earnings histories for HRS respondents. It compares tax payments and the present values of Social Security benefits from own work, spouse and survivor benefits associated with own work, and benefits from the spouse's employment. Redistribution under a prorated system is also explored. Income and wealth distributions for immigrants and native born are examined in section 8.6. Section 8.7 considers participation in transfer programs by immigrants and native born. Social Security benefits and tax contributions are compared for U.S. born and foreign born in section 8.8. Section 8.9 asks whether, on a purely selfish basis, native-born participants would favor having foreign-born individuals participate in the system. Section 8.10 concludes the paper.

8.2 How the Social Security Benefit Formula Differentially Affects U.S. Born and Foreign Born

8.2.1 The Social Security Benefit Calculation

Social Security benefits are determined from past covered earnings history, where past earnings are indexed to age 60 and are averaged to a summary statistic called the average indexed monthly earnings (AIME). For those reaching age 62 after 1991, AIME is calculated using the highest 35 years of indexed earnings. If an individual has covered earnings for fewer than 35 years, then zeros are entered into the AIME calculation for the remaining years.

To illustrate the fundamentals of the calculation, assume that an individual works x_s years under Social Security and that the individual's annual earnings, w_t, increase proportionately to the average wage index. This implies that the indexed wage used in the AIME calculation is either the average wage multiplied by the ratio of years worked divided by 35, or is a constant, w.[1]

The AIME is given in equation (1).

$$
(1) \qquad \text{AIME} = \begin{cases} \dfrac{x_s w}{35} & \text{if } x_s < 35 \\[2ex] \dfrac{35w}{35} = w & \text{if } x_s \geq 35. \end{cases}
$$

From the AIME, the basic benefit, called the primary insurance amount (PIA), is computed. As seen in equation (2), the PIA is a quasi-concave function of the average indexed monthly earnings, where for those reaching 62 in 1997, the function f is 90 percent of the first $455 of AIME, 32 percent of AIME between $455 and $2,741, and 15 percent of AIME over $2,741. Forty quarters of coverage are required to be eligible for benefits.

$$
(2) \qquad \text{PIA} = f(\text{AIME}).
$$

8.2.2 Benefits and Taxes

If the number of years worked under Social Security is equal to x, the number of years since entering the United States at age a_0, the value of the stream of Social Security benefits at age 62, less the value of the contributions, is given by

---

1. This assumption is only approximate. The rules state that wages before age 60 are indexed up to age 60 for the AIME formula, and that wages after age 60 enter the formula unindexed.

(3) $$V = g(a_0 + x)\text{PIA} - \int_{a_0}^{a_0+x} bwe^{-(r-g)(t-62)}dt.$$

In the first term, $g(a_0 + x)$ is the annuitized value of the Social Security benefits for each \$1 of PIA, adjusted for the early retirement penalty or late retirement credit, and discounted to age 62. For example, if the individual retires at age 63, the value of a \$1 annuity starting at age 63 and discounted to age 62 would be \$13.61.[2] The individual would be eligible for 86.7 percent of the PIA (because he retired two years before the normal retirement age), so the value of the function g would be \$13.61 times 86.7 percent, or \$11.80.

In the second term, b is the Social Security contribution rate. At the time of writing, the rate levied to support old age and survivors benefits is 10.6 percent.[3] The expression $bwe^{-(r-g)(t-62)}$ represents the value of the contributions paid at age t, discounted to age 62.[4]

8.2.3 Differences in Returns to Social Security between U.S. and Foreign Born Arising from Social Security's Progressive Benefit Structure

Table 8.1 illustrates benefits when earnings fall in different brackets of the Social Security formula. The illustration begins with a calculation, looking forward, for a person who is 21 in 1997 and will earn the 1997 maximum taxable wage of \$65,400 in real terms for his entire working life. If the 1997 formula continued in place and the 21-year-old spent his entire working life under the U.S. Social Security system, the individual's real yearly retirement benefit at age 65 would be \$18,759.[5] Twenty-six percent of the benefit, or \$4,914, is due to the first \$5,460 worth of earnings, 8 percent of total covered earnings. The next 47 percent of the total benefit is due to earnings in the second bracket, between \$5,460 and \$32,892. That is, the next 42 percent of total earnings generates 47 percent of the total

---

2. This calculation uses a 2.3 percent real interest rate, consistent with the assumptions of the Social Security Trustees.

3. More precisely, from the year 2000 and thereafter, the combined employer and employee rate will be 10.6 percent. Currently it is 10.52 percent. (See Social Security Administration 1996, table 2.A3.)

4. It is also possible to analyze how the change in the value of benefits minus payroll tax payments varies with the amount of time spent outside the United States. Formally, one can conduct such an analysis by differentiating V in eq. (3) with respect to a_0. We do not believe that the timing of immigration decisions is based substantially on the change in the value of Social Security with respect to the date of immigration and do not explore that relationship here. For a related calculation in the context of the decision to participate in a privatized Social Security system, see Gustman and Steinmeier (1998).

5. Given the current financial condition of the Social Security system, the current benefit formula and payroll tax are likely to be changed in the future. But these changes are tangential to the question of how immigrants and U.S. born are treated under Social Security. Thus, the present discussion uses the current parameters of the system. For further discussion of some of the possible changes in the system, see the collected papers in Feldstein (1998).

| Table 8.1 | Illustrative Calculation of the Role of Brackets in the Social Security Benefit Formula for U.S. Born and Foreign Born for a Person with Constant Real Yearly Earnings of $65,400 |

	First Bracket	Second Bracket	Third Bracket
1. AIME upper limit	$455	$2,741	$5,450
2. AIME upper limit times 12	$5,460	$32,892	$65,400
3. Share of total earnings accounted for by earnings in indicated bracket	.08	0.42	0.5
4. Yearly benefit due to earnings in indicated bracket	$4,914	$8,778	$5,067
5. Share of total benefit due to earnings in bracket	0.26	0.47	0.27
6. Effective upper bracket limit for foreign born who is a U.S. resident for 10 years	$19,110	$115,122	$228,900
7. Effective upper bracket limit for foreign born who is a U.S. resident for 20 years	$9,555	$57,561	$114,450
8. Effective upper bracket limit for foreign born who is a U.S. resident for 30 years	$6,370	$38,374	$76,300

benefit. The remaining 27 percent of the benefit comes from the 50 percent of covered earnings between $32,892 and $65,400.

In the case of an otherwise comparable immigrant who has been in the United States for less than the full 35 years, the Social Security benefit formula counts all years of work outside the United States as years of zero earnings. The effect is to widen the brackets for calculating the average indexed monthly earnings. The extent of widening will depend on how long the immigrant works in covered U.S. employment.

Consider the case illustrated in row 6 of table 8.1, for a foreign-born individual who will divide a full-time work life between his country of origin and the United States, and who also will earn today's maximum covered earnings in real terms in each year of work. Suppose this individual will be in the United States for 10 years. Applying the current formula, the AIME includes as the highest 35 years of earnings, 10 years of maximum earnings and 25 years of zeros. Therefore, instead of receiving benefits that are 90 percent of the first $5,460 per year earned in each year of work, row 6 in table 8.1 indicates that an immigrant who worked 10 years in the United States will have the 90 percent replacement rate extend through the first $19,110 earned per year in the United States. That is, a person who earned $19,110 in real terms in each year of his 10 years in the United States will receive yearly benefits worth 90 percent of the AIME. Analogously, for a person who has been in the United States for 20 years, average earnings for the first 20 years of up to $9,555 will have a replacement rate of 90 percent. For a person in the United States for 30 years, because 5 years of zeros are mixed into the AIME formula, earnings of up to $6,370 will be subject to a 90 percent replacement rate. The upper limit on the second bracket is raised to $115,122 for a person who has been here for 10 years, $57,561 for a person who has been here for 20 years, and $38,374 for a person who has been here for 30 years. These numbers are reported in the last two rows of table 8.1. Because only $65,400 of income is counted in any year, that means that a person who has been in the United States for 10 years and who has maximum covered earnings in each year will have all income subject to the payroll tax replaced at a marginal rate of at least 32 percent, never entering the third bracket. A person who has been in the United States for 20 years with maximum earnings will have covered earnings replaced at 15 percent only for $7,800 ($65,400 − $57,561) of earnings, with most of his or her benefits calculated using either the 90 percent or the 32 percent marginal rate. Even a person who has been in the United States for 30 years has wider brackets than would apply for the U.S.-born citizen, and would thus enjoy a higher marginal replacement rate than the counterpart U.S.-born citizen.

Using data from the Health and Retirement Study, to be examined in much more detail below, figure 8.1 shows the share of the foreign born who were between the ages of 51 and 61 in 1992; who have more than $5,000 in yearly earnings in years that they worked, so they have earnings spanning more than one bracket; and who will retire with about 10, 20, or 30 years of coverage. Table 8A.1 in the appendix reports the distribution of immigrants in the HRS by the decade of immigration and average real covered earnings in all years worked. According to the numbers in the HRS for sample-age eligibles, about 13 percent of foreign-born men and 9 percent of foreign-born women entered the United States in 1980 or later and earn more than $5,000 per year. These immigrants will end up with about a decade or a bit more of covered work by the time they retire, on average around 1998. About 23 percent of foreign-born men and 16 percent of foreign-born women entered in the 1970s and have average yearly earnings above $5,000 per year; they will end up with about two decades of coverage. And 31 percent of foreign-born men and 29 percent of foreign-born women entered the United States in the 1960s and have average earnings in years worked above $5,000; they will end up with three decades of coverage by the time they retire.

Before examining the actual data on benefits for immigrants and foreign born in the HRS cohort, which depend on the precise history of Social Security rules governing covered earnings and the age and work history of the respondent, it is helpful to determine how the benefit schedule itself works. With a better feeling for how benefits vary with time in the United States and with the earnings for simple, standardized cases, it will be easier

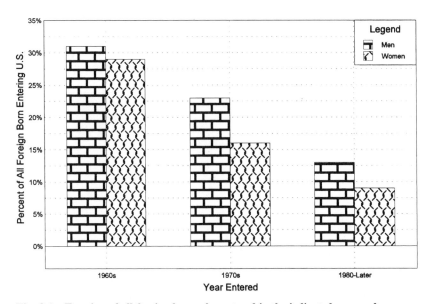

Fig. 8.1   Fraction of all foreign born who entered in the indicated year and earn more than $5,000 per year

to understand what underlies the actual distributions in the population. Moreover, the differences in benefits between immigrants and U.S. born will be not be the same in the future as they were in the past. Maximum covered earnings have increased sharply from levels in earlier decades. Accordingly, because these calculations are forward looking, they generate different relationships between benefits and taxes than will be found in the HRS data examined below.[6]

Simple comparisons may be constructed by assuming various, constant levels of lifetime earnings, and comparing benefits over different periods of covered earnings. The comparisons we make are for a 22-year-old who we assume will retire at age 62 after having constant levels of real yearly earnings, using alternative hypothetical real earnings of $5,000, $10,000 to $60,000 at $10,000 increments, and at the 1997 maximum of $65,400. As above, we will examine outcomes at 10, 20, 30, and 40 years of covered earnings.

Table 8.2 reports benefits that would be received by decades of covered work in the United States at the indicated yearly earnings. One hallmark of the Social Security benefit structure is its progressivity. Comparing benefits for those earning the 1997 maximum covered earnings of $65,400

---

6. Members of the IIRS were subject to relatively low covered earnings in their early work years. As a result, there are smaller advantages to late-arriving immigrants in the HRS than will be true for late-arriving immigrants in younger cohorts.

Table 8.2   **Yearly Social Security Retirement Benefits Earned, by Years of Work in the United States, for Hypothetical, Constant Real Yearly Earnings**

Real Yearly Earnings	Years of Work under Social Security			
	10 Years	20 Years	30 Years	40 Years (U.S. Born)
$5,000	$1,286	$2,571	$3,857	$4,500
$10,000	$2,571	$4,995	$5,910	$6,367
$20,000	$4,995	$6,824	$8,653	$9,567
$30,000	$5,910	$8,653	$11,395	$12,767
$40,000	$6,824	$10,481	$13,901	$14,758
$50,000	$7,738	$12,310	$15,187	$16,258
$60,000	$8,653	$13,901	$16,473	$17,758
≥ $65,400	$9,146	$14,364	$17,167	$18,568

with those earning $5,000 a year over a 40-year work life, an income difference of 13 to 1 is associated with a comparable ratio of benefits of 4 to 1. Except for those in the very lowest income brackets, each successive decade of work contributes less than the previous decade's work to the Social Security benefit. The last 10 years of work, although they account for a quarter of the payroll taxes paid, contribute much less to benefits than work in either of the three previous decades. It is not only that the Social Security formula is progressive; once 35 years of work have been accumulated, additional years of work result in a higher payroll tax, but they have no effect on the benefit computation.[7]

Each of the first three decades of work adds about the same amount to yearly Social Security benefits for those earning $5,000 per year. The reason is that those with very low incomes remain in the 90 percent bracket for most of the work life. Those with incomes low enough to remain in the first bracket through their entire work lives are the exception, however. For those earning $20,000 to $40,000 a year, the second and third decades of work contribute roughly the same amount to benefits, which is much less than the contribution from the first decade of work. For those whose real yearly earnings are $20,000 or more, working in the United States for 10 years will entitle them to about half of the total benefit that will be received by a U.S. worker covered for the full career. For those earning $20,000 or more, a second decade in the United States accounts for another 20–30 percent of benefits. The third quarter of work contributes around 15 to 20 percent of the benefits received by a U.S.-born worker covered for 40 years. The final 10 years of work account for a lower share of benefits for all income classes. For all but those earning $5,000 a year,

---

7. If real earnings in later years were higher than earnings in earlier years, Social Security benefits might increase as a result of additional work after 35 years of work had been accumulated. But such effects are typically modest. See Gustman and Steinmeier (1985, 1991).

the last quarter of covered employment, and of taxes paid, generates 10 percent or less of the total benefits paid as a result of 40 years of work. For those earning $50,000 or above, each decade of work contributes successively less to benefits.

Except for the very first bracket, for working under Social Security for half of the time of a U.S.-born worker, a foreign-born worker earning $10,000 a year or more receives 70–80 percent of the benefit paid to a U.S.-born worker. Only half of the payroll taxes charged to a U.S. worker with comparable earnings over 40 years have been paid by a foreign-born worker and his employer after 20 years of work, however.

8.3 Social Security Benefits When Benefits Are Prorated Based on Time in the United States

There is an alternative to the current system that would maintain the progressive Social Security benefit formula but would no longer provide higher benefit/tax ratios to those who have been in the country for fewer years. The approach involves prorating the benefits of immigrants. Their benefits are reduced for time during prime working age spent in their country of origin, rather than counting such time as years of zero earnings.

8.3.1 Totalization Agreements

Prorating benefits for immigrants is not a new idea. There is a very small program, called totalization, that prorates immigrants' Social Security benefits.[8] The central purpose of totalization agreements is to allow workers who are working abroad to qualify for benefits, even though they have accumulated less than the required 40 quarters of covered earnings under Social Security. Totalization agreements also have the purpose of avoiding double taxation of citizens of one country who are stationed abroad, allowing crediting under one system or the other. In 1995, there were only 36,000 retired worker recipients whose eligibility was based on international agreements, and 51,000 total recipients under totalization agreements. Their average monthly benefit was only $155 (Social Security Administration 1996, 269). The very small size of the population subject to totalization agreements is apparent when it is realized that, overall, there are 2.76 million foreign born in the United States over the age of 65. Of these, 1.7 million are naturalized citizens and 1.05 million are not (U.S. Bureau of the Census 1997, 3).[9]

---

8. Seventeen countries have totalization agreements, which are bilateral agreements with the United States.

9. Other groups who are outside the Social Security system for part of their work lives have their benefits calculated using special formulas that are designed to limit double dipping. The best known of these formulas limits double dipping by those government workers who were not covered by Social Security. Under windfall elimination provisions, some adjustments

Under totalization, the first decade of work in the United States results in 10/35 of total benefits, each of the next two decades of work increases benefits by another 10/35 of the total PIA, and the last decade of covered work brings in an additional 5/35 of the PIA. In contrast, the formula for prorating proposed below computes the average indexed monthly earnings only over the time the immigrant has spent in the United States, computes the associated primary insurance amount, and then multiplies the PIA by the ratio of years spent inside the United States divided by 35 or 40.[10] Thus, totalization agreements adjust a hypothetical PIA, computed as if the individual worked a lifetime in the United States, in accordance with the ratio of years *worked* to 35. In contrast, the prorating system examined here adjusts the hypothetical PIA to reflect years *residing* in the United States, rather than years worked in the United States.[11] This will preserve the favorable treatment under the Social Security system of those who do not work every year.[12]

---

may also be made to the Social Security benefits received by immigrants to the United States who report that they received pension or Social Security benefits based on work that was not covered by the U.S. Social Security system. Specifically, for those receiving a pension or Social Security from uncovered foreign work, and who worked fewer than 20 years in the United States, the replacement rate in the first bracket of the formula determining the Social Security benefit is lowered from 90 percent to 40 percent. This reduces the degree of redistribution under the formula. For those who worked between 20 and 30 years, the bracket replacement rate is prorated between 40 percent and 90 percent. Those who were in covered employment for more than 30 years receive the full 90 percent replacement rate. The reduction is limited to half the benefit under the pension that was not covered by Social Security. Importantly, the factor is not reduced when calculating survivor benefits. Another way that Social Security may be reduced is by a government pension offset. Spouse or survivor benefits are reduced for individuals who worked outside of the Social Security system by the amount of their pension from uncovered work (see Social Security Administration 1997). According to data from the Office of the Actuary supplied to us by the Division of Payment Policy at the Social Security Administration, in June 1996 there were 22,242 primary beneficiaries and 5,547 auxiliary beneficiaries who were subject to windfall elimination provisions but were not former state, local, or federal government employees.

10. For further information, see Social Security Administration, Office of International Policy (1997). These provisions are triggered upon application by the individual.

11. If benefits are to be based on the period spent in residence, rather than spent in employment, it is necessary to define when the period of permanent residence begins. A claimant for old-age insurance already must file proof of age. Prorating benefits would require, for those born outside the United States, that they also show proof indicating the year they first arrived to establish residence. The extensive back and forth flow between California and Texas and elsewhere in the United States and Mexico means that the period of residence is not always continuous. This will complicate the calculation for some, perhaps requiring the adoption of crude or pragmatic criteria for initial residence. According to the HRS data, about 10 percent of foreign born have a first year of Social Security earnings before the year they report coming to the United States, suggesting multiple trips for these respondents.

12. The present procedure under totalization agreements, where benefits are multiplied by the ratio of covered years of work to 35, reduces the level of benefits, and thus the progressivity of the system, for those who only work part of the time they spend in the United States, remaining out of the labor market for the other years. Multiplying benefits by the ratio of years resident in the United States divided by 35 would allow the current progressivity to apply to those who work only a part of their lifetime spent in the United States.

The method used under totalization also ignores the extra taxes paid by U.S. residents who work more than 35 years under Social Security. Therefore, we also examine the alternative of multiplying the PIA by the ratio of years spent in the United States until age 62 divided by 40.[13] Throughout this paper, we will focus on the vast majority of foreign born, who are not subject to totalization agreements, and who we assume do not report that they are entitled to and are receiving pension or Social Security benefits from their country of origin.

8.3.2 Basic Features of Benefit Determination under a Prorated System

Equation (4) is the formula for the modified AIME under a prorated system. It would replace the AIME calculation in equation (1). In calculating the AIME, we exclude, from both the numerator and denominator of the AIME calculations, years in which the individual resided outside of the United States.[14]

$$(4) \qquad \text{AIME} = \begin{cases} \dfrac{wx_s}{x} & \text{if } x < 35 \\[2ex] \dfrac{wx_s}{35} & \text{if } x \geq 35 \text{ and } x_s < 35 \\[2ex] w & \text{if } x_s \geq 35. \end{cases}$$

In equation (4), x again is the total number of years the individual is resident in the United States, and x_s is the number of years spent in work covered by Social Security. Note that if the immigrant works all of the years he or she is in the United States, the AIME will always be w with this formula. Thus, in contrast to the present formula, the denominator is reduced by the number of years the individual is out of the country.

The PIA under a modified system would remain a quasi-concave function of the AIME where in the current year the function f is 90 percent of the first \$455 of AIME, 32 percent of AIME between \$455 and \$2,741, and 15 percent of AIME over \$2,741. The PIA modified for different years of participation is given in equation (5).

---

13. When there is a totalization agreement, windfall gain provisions usually do not apply, and coverage may depend on whether the citizen of one country is stationed for a definite period or indefinitely in the other country.

14. It would be unfair simply to exclude years that the individual is outside the country from the calculations, while still using the high, 35 out of 40 years of earnings. This approach would impose a double penalty for the years out: First, the AIME would be proportionately reduced because of the years out of the system, since zeros would effectively replace years with earnings; and second, the PIA would be proportionately reduced.

Table 8.3   **Ratio of Benefits under a Prorated System with a 35-Year Base to Benefits under the Current System**

	Years of Work under Social Security			
Real Yearly Earnings	10 Years	20 Years	30 Years	40 Years (U.S. Born)
$5,000	1.00	1.00	1.00	1.00
$10,000	0.71	0.73	0.92	1.00
$20,000	0.55	0.80	0.95	1.00
$30,000	0.62	0.84	0.96	1.00
$40,000	0.62	0.80	0.91	1.00
$50,000	0.60	0.75	0.92	1.00
$60,000	0.59	0.73	0.92	1.00
≥ $65,400	0.58	0.74	0.93	1.00

Note: Years of work under Social Security are taken to be identical to years resident in the United States for purposes of these illustrative calculations.

$$(5) \qquad \text{PIA} = \begin{cases} \left(\dfrac{x}{35}\right) f(\text{AIME}) & \text{if } x < 35 \\ f(\text{AIME}) & \text{if } x \geq 35. \end{cases}$$

The first factor on the right-hand side of equation (5) simply reflects that the PIA is reduced proportionately for years out of the system.

Table 8.3 reports the ratio of benefits under the prorated system to benefits for the same individuals under the current system. Prorating makes no difference to the benefits of those whose earnings fall entirely in the first earnings bracket, as is the case for those who earn $5,000 per year. For those making $10,000 or more, relative benefits are reduced more when they are prorated, the fewer the years spent in the United States. Those in the United States for 10 years who earned $20,000 or more per year would experience a fall in benefits of 38–45 percent under a prorated system with a 35-year reference period. Among those in the United States for 20 years, for those earning more than $5,000 per year, benefit reductions under a prorated system range from 16 to 27 percent. At 30 years of work in the United States, benefits for those earning more than $5,000 per year would be reduced by 4–9 percent.

One could also argue that one should prorate benefits by multiplying the PIA in equation (5) by the ratio of years of residence in the United States divided by 40. This would recognize that U.S. workers who are employed for more than 35 years pay payroll taxes over the additional years of employment but do not have their benefits increased. All of the figures from table 8.2 for those working less than 40 years would be reduced by 12.5 percent in view of the division of benefits by a higher denominator. For those who work 10 years in the United States and earn $20,000 or more, prorating over a 40-year period reduces benefits to about half of their value from the current system.

8.3.3   Issues Raised by Spouse and Survivor Benefits for Prorating of Social Security Benefits

It is possible to establish a taxonomy in which (1) the husband and wife are both immigrants, (2) the husband only is an immigrant, or (3) the wife only is an immigrant. For each group we then can analyze benefits according to whether families fall in one of three groups: (a) the spouse with lowest earnings has not worked enough to qualify for any benefits based on own earnings, (b) the spouse with lowest earnings has earned enough to be a dual beneficiary, or (c) the spouse with lowest earnings is entitled to benefits from own work only, at least until the higher earner dies. One then could examine outcomes for each of these nine cases under a number of alternatives: (i) the present system, (ii) a system where own benefits and benefits payable to the individual's spouse and survivors are reduced when benefits are computed on a prorated basis for foreign born, or (iii) a system where own benefits, entitlement to benefits as a spouse or survivor, and benefits payable to one's own spouse or survivor are all reduced when benefits are computed on a prorated basis for foreign born. Without going through each of the possible cases, we discuss some of the major considerations.

In the U.S. Social Security system, there are specific rules for determining spouse and survivor benefits. When an individual is entitled both to old-age benefits based on own earnings and also to spouse or survivor benefits, the procedure is to pay benefits based on own earnings first. If spouse or survivor benefits are below benefits based on own earnings, no spouse or survivor benefits are paid. If spouse or survivor benefits exceed benefits based on own earnings, then the difference is paid on top of the payment based on own earnings, and the recipients are called dual beneficiaries. In the end, the individual receives the highest level of benefits to which he or she is entitled.[15]

The structure of the Social Security benefit formula increases the likelihood of a spouse collecting benefits based on own earnings rather than on the record of the primary earner. For example, the progressivity of the benefit formula makes it easier for the secondary earner in a household to earn at least half of the benefits of the primary earner. To be entitled to

---

15. The relative sizes of the different groups among the retired in the overall U.S. population in 1994, when there were 20.8 million women beneficiaries age 62 or over, are as follows: group 1, 8 million women 62 or older in 1994 were entitled to benefits as a wife or widow, not having worked enough to qualify for any benefits based on own earnings history; group 2, 5.3 million were dual beneficiaries, receiving spouse or survivor benefits; and group 3, 7.5 million were entitled to workers benefits only (from Social Security Administration 1996, table 5.A.14).

half of the benefits of the primary earner, the spouse of a primary earner whose indexed yearly earnings fall at the second bracket amount or beyond—that is, whose average indexed monthly earnings multiplied by 12 is $32,892 or more in 1997—must earn one-third of the amount earned by the primary earner.[16] However, from the perspective of the secondary earner, total benefits accrued as a result of own earnings are not much bigger than the spouse benefits called for under the system.

Accordingly, under the current system, the spouse can easily recover half of the benefits that would be earned by a primary earner in the household. This means that should a rule be adopted that reduces primary, spouse, and survivor benefits for a foreign-born individual on the basis of years spent out of the country, a working spouse would not experience a proportionate loss in benefits, especially if the spouse were U.S. born. It also means that unless a foreign-born spouse has not only own benefits but also spouse and survivor benefits reduced by years spent outside the United States, then in the case of families with one immigrant and one U.S.-born spouse, having worked outside of the United States would continue to present a special advantage. More generally, if only own benefits are reduced for immigrants on the basis of time spent overseas, but spouse and survivor benefits are not reduced, the adjustment in benefits on the basis of immigrant status would be mitigated, as roughly one-third of benefits earned by foreign-born men accrue in the form of spouse and survivor benefits. Analogously, one might wish to adjust benefits for spouses and survivors who are immigrants when the primary earner in the family is not an immigrant.

When simulating the effects of prorating benefits, we assume that spouse and survivor benefits deriving from the benefits of a principal earner are adjusted whenever the principal earner's benefits are adjusted. But we do not reduce spouse and survivor benefits for a foreign-born spouse when the primary earner does not experience a reduction in benefits.

8.4 Labor Force Patterns and Earnings for Immigrants and Native Born

Before comparing the Social Security outcomes between U.S. born and foreign born, it is useful to compare these populations with regard to various labor market outcomes. Table 8.4 makes this basic comparison using data from the Health and Retirement Study.

The HRS population includes households in which there is a person

16. For a family whose primary earner has earnings at the second bracket point—that is, who has indexed earnings of $32,892 per year—the primary earner will receive $13,692 per year. To earn half of those benefits, $6,841, the secondary earner must have average indexed yearly earnings of $11,482. The calculation for the primary earner who has $50,000 in average indexed yearly earnings also shows that it takes about 30 percent of the primary earner's income for a spouse to be entitled to half the benefit.

Table 8.4   Work, Retirement, and Related Descriptive Statistics

	All		U.S. Born		Foreign Born	
	Men	Women	Men	Women	Men	Women
No current job (%)	20.6	38.9	20.6	38.0	20.1	46.6
Working < 400 hours/year (%)	1.0	2.0	1.0	2.1	0.5	1.2
Working 400–1,499 hours/year (%)	6.5	13.3	6.4	13.7	7.6	9.8
Working 1,500 hours or more (%)	70.9	45.2	70.9	45.6	71.3	41.0
Average hours of work by employed	2,222	1,829	2,227	1,824	2,168	1,884
Percent in agriculture	4.9	1.3	4.7	1.2	6.6	2.3
Percent union	24.8	18.9	24.9	18.5	23.6	22.3
Percent self-employed	23.3	13.9	23.3	13.6	22.4	16.3
Percent retired	12.4	11.9	12.9	12.5	6.9	6.4
Percent partially retired	7.6	5.1	7.8	5.4	5.7	2.6
Percent not retired	77.3	66.6	76.6	66.6	85.2	66.8
Average age	55.9	55.9	55.9	55.9	55.6	55.8
(Expected) full retirement age	63.6	63.2	63.5	63.2	64.3	63.6
Percent never retire	11.9	9.5	12.2	9.7	9.1	7.8
Percent < high school	24.4	25.9	22.8	23.8	40.8	44.7
Percent high school degree	32.7	40.1	34.2	41.8	17.6	24.4
Percent some college	19.1	18.9	19.8	19.5	11.8	13.9
Percent college degree	10.4	7.3	10.3	7.0	11.7	9.9
Percent graduate school	13.4	7.8	12.9	7.9	18.2	7.1
Percent married	83.4	68.6	83.1	68.6	86.5	68.2
Husband's age minus wife's age	3.7	3.1	3.7	3.1	4.0	3.8
Percent white and other	84.9	81.9	87.6	85.1	57.5	53.9
Percent black	8.4	10.6	8.8	11.1	4.6	6.1
Percent Hispanic	6.7	7.4	3.6	3.8	37.9	40.0
Percent spouse foreign born	8.2	5.7	3.1	1.7	60.9	41.5
Percent receiving Social Security	5.2	4.9	5.4	4.9	3.1	5.4
Percent expecting Social Security	87.0	84.9	87.2	85.6	85.5	79.2
Average 1991 earnings ($)	40,500	19,246	40,076	19,126	44,847	20,485
Unweighted observations	4,589	5,164	4,152	4,617	437	547

Source: Health and Retirement Study, wave 1.

Note: Sample is all age eligibles. Percentages in each category will not add to 1.0 if information for particular variables is missing for some observations.

who is 51–61 years old in 1992. There are 12,652 observations, but only 9,824 of these household members were born between 1931 and 1941. Of these, 9,753 are in households where the person designated as the financially knowledgeable respondent has cooperated with the survey.[17]

On average, it can be seen that the immigrant population does not differ sharply from the population of U.S. born. Notice that almost 80 percent of U.S.- and foreign-born men are working. There are fewer (53 percent) foreign-born women working than native-born women (61 percent). U.S.-born men and women are twice as likely to call themselves retired as are the foreign born. Among those working, U.S.-born men work more hours, while U.S.-born women work fewer hours than do foreign-born men and women respectively, but the differences in hours of work are small. The U.S.-born men are less likely to have earned a graduate degree (13 percent versus 18 percent), but the U.S.-born men and women are also much less likely to report having earned less than a high school degree (41 percent versus 23 percent among men, and 45 percent versus 24 percent among women). Foreign born are roughly 38 percent Hispanic, versus about 4 percent for U.S. born.

Three other figures in table 8.4 are particularly noteworthy. First, 61 percent of the foreign-born men and 42 percent of the foreign-born women in the HRS sample, have a foreign-born spouse.[18] This means that the question of how to treat Social Security spouse and survivor benefits in a household with only one immigrant is an important issue. Second, there is only a small difference in the proportions of U.S. born and foreign born who expect to receive Social Security benefits when they retire. While 87 percent of U.S.-born men expect to receive Social Security benefits in the future, 86 percent of foreign-born men expect to receive Social Security benefits; and for women, the comparable figures are 86 percent for U.S. born and 79 percent for foreign born. The last point to make with the data in table 8.4 is that earnings between U.S. born and foreign born are roughly comparable. Earnings for U.S.-born men in 1991 were $40,076, while they were $44,847 for foreign-born men. The medians are closer, as

---

17. In those parts of our analysis that pertain to the household, or in which spouse benefits are relevant, we include information for spouses who are out of age range. When one spouse in a household refuses to cooperate with the survey, the data for the missing spouse is hot decked. When spouses are hot decked, we run through the procedure twice and average the results. Observations are dropped when the spouse who refuses to cooperate is designated to report financial data. Data on earnings in years from the survey date until the expected retirement date are stochastically estimated using earnings from the years before the survey. Consequently, there are small differences in means that depend on the precise match that is made by the stochastic routine. Thus, one should expect some measures of central tendency for economic variables reported in these tables to differ slightly from those in other studies based on the HRS wave 1 responses.

18. When spouses are hot decked, for those in the survey with a spouse who would not be interviewed, immigrant status is one of the criteria used. The probability of having a foreign-born spouse for each group (natives and immigrants, male and female) is taken from table 8.4.

are the comparable figures for U.S.- and foreign-born women, suggesting that we are not dealing here with two populations that have very different overall levels of income. Any disparate treatment of immigrants and native born by Social Security will reflect program differences, rather than differential treatment under Social Security of those with major differences in incomes. We return to these issues below when we examine the distributions of income and wealth for U.S. born and foreign born.

8.5   Social Security Benefits for the Sample of Immigrants in the Health and Retirement Study

8.5.1   Current System

A major strength of the HRS for use in the present analysis is that it provides Social Security earnings records for survey participants, as well as a great deal of information on the labor market history, income, and wealth of survey respondents.[19] Also, the HRS oversamples Hispanic respondents, increasing the number of observations available for the immigrant portion of the sample. Altogether, about 10 percent (1,294) of the sample of 12,652 HRS respondents, and 9 percent of the weighted count, are foreign born.[20] The mean time of arrival in the United States is mid-1966, which means that by age 62, the average foreign-born sample member will have been in the United States for 30 years.

Social Security records were obtained from the Social Security Administration for 6,950 observations, amounting to 70 percent of the full within-age-range HRS sample. For those without an earnings history, the work history was estimated from the self-reported job history in wave 1, and from a battery of questions in wave 3 inquiring about years of previous work and the years of work that were not covered by Social Security.

Table 8.5 describes covered work history by gender and immigrant status. Three types of information are reported in the table: percent of years with nonzero Social Security earnings, quarters of Social Security coverage, and average real covered earnings in nonzero years of coverage.[21] From table 8.5, the ratio of foreign-born women to men is 1.25 to 1 (547/

19. For detailed discussions of the labor market, Social Security, pension, and wealth data in the HRS, see Gustman et al. (forthcoming).

20. Among the foreign born in the HRS sample, 97 are from Asia, 62 are from Canada, 112 are from the Caribbean, 60 are from Central America, 117 are from Cuba, 67 are from Germany, 53 are from Great Britain, 318 are from Mexico, and 85 are from South America. The average age at arrival is about 30. These data are taken from simple tabs of variables produced at the Institute for Social Research. The country of origin is suppressed on the special version of the HRS 1 tape that is supplied with the restricted Social Security earnings histories. As a result, we will not be able to conduct any analysis of the relation between Social Security variables and country of origin.

21. The results are very close between the full sample and the subsample with an attached Social Security record.

Table 8.5   Work History from Social Security Record Including Imputations for Those
                   without a Social Security Record

	All		U.S. Born		Foreign Born	
	Men	Women	Men	Women	Men	Women
Percent of years with nonzero earnings since age 21	82.0	51.7	84.1	53.3	60.4	37.6
Quarters of coverage	119.0	72.0	122.4	74.4	83.4	50.0
Average earnings in nonzero years of coverage ($)	24,635	12,296	24,702	12,368	23,954	11,653
Observations	4,589	5,164	4,152	4,617	437	547

Source: Health and Retirement Study, age-eligible individuals for whom a Social Security earnings record was obtained.

437), while the ratio of U.S.-born women to men is 1.11 to 1 (4,617/4,152). Foreign-born men have about 72 percent of the years of nonzero earnings of U.S.-born men (60.4/84.1). Foreign-born women have 71 percent of the years of nonzero earnings of U.S.-born women (37.6/53.3). The shares of quarters of coverage are 68 percent for foreign- versus U.S.-born men (83.4/122.4), and 67 percent for women (50.0/74.4).

In table 8.4, average earnings in nonzero years of coverage are roughly comparable for U.S.- and foreign-born respondents. For males, U.S. born average $24,702 in covered earnings, while foreign born average $23,954. Comparable figures for women are $12,368 for U.S. born and $11,653 for foreign born. In contrast to the Social Security earnings in table 8.5, in table 8.4, 1991 self-reported earnings were slightly higher for foreign born than for U.S. born of the same gender.

U.S.-born women had exactly half of the covered earnings of men in years that they worked ($12,368/$24,702) and 61 percent (74.4/122.4) of the quarters of coverage of U.S.-born men, while foreign-born women had 49 percent of the earnings of foreign-born men ($11,653/$23,954) and 60 percent of the quarters of coverage (50.0/83.4). Thus, relative differences in covered earnings and quarters of coverage between immigrants and native born do not vary by gender.

To provide further insight into the work histories of immigrants, table 8.6 reports these same data by decade of arrival into the United States. By raw count, 55 percent of the immigrants in the HRS entered the United States between 1960 and 1980 (529/957). Forty percent of the immigrants (379/957) arrived in the United States after 1970, which means they typically will have a decade or two of coverage under Social Security when they retire. Earnings of those arriving since 1970 are lower than the earnings of those arriving in earlier years.

Table 8.7 reports the present discounted value of taxes paid to date and

Table 8.6   **Work History from Social Security Record by Year of Entry to United States**

	Before 1940		1940–49		1950–59		1960–69		1970–79		1980 or later	
	Men	Women	Men	Women	Men	Women	Men	Women	Men	Women	Men	Women
Percent nonzero earnings years since age 21	83.1	54.0	86.8	61.9	83.2	44.1	70.1	45.9	45.2	28.7	18.1	8.9
Quarters of coverage	125.5	83.4	129.9	82.5	117.3	61.0	95.0	59.4	61.8	37.0	24.4	11.7
Average of nonzero covered earnings ($)	26,751	12,469	26,333	13,577	25,514	12,376	27,316	13,632	22,911	9,983	15,646	6,933
Observations	3	8	16	26	94	125	134	172	108	115	73	83

Source: Health and Retirement Study, age-eligibles who said yes to being born outside the United States and reported year when they entered.

Note: When Social Security records are not reported, earnings histories are estimated from self-reported data.

Table 8.7   Social Security Taxes Paid and Value of Benefits, Assuming Retirement at Expected Age

	All		U.S. Born		Foreign Born	
	Men	Women	Men	Women	Men	Women
Discounted taxes ($)	124,630	46,836	127,395	47,917	96,253	37,140
PIA (1992$)	9,708	4,996	9,856	5,096	8,196	4,095
	Benefits: Based on Respondent Earnings ($)					
Own	76,925	48,512	78,132	49,537	64,542	39,309
Spouse	5,641	309	5,686	319	5,180	218
Survivor	18,218	460	18,469	453	15,634	518
Total	100,784	49,281	102,287	50,310	85,356	40,045
	Benefits: Based on Spouse Earnings ($)					
Own	37,876	57,157	38,456	57,997	31,925	49,622
Spouse	425	5,468	424	5,528	440	4,931
Survivor	672	16,532	669	16,699	701	15,029
Total	38,973	79,157	39,549	80,224	33,066	69,582
Total household taxes ($)	162,316	131,769	165,788	134,617	126,681	106,207
Total household benefits ($)	139,757	128,438	141,836	130,534	118,422	109,627
Observations	4,589	5,164	4,152	4,617	437	547

Source: Health and Retirement Study, age-eligibles.

Note: For those without a Social Security record, benefits are imputed based on self-reported earnings histories in waves 1 and 3. Payroll tax payments are inflated to 1992 values using the interest rate on 10-year U.S. government bonds. Benefits are deflated using real interest rates from Social Security Administration intermediate projections (Federal Old Age and Survivors Insurance and Disability Insurance Trust Fund 1995, table II.D1).

benefits to be received, by immigrant status.[22] The calculation assumes that immigrants retire at their expected retirement ages.[23] In computing benefits for each spouse in a marriage, we follow the rules that provide the highest benefits to which a spouse is entitled. The spouse and survivor benefits attributed to the male in the family consist only of the additional benefits the spouse has coming beyond the benefits paid based on the female's own work. Only if the wife had no earnings would the spouse and survivor benefits represent the full amount of benefits the wife will receive. Husbands' benefits are treated symmetrically.

By the time they retire, all men have paid taxes averaging $124,630 in 1992 dollars.[24] The respondent's own benefits add up to $76,925 for men. Spouse and survivor benefits due to their earnings history also generate an additional $23,859 in benefit value from the earnings of men. Women pay $46,836 in taxes and have accrued own benefits worth $48,512, while the spouse and survivor benefits that women have earned from their own work are worth only $769. Altogether, when the calculation is made for all households with a male in them, household benefits average $139,757 and taxes paid amount to $162,316, while when the calculation is made for all households with a woman in them, benefits average $128,438 per household and taxes average $131,769.

22. In computing accrued benefits, we count the value of benefits for all respondents who will accrue 32 covered quarters by the time they reach their expected retirement age. Quarters of coverage are based on earnings. Specifically, in 1997, each $670 earned generates one-quarter of coverage. Thus, our calculations assume that someone who is within 8 quarters of coverage when reaching expected retirement age would be willing to earn another $2,680 per year in real terms over the next two years in order to qualify for Social Security benefits.

23. As noted in table 8.4 above, foreign-born men expect to retire about 0.8 of a year later than U.S.-born men, while foreign-born women expect to retire 0.4 of a year later. However, 12.2 percent of U.S.-born men report they never expect to retire, compared to 9.1 percent of foreign-born men. The comparable figures for U.S.- and foreign-born women are 9.7 percent and 7.8 percent, respectively.

In constructing table 8.7 and subsequent tables, if an individual reported an expected age of retirement over 70, or if the individual expected never to retire, the expected retirement age was taken to be 70. If the individual did not report an expected retirement age, the expected retirement age was taken to be 62. 1991 is the last year in the Social Security record. If the retirement age was less than current age, no projection was made. The individual was assumed to be retired, and the value as of 1991 was used. As previously, we counted as zero any benefits accruing to those who will have less than 32 quarters of coverage by the time they retire. Post-1991 earnings are randomly chosen from the five-year period 1987–91 for all years up to the individual's expected retirement age. The expected date of retirement question (K13) inquires about date of complete retirement. To the extent that some individuals will partially retire, and have not done so by 1991, this will cause some overstatement of earnings, taxes, and, perhaps, benefits.

24. Nominal taxes paid in earlier years are inflated to 1992 values using the nominal interest rate on 10-year government bonds. As we will see below, only modest differences result when taxes are inflated using the interest rate realized on the Social Security portfolio. Benefits are deflated to 1992 values using the Social Security Administration's intermediate forecast of a future interest rate (Federal Old Age and Survivors Insurance and Disability Insurance Fund 1995, table II.D.1). Many other assumptions may be made in making money's worth calculations. See Leimer (1995) for a further discussion.

Table 8.8 reports similar data by decade of entry into the United States.[25] Men entering the United States between 1970 and 1979 have paid 55 percent ($69,985/$127,395) of the taxes paid by U.S. born. However, they have accrued 67 percent ($68,330/$102,287) of the benefits that will be paid to U.S. born and their spouses based on own earnings, and 70 percent ($54,382/$78,132) of the man's benefit earned from own work.

Table 8.9 reports the ratios of taxes paid by foreign born to taxes paid by U.S. born and the ratios of benefits to be received, as of 1992, all assuming retirement at the expected date. Tax payments reported in column (1) are assumed to be the same whatever the system in place. Thus, columns (1) and (2) report the taxes and benefits under the current system. Given the earlier finding that those who will be in the United States for only a decade or two receive the most favorable treatment under Social Security, data are reported separately for those who arrived in the United States in the 1970s and after 1980. Table 8.10 reports the ratio of the value of benefits, assuming work to retirement date, over the value of taxes paid. Columns (1) and (4) report the results under the current system.

By the time they retire, foreign-born men in the HRS cohort will pay about 76 percent ($96,253/$127,395) of the taxes paid by U.S.-born men, while total benefits based on own work will be about 83 percent ($85,356/ $102,287) of the benefits received by U.S.-born men. Foreign-born women will pay 78 percent ($37,140/$47,917) of the taxes paid by U.S.-born women, and will receive 80 percent ($40,045/$50,310) of the benefits.

Consider men who entered the United States in 1970 to 1979. At retirement, discounted taxes paid will amount to $69,985. The comparable figure for U.S. born is $127,395. Thus, the foreign-born male who entered in the 1970s will pay 55 percent of the taxes paid by a U.S.-born male. Total family benefits from own earnings for the foreign-born male who entered the United States in the 1970s are $68,330. This amounts to 67 percent of the family benefits from own earnings of $102,287 for U.S. born. A part of this difference is due to the difference in covered earnings. As seen in table 8.6, a foreign-born man who entered the United States in the 1970s earns $22,911 in average nonzero covered earnings, while for the U.S.-born male, nonzero covered earnings averaged $24,024. A foreign-born woman who entered in the 1970s will pay 57 percent ($27,419/$47,917) of the taxes paid by a U.S.-born woman. Benefits will be 67 percent ($33,456/$50,310) of the benefits received by a U.S.-born woman.

By the time he reaches his expected retirement age, a man who entered

---

25. The differences in table 8.8 between taxes paid and benefits do not vary as sharply with date of arrival as did the differences discussed in section 8.2. The calculations in section 8.2 were steady state calculations made under a constant tax structure. Those in the HRS were affected by a changing Social Security tax structure, where covered earnings and tax rates increased over time. Therefore, differences in taxes paid would not be proportionate to years spent in covered employment, even if earnings were held constant over time.

Table 8.8 Social Security Taxes Paid and Value of Benefits, Assuming Retirement at Expected Age, by Year Immigrant Entered the United States

	Before 1940		1940–49		1950–59		1960–69		1970–79		1980 or later	
	Men	Women	Men	Women	Men	Women	Men	Women	Men	Women	Men	Women
Discounted taxes	146,735	41,706	138,374	59,919	131,151	41,405	116,527	48,639	69,985	27,419	23,847	8,460
PIA (1992$)	10,642	4,402	10,141	5,954	10,098	4,337	9,608	5,125	6,926	3,407	3,565	1,614
Benefits: Based on Respondent Earnings ($)												
Own	82,433	47,183	83,003	57,282	79,387	42,795	75,992	48,314	54,382	32,462	26,733	15,014
Spouse	7,950	0	11,152	451	7,743	125	5,517	89	2,904	479	2,114	331
Survivor	13,607	821	26,819	255	22,882	540	16,415	623	11,044	514	6,784	318
Total	103,989	48,003	120,974	57,989	110,013	43,459	97,924	49,026	68,330	33,456	35,632	15,664
Benefits: Based on Spouse Earnings ($)												
Own	45,416	83,839	20,641	52,146	28,367	64,479	38,700	54,026	36,991	41,612	18,166	18,837
Spouse	0	9,199	0	3,043	545	7,219	56	5,099	464	3,812	1,037	2,150
Survivor	29	23,708	57	15,400	458	21,305	793	14,734	685	12,917	1,069	6,627
Total	45,445	116,746	20,698	70,589	29,370	93,002	39,550	73,859	38,139	58,341	20,272	27,614
Total household taxes ($)	173,982	155,951	155,768	137,723	156,634	133,320	155,151	127,893	107,665	80,873	37,766	28,017
Total household benefits ($)	149,434	164,750	141,673	128,578	139,383	136,462	137,474	122,884	106,470	91,797	55,904	43,278
Observations	3	8	16	26	94	125	134	172	108	115	73	83

Source: Health and Retirement Study, age-eligibles who said yes to being born outside the United States and reported year when they entered.

Note: See table 8.7 for details on the construction of the present value measures.

Table 8.9   **Ratios of Social Security Taxes for Foreign Born to U.S. Born, and of Benefits, under Different Schemes for Prorating Benefits of Foreign Born**

		Ratio of Benefits		
Relevant Group	Ratio of Taxes (1)	Current Rules (2)	Prorate over 35 Years (3)	Prorate over 40 Years (4)
All foreign-born men	0.76	0.83	0.78	0.72
All foreign-born women	0.78	0.80	0.74	0.68
Foreign-born men arriving in 1970s	0.55	0.67	0.55	0.48
Foreign-born women arriving in 1970s	0.57	0.67	0.57	0.50
Foreign-born men arriving in 1980s	0.19	0.35	0.24	0.21
Foreign-born women arriving in 1980s	0.18	0.31	0.21	0.18

Note: Calculations are made on the basis of expected retirement dates using HRS data. See table 8.7 for details on the construction of the present value measures.

the United States in the 1980s will pay taxes of $23,847. This is 19 percent ($23,847/$127,395) of the taxes paid by U.S. born. Benefits based on own earnings are $35,632 for a man entering in the 1980s, or 35 percent ($35,632/$102,287) of the benefits for a U.S.-born man. For the man entering in the 1980s, benefits well exceed taxes, while the opposite is true for the U.S. born. A foreign-born woman who entered in the 1980s will pay 18 percent ($8,460/$47,917) of the taxes paid by a U.S.-born woman. Benefits for the late entrant are 31 percent ($15,664/$50,310) of the benefits of a U.S.-born woman.

As seen in columns (1) and (4) in table 8.10, on average, both U.S.-born men and foreign-born men pay more in taxes than they will receive in benefits: Benefits are 80 percent ($102,287/$127,395) of taxes for U.S.-born men and 89 percent ($85,356/$96,253) for foreign-born men. Women receive slightly higher benefits than they pay in taxes whether U.S.-born or foreign born: Benefits are 105 percent ($50,310/$47,917) of taxes for U.S.-born women and 108 percent ($40,045/$37,140) for foreign-born women.

For those men who entered in the 1970s, their benefits are just slightly below taxes paid. For men entering in 1980 or later, benefits are 49 percent ($35,632/$23,847) higher than taxes paid, rather than 80 percent of taxes, as they are for U.S. born. For women entering 1980 or later, benefits are 85 percent higher than taxes paid ($15,664/$8,460).

8.5.2   Benefits under a Prorated System

The easiest way to isolate the effects of the progressive benefit formula on the benefits and costs of Social Security for U.S. born and foreign born

Table 8.10   Ratios of Social Security Benefits from Own Earnings to Social Security Taxes Paid for U.S. Born and Foreign Born

Relevant Group	Men			Women		
	Current Rules (1)	Prorate over 35 Years (2)	Prorate over 40 Years (3)	Current Rules (4)	Prorate over 35 Years (5)	Prorate over 40 Years (6)
U.S. born	0.80	0.80	0.80	1.05	1.05	1.05
All foreign born	0.89	0.83	0.77	1.08	1.00	0.92
Immigrants arriving 1970–79	0.98	0.81	0.71	1.22	1.05	0.92
Immigrants arriving after 1980	1.49	1.02	0.90	1.85	1.23	1.08

Note: Calculations are made on the basis of expected retirement dates using HRS data. See table 8.7 for details on the construction of the present value measures.

is to compute benefits using a prorated formula and to compare the pro-rated benefits with benefits under the current system. The approach we take to prorating is consistent with equations (4) and (5) above. For each respondent, we take the earlier of the year entering the United States or the first year with positive Social Security earnings. That year is subtracted from the year the individual turns 62. This difference indicates how many years are to be counted in computing the AIME. Earnings are then aver-aged over the indicated period, whether there are covered earnings in each year or not. The average AIME is then inserted into the PIA formula in equation (5), where the AIME is multiplied by the ratio of the years spent in the United States divided by 35.

Tables 8.11 and 8.12 report benefits at the expected retirement age when this prorated formula is used with a 35-year base period. Table 8.13 reports the percentage point reduction from prorating benefits of immigrants. If benefits were prorated for the foreign born in the HRS sample using a 35-year base period, foreign-born men would have benefits at the expected retirement age reduced by 6.8 percent ($79,575/$85,356), while they would be reduced by 7.3 percent ($37,108/$40,045) for foreign-born women.

From table 8.11, column (4), we see that on average, having paid 76 percent ($96,253/$127,395) of the taxes paid by U.S. born, after prorating their benefits, foreign-born men and their spouses would receive 78 per-cent ($79,575/$102,309) of the benefits for their families that are received by U.S. born (total household benefits of households with a foreign-born male would also be 78 percent [$111,045/$141,804] of those for U.S. born).[26] As seen in table 8.9, the benefit ratio is down from a ratio of 83 percent for benefits received by foreign- versus U.S.-born men at the ex-pected retirement age under the current formula. Some difference remains between the ratios of benefits received and taxes paid of foreign- to U.S.-born men in the face of prorating. The source of that difference is the extra taxes paid by U.S. residents who work more than 35 years.

Prorating over a 35-year base period, foreign-born women pay 78 per-cent ($37,140/$47,917) of the taxes paid by U.S.-born women, while receiv-ing 74 percent ($37,108/$50,313) of the benefits. Thus, the 35-year base period is adequate for adjusting for differences in benefit and tax ratios between U.S.- and foreign-born women.

Comparing table 8.12 with table 8.8, it can be seen that for foreign-born men who entered the United States in the 1970s, as a result of prorating benefits for the years spent in the United States out of a 35-year base period, total accrued benefits based on own earnings would fall to $56,519

---

26. Notice that benefits received by U.S. born differ slightly between tables 8.7 and 8.11. The reason is that foreign-born spouses of U.S. born have their benefits based on own earn-ings reduced under prorating. As a result, the spouse and survivor benefits credited to the U.S.-born spouse increase. These differences are very small, however. For example, for U.S.-born men, the survivor benefit increases under prorating from $18,469 to $18,485.

Table 8.11 Social Security Taxes Paid and Value of Benefits Assuming Retirement at Expected Age, Prorating Benefits for Foreign Born with a 35-Year Base Period

	All		U.S. Born		Foreign Born	
	Men	Women	Men	Women	Men	Women
Discounted taxes	124,630	46,836	127,395	47,917	96,253	37,140
PIA (1992$)	9,660	4,966	9,856	5,096	7,658	3,803
Benefits: Based on Respondent Earnings ($)						
Own	76,545	48,227	78,132	49,537	60,257	36,470
Spouse	5,622	307	5,692	320	4,903	198
Survivor	18,124	454	18,485	456	14,415	441
Total	100,291	48,989	102,309	50,313	79,575	37,108
Benefits: Based on Spouse Earnings ($)						
Own	37,690	56,843	38,406	57,946	30,343	46,938
Spouse	424	5,451	423	5,522	434	4,812
Survivor	669	16,434	666	16,675	693	14,263
Total	38,783	78,727	39,495	80,144	31,470	66,012
Total household taxes ($)	162,316	131,769	165,788	134,617	126,681	106,207
Total household benefits ($)	139,074	127,716	141,804	130,457	111,045	103,120
Observations	4,589	5,164	4,152	4,617	437	547

Source: Health and Retirement Study, age-eligibles.

Note: See table 8.7 for details on the construction of the present value measures.

Table 8.12   Social Security Taxes Paid and Value of Benefits Assuming Retirement at Expected Age, Based on Year Immigrant Entered the United States and Prorating Benefits for Foreign Born with a 35-Year Base Period

	Before 1940		1940–49		1950–59		1960–69		1970–79		1980 or Later	
	Men	Women	Men	Women	Men	Women	Men	Women	Men	Women	Men	Women
Discounted taxes	146,735	41,706	138,374	59,919	131,151	41,405	116,527	48,639	69,985	27,419	23,847	8,460
PIA (1992$)	10,642	4,294	10,113	5,755	10,036	4,222	9,255	4,858	5,834	2,938	2,504	1,075
Benefits: Based on Respondent Earnings ($)												
Own	82,433	46,016	82,737	55,350	78,903	41,687	72,997	45,663	45,705	27,882	18,685	9,942
Spouse	7,950	0	11,137	360	7,846	125	5,382	109	2,311	403	1,336	274
Survivor	13,607	751	26,747	225	22,931	448	15,593	578	8,504	385	4,279	228
Total	103,989	46,767	120,621	55,935	109,681	42,260	93,972	46,350	56,519	28,671	24,300	10,445
Benefits: Based on Spouse Earnings ($)												
Own	45,416	83,839	20,641	51,968	27,813	63,992	37,398	51,724	33,900	35,791	15,992	14,070
Spouse	0	9,199	0	3,376	543	7,363	88	5,092	397	3,286	1,051	1,634
Survivor	29	24,164	63	16,136	457	21,190	759	14,289	707	10,816	1,066	4,993
Total	45,445	117,202	20,705	71,480	28,813	92,545	38,246	71,104	35,004	49,893	18,109	20,698
Total household taxes ($)	173,982	155,951	155,768	137,723	156,634	133,320	155,151	127,893	107,665	80,873	37,766	28,017
Total household benefits ($)	149,434	163,970	141,326	127,415	138,494	134,805	132,217	117,454	91,523	78,563	42,409	31,143
Observations	3	8	16	26	94	125	134	172	108	115	73	83

Source: Health and Retirement Study, age-eligibles who said yes to being born outside the United States and reported year when they entered.

Note: See table 8.7 for details on the construction of the present value measures.

Table 8.13   **Percentage Point Reduction in Immigrants' Benefits Due to Prorating**

Relevant Group	Base Period 35 Years		Base Period 40 Years	
	Men	Women	Men	Women
All foreign born	6.8	7.3	13.6	15.1
Immigrants arriving 1970–79	17.3	14.3	27.6	24.9
Immigrants arriving after 1980	31.8	33.3	40.0	41.7

Note: Calculations are made on the basis of expected retirement dates using Health and Retirement Study data. See table 8.7 for details on the construction of the present value measures.

from $68,330. Thus, from table 8.13, accrued benefits for foreign-born men would be reduced by 17.3 percent for those men who entered in the 1970s. As a result, from the third row of table 8.9, it can be seen that foreign-born men who entered in the 1970s would pay 55 percent of the taxes paid by U.S. born ($69,985/$127,395), and that if benefits were prorated using a 35-year base period, they and their spouses would receive 55 percent of the benefits ($56,519/$102,309). For those men who entered in the 1980s, if benefits were prorated using a 35-year base period, accrued benefits would fall from $35,632 to $24,300, with the decline seen in table 8.13 to be 32 percent. From the fifth row of table 8.9, men who entered the United States in the 1980s would pay 19 percent of the taxes paid by U.S. born ($23,847/$127,395), while they and their spouses would receive 24 percent of the benefits ($24,300/$102,309) received by U.S. born. From table 8.13, women who entered the United States in the 1970s would find their benefits reduced from prorating by 14 percent ($28,671/$33,456), while women who entered the United States in the 1980s would find prorating using a 35-year period reduced their benefits by 33 percent ($10,445/$15,664).

In table 8.10, we see that the ratios of benefits to taxes paid for foreign born begin to approach the ratios for U.S. born once benefits are prorated using a 35-year base. For example, in the second row, columns (2) and (5), respectively, after prorating using a 35-year base period, for all foreign-born men the ratio of benefits to taxes falls to 0.83, while for foreign-born women it falls to 1.0.

Because a 35-year base period may be too short—in that it leaves some U.S.-born taxpayers paying taxes for a few years while benefits do not accrue and, therefore, foreign-born men still have a higher benefit-tax ratio than U.S-born men—it is of interest to consider the effects when the base period over which benefits are prorated is taken to be 40, rather than 35, years. That is, in equation (5), the primary insurance amount is multiplied by the number of years spent in the United States divided by 40. As seen in table 8.13, prorating over 40 years reduces benefits for foreign-born men by 13.6 percent, and by 15.1 percent for foreign-born women. As seen in table 8.9, in this case, foreign-born men would pay 76 percent ($96,253/ $127,395) of the taxes paid by U.S. born and would receive 72 percent ($73,725/$102,340) of the benefits. For women, the comparable percentages are 78 percent ($37,140/$47,917) of taxes and 68 percent ($34,004/ $50,315) of benefits. Using a 40-year base period to prorate benefits, a man arriving in the United States in the 1970s pays 55 percent ($69,985/ $127,395) of the taxes paid by a U.S.-born resident, while receiving 48 percent ($49,440/$102,340) of the benefits. A man arriving in the United States in the 1980s pays 19 percent ($23,847/$127,395) of the taxes paid by a U.S.-born resident, while receiving 21 percent ($21,369/$102,340) of the benefits.

These numbers suggest that a 40-year base period for prorating benefits of foreign born may be a bit too long, at least for the HRS cohorts. As seen in columns (3) and (6) of table 8.10, the ratio of benefits to taxes paid for all foreign-born men and women falls below the ratio for U.S.-born men and women when benefits are prorated over a 40-year period. Consistent with the earlier finding from table 8.5, on average, a U.S.-born man will not accumulate a full 40 years of covered quarters.[27] Of course, one may also argue that since many U.S. born will pay payroll taxes for 40 years or more, 40 years is still an appropriate base period for prorating.

8.6 Income and Wealth for Immigrants and Native Born

If the immigrant population were uniformly poor, then one might be less concerned about an additional transfer created by the Social Security system to some members of that population. Although the immigrant population is heterogeneous, on average it is similar to the population of U.S. born. Moreover, as we have already shown, the transfers under the Social Security benefit formula accrue disproportionately to immigrants with higher rather than lower incomes.

To better understand the heterogeneity of wealth and income in the immigrant population, and how the immigrant population compares to U.S. born, we present data from the Health and Retirement Study. Table 8.14 indicates the distribution of income and total net wealth for U.S. born and for foreign born. Total net wealth also includes Social Security, pension wealth calculated from the detailed pension plan description obtained from employers, retiree health insurance, housing wealth, business assets, financial assets, and retirement assets (IRAs and Keoghs). Pension and Social Security wealth are based on work to date. The Social Security

---

27. U.S.-born male respondents with earnings histories have an average of 122 quarters of coverage, or 30.5 years. This means that they will average 38 years of coverage by the time they retire. For the HRS sample, the extra 3 years that U.S. born were paying taxes occurred at the beginning of their career, when real covered earnings were low and when the tax rates were half of what they are today.

Table 8.14   Household Total Income and Total Net Wealth by Place in the Respective Distribution

Income or Wealth Percentile	Income Distribution ($thousands)			Total Net Wealth Distribution ($thousands)		
	All	All U.S. Born	Any Foreign Born	All	All U.S. Born	Any Foreign Born
0–5	495	617	85	2,820	6,004	−1,142
5–10	4,244	4,672	1,883	43,706	49,614	11,722
10–25	12,041	12,682	8,240	104,993	112,848	56,751
25–50	26,287	26,657	22,963	240,942	248,638	179,268
50–75	47,182	47,557	44,536	452,362	457,091	409,118
75–90	72,628	72,265	75,540	758,026	758,839	752,288
90–95	101,522	100,260	110,275	1,151,061	1,146,787	1,179,163
95–100	197,330	190,352	248,258	2,495,418	2,491,024	2,536,617
45–55	35,828	36,202	33,131	331,460	337,861	275,265
Mean	46,249	46,082	47,500	487,450	491,864	454,391

Source: Authors' calculations using Health and Retirement Study, wave 1.

Note: All data are weighted by HRS sample weights. Base year is 1992 for wealth and 1991 for income.

value is computed from the work history through 1992; the pension value is calculated as of the date of expected retirement and then prorated to 1992. Household income measures similarly include pension and Social Security accrual and the value of health insurance, in addition to labor earnings, income from assets, government transfer income, and so forth.[28]

From table 8.14, it can be seen that the mean total wealth of immigrants is 92 percent ($454,391/$491,864) of the mean total wealth of U.S. born. Not shown in the table, the Social Security wealth of immigrants is 86 percent ($98,115/$114,212) of the Social Security wealth of U.S. born. Social Security wealth accounts for 23 and 22 percent of the wealth of U.S. born and immigrants, respectively.

Incomes of immigrants are even closer to those of U.S. born. Indeed, at the mean, immigrants have higher incomes than U.S. born in the HRS, exceeding the incomes of U.S. born by 3 percent ($47,500/$46,082). At the medians of the relevant distributions, incomes of foreign born are 92 percent ($33,131/$36,202) of the incomes of U.S. born.

The heterogeneity of the income and wealth distributions is readily apparent in these data. The top quarter of foreign born have higher incomes than the top quarter of U.S. born, and there is an even larger difference for the top 5 percent of each distribution. The top quarters of the wealth distributions for foreign born and U.S. born are very similar, as are the figures for the top 5 percent of each distribution. However, among the bottom quarter of the wealth and income distributions, foreign born are substantially poorer than U.S. born.

8.7   Participation in Transfers by Immigrants and U.S. Born

The Social Security system will save more than taxpayers will from prorating benefits paid to immigrants on the basis of time spent in the United States. Many immigrant families are eligible for Supplemental Security Income (SSI) and for other income-tested programs such as food stamps and Medicaid. To the extent that benefits from Social Security are reduced for foreign born, benefits from SSI and other taxpayer-supported means-tested programs will be increased.[29]

Information on current participation in transfer programs is presented in table 8.15. With the exception of food stamps, foreign born in the HRS are making less rather than more use of transfer programs than U.S. born. U.S.-born men are 4.6 percent more likely than foreign-born men to report

28. For further details on the construction of the wealth and income variables, see Gustman et al. (forthcoming).

29. Because 40 quarters of covered work are required to be eligible for Social Security, despite laws restricting eligibility to SSI by some immigrants, reductions in Social Security benefits will result in increases in SSI and other benefits for those whose earnings fall below break-even levels and who qualify in other ways for these transfer programs.

Table 8.15   **Transfer Statistics**

	All		U.S. Born		Foreign Born	
	Men	Women	Men	Women	Men	Women
	Percentages					
Permanent health problems	19.6	20.0	20.1	20.0	14.7	19.9
DI or SSI disability	6.9	4.8	7.2	4.9	3.5	4.0
Other disability	0.3	0.1	0.3	0.1	0.3	0.3
Medicaid	2.2	4.0	2.1	4.0	2.9	4.6
UI income	6.3	3.7	6.3	3.5	6.2	5.6
SSI income	2.4	2.8	2.4	2.7	2.6	3.4
Welfare income	0.8	1.9	0.7	1.9	1.5	2.7
Disability income	4.8	3.1	5.1	3.1	2.0	3.7
Food stamps	3.7	6.1	3.4	6.0	6.7	7.5
Potential SSI	14.8	20.1	13.5	19.2	29.9	29.1
Observations	3,251	3,699	2,970	3,364	281	335
	Average Amount Received among Recipients ($)					
UI income	2,725	2,120	2,735	2,090	2,607	2,313
SSI income	1,879	1,216	2,012	1,048	517	2,662
Welfare income	1,644	2,535	1,758	2,465	992	3,053
Disability income	7,921	5,051	8,026	5,208	4,851	3,687
Food stamps	1,032	1,296	985	1,286	1,307	1,380

Source: Health and Retirement Study, wave 1.

a health problem, and they are 3.5 percent more likely to be participating in a disability program.

In table 8.15, we report the potential population of recipients of SSI. One criterion we use to establish potential eligibility is that the individual will receive Social Security benefits below $422 per month ($633 for couples) times 1.468 to reflect the size of state supplements. Additionally, the household has to have less than $10,000 in financial assets (business, financial, IRA, and pension assets), increased to $15,000 for couples.[30] This represents five times the asset limits of $2,000 for singles and $3,000 for couples. Using these criteria, we see from table 8.15 under the heading *Potential SSI* that 14 percent of U.S.-born men will qualify for benefits, as will 19 percent of U.S.-born women. In contrast, 30 percent of foreign-born men and 29 percent of foreign-born women will qualify for SSI benefits.

30. In January 1996, the basic benefit for SSI was $470 per month for an individual and $705 for a couple. Beyond a small disregard, Social Security benefits and other sources of income are subtracted from the SSI benefit. Earnings beyond the disregard are taxed at 50 percent. The average amount of the federal SSI benefit is $250 per month, while the state supplement averages $117 per month. We cannot be too precise about the relation of these rules to the immigrant population due to restrictions on the data in the HRS. Specifically, as of the date of writing this paper, researchers who are using the Social Security records in the HRS will not be provided with detailed information on state of residence.

SSI also has the effect of reducing the work incentives for those who are in the lowest income brackets. It especially reduces work incentives for those eligible for SSI among the foreign born who have been here for the fewest years—that is, the same individuals for whom Social Security creates the greatest increase in work incentives. Of course, those within hailing distance of 40 quarters of coverage have a greatly enhanced incentive to postpone retirement because of the spike in the present value of Social Security benefits, to establish Medicare eligibility, and because eligibility for income-tested programs requires at least 40 quarters of covered employment.[31]

8.8 Money's Worth Calculations

The comparisons of present values of Social Security benefits and taxes presented in this paper indicate that for the members of the HRS cohort, Social Security is not a good deal. That result is consistent with some money's worth calculations made by Leimer (1994, app. E), but it is not consistent with money's worth calculations that use the same low, constant interest rate to inflate tax payments and discount benefits. A major reason for the difference is that we are inflating the nominal value of taxes paid to the Social Security system by the rate of interest already realized for tax payments made before 1992 (Council of Economic Advisers 1995, table B-72), and we are using the intermediate assumptions for interest rates from the Social Security Administration (Federal Old Age Survivors Insurance and Disability Insurance Trust Fund 1995, table II.D1) for tax and benefit payments made after 1992. This interest rate starts at 7.1 percent (4.2 percent real) in 1992 and falls to a steady state real rate of 2.3 percent in 2009. For the HRS cohort, the very high real interest rates realized throughout the 1980s far exceed the long-term real interest rate at which future benefits are discounted under the Social Security Administration's intermediate scenario.

Table 8.16 indicates the present values of benefits and taxes, and resulting benefit tax ratios for all U.S.- and foreign-born households. Adopting the assumption used so far in this paper, row 1 indicates the present value of benefits, discounted to 1992, using the Social Security Administration (SSA) intermediate assumptions to project future interest rates. In row 2, tax payments made by respondents are inflated to 1992 values by the interest rate on 10-year government bonds. The resulting present values of benefits fall below the present values of tax payments for both U.S. and foreign born. Benefit tax ratios are reported in row 3. They indicate

---

31. Medicare is not valid outside the United States, so it will not enhance work incentives for those approaching age 65 with fewer than 10 years of covered quarters but who intend to return to their country of origin.

Table 8.16   **Money's Worth Calculations**

	All	U.S. Born	Foreign Born
Benefits discounted with SSA interest rate projection			
1. PV benefits ($)	120,279	122,397	100,182
Taxes inflated by 10-year government bond rate			
2. PV taxes ($)	133,739	136,836	104,348
3. PV benefits/PV taxes	0.899	0.894	0.960
Taxes inflated by return on Social Security portfolio			
4. PV taxes ($)	127,265	130,022	101,103
5. PV benefits/PV taxes	0.945	0.941	0.991
Benefits and taxes calculated with 2.3 percent real interest			
6. PV benefits ($)	141,675	144,148	118,213
7. PV taxes ($)	117,692	120,390	92,091
8. PV benefits/PV taxes	1.204	1.197	1.284

Note: PV = present value. All values are calculated assuming work until expected retired date, discounted to 1992.

that the present value of benefits falls below the value of tax payments by about 10 percent for U.S. born, and that benefits fall below taxes by about 4 percent for foreign born.

Row 4 of table 8.16 reports the value of taxes when their value is inflated by the return on the Social Security portfolio.[32] The ratio of benefits in row 1 to this measure of taxes suggests that Social Security benefits paid to members of the HRS cohort who were born in the United States fall below the value of taxes paid by about 6 percent. For foreign born, benefits fall below taxes by about 1 percent.

An alternative approach implicit in some calculations made in discussing the money's worth of Social Security would use the same real interest rate to blow up taxes and discount benefits. As seen in rows 6–8 of table 8.16, when we use a constant 2.3 percent real interest rate to deflate benefits and to inflate tax payments, the present value of benefits exceeds the value of tax payments by 20 percent for U.S. born, and by 28 percent for foreign born.

8.9   Would U.S. Born Prefer That Immigrants Participate in Social Security?

To this point, we have focused on differences in the relative treatment of immigrants and U.S. born by the Social Security system. The data on the present values of benefits and tax contributions can be used to answer a different question. If we were to evaluate the participation of immigrants in Social Security from the purely selfish perspective of U.S. born, would

---

32. The average return in each year to Social Security investments is taken from the home page of the Office of the Chief Actuary (http://www.ss.gov/OACT/).

the U.S. born prefer that immigrants participate in the Social Security system? [33]

One part of the answer to this question turns on the money's worth calculation as applied to immigrants. An additional part of the answer turns on the amount that immigrants who leave the country without collecting benefits, but having paid taxes, contribute to the Social Security system. That is, although the amount paid by immigrants who leave the country without collecting benefits is not relevant to determining whether the current system favors *immigrants who stay* relative to U.S. born, it is relevant to calculating whether the total contributions from all immigrants exceed or fall short of total taxes paid by all immigrants.

We have found that immigrants in the HRS cohort receive a better deal than U.S. born in that cohort. However, we have also found that the deal immigrants receive is poor enough that immigrants in the HRS cohort pay more in taxes than they receive in benefits.[34] Once we add in the contributions made by immigrants who returned to their country of origin without becoming eligible for Social Security benefits, the tax contributions are much greater than benefits received, and should lead native born to favor including immigrants in the Social Security system.

Duleep (1994) reports that calculations by the SSA assume that the emigration rate is 30 percent, implying that roughly half the number of current resident immigrants returned to their country of origin. Her own calculations are consistent with the SSA assumptions.[35] According to the National Research Council (1997, 7-6), about 30 percent of immigrants return to their country of origin, most within a decade of arriving in the United States. Our own very rough calculation is consistent with an emigration rate of 30 percent.[36]

33. When we answer the question of whether U.S. born would prefer that foreign born participate in Social Security, it is not on the basis of the flow of funds. Rather, we focus on the present value of the immigrants' contributions and benefits.

34. In table 8.16, tax payments made by immigrants exceed the value of benefits as long as, counter to the experience of the HRS cohort, we do not assume a low, constant interest rate.

35. However, with the change in country of origin from Europe for recent immigrants, Duleep (1994) is skeptical that the 30 percent emigration rate will continue.

36. We begin by summing the number of legal immigrants to the United States from 1931 to July 1992 who were born from 1931 to 1941. That figure is 2.983 million. We then turn to estimating the current population of immigrants who were born between 1931 and 1941. According to the 1990 Census of Population and Housing, there were 2.389 million immigrants who were age 49–59 in 1990. Next, we adjust the number of resident immigrants born from 1931 to 1941 for illegal immigration. Dividing INS estimates of the number of illegal immigrants in the United States by the CPS immigrant population, we find a rate of about 17 percent. Data from Warren (1997) and Passel, Bean, and Edmonton (1990) suggest that about 15 percent of foreign-born residents are illegal immigrants. Data from the National Research Council (1997) suggests a rate of about 16 percent. Adjusting the number of foreign born downward by 15 percent to isolate the number of legal foreign-born residents in the United States leaves 2.031 million. Dividing the number who remain by the number ever immigrating, we have .68, or an emigration rate of just over 30 percent.

Based on the information from the HRS and the evidence provided by Duleep, it is possible to guess at the tax contributions made by immigrants who will not collect benefits. Duleep finds that five-sixths of emigrants are not qualified for Social Security, probably having worked for fewer than five years. Accordingly, the 30 percent (or less) of immigrants who emigrate are likely to have contributed much less to Social Security taxes than their numbers would suggest.

Duleep also finds that most immigrants who leave before 10 years appear to emigrate within the first five years of U.S. residence (1994, 31). Since immigrants who remain in the United States have over 80 quarters of coverage, then if returnees had as many as five years of coverage, or about 20 quarters of coverage, their quarters of coverage would amount to about one-fourth of the quarters accrued by those immigrants who remain. Assume that those who return within a decade have half of the earnings of those who stay.[37] Then the taxes paid by emigrants who receive no benefits will amount to about 5 percent of the taxes paid by immigrants who remained in the United States $[(.5) \times (5/6) \times (.25) \times (.5)]$. Adopting these assumptions, in determining whether U.S. born would prefer to have foreign born participate in the Social Security system, the tax contributions of foreign born should be increased by about 5 percent.

The addition of 5 percent to taxes collected from emigrants would reduce the benefit-cost ratio of foreign born from 0.960 ($100,182/$104,348) to 0.914 [$100,182/($104,348 $\times$ 1.05)]. Thus, from an ex ante perspective, asking what the value of participating in Social Security is to a new immigrant who does not yet know if he will return to his country of origin, the benefit-cost ratio of participating in Social Security is 91.4 percent. Both benefit-cost ratios for immigrants exceed the benefit-cost ratio for U.S. born of 0.894 ($122,397/$136,836).[38]

8.10 Conclusions

It is useful to estimate, if only roughly, the overall reduction in Social Security payments from prorating benefits of immigrants over a 35- or 40-year period. According to the Social Security Administration's Annual Statistical Supplement (1996, 196), there are 10.1 million insured men and 8.5 million insured women who were age 55–64 in 1996 (51–60 in 1992),

37. Duleep (1994, 20) cites statistics suggesting that four-fifths of those who emigrate within the first 10 years do so within the first 5 years. This means that the assumption of 20 quarters of work by emigrants may be too high. We assume that earnings of emigrants are half the rate of the earnings of those who stay in view of the short period of time for them to find a good job match and experience earnings growth.

38. Again, from the perspective of providing comparable returns to U.S.-born and foreign-born Social Security beneficiaries, there is no reason for the tax payments made by immigrants who leave the United States to be credited toward the accounts of immigrants who stay.

representing roughly 10/11 of the HRS cohort.[39] Approximately 9 percent of these are foreign born, amounting to 0.91 million foreign-born men and 0.77 million foreign-born women. Comparing tables 8.7 and 8.11, when prorating using a 35-year period, benefits from own earnings are reduced by \$5,781 (\$85,356 − \$79,575) for foreign-born men, and by \$2,937 (\$40,045 − \$37,108) for foreign-born women. Multiplying by the number of insured foreign-born men and women yields a total difference in benefits of \$7.5 billion for the 91 percent of the HRS cohort who were born from 1932 to 1941.[40] When prorating using a 40-year period, benefits from own earnings are reduced by \$11,631 (\$85,356 − \$73,725) for foreign-born men, and by \$6,041 (\$40,045 − \$34,004) for foreign-born women. Multiplying by the number of insured foreign-born men and women yields a total difference in benefits of \$15 billion for the 91 percent of the HRS cohort born from 1932 to 1941.[41]

Turning from the HRS population to the full population, the cohort born from 1932 to 1941 represents one-seventh of those who are now age 25–64.[42] Thus, although the earnings histories and populations are quite different, if the HRS population provides any basis for projecting to the full working-age population, the saving from prorating Social Security benefits of immigrants may amount to a present value of \$50-\$100 billion.

8.10.1   Are There Reasons for Providing Higher Returns under Social Security for Foreign Born?

There are a number of possible arguments to be made in favor of providing a higher return under Social Security for foreign born than for U.S. born. One might cite need as a basis for providing a higher return to immigrants. But we show that mean annual earnings of immigrants are similar to the earnings of U.S. born. Nevertheless, it may be argued that most immigrants will not receive retirement benefits from work in their countries of origin. A central problem with this rationale, however, is that the current system disproportionately benefits high-wage immigrants who have been in the United States for only a decade or two. If one wishes to redistribute toward poor immigrants, it is much more efficient to do so using other income-tested policies, such as Supplemental Security Income

---

39. The figures for covered population cited in the *Annual Statistical Supplement* (Social Security Administration 1996) pertain to those age 51–60 in 1992, while the HRS pertains to those 51–61 in 1992. Roughly speaking, the number of covered workers cited in the *Annual Statistical Supplement* therefore represents 91 percent (10/11) of the HRS cohort.

40. Therefore, multiplying \$7.5 billion by (11/10) and prorating over 35 years would reduce benefits for the full HRS cohort by approximately \$8.25 billion.

41. Multiplying \$15 billion by (11/10), the projected saving for the full HRS cohort is \$16.5 billion.

42. Earnings are lower for cohorts who arrived in the United States after the HRS cohort, reducing the effects of prorating on their benefits. On the other hand, younger cohorts experienced a higher ceiling on covered earnings throughout their work lives.

(SSI). Such programs are bound to be more target efficient than is a scheme that automatically counts any year spent outside the United States as a year of zero earnings, and then redistributes benefits based on that calculation using the Social Security formula.[43]

Another possible argument for redistributing in favor of immigrants is that some immigrants, those who only spend a few years in the United States, pay Social Security payroll taxes but receive no benefits. The obvious question is, Why should *only* those immigrants who stay receive the credit for taxes paid by other individuals, those immigrants who emigrate before becoming eligible for benefits? Shouldn't we credit tax payments made by immigrants who will not collect benefits due to emigration not only to immigrants who stay but also to U.S. born? Although relevant to an ex ante calculation of the value of Social Security to an immigrant who has yet to enter the United States, it is not any more justified to credit the loss of tax payments by those who emigrate only to immigrants who stay in the United States than it is to credit the tax payments made by U.S. born who do not qualify for benefits only to U.S. born who do.[44]

A related argument might cite the long vesting period under Social Security as a reason for treating immigrants who qualify for benefits more favorably than U.S. born.[45] Mitigating this argument, the 10-year vesting under Social Security is more flexible than vesting under private pensions. Social Security counts work with any employer as part of the vesting period and uses a very low threshold of earnings to establish a quarter of work, while pensions usually require full-time work for a single employer.[46] For clarity and equity, issues of vesting and of benefit determination should be treated separately.

43. Under the welfare reform adopted in 1996 (Personal Responsibility and Work Opportunity Reconciliation Act of 1996), Congress denied SSI benefits to many noncitizen immigrants. These provisions are not central to this discussion because the restriction does not apply to immigrants who have worked 10 years or more in the United States, which is the same as the requirement for eligibility for Social Security benefits.

44. Another possible argument for maintaining the favorable treatment of immigrants would cite the windfall benefits from Social Security that accrued to the parents of U.S. born but not to the parents of foreign born. For balance, this argument, if extended, would require that we somehow divide the capital formed from expenditures undertaken throughout U.S. history and determine which part should be billed to immigrants. Moreover, in contrast to the spirit of this argument, the redistribution under the current formula is toward those immigrants who are in the United States for fewer years, and thus toward those who pay fewer taxes, rather than toward immigrants who are paying taxes for most of their work life.

45. The 40-quarter vesting period required for immigrants to vest in Social Security is longer than the maximum vesting period under U.S. pension law. Although initially a 10-year vesting was required under ERISA for private pension plans, the Tax Reform Act of 1986 shortened the vesting period to 5 years (5-year cliff vesting or 7-year graded vesting).

46. Social Security treats those who have worked for short periods early in their lifetimes much more favorably than they are treated under defined-benefit pension plans offered in the private sector. This favorable treatment results not only from the progressivity of the Social Security benefit formula but also because Social Security benefits are computed from indexed, rather than nominal, yearly earnings.

Thus, it is difficult to justify the kind of redistribution fostered by the current Social Security system.

8.10.2 Implications

The Social Security system treats years of residence outside the United States as years of zero earnings. The resulting redistribution is not target efficient. It increases benefits not only for those with low lifetime earnings who are meant to gain from redistribution under the progressive Social Security benefit formula, but also for many immigrants who have similar wealth and incomes as U.S. born, especially those with high incomes who have only been here for a decade or two by the time they retire. Statistics on income and wealth demonstrate that as a group, immigrants are not much worse off than native born and, indeed, that the rich among the immigrants are as wealthy and have higher incomes than the rich among U.S. born. It is very hard to justify the disproportionately high Social Security benefits for immigrants who have relatively high earnings and who have been in the United States for shorter periods of residence. Yet this is the consequence of the mechanical application of a uniform Social Security formula that fails to distinguish years of zero earnings from time spent outside the United States.

A system of prorating Social Security benefits for immigrants on the basis of the fraction of a 35- to 40-year base period spent in residence in the United States would eliminate the very high returns enjoyed under Social Security by some immigrants. Aid under SSI will mitigate the effects of the benefit reduction on the poorest of the immigrants. Prorating the benefits of immigrants based on the share of the base period spent in residence could be accomplished by modifying the approach now taken under totalization agreements already adopted under Social Security.

All of this said, the Social Security system has benefited financially from having immigrants in the HRS cohort participate. Despite the better deal they receive, like U.S.-born participants in the HRS cohort, most immigrants in the HRS cohort who remain in the United States will pay more in taxes than they will receive in benefits, although just barely. From the perspective of U.S.-born participants, taxes received from immigrants who subsequently emigrate without collecting benefits tip the balance in favor of having included immigrants from the HRS cohort in the Social Security system.

Appendix

Table 8A.1   **Distribution of Immigrants by Decade of Immigration and Average Real Covered Earnings in Years Worked**

Year Immigrated	Real Covered Earnings in Year Worked					Sum of Columns
	<$5,000	$5,000–$10,000	$10,000–$20,000	$20,000–$30,000	> $30,000	
Men						
Before 1940	0	0	1	0	2	3
1940–49	0	0	4	6	6	16
1950–59	3	5	23	37	25	93
1960–69	3	7	38	33	53	134
1970–79	9	12	33	25	25	104
1980 or later	10	17	24	9	6	66
Sum of rows	25	41	123	110	117	416
Women						
Before 1940	1	0	3	3	0	7
1940–49	5	11	5	1	3	25
1950–59	17	35	39	20	5	116
1960–69	26	36	54	28	14	158
1970–79	22	22	35	8	6	93
1980 or later	11	12	24	3	1	51
Sum of rows	82	116	160	63	29	450

References

Council of Economic Advisers. 1995. *Economic report of the president.* Washington, D.C.: U.S. Government Printing Office.

Duleep, Harriet O. 1994. Social Security and the emigration of immigrants. Working paper, Social Security Administration, Office of Research and Statistics, Washington, D.C.

Federal Old Age and Survivors Insurance and Disability Insurance Trust Fund. Board of Trustees. 1995. The annual report of the federal old-age and survivors insurance and disability insurance trust fund. Washington, D.C.: U.S. Government Printing Office.

Feldstein, Martin, ed. 1998. *Privatizing social security.* Chicago: University of Chicago Press.

Gustman, Alan L., Olivia S. Mitchell, Andrew A. Samwick, and Thomas L. Steinmeier. Forthcoming. Pension and Social Security wealth in the health and retirement study. In *Wealth, work and health, innovations in measurement in the social sciences,* ed. James Smith and Robert Willis. Ann Arbor: University of Michigan Press.

Gustman, Alan L., and Thomas L. Steinmeier. 1985. The 1983 Social Security reforms and labor supply adjustments of older individuals in the long run. *Journal of Labor Economics* 3:237–53.

———. 1991. Changing the Social Security rules for work after 65. *Industrial and Labor Relations Review* 44 (4): 733–45.

———. 1998. Privatizing Social Security: First round effects of a generic, voluntary, privatized U.S. Social Security system. In *Privatizing Social Security,* ed. Martin Feldstein. Chicago, University of Chicago Press.

Leimer, Dean R. 1994. Cohort-specific measures of lifetime net Social Security transfers. Social Security Administration, Office of Research Working Paper no. 59. Washington, D.C.: Social Security Administration.

———. 1995. A guide to Social Security money's worth issues. *Social Security Bulletin* 58 (2): 3–20.

National Research Council. 1997. *The new Americans: Economic, demographic, and fiscal effects of immigration,* ed. James P. Smith and Barry Edmonston. Washington, D.C.: National Academy Press.

Passel, J. S., F. D. Bean, and B. Edmonston. 1990. Undocumented migration since IRCA: An overall assessment. In *Undocumented migration to the United States: IRCA and the experience of the 1980s,* ed. F. D. Bean, B. Edmonston, and J. S. Passel. Washington, D.C.: The Urban Institute.

Social Security Administration. 1996. *Annual statistical supplement to the Social Security bulletin.* Washington, D.C.: U.S. Government Printing Office.

———. 1997. A pension from work not covered by Social Security. Washington, D.C.: U.S. Government Printing Office.

———. Office of International Policy. 1997. Computation of U.S. pro rata benefit amounts under international Social Security agreements. Washington, D.C.: U.S. Government Printing Office.

U.S. Bureau of the Census. 1997. *Current Population Reports,* Washington, D.C.: U.S. Government Printing Office. Kristin A. Hansen and Carol S. Farber. Report no. P-20-494. Washington, D.C.: U.S. Bureau of the Census.

Warren, R. 1997. Estimates of the unauthorized immigrant population residing in the United States: October 1996. Washington, D.C.: Immigration and Naturalization Service, Office of Policy and Planning.

The Role of Deportation in the Incarceration of Immigrants

Kristin F. Butcher and Anne Morrison Piehl

9.1 Introduction

The small empirical literature on the effects of immigration on crime and criminal justice has produced several stylized facts. While any amount of immigration must increase the total number of crimes in the United States, Butcher and Piehl (1998b) reported that increasing immigration did not increase crime *rates* in the largest U.S. cities. In an analysis of the effects of immigration on the behavior of the native born, Grogger (1998) showed that there did not appear to be "spillovers" from the labor market competition of immigrants onto the criminality of African American youth. Butcher and Piehl (1998a) found that more-recent immigrants appeared to be less criminal (relative to the native born) than earlier arrivals. This is in spite of the fact that recent immigrants fare relatively poorly in the labor market. Furthermore, the same paper documented that immigrants were much less likely to be institutionalized than one would expect given their relatively low levels of education.

Kristin F. Butcher is assistant professor of economics at Boston College. Anne Morrison Piehl is associate professor of public policy in the Kennedy School of Government at Harvard University and a faculty research fellow of the National Bureau of Economic Research.

The authors are grateful to Daniel Kanstroom and David Cory for help with interpretation of the immigration laws. They thank John Berecochea and the Research Branch of the California Department of Corrections for access to and assistance with the data. The findings presented here should not be construed as representing the views of the State of California or the Department of Corrections. Mark Fassold provided excellent research assistance. The authors appreciate helpful comments from David Card, Jeffrey Grogger, Hilary Hoynes, Stephen Legomsky, Gilbert Metcalf, Dan Noelle, and seminar participants at UC Berkeley, Tufts University, and the NBER conference. Butcher appreciates support from the Industrial Relations Section at Princeton. Piehl appreciates the support of the Robert Wood Johnson Foundation. All errors are the authors'.

This literature has left unanswered many questions relevant to public policy about immigration and, in particular, about immigrants in the criminal justice system. Policies toward immigrants who commit crimes in the United States may affect which immigrants choose to enter the country, the extent to which immigrants become naturalized citizens, and the extent to which immigrants in the country engage in illegal activity. While these are important topics, there are more basic questions about current conditions about which we know very little. Do immigrants and natives commit similar types of offenses? Are the foreign born treated differently than natives within the criminal justice system? And if so, how does that affect costs? In this paper, we address these questions while documenting the legal consequences of criminal activity for immigrants and how these consequences have changed over time.

There are many reasons to be concerned about the treatment of criminal aliens in the United States. First, the past 25 years have seen the largest numbers of immigrants since the early 1900s and the quadrupling of the prison population. Consequently, the absolute number of incarcerated immigrants is large and growing. Second, congressional legislation has dramatically expanded the types of criminal acts that "qualify" noncitizens for deportation, while at the same time increasing the resources for identifying and processing criminal aliens. These acts impose conditions on the states, which have traditionally maintained primary responsibility for law enforcement. The consequences of these laws, intended or not, are considerable. Third, several court cases have restricted the use of certain modes of punishment for noncitizens, for example, early release and low-security facilities, which are widely used for citizens. While not everyone will be concerned about horizontal equity associated with differential punishment by nativity for similar criminal acts, concern about the efficient use of the public purse is widespread. To the extent that costs of the restrictions on the terms of confinement are not offset by savings due to increased vigilance in implementing deportation, the increase in the use of public resources in the incarceration of aliens could be substantial.

We analyze the experience of one jurisdiction (California) particularly affected by the costs of incarcerating foreign-born inmates. While California may not be representative of the nation, it is emblematic of this particular social policy issue. Using data on all new admissions to state prisons for three points in time, we analyze the offenses of the foreign born and of natives. We find that the foreign born are very different from native-born inmates in terms of their crime mix, with foreigners much more likely to be serving time for drug offenses. The Immigration and Naturalization Service (INS) appears to be much more involved with the incarcerated foreign born in 1996 than it was in 1986. This is the result of the war on drugs as well as changes in public law and in the level of resources appropriated for enforcement activities targeting deportable aliens. Inmates designated by the California Department of Corrections (CADOC) to be released to INS custody (called "INS holds") had sentences about 40 percent longer than natives in 1986, which may reflect that those foreigners had committed more serious offenses. By 1996, the definition of "deportable" was expanded such that it should cover all noncitizens in the CADOC. We find that, even at the end of the period, those foreign born with INS holds served substantially longer terms (conditional upon sentence length) than natives or other "similar" foreigners. These longer terms of incarceration impose substantial costs on the state.

The paper is organized as follows. Section 9.2 compares foreign-born inmates to native-born inmates in California. Section 9.3 considers federal jurisdiction. Section 9.4 describes the legal and law enforcement environment with respect to noncitizens involved in criminal activity. Section 9.5 contains a multivariate analysis of criminal justice outcomes in California, and section 9.6 concludes.

9.2 California Inmates: Foreign Born and Native Born

This section introduces the data used in the paper and provides a description of inmates in California prisons over time, focusing on the differences between foreign-born and U.S.-born offenders.

9.2.1 California Department of Corrections Data

We use administrative data from the CADOC from 1986, 1990, and 1996. These are administrative data used to keep track of inmates while they are in the custody of the Department of Corrections. The admission cohorts contain all individuals who were admitted to the prison system with new crimes in each year.[1] These data were constructed from the CADOC master file as of June 1997, so we observe whether an inmate was released by that date. We focus on the subsample of offenders with completed terms when we analyze differences in time served across groups.

Because the purpose of these data is to keep track of inmates, the number of variables included in the master data set is enormous and rich in details about the inmates' appearance (e.g., hair and eye color) and movements (e.g., to and from the dentist). However, many of these variables are not of interest here, and much information that we would like is unavailable. The available demographic data include the inmates' age at admission, race and ethnicity, and country of origin. Additionally, we have information on the principal commitment offense category, the length of sentence, and the actual time served for those who are released during the period.

---

1. The restriction to "new admissions" means that offenders entering prisons for violating the conditions of probation or parole are not included in the sample.

There is potentially important information that we do not have, most notably criminal history. The data also contain no information on educational attainment, which for some purposes is a useful control variable. Also, we have no information on presentencing confinement or behavior in prison, both of which could impact the time actually served for a particular sentence length. We discuss the impact of these data shortcomings on interpretation as they arise.

While we have information on country of origin, we have no information on citizenship status. In the labor economics literature, it is common to use the terms "foreign born" and "immigrant" interchangeably. Here, however, it is important to recognize the differences. The foreign born who have become citizens are not subject to deportation, so one would not expect changes in policies surrounding deportation to affect their criminal justice outcomes. Secondly, some of the foreign-born inmates may be individuals who were expecting to be in the United States temporarily (e.g., tourists or business travelers), some of whom may have entered for the purpose of committing a crime and are therefore not "immigrants."[2]

When we analyze those inmates who have been released, we break the foreign born into three groups, depending on their status with the INS. When a foreigner is sentenced, the INS is supposed to begin proceedings to determine his or her deportation status. If the INS either determines that the individual is deportable or is continuing its investigation into whether he or she is deportable, an INS "hold" is placed on that person. Our data contain information on whether someone is in this "INS hold" category. For some individuals, an INS hold was placed on them *after* their release date, because the INS did not discover until late in the process that the person was potentially deportable. We label those with INS holds prior to their release from prison as "INS hold." Those with holds after their release date are labeled "late holds." Those with no INS holds on their records are labeled "no hold."

We dropped a number of observations from the sample because of missing or invalid data. Individuals who had an invalid year for admission or release, those who were released on the same day as they were admitted, and people who were sentenced for less than one year were dropped. This latter exclusion is because individuals are only supposed to be remanded to the prison system for terms of one year and higher (others are remanded to jails operated by counties). "Lifers"—those in for murder—were excluded because they do not have determinate sentences.[3]

---

2. If, for example, many of the incarcerated aliens were admitted on tourist or business visas, there would be little implication that the United States should change the number or criteria for admission of those seeking to become permanent resident aliens. Unfortunately, information on visa status is not available.

3. California's 1982 Determinate Sentencing Law requires specific terms of punishment for all offenses other than murder. The actual time served for those with indeterminate sentences is determined by a parole board.

We further excluded some individuals because of difficulty in interpreting their information. We dropped individuals whose principal commitment offense was "escape," since we do not have information on the crime that landed them in prison in the first place. We also deleted people who served more than 100 percent of their sentence and those whose sentencing date was later than their admission date. The first group is likely to be those with extremely bad behavior while in prison. The latter group is those who were sentenced for an additional offense while in prison. Since we have no information on behavior in prison, these individuals complicate the analysis. Finally, we dropped individuals born in outlying areas of the United States (Puerto Rico), and the native born who had an INS hold placed on their record, since neither fit cleanly into the groups under study.[4] In all of the subsamples we analyze, only 3 to 4 percent are lost because of these sample restrictions.

9.2.2 Descriptive Statistics

Panel A of table 9.1 shows information for those men admitted in 1986, 1990, and 1996. The number of men admitted in 1986 was approximately 21,000. By 1996, the number of new admissions had increased to about 39,000. The fraction of the admission cohorts that was foreign born also increases, rising from about 19 percent in 1986, to 25 percent in 1990, to 27 percent in 1996. While foreign-born men represent a sizable fraction of the flows into prison in California, they also represent a large fraction of the population overall. In 1980, the foreign born made up about 18 percent of the 18-to-40-year-old male population (roughly comparable to the group most likely to be in prison); by 1990, they had risen to about 24 percent of this population.[5] So foreign-born men's representation in the admission flows into prison in California is roughly equal to their representation in the state as a whole, despite the fact that based on their average education, for example, one might expect them to have higher incarceration rates (see Butcher and Piehl 1998a).

There are substantial differences between the characteristics of native-born and foreign-born men in these admission cohorts. Foreign-born men are slightly younger than native-born men, and this difference increases slightly over the time periods studied here. There are striking differences in the race and ethnicity categories, and these differences increase over time. Among the native born, the percentage white non-Hispanic was 37 percent in 1986 and rose slightly to 40 percent in 1996. Among the foreign born, the overwhelming majority of inmates are Hispanic. In 1986, Hispanics represent 72 percent of the foreign-born inmates admitted. This

4. In neither of these two cases do these omissions affect the substantive results. Dropping these final two categories of inmates eases the discussion of the results.

5. By 1996, over 30 percent of the 18- to 44-year-olds (male and female) in California were foreign born (published tabulations from the 1996 March CPS). See http://www.bls.census.gov/cps/.

Table 9.1   **Descriptive Statistics for Admissions Cohorts**

	1986		1990		1996	
	Native Born	Foreign Born	Native Born	Foreign Born	Native Born	Foreign Born
			A. Men			
Age at admission	29.49	28.49*	30.65	28.77*	32.13	30.24*
	(0.067)	(0.131)	(0.056)	(0.088)	(0.056)	(0.082)
White	0.3688	0.0945*	0.3706	0.0488*	0.3952	0.0405*
	(0.0037)	(0.0046)	(0.0030)	(0.0023)	(0.0029)	(0.0019)
Black	0.3912	0.0459*	0.3838	0.0290*	0.3201	0.0175*
	(0.0037)	(0.0033)	(0.0030)	(0.0018)	(0.0028)	(0.0013)
Hispanic	0.2170	0.7214*	0.2249	0.8473*	0.2596	0.8680*
	(0.0032)	(0.0071)	(0.0026)	(0.0039)	(0.0026)	(0.0033)
Mexican	0.2010	0.6946*	0.1943	0.7622*	0.1845	0.7472*
	(0.0031)	(0.0073)	(0.0025)	(0.0046)	(0.0023)	(0.0042)
Sentence length	47.14	42.93*	41.12	39.70*	45.19	45.37
	(0.436)	(0.669)	(0.318)	(0.380)	(0.407)	(0.777)
[Median]	[36]	[36]	[24]	[32]	[32]	[36]
Property offense	0.3901	0.3004*	0.3028	0.2041*	0.2860	0.1797*
	(0.0037)	(0.0073)	(0.0029)	(0.0044)	(0.0027)	(0.0037)
Assault offense	0.2639	0.2260*	0.2095	0.1587*	0.2227	0.1792*
	(0.0034)	(0.0066)	(0.0025)	(0.0040)	(0.0025)	(0.0037)
Drug offense	0.2046	0.3315*	0.3010	0.4528*	0.3249	0.4583*
	(0.0031)	(0.0075)	(0.0029)	(0.0054)	(0.0028)	(0.0048)
Drug possession	0.0726	0.0639	0.1117	0.0944*	0.1512	0.0990*
	(0.0020)	(0.0039)	(0.0020)	(0.0032)	(0.0021)	(0.0029)
Manslaughter	0.0413	0.0524*	0.0277	0.0360*	0.0246	0.0284*
	(0.0015)	(0.0036)	(0.0010)	(0.0020)	(0.0009)	(0.0016)
Sex offense	0.0633	0.0546*	0.0435	0.0408	0.0424	0.0469
	(0.0019)	(0.0036)	(0.0013)	(0.0021)	(0.0012)	(0.0020)
INS hold	0	0.3054*	0	0.6832*	0	0.7495*
		(0.0073)		(0.0051)		(0.0042)
N	17,100	3,991	25,821	8,482	28,450	10,763
Fraction foreign born	0.1892		0.2473		0.2745	
	(0.0027)		(0.0023)		(0.0023)	
			B. Women			
Age at admission	30.98	31.49	31.83	32.69	34.13	33.55
	(0.185)	(0.725)	(0.136)	(0.524)	(0.118)	(0.390)
White	0.3968	0.2180*	0.3807	0.1732*	0.4111	0.1179*
	(0.0118)	(0.0359)	(0.0086)	(0.0238)	(0.0075)	(0.0151)
Black	0.2986	0.0677*	0.3857	0.0787*	0.3387	0.0437*
	(0.0110)	(0.0219)	(0.0086)	(0.0169)	(0.0072)	(0.0096)
Hispanic	0.2526	0.5113*	0.1981	0.5787*	0.1947	0.6638*
	(0.0105)	(0.0435)	(0.0070)	(0.0310)	(0.0060)	(0.0221)
Mexican	0.2363	0.4962*	0.1757	0.5079*	0.1022	0.5218*
	(0.0103)	(0.0435)	(0.0067)	(0.0314)	(0.0046)	(0.0234)
Sentence length	32.75	30.74	29.33	33.78*	30.54	37.70*
	(0.577)	(1.222)	(0.323)	(1.596)	(0.377)	(1.574)
[Median]	[24]	[24]	[24]	[24]	[24]	[32]

Table 9.1   (continued)

	1986		1990		1996	
	Native Born	Foreign Born	Native Born	Foreign Born	Native Born	Foreign Born
Property offense	0.4866	0.3459*	0.3543	0.3307	0.3621	0.2336*
	(0.0121)	(0.0414)	(0.0084)	(0.0296)	(0.0073)	(0.0198)
Assault offense	0.1409	0.1053	0.0964	0.0827	0.1158	0.1179
	(0.0084)	(0.0267)	(0.0052)	(0.0173)	(0.0049)	(0.0151)
Drug offense	0.2724	0.4812*	0.4747	0.5157	0.4560	0.5721*
	(0.0107)	(0.0435)	(0.0088)	(0.0314)	(0.0076)	(0.0231)
Drug possession	0.1234	0.1203	0.2308	0.1299	0.2594	0.1507*
	(0.0079)	(0.0283)	(0.0074)	(0.0211)	(0.0067)	(0.0167)
Manslaughter	0.0471	0.0301	0.0258	0.0276	0.0146	0.0262
	(0.0051)	(0.0149)	(0.0028)	(0.0103)	(0.0018)	(0.0075)
Sex offense	0.0128	0*	0.0044	0*	0.0032	0.0022
	(0.0027)		(0.0012)		(0.0009)	(0.0022)
INS hold	0	0.1805*	0	0.5827*	0	0.3319*
		(0.0335)		(0.0310)		(0.0310)
N	1,718	133	3,215	254	4,325	458
Fraction foreign born	0.0718		0.0732		0.0958	
	(0.0060)		(0.0044)		(0.0043)	

Note: Authors' calculations from California Department of Corrections data. See text for description of the data and sample restrictions. Mexican is a subset of Hispanic. Drug possession is a subset of the drug offense category. "Other" offenses are omitted. An asterisk indicates the mean is different from the mean in the previous column at the 5 percent level of statistical significance. Numbers in parentheses are standard errors.

rose to 85 percent in 1990, and 87 percent in 1996. Hispanics, both native and foreign born, were predominantly of Mexican descent.

One of the unanswered questions in the literature on immigration and crime is whether the foreign born and natives commit different types of crimes.[6] These data allow us to address this question, at least in part. These data, of course, do not allow us to answer questions about those who commit crimes but are never apprehended or convicted. To the extent that there are differences in apprehension and conviction rates between the foreign born and natives, these data will give a distorted view of the crimes committed by these two groups.

There are statistically significant differences, in all years of admission data, in the types of crimes for which foreigners and natives are committed

6. Smith and Edmonston (1997) show the distribution of offense types for the nation as a whole, by citizenship. Noncitizens are more likely (than citizens) to serve time for drug offenses and less likely to serve time for property and violent offenses. Denominating by the male population age 18–54, they find that noncitizens have incarceration rates for violent offenses about half those of citizens; for property offenses, noncitizens have incarceration rates about one-third the native rate; while for drug offenses, noncitizens have double the incarceration rate of natives (Smith and Edmonston 1997, 388).

to prison. The foreign born were less likely to be in prison for property and assault offenses. In 1986, they were less likely to be serving time for sex offenses. Although the fraction of the admission cohort that was incarcerated for manslaughter is low overall (and falling), the foreign born were slightly more likely to have this as their principal commitment offense. There is a striking difference in the fraction sentenced for drug offenses. In 1986, 20 percent of the natives and 33 percent of the foreign born were committed for drug offenses. By 1996, this rose to 32 percent of the native born and 46 percent of the foreign born. The category "drug possession" is a subset of the "drug offenses" group. The foreign born were significantly less likely in 1990 and 1996 to be incarcerated solely on possession charges.

In 1986 and 1990, foreign-born men had significantly shorter sentences than native-born men. The average sentence length among the native born was 47 months in 1986, fell to 41 months in 1990, and rose again to 45 months in 1996. Among the foreign born, the average sentence length was 43 months in 1986, 40 months in 1990, and 45 months in 1996. The shorter sentences for the foreign born in 1986 and 1990 may reflect differences in the offense types. The increase in the relative sentence length up to equality with the native born by 1996 may be due to several factors: changes in the offense type or severity, changes in the enforcement and punishment of certain offenses, or changes in the treatment of immigrants per se. These possibilities are explored in section 9.4.

Near the bottom of panel A of table 9.1 is the fraction of the foreign born with an INS hold on their records. As described previously, this indicates that the INS had either determined that the individual is deportable[7] or was in the process of investigating his or her status. The fraction of the foreign-born population that has an INS hold on record increased dramatically over this time period, rising from approximately 30 percent in 1986, to 68 percent in 1990, to 75 percent in 1996. In addition, the swiftness with which INS hold orders are placed increased as well. In 1986, 75 percent of those inmates who would eventually have INS holds (including those for whom INS holds were filed after their release) had those holds on record within 766 days. In 1990, 75 percent of those who would eventually have INS holds placed on their records were identified within 152 days.

Panel A of table 9.2 gives details on the offense categories, sentence length, and actual time served for four groups: the native born and three subgroups of the foreign born. The data here are for the men admitted in 1986 and 1990 and released within six years of admission. Restricting the

---

7. Technically, some in this category may be "excludable" rather than "deportable." "Exclusion" applies to those foreigners who are in the United States awaiting formal admission, such as refugees. They may be deemed excludable and returned to their country of origin.

Table 9.2 Descriptive Statistics for Inmates Released within Six Years of Admission, by Admission Year

A. Men

| | 1986 | | | | 1990 | | | |
| | Native | Foreign Born | | | Native | Foreign Born | | |
		No Hold	INS Hold	Late Hold		No Hold	INS Hold	Late Hold
Fraction of sample	0.810	0.101	0.056	0.034	0.752	0.065	0.169	0.014
Sentence length	40.10	32.97	53.96	27.05	36.20	33.26	38.66	27.81
	(0.204)	(0.461)	(0.826)	(0.565)	(0.167)	(0.504)	(0.327)	(0.652)
[Median]	[36]	[24]	[48]	[24]	[24]	[24]	[36]	[24]
Time served	18.01	13.96	25.32	11.41	15.94	14.20	17.37	11.59
	(0.103)	(0.218)	(0.405)	(0.290)	(0.078)	(0.242)	(0.162)	(0.351)
[Median]	[13.63]	[11.33]	[22.41]	[10.35]	[11.76]	[10.81]	[13.88]	[9.95]
Property offense	0.402	0.326	0.212	0.409	0.308	0.218	0.193	0.332
	(0.004)	(0.010)	(0.012)	(0.019)	(0.003)	(0.009)	(0.005)	(0.022)
Assault offense	0.258	0.211	0.281	0.162	0.204	0.166	0.152	0.180
	(0.003)	(0.009)	(0.013)	(0.014)	(0.003)	(0.008)	(0.005)	(0.018)
Drug offense	0.212	0.336	0.320	0.389	0.308	0.271	0.537	0.362
	(0.003)	(0.010)	(0.014)	(0.019)	(0.003)	(0.010)	(0.007)	(0.022)
Drug possession	0.075	0.071	0.039	0.092	0.114	0.079	0.100	0.131
	(0.002)	(0.006)	(0.006)	(0.011)	(0.002)	(0.006)	(0.004)	(0.016)
Manslaughter	0.034	0.033	0.081	0.013	0.023	0.034	0.031	0.017
	(0.001)	(0.004)	(0.008)	(0.004)	(0.001)	(0.004)	(0.002)	(0.006)
Sex offense	0.056	0.042	0.088	0.009	0.039	0.054	0.034	0.008
	(0.002)	(0.004)	(0.008)	(0.004)	(0.001)	(0.005)	(0.002)	(0.004)
N	16,483	2,052	1,142	684	25,200	2,173	5,662	473

(continued)

Table 9.2 (continued)

B. Women

| | 1986 | | | | 1990 | | | |
| | | Foreign Born | | | | Foreign Born | | |
	Native	No Hold	INS Hold	Late Hold	Native	No Hold	INS Hold	Late Hold
Fraction of sample	0.928	0.054	0.013	0.005	0.927	0.028	0.043	0.003
Sentence length	31.50	27.56			28.95	26.60	38.20	
	(0.461)	(1.230)			(0.298)	(1.440)	(2.167)	
[Median]	[24]	[24]			[24]	[24]	[24]	
Time served	13.79	10.94			12.06	10.88	15.84	
	(0.235)	(0.606)			(0.150)	(0.804)	(1.002)	
[Median]	[11.10]	[9.94]			[9.94]	[8.38]	[11.63]	
Property offense	0.491	0.354			0.355	0.402	0.259	
	(0.012)	(0.048)			(0.008)	(0.050)	(0.036)	
Assault offense	0.142	0.121			0.096	0.082	0.088	
	(0.008)	(0.033)			(0.005)	(0.028)	(0.023)	
Drug offense	0.274	0.475			0.476	0.392	0.612	
	(0.011)	(0.050)			(0.009)	(0.050)	(0.040)	
Drug possession	0.124	0.141			0.232	0.155	0.109	
	(0.008)	(0.035)			(0.007)	(0.037)	(0.026)	
Manslaughter	0.041	0.010			0.025	0.021	0.034	
	(0.005)	(0.010)			(0.003)	(0.015)	(0.015)	
Sex offense	0.012	0			0.004	0	0	
	(0.003)				(0.001)			
N	1,703	99	24	10	3,204	97	147	9

Note: Authors' calculations from California Department of Corrections data. See text for description of the data and sample restrictions. Drug possession is a subset of the drug offense category. "Other" offenses are omitted. Numbers in parentheses are standard errors.

analysis in this way allows us comparable groups for the 1986 and 1990 admission cohorts. The vast majority of inmates serve fewer than six years—from 96.5 percent to 99.7 percent of our various admission cohorts. Nonetheless, these results are not generalizable to the inmate population serving the longest terms.[8]

Since most inmates serve fewer than six years, the means for most variables are essentially the same as in panel A of table 9.1. Here we focus on time served but repeat some other variables so they can be compared for a consistent sample. For example, the crime mix is somewhat different from the earlier table.

The foreign born are divided into the three categories described earlier: those with no INS hold, those with an INS hold on record, and those for whom the INS hold was placed on their record after their release to parole ("late hold"). In 1986, the "INS hold" group had by far the highest sentence length, averaging 54 months. Those foreign born without holds, or those deemed deportable after release, had the lowest sentences (33 and 27 months, respectively). Under the California Determinate Sentencing Law, an inmate is supposed to serve at least 40 percent of his sentence. In practice, actual time served in prison depends on several factors. The exact amount depends on rewards for behavior in prison, often referred to as "good time." In addition, some of those admitted to prison were not able to make bail and thus were confined in county jails prior to their sentencing. These individuals may receive "credit" for this presentencing confinement and, as a result, may not serve as much time in the state system. These complications notwithstanding, the correlation between sentence length and actual time served is strong. The INS-hold foreigners served 25 months in 1986, compared to 18 months for the native born. Foreigners without INS holds served 14 months, and "late holds" served 11 months. There is also evidence that in 1986 the INS-hold foreigners were committed for more serious crimes. A higher proportion of them were incarcerated for assault, manslaughter, and sex offenses. In 1986, deportation appears to have been pursued largely for the most serious offenders.

By 1990, quite a lot had changed. The immigrants with INS holds had sentences that were only slightly higher than the native born (39 months versus 36 months). The offense distribution for the "INS holds" changed as well. Now 54 percent were incarcerated for drug offenses, and the proportion incarcerated for assault dropped well below that for the native born and slightly below that for the other groups of foreign born. The proportion committed for manslaughter fell from 9 percent in 1986 to 3.4 percent in 1990, which is below the rate for the native born. The proportion of sex offenders has also fallen below that for the native born.

In all, panel A of table 9.1 and panel A of table 9.2 suggest that there

---

8. The restriction excludes 2–5 percent of men and less than 1 percent of women.

has been a significant increase in the proportion of the foreign-born prison population that is "deportable." Panel A of table 9.2 suggests that the types of crimes committed by this "deportable" group has shifted from serious violent crimes to more drug offenses. Section 9.4 below details some of the reasons this segment of the foreign-born inmate population increased so dramatically during this time period, and why the principal commitment offenses may have changed. Before moving to that section, we examine the analogous data for women.

Panel B of table 9.1 shows the fraction foreign born, demographic information, and offense distribution for women in the 1986, 1990, and 1996 admission cohorts. Note that the sample sizes are dramatically smaller for women than for men. Although the number of incarcerated women has been increasing, by 1996 they still represented only 10 percent of the prison admissions. The next striking thing to note is the fraction foreign born: in 1986, 7 percent of the women were foreign born; by 1996, this increased to approximately 10 percent. By 1996, foreign-born women made up about 25 percent of the female population in California.[9] It is clear that foreign-born women are vastly underrepresented in the inmate inflow rates. Foreigners with an INS hold on record were 18 percent of those admitted in 1986, 58 percent in 1990, and 33 percent in 1996. It is difficult to know if this fluctuation reflects changes in enforcement or changes in the underlying population, or if it is merely due to the small samples. The small sample sizes for women limit the extent of the analyses we can perform. Throughout the paper, we report only as much as we feel the data justify.

Relative to the male inmates, women were more likely to be incarcerated for property and drug offenses and less likely to be in for violent offenses. Within gender, however, the comparisons between foreign born and native born are similar. It is worth noting the large increase in the proportion of women who were committed for drug offenses. By 1996, 46 percent of the natives and 57 percent of the foreign born were admitted to prison for drug offenses.

Panel B of table 9.2 presents means for those released within six years. There are not enough of the "INS hold" and "late hold" foreign born to break them out separately in both years. In 1990, one can see that, as with the men, the INS-hold foreigners had the longest sentence length and the longest time served. The offense distribution overall looks almost identical to the admission cohorts since very few women are truncated by our sample restriction of serving fewer than six years. As with the men, in 1990 women with INS holds were much more likely to be in for drug offenses than were other women.

Offenders who have committed crimes in California may also be incarcerated in the federal Bureau of Prisons. In order to complete the descrip-

9. See published tabulations from the March 1996 CPS at http://www.bls.census.gov/cps/.

tion of immigrant/nonimmigrant differences in incarceration, the next section considers the effect federal jurisdiction has on inmate populations at the state level.

9.3 Federal Jurisdiction

Although state and federal jurisdiction are often analyzed in isolation, there are important reasons to consider them jointly. The responsibility for arresting, trying, and punishing criminal offenders rests primarily with state and local governments, yet there are several relevant categories of offenses that fall solely under federal jurisdiction, namely immigration offenses and treason.[10] Anti-immigrant advocates often overlook this definitional issue. For example, the Federation for American Immigration Reform (FAIR) in its literature often cites that 25 percent of federal inmates are noncitizens[11] without noting either that the federal system incarcerates only about 7 percent of the nation's inmates (Glaeser, Kessler, and Piehl 1998) or that 13 percent of the noncitizens are incarcerated for immigration violations—crimes that come only under federal jurisdiction and for which citizens (generally) are not at risk.[12]

Most violations of other areas of federal law are also violations of state laws. The practical consequences of this concurrent jurisdiction have not been well researched, however (see Glaeser, Kessler, and Piehl 1998). Concurrent jurisdiction is particularly important in the area of drug crimes, since criminal acts could be prosecuted under either the relevant state law or federal law, potentially with very different consequences for the offender.[13] Time served in the federal system for the same crime is likely to be twice as long as in a state prison because federal law requires that inmates serve 85 percent of their nominal sentences. Also, federal inmates generally serve time in prison much further from home, which makes visits from family and friends much less likely.

The existence of the federal criminal justice system raises two important questions for our analysis of immigration and state inmates. Are there native/foreign born differences in the mix of inmates serving time on "federal only" offenses? For those offenses with concurrent jurisdiction, does

10. The federal government has also been particularly interested in regulating offenses by or against federal officials or committed on federal property (DiIulio, Smith, and Singer 1995).

11. See FAIR's Web page, "Government Studies on Criminal Aliens," at http://www.fairus.org/04111604.htm.

12. The percentage of noncitizens entering the prison system with immigration crimes is 26 percent. This number differs substantially from the percentage of the stock of inmates since sentences for immigration offenses are generally shorter than for drug and violent offenses (Scalia 1996, tables 9 and 12).

13. While it is constitutional to bring charges against a defendant under both sets of laws for the same act, this is rarely done in practice. For a discussion of these jurisdictional issues plus a model of the incentives for prosecutors to choose different cases in the two systems, see Glaeser, Kessler, and Piehl (1998).

the margin for moving into the federal jurisdiction differ between the foreign born and natives? Because data comparable to our California sample do not exist, this section reviews data from several sources, all of which require approximations to the concept of nativity used elsewhere in this paper.

Table 9.3 reports information from the U.S. Sentencing Commission monitoring database of all cases resulting in conviction in U.S. district courts in 1994–95.[14] This table shows that noncitizens were overrepresented among those from California convicted in U.S. courts. Noncitizens were primarily convicted of immigration and drug violations. Furthermore, there are important differences between legal and illegal immigrants—nearly 60 percent of the illegal immigrant males were convicted of immigration violations. However, excluding immigration offenses, drug violations were very important to each group, and constitute a larger proportion of the noncitizens' offenses than of the citizens'. Therefore, these high proportions of immigrant drug offenders may indicate that the foreign born are differentially "missing" from analyses of state prison populations.

A report from the Bureau of Justice Statistics suggests that, for drug offenders, the margin for noncitizens to move into federal jurisdiction may have been lower than for citizens (Scalia 1996). Scalia notes that "noncitizens convicted of a Federal drug offense were more likely than citizens to have played a minor role in the drug conspiracy. Approximately 29% of noncitizens convicted of a drug offense received a downward sentencing adjustment for 'mitigating role,' compared with 14% of U.S. citizens" (Scalia 1996, 1). While these findings have implications for the costs of incarcerating the foreign born in the federal criminal justice system, the existence of this system also has implications for the interpretation of results for states. If we were able to cleanly connect the data for both prison systems, we would find that the California data underestimate the disproportionate representation of the foreign born among drug offenders and the longer time served by the foreign born (which we show below).

9.4 Laws and Enforcement

The information presented in tables 9.1 and 9.2 makes clear that the fraction of inmates who were foreign born, and the fraction of the foreign born with an INS hold on record, increased for both men and women. To understand why this happened, it is worth distinguishing the factors that affect the criminal justice system in general from those that determine whether an immigrant is deportable.

---

14. The coverage of these data is somewhat broader than statistics on the flow of inmates into the Bureau of Prisons, since some of those convicted are not sentenced to incarceration.

Table 9.3   Offense Distribution: Convictions in U.S. District Courts, 1994

	Men			Women		
	Citizens	Legal Residents	Illegal Immigrants	Citizens	Legal Residents	Illegal Immigrants
Assault/murder	.028	.003	.007	.010	.002	0
Bank robbery	.061	.013	.002	.019	.002	0
Larceny/fraud	.243	.163	.066	.424	.208	.113
Racketeering/extortion	.090	.060	.020	.152	.122	.074
Drug offenses	.401	.610	.285	.308	.493	.385
Immigration	.005	.081	.586	.008	.100	.377
Firearms	.097	.026	.016	.020	.010	.004
Burglary/theft	.009	.002	.0005	.0006	0	0
N	23,834	2,960	3,841	4,735	418	231
(Fraction of total)	(.78)	(.10)	(.13)	(.88)	(.08)	(.04)
California						
N	1,621	573	1,231	350	84	43
(Fraction of total)	(.47)	(.17)	(.34)	(.73)	(.18)	(.09)

Source: Authors' calculations using the United States Sentencing Commission monitoring database, 1994–95.

During the past decade, several changes have taken place in criminal justice policy that, while not aimed at immigrants directly, may nonetheless have had a disproportionate impact on their incarceration. A plethora of acts under the heading of the "war on drugs" has increased enforcement and penalties for violations involving controlled substances (see Forst 1995; Tonry 1995). Data from our earliest time period, 1986, show that immigrants were disproportionately incarcerated for drug-related activity. If one interprets that to mean that the foreign born were disproportionately involved in drug crimes, then, as enforcement increased with the "war on drugs," a disproportionate number of foreign born would be caught in the net.

Furthermore, immigrants and others with low levels of income and education may have poor (or no) representation in court. Because of language and cultural barriers, the foreign born may be particularly less likely to aid adequately in their own defense. Further, with few exceptions, federal law prohibits agencies from using funds from the Legal Services Corporation to represent aliens. With the increasing numbers of aliens requiring legal services and the expense of providing representation (due to the remote location of many detention facilities and prisons), the availability of pro bono representation is scarce.[15] Thus, aliens may be more likely to be convicted than the native born who commit similar crimes.

There are also changes in the enforcement environment that may have had a specific impact on the foreign born. Consider the "war on drugs" again. There is a trivial reason this may have disproportionately affected the foreign born. Since drugs tend to come from abroad, the couriers are often foreign born. As enforcement against drug smugglers increased, it is likely that the proportion of foreign born who are apprehended, convicted, and incarcerated also increased. As discussed earlier, this connection is worth keeping in mind, since these individuals are not necessarily among the some 1 million immigrants admitted for legal permanent resident status each year; rather, they are among the some 25 million people admitted each year on student, business, and tourist visas. As the discussions of immigration and crime become intertwined, it is worth noting that not all of the foreign born who are incarcerated were necessarily admitted under the U.S. family-based admission criteria for permanent residents.

There have also been changes in U.S. policies toward criminal immigrants. Since the United States stopped its open border policy in the 1870s, criminal activity has been a basis for both exclusion and deportation of those who, until that point, had been legal residents.[16] Only those

15. These comments were provided in personal communication from Stephen Legomsky, 31 January 1998.

16. See Borjas (1990, 27) for a summary of early immigration restrictions. In fact, the first attempted regulation of immigration was the Aliens Act of 1798. It legalized the deportation of "any alien deemed 'dangerous' to the peace and safety of the country."

immigrants who have become naturalized citizens are immune to deportation. Although "crimes of moral turpitude" and a host of other criminal activities have always been grounds for deportation, deportation was pursued rather selectively. As our 1986 data reveal, the foreign born with INS hold orders in 1986 were disproportionately incarcerated for violent crimes, and officials took longer in placing INS holds on inmates' records compared to later years.

Congressional legislation during the 1980s took away some of the INS's discretion over deportation proceedings, enlarged the categories of criminal activity for which deportation was required, and increased the resources of enforcement agencies.[17] The Immigration Reform and Control Act (IRCA) of 1986 required the INS to start deportation proceedings as soon as possible after the conviction of a noncitizen. The Anti–Drug Abuse Act of 1988 introduced the term "aggravated felon" and required deportation of all noncitizens convicted of aggravated felonies. As originally defined, an aggravated felony consisted of such crimes as murder, drug or firearms trafficking, and money laundering. However, the term was amended and broadened in 1990 and 1994. By 1996, with the Illegal Immigration Reform and Immigrant Responsibility Act, the term "aggravated felon" applied to crimes of theft or burglary, provided the court imposed a sentence of at least one year;[18] a conviction for fraud or deceit is now an aggravated felony if the loss is $10,000 (Brady and Kesselbrenner 1997, 6). The Anti-Terrorism and Effective Death Penalty Act of 1996 contained some overlapping provisions. Specified grounds for deportation in this act included several provisions: "conviction of an aggravated felony, conviction of a controlled substance offense, drug addiction or abuse (no conviction necessary), conviction of a firearm offense," and several other miscellaneous crimes (Brady and Kesselbrenner 1997, 4).

Note that these convictions need not result in prison time in order for a defendant to be "deportable." A conviction for a qualified offense that resulted in a suspended sentence or a sentence of probation meets the grounds for deportation. In addition, aggravated felonies need not be committed within any given time period following immigration. Therefore, a legal resident with one conviction after 20 years in the country would qualify for deportation. (In contrast, only those moral turpitude crimes committed within 5 years after admission are "qualifying offenses.") In 1996, the crim-

17. In fiscal year 1984, the United States budget reports the INS's total obligations to be $518,058,000 (Executive Office of the President 1985, I-N16). By 1996, the total obligations are reported to be $2,291,000,000 (Executive Office of the President 1997, 684). In 1994, a new section was added to the INS budget entitled "Violent Crime Reduction Programs." In fiscal year 1998, this additional funding was $732,251,000 and was "to remain available until expended" on programs to combat crime through immigration control.

18. These rules create potential horizontal inequities across noncitizens depending on their state of residence. In states with longer sentences, immigrants will be more likely to meet the grounds for deportability.

inal grounds for deportability became retroactive, so a legal resident who had committed one of these offenses in the past, even if it was not grounds for deportation at the time, is now subject to deportation.[19]

In addition to the changes in the definition of the grounds for deportation, Congress also appropriated more funds for enforcement. The Institutional Hearing Program (IHP) was established in response to the IRCA requirement that deportation proceedings be initiated more quickly.[20] The process is supposed to work as follows: corrections officials identify new prisoners as foreign born; INS agents screen these prisoners for deportability; if an inmate is deportable, a detainer is filed requiring the inmate to be released to INS custody upon release from prison; deportation hearings are scheduled. The hope was that most deportable inmates would complete the entire process during the term of incarceration, and deportation would occur at the inmate's prison release date. (In practice, however, many deportable inmates were not identified by this process.)[21]

The increases in resources to the INS coupled with increasing managerial attention to criminal aliens have yielded large increases in the numbers removed from the United States. Only 30,464 aliens were deported for criminal and narcotics violations over the entire decade of the 1980s (U.S. Department of Justice 1993); in 1997 alone, 50,165 criminal aliens were removed (U.S. Department of Justice 1997b). Among the removed criminal aliens, 61 percent had been convicted of aggravated felonies and 43 percent had drug convictions (U.S. Department of Justice 1997b). Fewer than 15,000 of the criminal aliens were removed through the Institutional Hearing Program (e.g., directly from a correctional institution), evidence of incomplete implementation (U.S. Department of Justice 1997c).

Negotiated arrangements for expediting the processing of criminal aliens continue to develop between local offices of the INS and state and local law-enforcement agencies. A recent INS effort, the Law Enforcement Support Center, has pilot programs for improving the identification of illegal aliens who commit crimes (McDonald 1997). Because law enforcement is organized locally, and because populations vary substantially, systems must be adapted to the practices of police departments, sheriffs'

---

19. The law gets quite complicated. According to Legomsky (1997a, 448), "it is necessary . . . to distinguish between the effective date of a change in the *definition* of 'aggravated felony' and the effective dates of the various specific *consequences* of conviction of an aggravated felony" (Legomsky's emphasis).

20. The discussion of the IHP in this paragraph draws heavily from General Accounting Office (GAO, 1997).

21. A GAO audit of the process found that, during the final six months of 1995, 40 percent of a sample of potentially deportable foreign-born inmates had a final deportation order upon release from prison and 52 percent had the process completed after release from prison. GAO estimated that $63 million in detention costs could have been saved if the deportation process had been completed while inmates were incarcerated (GAO 1997).

offices, and departments of corrections.[22] While removal is generally not permitted before the sentence is served, 1996 legislation increased the discretion of the attorney general to remove nonviolent offenders early (Legomsky 1997a, 730).

The Violent Crime Control and Law Enforcement Act of 1994 provided "reimbursement" to states for incarceration of undocumented alien inmates. This reimbursement gives state officials an incentive to notify the federal authorities of suspected illegal immigrants.[23] This act also increased funding to the INS to proceed with deportation hearings against criminal aliens.

Although only some of these laws were in effect by the time individuals in our sample were convicted, they demonstrate the rapidly changing attitude toward criminal aliens. During the intervening years between each of our data sets, new laws were passed either to broaden grounds for deportation of criminal aliens or to increase funding to the INS to initiate deportation proceedings. We observe changes in our data that correspond to these changes in policy. The expansion in offenses requiring deportation is reflected in the extent to which less-serious offenders increasingly have INS holds on record (i.e., comparing 1990 and 1996 to 1986) and in the upswing in the numbers of criminal aliens awaiting deportation. Additionally, our data are consistent with these procedures' becoming more systematic over time. One measure of this is the speed with which the INS hold orders were filed.

There are also several reasons to believe that the foreign born may be treated differently within the criminal justice system. These differences in treatment may, among other things, increase the costs of incarcerating the foreign born.[24] For example, in the 1992 decision *United States v. Restrepo,*[25] it was determined that noncitizens held in the (federal) Bureau of Prisons are not allowed to serve any portion of their sentence in minimum security facilities or halfway houses. While this decision may be warranted if immigrants pose a much greater escape or flight risk than do citizens, it will materially increase the costs of incarcerating them.[26]

---

22. McDonald reports that an assessment of practices related to identifying and processing criminal aliens in five states found "wide variations in the nature of cooperation between federal, state, and local agencies" (1997, 7).

23. In practice, the State Criminal Alien Assistance Program partially reimburses states for expenses of incarcerating certain criminal aliens (convicted of one felony or two misdemeanors). In fiscal year 1996, the reimbursement rate was 60 cents for each dollar claimed (U.S. Department of Justice 1997a).

24. In this paper, we focus on postconviction treatment of foreigners. For discussions of differential treatment at earlier stages in the criminal justice process, see Hagan and Palloni (1997).

25. *United States v. Restrepo,* 802F. Supp. 781 (U.S. Dist. 1992).

26. This also means that noncitizens will serve their sentences under more severe circumstances than citizens convicted of identical crimes.

Additionally, there are reasons deportable noncitizens may serve longer sentences for the same crime than do citizens. In *Rodriguez v. United States* (1993),[27] the second circuit court, relying on the statutory language from the Immigration and Nationality Act, determined that while the INS must begin any deportation proceeding as quickly as possible, alien prisoners will be required to serve their complete terms before they may be deported. Thus, noncitizens may be required to serve more of their sentences than citizens.[28] Deportable aliens will spend more time behind bars than citizens for two additional reasons. First, they must wait in detention until the INS authorities come to get them, so any administrative delay will protract their time served. Second, once the INS authorities collect them, they are transferred to INS detention centers awaiting final decisions on their deportation status and removal to their country of origin.[29]

9.5   Multivariate Analysis of Sentence Length and Time Served

The previous section reviewed the case law and legislation that both increased the number of deportable aliens and, potentially, increased the time they serve on a given sentence relative to citizens and other aliens. In this section, we use data from the California Department of Corrections to analyze the effect of an INS hold order on time served for noncitizens relative to comparable inmates.

9.5.1   The Effect of Deportation Holds on Sentence Length and Time Served

In anticipation of our analysis of time actually served, we begin with an examination of the effect of INS status on sentence length because the sentence is a potentially important control for criminal activity. We control for six offense categories, race and ethnicity, and three categories of foreign born. The policies outlined above should not increase deportable immigrants' sentence lengths if we had perfect controls for the details of their crimes and their criminal history, and if there were equal treatment under the law. We do not have access to information on the first two of these, and the last is in some doubt.

We control for six broad offense categories: manslaughter, property, assault, sex, drug, and other offenses. Although additional offense categories

---

27. *Rodriguez v. United States,* 994 F 2d 110 (2d Cir. 1993).

28. As corrections agencies and the INS make and implement arrangements as to what constitutes "serving one's sentence," the extent to which criminal aliens serve more time in custody should decline.

29. While the latter will not be picked up in the analysis in this paper, the approach taken in Butcher and Piehl (1998a) does capture the institutionalization of those in deportation facilities.

are available in the data,[30] offense severity is one dimension along which bias in the criminal justice system may be manifested. Under determinate sentencing, the conviction offense should map into the sentence.[31] In practice, the conviction offense is reached through the discretion of the prosecutor and plea bargaining. Kessler and Piehl (1998) recommend "stepping back" from the crime of conviction to that of the original charge in order to get closer to the actual action that led to arrest. Since we do not have this earlier information, we use these broader offense categories to avoid overcontrolling for the sentence.

We include several other control variables. Since the foreign born tend to be members of racial and ethnic minorities, we control for black, Hispanic, and other race. We also include controls for age at admission and age at admission squared. Age may affect sentence length, because the older an individual is, the more likely she or he will have a longer criminal history.

We also control for three categories of the foreign born: all foreign born, those foreign born with "INS holds," and the foreign born with "late holds." There are reasons to use each of these comparison groups. First, all foreign born in California are likely to have difficulty speaking and understanding English. To the extent that this hampers their ability to aid in their own defense, they may be more likely to be convicted or to receive longer sentences upon conviction.[32] Secondly, the foreign born are likely to have had less time in the United States, and thus have shorter (domestic) official criminal records. The "late" INS holds are interesting because they may have unobservables similar to those of the INS-hold foreign born, since both are eventually deemed "deportable."

Table 9.4 presents the ordinary least squares (OLS) regressions for sentence length for men in 1986 and 1990, for all offenses, drug offenses, and property offenses. The left-hand-side variable is the natural log of sentence length. One would like to estimate the sentence length for all crime

30. These categories, however, are of questionable usefulness. They appear to be designed more for political than research purposes (e.g., many types of drug and sex offenses are delineated, while there are few categories of other violent and property crimes).

31. Generally, there are three sentence lengths from which a judge may choose. Adjustments to these may be made for other circumstances, such as particular characteristics of the crime (such as the use of a firearm) or particular characteristics of the defendant (such as having a previous conviction for a violent crime).

32. A defense lawyer who is aware of the immigration consequences of different convictions may use these to negotiate with prosecutors. For example, knowing that a particular type of charge sets into motion required deportation proceedings, a defense attorney may bargain for slightly more time in return for a different charge. This would increase the sentence length of the "nondeportable" foreign born relative to those with INS holds. While this type of deal making does occur, immigration law is a specialty within law and court appointed defense attorneys (and their clients) are often not aware of the deportation consequences of various convictions. Also, it is unclear how acceptable such offers are to district attorneys.

Table 9.4   **Determinants of Log Sentence Length: Men Released within Six Years of Admission, by Admission Year**

	All Offenses		Drug Offenses		Property Offenses	
	1986 (1)	1990 (2)	1986 (3)	1990 (4)	1986 (5)	1990 (6)
INS hold	0.396	0.145	0.372	0.152	0.453	0.083
	(0.0157)	(0.0116)	(0.0231)	(0.0204)	(0.0366)	(0.0256)
"Late" hold	-0.083	-0.089	-0.068	-0.116	-0.090	-0.125
	(0.0164)	(0.0198)	(0.0234)	(0.0350)	(0.0257)	(0.0334)
Foreign born	-0.127	-0.046	-0.052	0.028	-0.139	-0.055
	(0.0107)	(0.0104)	(0.0169)	(0.0200)	(0.0179)	(0.0219)
Black	-0.074	-0.010	-0.052	0.048	-0.104	-0.076
	(0.0086)	(0.0071)	(0.0171)	(0.0127)	(0.0134)	(0.0121)
Hispanic	-0.055	-0.051	-0.043	-0.045	-0.057	-0.030
	(0.0092)	(0.0075)	(0.0181)	(0.0145)	(0.0143)	(0.0132)
Other race	0.008	0.038	-0.053	0.013	0.033	0.038
	(0.0169)	(0.0158)	(0.0290)	(0.0298)	(0.0315)	(0.0291)
Offense groups	yes	yes	—	—	—	—
R^2	0.2831	0.2580	0.0704	0.0224	0.0385	0.0100
N	20,361	33,508	4,817	11,549	7,818	9,474

Notes: Data are from the California Department of Corrections for men who were admitted in 1986 and 1990 and released within six years. "Late hold" indicates individuals for whom the "INS hold" was enacted after they had been released. All regressions include age at admission, age squared, and a constant. The offense groups in the first two columns include manslaughter, assault, sex, drug, property, and other offenses. Numbers in parentheses are standard errors.

categories separately because there were changes in punishments associated with these crime categories over these years. However, we only have sufficient data to estimate the two largest crime categories separately.

Before turning to estimates for the groups of the foreign born, note the effects of race and ethnicity. African Americans had significantly shorter sentences, all else equal, overall and for property offenses. In 1990, blacks convicted of drug offenses had longer sentences than non-Hispanic whites. The indicator for Hispanic was negative and significant in all specifications. The "other race" indicator was insignificant in most cases.

The "INS hold" coefficient was large, positive, and significant across all specifications. The effect was larger in 1986 than in 1990. The coefficient implies that those with INS holds were serving 39.6 percent, 47.2 percent, and 45.3 percent longer sentences for all, drug, and property offenses, respectively, than other "similar" individuals. By 1990, the analogous figures were 14.5 percent, 15.2 percent, and 8.3 percent for all, drug, and property offenses, respectively. This is consistent with the fact that the list of deportable crimes was expanding during this time period to include less and less serious crimes.

How should we interpret this coefficient on "INS hold"? If the offense categories control for all pertinent aspects of an individual's criminal activity, then none of the other variables should matter. Clearly, this is not the case. As discussed above, there are several things that are relevant for sentencing for which we have no information: details about the exact criminal act and the individual's criminal history. To the extent that "foreign born" controls for criminal history, we want to control for it and assess the "INS hold" coefficient on its own. To the extent that "INS hold" merely indicates that these are the individuals who are committing more serious crimes, we may want to compare the "INS hold" to the "late hold" coefficient. These are both groups of people who turn out to be "deportable," and so may have similar underlying characteristics to their crimes. In this case, "INS hold" seems to add considerably to the sentence length since "INS hold" was positive and significant and "late hold" was negative and significant across all specifications. Of course, the fact that the "late hold" individuals were not determined to be deportable until after their release may indicate either that they had very short sentences and were in and out of the system before the INS could catch up with them, or that they committed lower priority crimes so no one immediately looked into their deportation status. If we want to compare the foreign born with INS holds to the native born, we need to add the "INS hold" coefficient to the coefficient on foreign born. INS-hold foreign born received 3–31 percent longer sentences than the native born, depending on the year and the specification.

Table 9.5 reports the results for sentence length for women in 1990, overall and for drug offenses. There were not enough observations to run

Table 9.5   **Determinants of Log Sentence Length: Women Released within Six Years of Admission, 1990**

	All Offenses (1)	Drug Offenses (2)
INS hold	0.295	0.350
	(0.0540)	(0.0732)
Foreign born	−0.060	−0.094
	(0.0373)	(0.0504)
Black	0.016	0.096
	(0.0174)	(0.0253)
Hispanic	−0.019	0.053
	(0.0193)	(0.0296)
Other race	−0.022	0.028
	(0.0360)	(0.0679)
Offense groups	yes	—
R^2	0.1876	0.0349
N	3,457	1,654

Notes: See notes for table 9.4.

the 1986 specifications for women, and there were not enough late-hold foreigners to include that variable in these regressions. INS-hold foreigners receive about 30–35 percent longer sentences than other foreigners, and they received about 24–26 percent longer sentences than the native born. These effects were similar in direction to those for the men, but they were larger than the 1990 effects for men.

In sum, the foreign born with an INS hold on record received significantly longer sentences than other groups. We do not have a particular interpretation to give to these results. Rather, they inform the upcoming results of our analyses of time served. To the extent that this reflects differences in criminal history or differences in the severity of the crime, we want to control for sentence length when we analyze actual time served. To the extent that the effect of "INS hold" reflects bias in the system against this group of noncitizens, we do not want to control for its effects when we analyze time served. We present both specifications in what follows.

Table 9.6 presents OLS regression results for the natural log of time served. All the controls we used in the sentence length regressions are included here. In the first regression for each pair, we add the log of sentence length and its square on the right-hand side.[33] The specifications that include all offenses show that the foreign born with INS holds served significantly longer sentences (by about 6 percent) than did other similar

---

33. When the log of sentence length is entered linearly, the coefficient is significantly different from one.

Table 9.6   Determinants of Log Time Served: Men Released within Six Years of Admission, by Admission Year

	All Offenses				Drug Offenses				Property Offenses			
	1986		1990		1986		1990		1986		1990	
	(1)	(2)	(3)	(4)	(5)	(6)	(7)	(8)	(9)	(10)	(11)	(12)
INS hold	0.060	0.508	0.061	0.228	0.038	0.452	0.058	0.239	0.077	0.594	0.131	0.226
	(0.0117)	(0.0209)	(0.0095)	(0.0160)	(0.0215)	(0.0331)	(0.0193)	(0.0295)	(0.0261)	(0.0502)	(0.0251)	(0.0390)
"Late" hold	0.009	−0.086	−0.063	−0.164	−0.035	−0.110	−0.081	−0.220	0.052	−0.050	−0.092	−0.235
	(0.0160)	(0.0236)	(0.0265)	(0.0361)	(0.0264)	(0.0364)	(0.0430)	(0.0621)	(0.0269)	(0.0374)	(0.0638)	(0.0775)
Foreign born	−0.033	−0.176	−0.034	−0.086	0.007	−0.051	−0.025	0.008	−0.038	−0.197	−0.079	−0.142
	(0.0104)	(0.0154)	(0.0097)	(0.0151)	(0.0153)	(0.0231)	(0.0213)	(0.0305)	(0.0202)	(0.0268)	(0.0240)	(0.0350)
ln(sentence)	1.361	—	1.711	—	1.011	—	1.755	—	1.085	—	1.332	—
	(0.0711)		(0.0788)		(0.1628)		(0.0838)		(0.1443)		(0.0989)	
ln(sentence)^2	−0.032	—	−0.080	—	0.015	—	−0.082	—	0.008	—	−0.028	—
	(0.0096)		(0.0110)		(0.0236)		(0.0113)		(0.0201)		(0.0135)	
Black	0.006	−0.079	−0.016	−0.027	−0.027	−0.085	−0.043	0.018	0.011	−0.107	−0.009	−0.097
	(0.0066)	(0.0118)	(0.0058)	(0.0100)	(0.0158)	(0.0248)	(0.0109)	(0.0187)	(0.0113)	(0.0191)	(0.0116)	(0.0181)
Hispanic	0.022	−0.040	0.022	0.037	−0.031	−0.079	−0.010	−0.061	0.029	−0.037	0.030	−0.004
	(0.0077)	(0.0128)	(0.0060)	(0.0103)	(0.0172)	(0.0259)	(0.0126)	(0.0212)	(0.0129)	(0.0204)	(0.0112)	(0.0185)
Other race	0.001	0.009	−0.007	0.036	−0.027	−0.085	−0.002	0.017	0.019	0.057	−0.021	0.022
	(0.0126)	(0.0226)	(0.0120)	(0.0203)	(0.0260)	(0.0402)	(0.0203)	(0.0392)	(0.0220)	(0.0415)	(0.0296)	(0.0454)
Offense groups	yes	yes	yes	yes								
R^2	0.7493	0.2096	0.7380	0.1841	0.6269	0.0523	0.6834	0.0243	0.6589	0.0313	0.6160	0.0169
N	20,361	20,361	33,508	33,508	4,817	4,817	11,549	11,549	7,818	7,818	9,474	9,474

Notes: See notes to table 9.4.

inmates in both years. For drug offenses, the coefficient on "INS hold" was .038 (insignificant) in 1986 and .058 in 1990. This figure was slightly larger for property offenses, with "INS hold" increasing time served approximately 8 percent in 1986 and approximately 13 percent in 1990. Those foreign born with a late hold or no hold served less time (in most specifications). Compared to other inmates with similar characteristics and the same sentence length, the INS-hold foreign born served significantly more time. When we look within drug and property offenses, we see that this effect was larger in 1990 than in 1986. This suggests that the penalty for being deportable was increasing over time.

As described above, if we want to compare the INS-hold foreign born to the native born, we need to add the coefficients on "INS hold" and "foreign born." Whether or not this is the right exercise depends on whether the INS-hold foreign born are more similar to other foreign born or to natives in terms of prior criminal history and behavior within the prison system. These data cannot answer this question, so it is worth noting that the differences in time served between the INS-hold foreign born and the native born were smaller than between the INS-hold foreign born and those foreign born without a hold order. However, except for the case of drug offenses in 1986, the INS-hold foreign born served significantly longer than the native born, and the differential was between 3 and 5 percent.

If one believes that all effects of "INS hold" on sentence length in the previous tables were the result of differences in the severity of the criminal act, then controlling for sentence length in these specifications should account for this source of differences. The effect of INS holds on time served in these specifications can only result from differences in preconfinement credits, behavior in prison, or differences in treatment within the criminal justice system. Preconfinement credits come about if the individual is held during trial. This is more likely if someone is unable to make bail or is more likely to have a trial. There is some evidence that noncitizens are less likely to be free on bail before trial (Hagan and Palloni 1997). The relationship between citizenship and plea-bargaining is more complicated. If noncitizens have poor legal representation, they may be more likely to accept a plea bargain. On the other hand, the current deportation consequences of a felony conviction may lead noncitizens to go to trial. In the latter case, the subsample of those convicted noncitizens will have longer average sentences (since they do not receive any discount from guilty pleas). Then, the inclusion of sentence length will tend to bias downward the coefficient on "INS hold."

We have no direct information on behavior in prison, but have no a priori reason to believe "INS hold" foreign born would have worse behavior than the other groups. The 1991 Survey of Inmates of State Prisons sheds some light on the question of behavior in prison, since it includes variables on "rule breaking" while incarcerated. For this check, we were able to compare citizens to noncitizens, which is not exactly comparable to our California analyses. Due to the small sample sizes, we could not always look at the desired level of detail. (For example, the survey contained no female noncitizens in California prisons who had broken a major rule.) In the national sample (with state fixed effects) there was no difference in the extent of rule breaking between citizen and noncitizen males when all offenders were considered together or among only drug offenders. Among women, citizens had statistically significantly higher rates of rule breaking. For male California inmates only, again there was no difference in behavior. In none of the specifications we ran for rule breaking was the coefficient on citizen negative. Thus, we do not believe that behavioral differences in prison explain the finding that those with INS holds serve a longer proportion of their sentences.

Another potential problem in the interpretation of the INS hold coefficient is reverse causality. Suppose that for some unknown reason (e.g., behavior in prison, preconfinement credits), some individuals stay in prison longer for a given sentence length. The INS would then have longer to identify who was deportable and then file hold orders. Longer time served would, in effect, *cause* inmates to be deemed deportable. We do not think our results are driven by reverse causation. As mentioned earlier, in 1986 it may have been the case that deportation holds were filed selectively and the longer one was in prison, the greater the chance that officials would decide to investigate one's deportation status. But by 1990, the placement of INS holds had become much more systematic. Over three-quarters of all holds were placed within the first four months of detention. As a further check for possible reverse causation, we reran the regressions in table 9.6 on the sample of individuals who were sentenced to at least two years in prison. We then limited the definition of "INS hold" to those whose hold was placed within three months of admission. Among this group, it cannot be the case that reverse causation drives our results, as reverse causation implies that those who stay in prison longer are more likely to be identified as deportable. This group serves a long sentence and the INS hold is filed almost immediately. Our results using this sample are very similar to the reported results in table 9.6. For example, inmates with INS holds served 11.2 percent longer in 1986 and 11.5 percent longer in 1990.

The final explanation for the positive relationship between "INS hold" and time served, that there are differences in treatment, is consistent with the idea that there are statutory reasons why these noncitizens must serve out their sentences prior to deportation, and that there might be some delay before the INS can transfer them to a deportation facility.

If one believes that the effects of "INS hold" on sentence length represent some sort of improper bias toward this group, then one would not

Table 9.7   **Determinants of Log Time Served: Women Released within Six Years of Admission, 1990**

	All Offenses		Drug Offenses	
	(1)	(2)	(3)	(4)
INS hold	0.119	0.459	0.034	0.445
	(0.0651)	(0.0905)	(0.0616)	(0.0967)
Foreign born	−0.114	−0.183	−0.038	−0.148
	(0.0623)	(0.0781)	(0.0552)	(0.0773)
ln(sentence)	1.278	—	1.375	—
	(0.1589)		(0.2241)	
ln(sentence)^2	−0.018	—	−0.028	—
	(0.0127)		(0.0308)	
Black	−0.004	0.015	−0.031	0.084
	(0.0170)	(0.0263)	(0.0233)	(0.0378)
Hispanic	0.005	−0.017	−0.026	0.037
	(0.0205)	(0.0302)	(0.0290)	(0.0453)
Other race	0.043	0.018	−0.016	0.018
	(0.0349)	(0.0544)	(0.0510)	(0.0926)
Offense groups	yes	yes	—	—
R^2	0.6249	0.1123	0.6455	0.0282
N	3,457	3,457	1,654	1,654

Notes: See notes to table 9.4.

want to control for it in the time-served regressions. The second column in each year/offense group shows the results excluding the log of sentence length and its square. In this case, the effect of having an INS hold on one's record is enormous. INS-hold foreign born served between 50 and 60 percent longer sentences in 1986. This effect was much smaller in 1990, only about 23 percent. This is undoubtedly because the list of offenses that were considered grounds for deportation increased dramatically in these two time periods, so the foreign inmates with INS holds have shorter sentences on average in 1990, although there are more of them.

Table 9.7 shows the results for time served for women. We could not perform identical analyses to those for the men because the sample sizes were too small. The results controlling for sentence length show that the foreign born with INS holds served about 12 percent more time when we consider all offenses together. Within drug offenses, there was a positive but insignificant effect. The race and ethnicity variables similarly have little effect here. Similar to the men, when sentence length is not included, the coefficient on "INS hold" was very large—this group serves about 45 percent longer.

9.5.2   Recent Evidence on the Effect of Deportation Holds

As described in section 9.4, policies toward criminal aliens have become increasingly severe. Although some of these policies took effect between

1986 and 1990, more were instituted between 1990 and 1996. It is worthwhile, then, to investigate more recent evidence.

While we have data from 1996, we only observe these inmates until 30 June 1997. In order to observe a completed spell of incarceration, an inmate would have had to serve approximately one year. In order to analyze comparable samples across the years, for each year we include only those who were admitted during the first six months of a year and released by the end of June of the following calendar year. This new subsample shifts the offense distribution of inmates away from violent crimes and toward drug and property crimes. Nonetheless, there are a substantial number of men who serve approximately a year in prison. For women, however, the sample sizes are too small to analyze such short terms.

Table 9.8 shows the OLS estimates for the natural log of time served for this sample of men serving short prison terms and, in the last row, the marginal effects of "INS hold" for being included in this subsample. These regressions are analogous to those in table 9.6, although the log of sentence length and its square are always included. Once again, we show the estimates for all offense groups combined, and for drug and property offenses separately.

The point of this exercise is to investigate the magnitude of the "INS hold" coefficient over time. The extent to which these coefficients are comparable depends on whether the underlying distributions of inmates are similar over the decade. This is a problem generally in periods when incarceration policy and enforcement environments are changing, but it may be a particular problem in these specifications since the sample is truncated to include only those with relatively short sentences. We will take up later the implications of the selection into this sample and whether these coefficients can be generalized to the broader prison population.

Looking across the columns of table 9.8, we can see that the effect of "INS hold" on time served dramatically increased from 1986 to 1996. In 1986, the foreign born with INS holds on record did not serve significantly different time from other inmates. By 1990, they served between 7 and 14 percent longer. By 1996, the foreign born under INS hold orders served 20–25 percent longer than other similar inmates.

Do these striking changes across the years represent a real change in the treatment of foreign-born inmates under INS hold orders, or do they result simply from a change in the underlying distribution of who is included in the short term sample? Consider the last row of the table. This reports the marginal effect of "INS hold" (estimated using a probit model) on being in this short term sample, controlling for the complete list of variables listed in the time-served regressions. For all offense groups combined and the subset of drug offenders, INS-hold foreign born were significantly less likely to be in this short term sample in 1986 and 1990. By 1996, the INS-hold inmates in these offense groups were no different from

Table 9.8   Determinants of Time Served: Men Who Served Short Terms, by Admission Year

	All Offenses			Drug Offenses			Property Offenses		
	1986 (1)	1990 (2)	1996 (3)	1986 (4)	1990 (5)	1996 (6)	1986 (7)	1990 (8)	1996 (9)
INS hold	-0.001	0.084	0.210	-0.106	0.066	0.238	0.029	0.138	0.245
	(0.0120)	(0.0226)	(0.0265)	(0.0731)	(0.0445)	(0.0558)	(0.0724)	(0.0477)	(0.0517)
"Late" hold	0.016	-0.083	-0.664	-0.104	-0.092	-0.793	0.076	-0.096	-0.387
	(0.0338)	(0.0552)	(0.1629)	(0.0611)	(0.0861)	(0.3218)	(0.0469)	(0.1051)	(0.1758)
Foreign born	-0.020	-0.019	-0.053	0.062	-0.006	-0.071	-0.033	-0.072	-0.113
	(0.0227)	(0.0232)	(0.0273)	(0.0330)	(0.0497)	(0.0580)	(0.0322)	(0.0461)	(0.0513)
ln(sentence)	4.978	4.157	4.273	7.369	8.592	5.600	6.075	6.432	8.423
	(0.6519)	(0.9286)	(0.7082)	(1.2084)	(1.1075)	(0.7287)	(0.7070)	(0.6287)	(1.0145)
ln(sentence)^2	-0.704	-0.543	-0.587	-1.096	-1.255	-0.801	-0.885	-0.917	-1.258
	(0.1054)	(0.1504)	(0.1135)	(0.1980)	(0.1811)	(0.1172)	(0.1163)	(0.1028)	(0.1665)
Black	-0.010	-0.034	-0.029	-0.035	-0.040	-0.058	-0.008	-0.007	-0.008
	(0.0182)	(0.0136)	(0.0157)	(0.0450)	(0.0242)	(0.0273)	(0.0239)	(0.0213)	(0.0259)
Hispanic	0.034	0.021	-0.035	0.023	0.016	-0.038	0.011	0.028	-0.021
	(0.0208)	(0.0131)	(0.0163)	(0.0454)	(0.0259)	(0.0279)	(0.0281)	(0.0214)	(0.0276)
Other race	0.042	-0.033	-0.003	0.002	0.026	-0.110	0.045	-0.054	0.024
	(0.0340)	(0.0367)	(0.0366)	(0.0706)	(0.0511)	(0.0820)	(0.0501)	(0.0737)	(0.0556)
Offense groups	yes	yes	yes	—	—	—	—	—	—
R^2	0.1316	0.1910	0.1319	0.1379	0.2115	0.1414	0.1390	0.1751	0.1427
N	4,360	8,745	8,808	1,188	3,033	3,289	2,238	3,241	2,993
Sample selection[a]	-0.025	-0.016	0.002	-0.079	-0.033	0.035	0.009	-0.009	-0.003
	(0.0078)	(0.0069)	(0.0063)	(0.0173)	(0.0109)	(0.0147)	(0.0291)	(0.0228)	(0.0178)

Notes: See notes to table 9.4. See text for description of sample.

[a] This is the marginal effect of "INS hold" from a probit regression for whether the individual is in this short term sample. The probits include the same variables as the OLS regressions for time served.

other inmates in terms of their probability of being in this sample. Thus, there is some evidence that the selection into this sample has changed over time.

How important is this for the comparability of these estimates? It is difficult to sign the "selection bias" without a great deal of further information.[34] However, note that the selection into the short term sample does not appear to have changed over time for the subset of inmates convicted of property offenses. An INS hold order has no significant relationship to the probability of being in the short term sample for any of the years for property offenders. Nonetheless, the coefficients on "INS hold" in the time-served regressions for property offenders show a very similar pattern to that in the other specifications: the impact increased steeply over time.

There are reasons to believe that the magnitude of these impacts may not generalize to the rest of the population. Suppose the "INS hold" effect comes mainly from bureaucratic delay—it takes time for the INS to complete deportation hearings and to take charge of a deportable alien. The length of this delay will be proportionally longer for those who are serving shorter periods of time overall. However, comparing the size of the "INS hold" effect in table 9.8 to that in table 9.6 further supports our interpretation that something fundamental has changed in the treatment of inmates based on their INS hold status, and our sample selection is not driving these results. In the former table, we have the experience of the one-fourth to one-fifth of the population serving the shortest terms. The effect of having an "INS hold" in 1986 was insignificant for those serving short terms, where it was positive in table 9.6. In 1990, however, there was little difference in the magnitude of the coefficients for "INS hold" between the short term and broader populations.

We were interested in whether the experience of Mexicans differed from that of other foreign-born inmates. In particular, it seemed likely that improvements in the processing of criminal aliens for deportation would be easiest to achieve for Mexican citizens, both because they constitute the largest number of foreign born in California prisons and due to the physical proximity of Mexico. Interestingly, we found no evidence (1) that those inmates with INS holds who were born in Mexico served a lower proportion of their sentence than other inmates with INS holds, or (2) that there

---

34. There are some examples where the selection would work to bias downward the impact of INS hold on time served in the short term sample. Consider the case where the reason for the impact of INS hold is purely due to bureaucratic delay. Suppose further that the prison authorities become better over time at identifying who is a deportable alien and moving them from the CADOC into INS custody and that bureaucratic delay is proportionately longer for shorter sentences. In the later period, a higher fraction of aliens under INS hold orders would be included in the short term subsample. Then, in the later period, the average proportion of sentence served will fall due to the addition of these people with longer sentences and therefore lower proportion served.

was a reduction (over time) in the proportion of sentence served by Mexicans relative to other inmates (all with INS holds).

9.6 Conclusion

Noncitizens are at risk for deportation if they are convicted of criminal offenses. The character of that risk has changed substantially over the past decade due to (1) legislation broadening the list of offenses that "qualify" for deportation and making certain provisions retroactive, (2) court decisions clarifying the terms of confinement for inmates facing deportation, (3) increases in resources for enforcement against criminal aliens, (4) shifting emphasis of enforcement toward drug crimes, (5) reductions in the discretion allowed the INS in enforcing deportation provisions of the law, and (6) the introduction of financial incentives for states to identify noncitizens in their prison populations.

Our analysis of the inmates in California state prisons documents the current environment for criminal aliens and the extent of the recent changes in that environment. The legislative changes have had a large impact on California's prisoners. Fully 75 percent of male, and 33 percent of female, foreign-born inmates entering the system in 1996 had INS holds on their records. Those inmates with INS holds served longer in prison than similar native- or foreign-born inmates. The results also suggest that the differential in time served has been increasing over time, at least for inmates with relatively short sentences. It is possible that these differentials will narrow with time, if their cause is administrative delay and improvements are made.

Yet even if these differentials are temporary, they impose substantial costs. First, the inmates themselves bear the cost of serving longer terms behind bars. Without a full accounting of how time served in prison interacts with time spent in detention centers, it is difficult to place a value on this cost. While it is possible that inmates are better off serving longer sentences because options for appeal are limited after deportation, there is no evidence that this time can be utilized by inmates for their appeals. More generally, we are not aware of any studies of the impact of the recent developments in the treatment of criminal aliens on the deportation due process or on living conditions in deportation centers. Given the abrupt shifts in policy in a period of high immigration, it would not be surprising to find multiple bottlenecks in the process. If that is the case, the costs described in this paper severely understate the social costs of recent legislation regarding criminal aliens.

Second, for criminal justice as a whole, there is the question of the opportunity cost of resources. How would these cells be used if noncitizens served the same terms as citizens? It is possible that there would be no replacement of these inmates in the system. In that case, the current costs are borne by the inmates and guards operating in overly crowded conditions, which may or may not be a cause for concern. It is not hard to imagine, however, that the opportunity cost of these cells is additional offenders on probation who might otherwise be incarcerated.

Third, our results suggest that the direct costs of incarcerating immigrants are increasing because of the increase in absolute numbers and the differential time served by deportable aliens. How are those direct costs allocated across jurisdictions? Criminal aliens under deportation orders are released from prison and transported to INS deportation facilities. If the additional time in California prisons is used to adjudicate their deportation cases, then this extra time in state prisons may result in less time in INS deportation facilities, saving the federal government money. From the inmates' point of view, it may not matter where one resides except to the extent that one environment is preferable to another. However, from the state's point of view, it may matter a great deal. The longer individuals are in their prisons, the more it costs the state. While the federal government has begun to allocate funds to compensate states for criminal aliens, currently the reimbursement rate is much less than one.

The Violent Crime Control and Law Enforcement Act of 1994 provided "reimbursement" to states for incarceration of undocumented alien inmates. This reimbursement gives state officials an incentive to notify the federal authorities of suspected illegal immigrants. In practice, the State Criminal Alien Assistance Program (SCAAP) partially reimburses states for expenses of incarcerating certain criminal aliens (convicted of one felony or two misdemeanors). In fiscal year 1996, the reimbursement rate was 60 cents for each dollar claimed (U.S. Department of Justice 1997a).

While 60 percent of these costs are being "reimbursed," it may not be sufficient to cover the costs associated with the longer terms served. First, capital costs are not included in the reimbursable amounts (U.S. Department of Justice 1997a). Second, the "extra" time served by deportable aliens is sufficient to overcome the benefits of SCAAP funds. Using the time served of the native born as a proxy for the "base cost" of incarceration in the absence of the INS deportation policy, the state loses money by identifying potentially deportable inmates when the multiplier on time served for deportable aliens is less than one over the reimbursement rate. Some of the estimates of the "time-served multiplier" in this paper suggest that even at a 60 percent reimbursement rate, California is close to the point of losing money by identifying deportable aliens. Further, the reimbursement rate is a function of the claims, since the appropriation for SCAAP is fixed. Therefore, if claims from states increase, the reimbursement rate could fall dramatically. So at the same time the federal government began to share in the cost of incarcerating alien inmates, it also passed additional laws governing the terms of incarceration that had substantial impacts on state governments.

References

Borjas, George J. 1990. *Friends or strangers: The impact of immigration on the U.S. economy.* New York: Basic Books.

Brady, Katherine, and Dan Kesselbrenner. 1997. Recent developments in the immigration consequences of crimes. *National Immigration Project Newsletter* 23 (4): 3–10.

Butcher, Kristin F., and Anne Morrison Piehl. 1998a. Recent immigrants: Unexpected implications for crime and incarceration. *Industrial and Labor Relations Review* 51 (4): 654–79.

———. 1998b. Cross-city evidence on the relationship between immigration and crime. *Journal of Policy Analysis and Management* 17 (3): 457–93.

Carling, Duane D. 1994. Recent development: J. Rodriguez v. United States—Adjustments to the length of incarceration for alien convicts expecting deportation. *Journal of Contemporary Law* 20:272–81.

Clark, Rebecca L., Jeffrey S. Passel, Wendy Zimmerman, and Michael E. Fix. 1994. *Fiscal impacts of undocumented aliens: Selected estimates for seven states.* Washington, D.C.: The Urban Institute.

DiIulio, John J., Jr., Steven K. Smith, and Aaron J. Singer. 1995. The federal role in crime control. In *Crime,* ed. James Q. Wilson and Joan Petersilia, 445–62. San Francisco: ICS Press.

Executive Office of the President. Office of Management and Budget. 1985. *Budget of the United States government, fiscal year 1986—Appendix.* Washington, D.C.: U.S. Government Printing Office.

———. 1997. *Budget of the United States government, fiscal year 1996—Appendix.* Washington, D.C.: U.S. Government Printing Office.

Forst, Brian. 1995. Prosecution and sentencing. In *Crime,* ed. James Q. Wilson and Joan Petersilia, 363–86. San Francisco: ICS Press.

General Accounting Office (GAO). 1997. *Criminal aliens: INS efforts to identify and remove imprisoned aliens need to be improved.* GAO Report no. GAO/T-GGD-97-154. Washington, D.C.: U.S. Government Printing Office.

Glaeser, Edward, Daniel Kessler, and Anne Morrison Piehl. 1998. What do prosecutors maximize? NBER Working Paper no. 6602. Cambridge, Mass.: National Bureau of Economic Research.

Grogger, Jeffrey T. 1998. Immigration and crime among young black men: Evidence from the National Longitudinal Survey of Youth. In *Help or hindrance: The economic implications of immigration for African Americans,* ed. Daniel S. Hamermesh and Frank D. Bean, 322–41. New York: Russell Sage Foundation.

Hagan, John, and Alberto Palloni. 1997. Sociological criminology and the myth of the Mexican criminal. University of Toronto, Toronto, Ontario.

Kessler, Daniel P., and Anne Morrison Piehl. 1998. The role of discretion in the criminal justice system. *Journal of Law, Economics and Organization* 14 (2): 256–76.

Legomsky, Stephen H. 1997a. *Immigration and refugee law and policy.* 2d ed. Westbury, N.Y.: Foundation Press.

———. 1997b. Non-citizens and the rule of law: The 1996 immigration reforms. *Research Perspectives on Migration* 1 (4): 1–7.

McDonald, William F. 1997. Crime and illegal immigration: Emerging local, state, & federal partnerships. *National Institute of Justice Journal,* no. 232: 2–10.

McShane, Marilyn D. 1987. Immigration processing and the alien inmate: Constructing a conflict perspective. *Journal of Crime & Justice* 10 (1): 171–94.

Sampson, Robert J., and Janet L. Lauritsen. 1997. Racial and ethnic disparities in crime and criminal justice in the United States. In *Ethnicity, crime, and immigration: Comparative and cross-national perspectives,* ed. Michael Tonry. Crime and Justice: A Review of Research, vol. 21. Chicago: University of Chicago Press.

Scalia, John. 1996. *Noncitizens in the federal criminal justice system, 1984–94.* U.S. Department of Justice, August.

Smith, James P., and Barry Edmonston, eds. 1997. *The new Americans: Economic, demographic, and fiscal effects of immigration.* Washington, D.C.: National Academy Press.

Tonry, Michael. 1995. *Malign neglect.* Oxford: Oxford University Press.

U.S. Department of Justice. 1993. *Statistical yearbook of the Immigration and Naturalization Service: 1993.* Washington, D.C.: U.S. Government Printing Office.

———. 1997a. *State criminal alien assistance program.* Bureau of Justice Assistance Fact Sheet. Washington, D.C.: U.S. Department of Justice.

———. 1997b. INS increases removals a record 62 percent over FY 1996. Immigration and Naturalization Service news release, 30 October.

———. 1997c. The year in review: Highlights of 1997. Immigration and Naturalization Service news release, n.d.

Contributors

Julian R. Betts
Department of Economics
University of California, San Diego
La Jolla, CA 92093

George J. Borjas
Kennedy School of Government
Harvard University
79 JFK Street
Cambridge, MA 02138

Kristin F. Butcher
Department of Economics
Carney Hall 145
Boston College
140 Commonwealth Avenue
Chestnut Hill, MA 02467

David Card
Department of Economics
University of California, Berkeley
549 Evans Hall #3880
Berkeley, CA 94720

Janet Currie
Economics Department
University of California, Los Angeles
405 Hilgard Avenue
Los Angeles, CA 90095

John DiNardo
Department of Economics
Social Science Plaza
University of California, Irvine
Irvine, CA 92697

Eugena Estes
Department of Economics
Princeton University
Princeton, NJ 08544

Edward Funkhouser
Department of Economics
University of California,
  Santa Barbara
Santa Barbara, CA 93106

Alan L. Gustman
Department of Economics
Dartmouth College
Hanover, NH 03755

Guillermina Jasso
Department of Sociology
New York University
269 Mercer Street, 4th Floor
New York, NY 10003

Edward P. Lazear
Graduate School of Business
Stanford University
Stanford, CA 94305

Magnus Lofstrom
Department of Economics
University of California, San Diego
La Jolla, CA 92093

Anne Piehl
School of Public Health
140 Warren Hall
University of California, Berkeley
Berkeley, CA 94720

Mark Rosenzweig
Department of Economics
University of Pennsylvania
3718 Locust Walk
Philadelphia, PA 19104

James P. Smith
RAND
1700 Main Street
PO Box 2138
Santa Monica, CA 90407

Thomas Steinmeier
Texas Technology University
Department of Economics
Lubbock, TX 79409

Author Index

Subject Index